Canada in Question:

FEDERALISM IN THE EIGHTIES

THIRD EDITION

McGraw-Hill Ryerson Series in Canadian Politics
General Editor—Paul W. Fox

Canada in Question:

FEDERALISM IN THE EIGHTIES

THIRD EDITION

Donald V. Smiley
Professor of Political Science
York University

McGraw-Hill Ryerson Limited
Toronto   Montreal   New York   St. Louis   San Francisco
Auckland   Bogotá   Guatemala   Hamburg   Johannesburg   Lisbon
London   Madrid   Mexico   New Delhi   Panama   Paris
San Juan   São Paulo   Singapore   Sydney   Tokyo

Canada in Question: Federalism in the Eighties, Third Edition

ISBN 0-07-077867-1

4 5 6 7 8 9 0 D 9 8 7 6 5 4 3

Printed and bound in Canada

Care has been taken to trace ownership of copyright material contained in this text. The publishers will gladly take any information that will enable them to rectify any reference or credit in subsequent editions.

Canadian Cataloguing in Publication Data

Smiley, Donald V., date
    Canada in question

(McGraw-Hill Ryerson series in Canadian politics)
Bibliography: p.
Includes index.
ISBN 0-07-077867-1

1. Federal government—Canada. 2. Canada—Politics and government—1963—   *. I. Title.

JL65 1972 S6 1980   321.020971   C80-094258-2

TABLE OF CONTENTS

This book is dedicated to Henry Angus, Dean Emeritus of Graduate Studies of the University of British Columbia, whose study of the Canadian Confederation extends over nearly seventy years of its history. His lucidity of analysis and exactness of expression are standards I should like sometime to meet.

FOREWORD TO
THE THIRD EDITION

This is the best edition yet of Professor Donald Smiley's popular and important text book on Canadian federalism. Perhaps it is because Canadian federal problems are getting more complex and therefore more intriguing. But more likely it is because the author's talents continue to grow with each edition.

No one has a better grasp of the fundamentals of Canadian federalism and the breadth and depth of the literature on the subject, nor a more personal concern with the outcome. Professor Smiley, who is a formidable scholar, keeps up with each new development and significant publication and melds it into his description, analysis, and conclusions. The latter are at the same time both objective and subjective, a mixture which gives his book a particularly piquant appeal.

This third edition carries his assessment of Canadian federalism into the 1980s. It is up-to-date, comprehensive, and even more penetrating in its analyses than the previous editions. Although it covers some important aspects of the topic at greater length and in more detail than formerly, it is not much enlarged since Professor Smiley has tightened up some of his material and skilfully reorganized a number of sections. Finally, while he may not thank me for saying so, I think it is worth noting that although this is a sober and realistic analysis of Canadian federalism in the current decade, the author seems to be more optimistic about the present and future than he was in the previous edition.

The chapters in the third edition vary from their predecessors in the following manner. Chapter 1 now serves as a general introduction to the book. Chapter 2, describing Canada's constitutional system of parliamentary and federal government, has been reorganized, substantially rewritten, and enlarged. The line of argument has been simplified and the philosophical principles more clearly delineated. Chapter 3 is more historical. The author has gone back to 1927 to commence tracing the story of explicit constitutional reform which he carries forward to 1978. He describes succinctly the various proposals which have been presented to the many federal-provincial constitutional conferences in the past half century and explains why the attempts to achieve a new constitution have failed.

Professor Smiley has enlarged Chapter 4 on executive federalism by adding new sections on regionalism and regulatory agencies. He also has extended his discussion of interprovincial relations and the net effect of the increase in the volume of federal-provincial executive relations and the creation of intergovernmental officials and secretariats such as the Federal-Provincial Relations office. He concludes soberly that such activities and agencies have led to greater contention between governments rather than to improved accommodation.

Professor Smiley has left most of Chapter 5 untouched, much to my satisfaction, since his description of the extent to which political parties have been cohesive or divisive elements in Canadian confederation seems to me to be one of the most interesting and innovative parts of the book. The author has enlarged the chapter, bringing the contents up-to-date and incorporating the discussion of interest groups which appeared elsewhere in the second edition. In doing so, he demonstrates his great talent for absorbing and synthesizing all the recent literature.

Chapter 6, which deals with the complicated maze of federal-provincial financial relations, has been completely restructured and extensively rewritten. Less attention is now paid to the details in agreements than to the principles underlying the system. The subject has been broadened to "the economic dimensions of Canadian federalism," as the new title of the chapter indicates. With a more extended and comprehensive sweep, Professor Smiley discusses not only the intra-Canadian aspects of federal-provincial fiscal relations, such as equalization and stabilization, but the international implications as well.

Chapter 7 on cultural duality bears the same title as its predecessor but it contains a much fuller description of the language policies pursued at Ottawa by the Trudeau government and in Quebec by the Bourassa and Lévesque regimes. Smiley analyzes carefully the major provisions in Bills 22 and 101 and gives an extensive, up-to-date detailed account of the Parti Québécois and its proposed sovereignty association and referendum.

Chapter 8 has been rearranged, considerably enlarged, and brought up-to-date. Its themes are also much more deeply argued. Contending that the current Canadian crisis involves the structure of government as well as its forms, Smiley focusses on three sets of relations: English-French, centre-periphery, and Canadian-American.

Each of these three axes of Canadian federalism is under such pressure that Canadian nationhood is threatened. Yet there is little disposition to accommodate differences. Smiley gives a masterful summary of the difficulties of sovereignty-association and why English Canadians could not accept it. He paints an equally clear picture of the West's position and problems and the stresses and strains between Canada and the United States.

These challenges to Canada's survival lead Smiley to pose the fundamental question which he takes as the title for his concluding Chapter 9, "Is There a Basis for a Political Community in Canada?"

His answer is cautious and qualified. He notes that as a people we are not inclined to indulge in philosophical reflections about even fundamental matters such as federalism, self-determination, and culture and language as the bases for the creation of a Quebec state or the reestablishment of a Canadian nation. He wonders whether cultural nationalism can be contained and he worries about the right to self-determination. Finally, he posits two prerequisites for the survival of Canada as a country: "first, there must be a recrudescence of Cartier's vision of a political nationality not based on culture and ethnicity," and "second, there must be a discriminating limitation of the powers of the state and a strengthening of the voluntarist institutions of society."

In an Appendix, Professor Smiley suggests some lines of investigation and thinking which should be pursued further.

I hope that this brief review gives some indication of the depth, breadth, and quality of Professor Smiley's third edition. It is a remarkable *tour de force* in a difficult, complex and critical area of Canadian government. It provides not only a comprehensive description of Canadian federalism at the beginning of the eighties but a lucid, incisive, and provocative analysis of where we are heading. It is an exemplary book on federalism and the definitive text on the Canadian form.

Paul Fox
General Editor

Erindale College,
University of Toronto,
February 25, 1980.

INTRODUCTION

Not much more than two years after the second edition of *Canada in Question* appeared, McGraw-Hill Ryerson and the General Editor of its Series in Canadian Politics asked me to begin a revision. This was in one sense gratifying but, in another, I have been made to feel somewhat like a small child sent back to his sums and told to get them right. Within the time limits imposed on me I have done my best, but I am not very satisfied with the results. Canadian federalism itself and the vast amount of argument and analysis which surrounds its workings have become so complex that it is somewhat presumptuous for one person to write on such diverse matters as, for example, federal-provincial party organization, the roles of the two orders of government in stabilization policy, and the interpretation of the trade and commerce power by the Supreme Court of Canada. The author of a book such as this is both an academic scavenger and a dilettante, and I can do no more in the body of the study than to acknowledge in the footnotes and bibliography my indebtedness to those who have written on more specialized matters and ask for their tolerance in the summary way I have dealt with these complexities.

I first turned my attention to Canadian federalism about two decades ago when I was at the University of British Columbia and I want to mention here the help over the years of four people I came to know at that university—Edwin Black, Alan Cairns, Peter Meekison, and Richard Simeon. All of these in their own ways have contributed to our common understanding of the Canadian federal system and I am immodest enough to believe that in each case I helped to kindle an interest in this subject. Black and Cairns have made distinguished contributions to the scholarly literature, and in fact *this* book may reasonably be regarded as a long footnote to Cairns' brilliant and iconoclastic 1977 Presidential Address to the Canadian Political Science Association. Meekison is now Deputy Minister of Federal and Intergovernmental Affairs in Alberta, employing his considerable talents in pressing the legitimate and other interests of that province in the Canadian and international contexts. Richard Simeon in a few short years has written prolifically and well about Canadian federalism and as Director of the Institute of Intergovernmental Relations at Queen's University has built on the firm foundations laid by his predecessor, Ronald Burns, another British Columbian, to establish a vital and much-needed focus for federal studies in Canada. I would like to add almost parenthetically that I regard as one of the few hopeful developments in the federal system the increasingly active role the government of British Columbia has come to play in Canadian affairs in the regime of Bennett Secundus. The history of British Columbia has been relatively free of English-French and Catholic-Protestant conflicts and there is less bitterness against the economic hegemony of Montreal-Toronto than in the prairie and maritime provinces. In a period of Canadian experience when there is much too much reactivation of ancestral antipathies among cultures and regions, there is ample room for the kind of detachment which British Columbians can bring to our common affairs.

All of us who are university teachers draw intellectual sustenance from our immediate academic environments. In my view, York University in the strength of its various related disciplines is the most vital environment there is for the study of Canadian affairs and I would like to thank the stimulation of these colleagues among others in my study—David Bell, Fred and Martha Fletcher, Tom Hockin, Peter Hogg, Ian Macdonald, Ken McRoberts, and Douglas Verney. I want particularly to express my appreciation to McRoberts for sharing with me his sophisticated appreciation of the society and politics of Quebec. And despite the dismaying prospects in job markets, we are able to attract to York a very able and diligent group of graduate students in political science from whom I have learned much.

I have had other help too. Rosalie Still has done an outstanding job of turning my longhand into a "clean" manuscript. As in the other editions of this book, the General Editor of this Series, Paul Fox, has been a model of good humour and informed scholarly judgment in prodding me to do what I had agreed to do. And my wife Gwyn and our daughters have also helped, most of all perhaps by their tolerance of the inexcusable churlishness which comes over me when I am writing.

The third edition of *Canada in Question* is somewhat shorter on self-indulgent polemic than was its immediate predecessor. This does not mean that I have become a convert to the cause of "value-free political science" for, despite prolonged and diligent efforts to do so, I have never been able to understand how the analysis of significant political matters could be neutral about values. And as the son and the grandson of clergymen I have an ancestral impulse to witness against error wherever I find it—although in very many cases I have paid little heed to the Christian admonition to "speak the truth in love" and in the absence of charity I have often offended the scholarly rule of basing judgments on evidence. Be that as it may, I have chosen to make some minimal attempts to separate analysis from evaluation of the more explicit kind.

All worthy scholarship is a partnership between the past, the present, and that which is to come. Those who now study the Canadian federal system owe very much to that remarkable group of men who first began the systematic investigation of this system in the interwar period. I have been privileged to have personal contacts with several of these scholars—Henry Angus, Alex. Brady, Alex. Corry, Eugene Forsey, and Frank Scott. And it has been good to be in contact with younger persons—André Bernard, Tony Careless, Bill Irvine, Daniel Latouche, Larry Pratt, Richard Schultz, Richard Simeon, and Reg Whitaker among others—whom one can reasonably expect to carry this tradition of inquiry well into the twenty-first century.

Donald Smiley
Toronto, August, 1979.

CHAPTER 1
FEDERAL SOCIETY AND FEDERAL GOVERNMENT

A federal nation is one in which the most politically salient aspects of human differentiation, identification and conflict are related to specific territories. Conversely, of course, in a non-federal nation these political differentiations, identifications, and conflicts are not territorially bounded. This definition of federalism can be clarified somewhat by describing what a federal nation is not, using a somewhat far-fetched example. If gender became the most important basis for social, economic and political demands and people identified themselves almost exclusively with members of their own sex, we would not have a federal country—except in the unlikely and unhappy event that all or almost all the women lived in one part of it and all the men in the other.

Every country has its own mix of federal and non-federal elements and the proportion of each is never static. For example, although there are some countervailing forces at work, the United States appears to be moving away from federalism in the way I have defined it towards a situation in which some or even most of the crucial political conflicts are between interests which are not territorially bounded. On the other hand, the resurgence of Scottish and Welsh nationalisms in the United Kingdom is somewhat weakening the influence of economic and social class in dividing people on non-territorial lines.

Canada: A Federal Country

Canada is in the most elemental way a federal country, and it seems that it is becoming increasingly so. The following general statements can be made, each of which will be elaborated in more detail in succeeding chapters of this book:

—Canada is made up of several provincial/regional economies of a very different nature, which are at very different stages of development, and offer residents of these areas widely varying average levels of income and ranges of economic opportunities. The economic, social and political relations among people in a region or province dominated by, say, wheat-farming are very different from those in areas where commercial and manufacturing activities are the source of most of the employment and income. And of course the nature of these sub-national economies decisively shapes the relations of their residents with the rest of Canada and the world outside Canada's borders.

—in regard to cultural and linguistic differences, all but a small proportion of Canada's French-speaking citizens live in Quebec and in areas contiguous to Quebec in Ontario and New Brunswick. There has been a long-run trend towards the increasing concentration of this population within what Richard Joy has called the "Soo-Moncton line," with its boundaries of Sault Ste. Marie at the eastern end of Lake Superior and Moncton in east-central New Brunswick.[1]

—in comparison with the citizens of other western nations, Canadians are more attached to their regional and provincial communities than to the country as such. There appears to be a relatively weak sense of national identity and national solidarity.

—the most important economic, social and political conflicts in Canada pit the regions and provinces against one another and against the federal government. Most crucially, struggles on such territorial axes frustrate cleavages on nation-wide lines.

Society and Government

There is an important distinction to be made, the distinction between Society and Government—with capital letters used here in both cases. Government—variously designated as "public government" or "the state apparatus"—is the complex of courts, legislatures, cabinets, public services, armed forces and police forces. Government is distinguished from other institutions in that its decisions—what David Easton has called "the authoritative allocation of values"—bind all persons physically present within its territorial boundaries, and that its will is enforced in the last analysis by its monopoly of the means of physical coercion. Society consists of those elements of human association other than Government. We here include the economy and the relations among individuals and groups involved in the production, distribution, and exchange of goods and services in the private sector.

Society also includes a host of private associations formed to pursue goals that are neither economic nor governmental—religious, recreational, educational and so on—including those organizations whose activities are devoted wholly or partly toward influencing governments. Society comprises also family and kinship groups. And although these do not fit very well into either the Government or Society categories, I include in the latter those affective cognitive and evaluative orientations towards the political system which some scholars call "political culture."

In practice, the distinction between Government and Society is a good deal less clear than has been indicated above. Where do we put Canadian universities drawing most of their revenues from governments, and operating under increasingly specific provincial controls? or public corporations like Air Canada? or interest groups like the Canadian Association of Consumers relying heavily on public funds? or joint public-private enterprise such as Syncrude, established with the participation of governments and business corporations? In Canada as in other nations, the line between the governmental and the non-governmental is becoming increasingly blurred. However, for purposes of this analysis it is assumed that the Government-Society distinction is clearer than in fact it is.

Canada is a federal society with a federal system of government. But what shapes what? Does Society decisively determine Government—or is it the other way round? In a formal sense, is Society the independent variable, and Government the dependent variable? Or, to put it yet another way, do the "causal arrows" run from Government to Society or in the other direction?

In the 1950s, an American political scientist, William S. Livingston, made an argument which subsequently became very influential among students of federalism, that "Federalism is a function not of governments but of societies."[2] Thus "The [governmental] institutions themselves do not provide an accurate index of the federal nature of the society which subtends them; they are only the surface manifestations of the deeper federal quality of the society which lies beneath the surface. The essence of federalism lies not in the constitutional or institutional structure but in the society itself. Federal government is a device by which the federal qualities of the society are articulated and protected."[3] Livingston's argument was directed against the "legal formalism and formal jurisprudence" which had up to that time dominated the study of federalism.

Most students of contemporary Canadian federalism have accepted either explicitly or implicitly the sociological determinism of Livingston's analysis. Let us take, for example, a commonly accepted explanation of the resurgence of Quebec nationalism since 1960 and the pressures of successive Quebec governments for autonomy, with of course the culmination in the formation of the Parti Québécois on a platform of sovereignty, and the coming of that party to office in 1976. According to one explanation, the actions of these governments are and have been a reflection of the changed class structure in Quebec in which a "new middle class" of engineers, university teachers, journalists, managerial personnel and so on has displaced the traditional Francophone elite of priests, physicians and lawyers.[4] The individual and collective interests of this new élite have been in the directions of a much more extensive role for the Quebec state, and a much wider range of independence of this state from federal control. This kind of analysis also asserts the importance of the much strengthened identification of Francophone Quebeckers with the Quebec community—the change in self-definition from French Canadians or Canadiens to Québécois—and a heightened assertion of cultural and linguistic affiliation in political organization and political allegiance. In this kind of explanation, the actions of Quebec governments in seeking to extend their autonomy are attributed almost entirely to changes *outside* the political system.

In his 1977 Presidential Address to the Canadian Political Science Association, Alan C. Cairns challenged the Livingston position in a vigorous way.[5] The task Cairns set for himself was to explain the continuing aggressiveness and vitality of the provincial governments of Canada. He said:

> The sociological perspective pays inadequate attention to the possibility that the support for powerful, independent provincial governments is a product of the political system itself, that it is fostered and created by provincial government élites employing the policy-making apparatus of their jurisdictions, and that such support need not take the form of a distinct culture, society, or nation as these are conventionally understood. More specifically, the search for an underlying sociological base, whatever its nature and source, as the necessary sustenance for viable provincial political systems, deflects us from considering the prior question of how much support is necessary. Passivity, indifference, or the absence of strong opposition from their environment may be all that provincial governments need in order to thrive and grow. The significant question, after all, is the survival of provincial governments, not of provincial societies, and it is not self-evident that the existence and support of the latter is necessary to the functioning and aggrandisement of the former. Their sources of survival, renewal, and vitality may well lie within themselves and in their capacity to mould their environment in accordance with their own governmental purposes.[6]

Although Cairns' analysis was devoted to explaining the power of the provinces, it could similarly be applied to the federal government to the effect that Ottawa's strength comes from the national political apparatus itself, rather than the cultural, economic or other underpinnings of the country-wide community or the emotional commitments of Canadians to that community. Writing on the basis of a decade of prior experience as Deputy Minister of Intergovernmental Affairs in the Quebec government, Claude Morin came to this latter conclusion in his book *Quebec versus Ottawa* published in 1972.[7] Morin's basic argument was that the relations between the provinces and the federal government are irrevocably adversarial, and that in such conflicts there is an inherent tendency for the latter to get its way. He did not advance a coherent explanation of why the federal system has such a pervasively centralist thrust, although here and there there is reference to the disposition of English-speaking Canadians for centralization and the majoritarian pressures so resulting, according to the aphorism of Michel Brunet that "the lion always gets the lion's share." Yet my reading of Morin's argument is that his explanation of Ottawa's power is based on the assumption that this arises from the bureaucratic and political institutions of the federal government itself.

The Place of Institutions

A related question is whether the way that power is organized *within* Government has important consequences for the global distribution of power and privileges within Society. Do political institutions in any crucial sense matter? Is it of great concern that in Canada legislative powers are distributed between Parliament and the provinces, that members of the House of Commons are elected by pluralities from single-member constituencies and that both federal and provincial governments are organized according to the British parliamentary model? One would of course give affirmative answers to such questions only if he were predisposed to agree with the general lines of Cairns' argument that in the contemporary Canadian context Government has an independent influence in shaping Society. If the contrary position of Livingston were accepted that federal political institutions are merely a "surface manifestation" of the underlying federalism of Society, the way in which these institutions are structured is of only incidental importance.

In an article published in 1975, Richard Simeon argued that political institutions in Canada *do* matter.[8] He referred to the kinds of territorially-based differences in Canadian Society that I have outlined above. However, Simeon asserted that political institutions are never neutral in the determination of what kinds of cleavage develop in a political system, and he quoted E. E. Schattschneider to the effect that "All forms of political organization have a bias in favor of the exploitation of some kinds of conflict and the suppression of others. . . . Some issues are organized into politics while others are organized out."[9] In general terms, the issues which are "organized into" politics in Canada are territorially bounded, while those issues which divide Canadians on other axes are "organized out." Simeon's general conclusion was this: "institutions are not simply the outgrowth or products of the environment and . . . they are not just dependent variables in the political system. They can also be seen as independent forces, which have some effects of their own: once established, they themselves come to shape and influence the environment."[10] He went on to point out that some of the most important institutional characteristics of the Canadian system of government did not evolve from Canadian society but were "imported and imposed" from Britain.

The Explanatory Perspective of This Book

Some readers of what I have written above will no doubt claim that this is the kind of sterile and irrelevant and misleading debate in which professors are alleged to engage. Surely, it might be said, Government and Society interpenetrate one another in a myriad of ways, and it gives a perverse and distorted view of the real world to suggest the decisive influence of one over the other. This is a commonsense view, but it is not wholly adequate.

The task of the serious student of politics is to explain why the political world is as it is and not otherwise. But what is the test of an explanation? What criterion do we use to judge the relative validity of two or more contradictory explanations of the same phenomenon? Where complex matters are involved—such as the influence of Government on Society, or whether political institutions have an independent effect in determining the pattern of political cleavages—the only defensible test is, I think, plausibility. This test is by scientific standards inadequate, but it is the best we have. Rigorously scientific knowledge proceeds by separating out variables. For example, a scientist attempting to discover the effect of a particular fertilizer on the growth of corn plants identical seed in identical plots of land under identical climatic conditions, adding fertilizer to one plot but not the other, and at the end measuring the differences in yield which can thus be attributed entirely to the fertilizer. Students of politics can seldom use such devices, although techniques similar to this are used to determine the independent effects of such variables as age, sex and occupation on the distribution of public attitudes. However, the variables cannot be sorted out in this way to answer the questions of, say, the independent effects of parliamentary-cabinet government on the scope of public activity, or of electoral systems on the behaviour of politicians.

Each student of politics will find some kinds of explanations more plausible than others. In part, this is a matter of fashion. For example, contemporary political scientists are not disposed to attribute much significance to geographical factors in determining the nature of national political systems, although I am not aware of any body of empirical evidence which would justify this disposition. The social scientist's definition of plausibility is also linked to his ideological commitments. Ideology is a combination of (1) an explanation of some broad constellation of social, political and economic conditions (2) an imperative to either change or preserve that state of affairs and (3) a strategy for pursuing the goal of change or preservation. For example, on the basis of their divergent ideological commitments, one observer will explain an industrial conflict in terms of the normal clash of equally legitimate interests while another will perceive it in terms of the class struggle. But it must be remembered that an ideology is not only an imperative but also an explanation, and the honest student who thinks in ideological terms—and we cannot escape interpreting the world in such terms— will be willing to modify his views when such a framework patently fails to explain what is happening in the political environment. Thus, for example, any variant of communist theory which asserted that armed conflict between communist nations was "by definition" impossible would obviously have to be amended in the light of the events of recent years.

Whatever the justification for such a perspective, *Canada in Question* follows the general spirit of Cairns' assertion that "contemporary Canadian federalism is about governments," and readers will find relatively slight attention paid to economic classes, interest groups, public attitudes and other elements which I have consigned to the category of Society. This emphasis, this preference for one kind of explanation over others, is tentatively held, and new evidence might at some later time convince me I was wrong. We *do* know all too little about Government-Society linkages. However, the reader has at least been given notice of the general perspective of this book.

Notes

1. *Languages in Conflict: The Canadian Experience*, Published by Richard Joy, Ottawa: 1967, Chapter IV.
2. William S. Livingston, *Federalism and Constitutional Change*, Oxford: Clarendon Press, 1956, p. 4.
3. *Ibid.*, p. 2.
4. For one such analysis along neo-Marxist lines, see Henry Milner, *Politics in the New Quebec*, Toronto: McClelland and Stewart, 1978, particularly Chapters III, IV and VII.
5. Alan C. Cairns, "The Governments and Societies of Canadian Federalism," *Canadian Journal of Political Science*, X, December 1977, pp. 695-726.

6. P. 699.
7. Claude Morin, Quebec Versus Ottawa, Toronto: University of Toronto Press, 1972.
8. Richard Simeon "Regionalism and Canadian Political Institutions," in J. Peter Meekison, ed., *Canadian Federalism: Myth or Reality?* Third Edition, Toronto: Methuen, 1977, pp. 292-303.
9. P. 294.
10. P. 297. For another analysis of the importance of institutional arrangements see M. J. C. Vile, *Constitutionalism and the Separation of Powers*, Oxford: Clarendon Press, 1967, particularly Chapters 1 and XI. Vile speaks of constitutionalism being "based on a belief that there are certain demonstrable relationships between given types of institutional arrangements and the safeguarding of important values" (p. 8). He says also: "The study of politics must . . . very largely consist of the examination of the ways in which constitutional and political institutions, and the social forces and movements in a particular society, interact with each other; of the limits upon the extent to which stable constitutional modes of behaviour can be developed and maintained; and of the effects they have in moulding behaviour" (p. 314).

CHAPTER 2

THE CANADIAN CONSTITUTIONAL SYSTEM: PARLIAMENTARY *AND* FEDERAL

The Basic Models

The Dominion of Canada was the first political community to combine federalism with British-type parliamentary institutions, with what some have called the "Westminster model." This combination was to be repeated in the founding of the Australian union in 1900, and in several nations of the new Commonwealth after the Second World War.[1] The Canadian system of government—and no doubt those of other parliamentary federations—cannot be understood unless one keeps in mind that it is *both* irrevocably federal by reason of territorially-bounded particularisms in government, economy and society, *and* that it is, at the same time, cabinet-parliamentary by the settled habits and deliberate preferences of its citizens.

Federalism as the term is now used was an American invention, one of the most important and original inventions in the history of the art of government. The British legal scholar, A. V. Dicey, in his classic *Law of the Constitution* published in 1885 gave these as the distinguishing characteristics of federalism: "the supremacy of the constitution—the distribution among bodies with limited and co-ordinate authority of the different powers of government—the authority of the Courts to act as interpreters of the constitution."[2] However, Dicey's definition was derived largely from the American experience itself, and when the representatives of the several states gathered in Philadelphia in the summer of 1787 to consider changes in the Articles of Confederation they had no such model to guide them. In widely varying degrees, there was agreement that fundamental changes were needed in the "confederate, congressional form of government under which the United States had muddled through the first years of its existence."[3] But in reforming these political institutions, there was a major hurdle: where was sovereignty to reside? Or, to put the matter concretely, was it theoretically or practically possible to establish a system of government for the United States without vesting ultimate powers in one set of governmental authorities? There were only two models. The first was what the Americans called "national," in which one common authority would be supreme and the powers of the constituent states would be held at the discretion of that authority. The second model was in the parlance of the day "federal" where, as under the Articles of Confederation, the central "government" was dependent on the states for its powers, its financial resources and the enforcing of its decrees.

The way in which the "men of Philadelphia" combined the national and federal principles in the Constitution of the United States has been told in loving and almost infinite detail by successive generations of American writers.[4] The new government of the United States would be genuinely national in that the powers conferred on it by the Constitution would bear directly on individual citizens rather than on the states, and that these powers would be exercised by a national legislature, executive and judiciary. But the solution was also federal in the sense that the states would retain a constitutionally-protected autonomy over the powers not explicitly conferred on the national government or reserved to the people. And the Constitution itself, as the "supreme law of the land," rather than either the states or the national government, would be the sovereign authority.

When the politicians of British North America assembled in Charlottetown and later in Quebec City in the latter part of 1864, they did of course have the model of the United States before them. But they deliberately rejected this model in both its federal dimension and in its separation of legislative and executive powers. So far as the latter was concerned, those colonies had less than two decades before won the struggle for responsible government in which the governor was required to choose his executive advisors from among those who retained majority support in the legislative assembly. But federalism in the American sense was also rejected, and some of the Fathers of Confederation attributed the ongoing civil war to the alleged constitutional error of 1787 in conferring a wide measure of sovereignty on the states.[5] As we shall see later in this chapter, most of the English-speaking Fathers very much preferred a "legislative union" in which the powers of whatever provincial or other governments there were would be held and exercised at the discretion of the central authority. Although the French-Canadian leaders and some of those from the Maritime Colonies refused a solution along these lines, even they were brought to agree on what I shall later discuss as the "quasi-unitary elements of the

Canadian constitution," which differed markedly from the American federal pattern.

The Reconcilation (?) of Federal and Parliamentary Principles

Critics of the Canadian constitutional system have on occasion claimed that it is impossible to reconcile the parliamentary and federal principles. Writing of the proposed plan for the union of the British North American colonies, the Nova Scotian leader, Joseph Howe, said in early 1865: "We had two examples to guide us, that of England and that of the United States. The delegates offer us the Constitution of neither. . . . This hybrid resembles nothing on this continent, or on the other. The fare presented to us is neither fish, flesh, nor good red herring."[6] In similar vein, Dicey wrote sourly in *The Law of the Constitution:*

> The preamble to the British North America Act, 1867, asserts with diplomatic inaccuracy that the Provinces of the present Dominion have expressed their desire to be united into one Dominion" with a constitution similar in principle to that of the United Kingdom." If preambles were intended to express anything like the whole truth, for the word "Kingdom" might have been substituted "States," since it is clear that the Constitution of the Dominion is modelled on that of the Union.[7]

Dicey's essential point was that one of the two fundamental principles of the constitution of the United Kingdom was parliamentary sovereignty (the other was the rule of law), and that this was irreconcilable with federalism. According to parliamentary sovereignty, Parliament (the Monarch, the House of Lords and the House of Commons acting together) has "the right to make or unmake any law whatever; and further, that no person or body is recognized by the law of England as having a right to override or set aside the legislation of Parliament."[8] Dicey's definition of federalism, as quoted earlier, posited two sets of governmental authorities which were legally co-ordinate and a supreme constitution authoritatively interpreted by the courts. In Dicey's view the essential constitutional principle of the British North America Act was federal, and thus the Canadian system was basically American rather than British.

The reconciliation between parliamentary sovereignty and federalism was effected in the Canadian constitution by provisions which, with some exceptions, embody what lawyers call an "exhaustive" distribution of legislative powers between Parliament and the provinces. Dicey quoted an aphorism that "it is a fundamental principle with English lawyers that Parliament can do anything but make a woman a man, and a man a woman." In a federal context this means that the totality of law-making powers is divided by the constitution between the central and regional governments. This general circumstance is subject to certain qualifications in the Canadian case, and there are exceptions to the exhaustiveness of the distribution of legislative powers in the sense that some powers are withheld from both Parliament and the provinces. Among the more significant of these exceptions are the following:[9]

—certain crucial parts of the constitution itself are amendable only by the Parliament of the United Kingdom.

—neither Parliament nor the provinces may restrict the rights of the English and French languages as specified in Section 133 or the rights of denominational minorities in education as provided for under Section 93.

—neither Parliament nor the provinces may tax the lands or property of the other (Section 121).

—neither Parliament nor the provinces may delegate their legislative powers to the other.

—by judicial decision, neither Parliament nor the provinces can enact "privative clauses" enjoining the review by the courts of laws or executive acts on matters of law.

The continuing adherence of Canadians to the traditions and practices of the Westminster model has both shaped the federal system, and precluded certain kinds of changes in that system.

First, judicial review of the constitution is almost entirely limited to delineating the division of legislative powers between Parliament and the provinces. This is in marked contrast with the American situation. In the past generation the American courts, most importantly of course the Supreme Court of the United States, have almost ceased determining the limits of the respective powers of the national and state governments, but have been very much involved in the constitutional protection of the rights of individuals and, to a lesser degree, delineating the powers of the various elements of the national government. In Canada, on the other hand, the only kind of constitutional question decided on by the courts is, with relatively rare exceptions, whether either Parliament or the legislature of a province has trespassed on the other's jurisdiction. If one defines the Canadian constitution broadly as the body of rules determining the basic structures and processes of government, only a relatively small but crucial part of the constitution is included in constitutional law enforced by the courts. As in the United Kingdom, the most important of the operating rules of the parliamentary system are in the realm of convention rather than law, although in a somewhat illogical fashion the British North America Act of 1867 and its subsequent amendments do contain some of those principles of parliamentary government. For example, Sections 44-48 regulate the office of the

Speaker of the House of Commons, Section 48 requires at least 20 members of the House to be present for its meetings to be held, and Section 54 requires that a bill for the raising or expenditure of revenues can only be introduced into the House by a "Message of the Governor General"—in effect, by a cabinet minister. However, for the most part the courts do not involve themselves in policing the internal operations of the federal and provincial governments.

Secondly, British-type parliamentary institutions preclude a bicameral national legislative assembly in which the chambers have roughly equal powers. In most federal systems, including the Canadian, one of the houses of the national legislature is elected on the basis of representation by population while the other is chosen so as to give special recognition to the states or provinces. Yet the relative weakness of the Canadian Senate is well known, despite the circumstance that with the one exception mentioned in the preceding paragraph, this body has under the British North America Act the same powers as the House of Commons. The basic situation here is that under the Westminster model the cabinet collectively and the ministers individually are responsible to the House of Commons alone. The first cabinet of the Dominion which took office on July 1, 1867, included no fewer than five Senators among its 13 members and Sir John Abbott, who was Prime Minister in 1891-92, was a Senator, as was Sir Mackenzie Bowell in 1894-96. However, under modern conditions the rule is that all the ministers heading important departments of government hold seats in the House of Commons, and largely because of this circumstance the House dominates the Senate both in power and in public attention. Thus a bicameral system of genuinely co-ordinate chambers as prevails in the United States is precluded by the Westminster model. Even in Australia where the Senate is popularly elected, the House of Representatives to which the cabinet is responsible is dominant.

Thirdly, the workings of parliamentary institutions at the national level tend to make the popularly-elected legislative assembly an ineffective outlet for sentiments and interests specific to particular provinces or regions. Under the Westminster model, the ministry has an unshared right to govern so long as it can command majority support in the House of Commons. Cohesion and discipline within each of the parties in the House result from the circumstance that the continuance of the executive in office is dependent on this support. The influences toward cohesion are particularly strong in the party in power, but also impinge on the opposition party as it seeks to establish its credibility among the voters as a future government. But at any one time the powers of government are unshared, and a particular province or region which returns relatively few MPs to the governing side of the House of Commons is left out of access to the most important centres of governmental decision. As we shall see in Chapter 8, the disabilities of the Canadian House of Commons in providing an effective outlet for territorially based particularisms are compounded by the working of an electoral system which often leaves particular provinces and regions virtually unrepresented in the governing party, even when the voters of these areas have given a significant proportion of their votes to that party.

Fourthly, the Westminster model in its Canadian variant, provides for unified executive power at both levels of government. Thomas A. Hockin argues that the tradition of a "collective central energizing executive as the key engine of the state" is the essential operating principle of the Canadian system and that this executive dominance prevails in both Ottawa and the provinces.[10] The workings of "executive federalism" will be discussed in Chapter 4 and only the general outline of the parliamentary tradition as it impinges on these relations will be given here. The cabinet is collectively responsible to the House of Commons for government policies, and ministers are individually responsible for actions taken in their respective departments. These kinds of collective and individual responsibilities require a particular kind of relation between the elected members of the cabinet and appointed officials. Appointed civil servants in the departments and agencies of government are "neutral" and "anonymous" in the sense that they carry out the will of their "political masters" and that these latter persons are held accountable by the House of Commons and the electorate for the acts of the bureaucracy. Some students of parliamentary institutions in Canada and elsewhere claim that with the scope of government activity which now prevails, the traditions of cabinet/ministerial responsibility which I have outlined are so far from reality that this theory is at best misleading and, at worst, a dangerous concealment of the actual powers wielded by appointed officials.[11] However, these traditions do in my view encompass a good deal of the actual operations of Canadian government. The executive in both its elected and appointed elements dominates the governmental process, and in particular there are no significant institutional barriers to first ministers and cabinets integrating the activities of their own administrations so that they can deal with other governments on a "one-to-one" basis.

Fifthly, to the extent that the *actual* locus of decision-making has shifted to a network of intergovernmental interactions—whether these involve foreign jurisdictions or governments within a particular country—parliaments are unable to make the political executive effectively accountable for such affairs. We need here to be reminded that, within the framework of the Westminister model, the Canadian House of Commons is not in any real sense a legislature precisely because the executive almost completely monopolizes the law-making function and, so far as measures of general public concern are involved, the proposed enactments brought before Parliament are with few exceptions framed by the cabinet and the appointed bureaucracy. (Between 1957 and 1974 inclusive, of 1,130 enactments of a public significance made law by Parliament, only 9 were private members' acts).[12] In John Stewart's terms "the House has a constitutional function: not to govern but *to support a government.*"[13] Stewart breaks down what he calls the "democratic function of the House" into four sub-functions: (1) "the House can prevent the clandestine exercise of power by the government," (2) "the House can serve as a proving ground for the administrative policies and legislative proposals of the government," (3) "the House can constrain the government between elections" and (4) "the House can serve to inform and educate the electorate."[14] There are many influences limiting the capacity of the House of Commons and other legislative assemblies to perform such functions effectively: for example, the complexity of contemporary public policy, the extensive bureaucratic resources that ministers and governments can command in fending off opposition attacks, long-standing traditions of governmental secrecy along with plausible justifications for such secrecy as a prerequisite for the effective working of parliamentary institutions, and the conservatism of legislative bodies in reorganizing their own procedures. With all this being said, the most persuasive justification for the Westminster model is that it provides at least some possibilities for making governments effectively accountable and, to quote our basic "constitutional strategy" as formulated by Stewart:

> We want a government with a high sense of responsibility. To cultivate such a responsibility we concentrate power. We place the duty of using power, not in the hands of scores of private members, each elected in his own isolated constituency, but in the hands of the prime minister and his ministerial colleagues. By concentrating power we make responsibility difficult to evade.[15]

Yet such patterns of responsibility break down when ministers and governments come before parliaments with policies which are in fact the resultants of negotiations with other governments, whether the latter are inside or outside the country.[16] In such circumstances the assembly is restricted to either giving its assent or taking actions which will withdraw its confidence from the government and perhaps lead to its resignation. Further, plausible reasons for secrecy in intergovernmental relations also work in the direction of weakening effective procedures of accountability.

In general terms, Canadians throughout their history have shown a pronounced disposition to adhere to a version of the Westminster model which provides for executive dominance. Even the more thoroughgoing plans for the reform of the institutions of Canadian government brought forward in recent years suggest, for the most part, that these patterns be perpetuated at least in some modified form. The Official Program of the Parti Québécois, it is true, proposes far-reaching changes in the constitution of Quebec closely patterned after the American congressional system. By virtue of Section 92(1) of the British North America Act, which gives the provinces exclusive authority to amend their own constitutions "except as regards the Office of Lieutenant Governor," there would seem to be no legal barriers to most of these changes being carried out within Confederation.[17] In a political sense, however, the government of a province which operated according to such arrangements might be at a relative disadvantage in dealing with executives which derive their dominance from the traditions of the parliamentary system.

What *Is* the Canadian Constitution?

Among students of law and politics the term "constitution" is used in two different ways. In the first sense we refer to a legal code which, within a geographically-delineated area, overrides all other enactments or acts of government and is usually amendable by a procedure less flexible than that related to other legislation. The second way we use the term constitution involves subject-matter, i.e., the laws and settled usages within a state which determine the respective powers and privileges of the various institutions of government and the essential aspects of the relations between citizens and the political community. In many circumstances the procedural and subject-matter definitions of what is constitutional will coincide, where the legal document prescribing the basic political relations of a community is both paramount over other political acts, and subject to amendment by procedures less flexible than those by which other laws can be changed. On the other hand, jurisdictions with codified constitutions sometimes include provisions about substantive public policy, as when the United States Constitution was amended in 1919 to prohibit the manufacture or sale of alcoholic beverages. Contrariwise, the United Kingdom does not have a codified constitution at all, and from time to time the most fundamental of political relations are determined by the Crown in Parliament through the same procedures by which enactments relating to the most trivial of public matters come into being. In general, the usual distinction between written and unwritten constitutions is not very helpful, and the most useful classification is between codified and uncodified constitutions, and between codified and uncodified elements of the same constitutional system.

But what *is* included in the Canadian constitution?[18] An amendment to the British North America Act enacted in 1949 conferred on Parliament the power to amend "the Constitution of Canada," with certain very important exceptions related to the powers of the provinces, rights of the English and French languages and of denominational minorities in education, and provisions related to annual sessions of the House of Commons and to the maximum five-year length of the life of each House. In broad terms, "the Constitution of Canada" in this sense is restricted to the structure and organization of the federal government as a concomitant to the powers of the provinces to amend their own constitutions. Although, as we shall see in the next chapter, the Fulton-Favreau formula was not enacted, this proposed procedure for constitutional amendment agreed upon by the federal and provincial governments in the fall of 1964 included this definition:

> 11. Without limiting the meaning of the expression "Constitution of Canada," in this Part that expression includes the following enactments and any order, rule or regulation thereunder, namely,
>   (a) the British North America Acts, 1867 to 1964;
>   (b) the Manitoba Act, 1860;
>   (c) the Parliament of Canada Act, 1875;
>   (d) the Canadian Speaker (Appointment of Deputy) Act, 1895, Session 2;
>   (e) the Alberta Act;
>   (f) the Saskatchewan Act;
>   (g) the Statute of Westminster, 1931, in so far as it is part of the law of Canada; and
>   (h) this Act.[19]

Beyond the Fulton-Favreau definition there are other important elements governing the procedures by which the powers are held and exercised. Some of these take the form of what has been called "constitutional statutes," enactments of the Parliament of Canada which in a strict legal sense are solely at the discretion of that body but which are constitutional in their subject matter. It is, however, unlikely that any group of students of such affairs could be brought to agreement on a list of Canadian constitutional statutes.[20] Certainly there should be included the War Measures Act, the Canadian Bill of Rights, and the Supreme Court Act. But should such a category include, for example, the Canada Elections Act and the Canadian Citizenship Act? Beyond constitutional statutes, the powers of the Prime Minister of Canada are detailed in a minute of the Privy Council of October 25, 1935—leading to the somewhat paradoxical situation in which the powers of this official could in formal terms be changed by action of a subsequent cabinet, although an alteration in the office of Deputy Speaker of the Senate could be effected only by formal constitutional amendment. The most crucial of the operating rules of the parliamentary system, including the dependence of the political executive on the continuing support of the House of Commons, are almost entirely within the realm of custom, convention and the procedural rules established by each chamber to govern its own operations.[21] And if we extended our notion of constitution broadly enough we would include the circumstance that leaders of the political parties, and by consequence first ministers, are chosen by representative party conventions according to procedures established by the parties themselves.

In his recent book *Constitutional Law of Canada*, Peter Hogg points out: "The one real disadvantage of a comprehensive constitutional document [in Canada] is that the rules of the constitution are not readily accessible to non-lawyers."[22] But even the lawyers do not give the rest of us sure and certain guidance here; in Hogg's excellent and comprehensive treatise, only one of 25 chapters is given over to a discussion of the parliamentary dimension of the constitutional system. Other lawyers define the constitution in even narrower terms, and the descriptive subtitles to two widely used case books on Canadian constitutional law are "Cases, Text and Notes on the Distribution of Legislative Power," and "Cases, Notes and Materials on the Distribution and Limitation of Legislative Powers under the Constitution of Canada."[23] It is understandable that lawyers will be disposed to give a narrow definition of the constitution to include only those provisions to which the courts of law will give meaning and effect. For the most part, this will confine constitutional law to provisions related to the distribution of legislative powers between Parliament and the provinces under Sections 91 and 92 of the British North America Act, along with safeguards for the rights of the French and English languages and of denominational minorities in education in Sections 133 and 93 respectively. Such a definition excludes even provisions of the British North America Act itself which are not in the normal course of events subject to judicial review. For example, Sections 35 and 48 specify the number of members of the Senate and House of Commons respectively which shall constitute a quorum of these bodies, but it is almost inconceivable that any Canadian court would involve itself in overturning an enactment because of such procedural requirements not having been met.

Despite the analytical difficulties in restricting the definition of the Canadian constitution to the distribution of legislative powers between Parliament and the provinces, there is everything to be said for emphasizing this dimension of the Canadian constitutional experience. *This* is where the action is, and has been from the beginning, and as we shall see in the next chapter, recent efforts to effect constitutional changes which do not come to terms with the division-of-powers question have been unsuccessful.

The Federal Division of Legislative Powers

The most characteristic aspect of a federal constitution is its division of law-making powers between the central and regional governments.

Contemporary federal systems have variegated institutional characteristics. Most, like Canada, have a unified judicial system; the United States has parallel structures of federal and state courts. In several federations, like the United States and the Federal Republic of Germany, the regional governments as such have important responsibilities related to the functioning of the central authority; in Canada it is otherwise. The older federations have had separate and autonomous central and regional bureaucracies; in some of the newer ones there has been reliance on a unified civil service. Despite these and other institutional differences, the distinguishing characteristic of a federation is the constitutional distribution of legislative powers between national and state or provincial governments. There are many kinds of such distributions. In Canada and most of the newer federations the national legislature is given the residual powers—i.e. those not explicitly conferred on the provinces or states—while there is a contrary tradition which defines the federal principle in terms of the national government having only those powers explicitly conferred on it by the constitution. Some federations have a large number of concurrent legislative powers which can be exercised by either or both levels of government, but in Canada explicit provisions for concurrency are limited. In some federations, such as Canada and Australia, the distribution of legislative powers is exhaustive or nearly exhaustive in the sense that if one level cannot enact a particular kind of legislation the other has power to do so, while in the United States there are important constitutional restrictions upon what any government can do. Some federations like the United States provide that all the constituent states/provinces have precisely the same law-making powers while, in others, like the Republic of India, not all the states or provinces have the same legislative authority. Despite these variations, all federal constitutions provide for a distribution of legislative powers which cannot be altered or amended at the unilateral discretion of either level.

Those who framed the British North America Act did not find it difficult to agree on a distribution of law-making powers between Parliament and the provincial legislatures. There have been several explanations of the relative ease with which the matter was resolved. In a study published in 1939, Donald Creighton suggested that, so far as economic affairs were concerned, the Fathers of Confederation made an implicit distinction between activities associated with land and activities associated with commerce, and on the basis of this distinction allocated powers to the provinces and the Dominion respectively.[24] The Report of the Quebec Royal Commission on Constitutional Problems, published in 1956, argued that in general the subjects given to the provinces were those in respect to which the traditions and interests of the English- and French-speaking communities were significantly different, while Dominion matters were believed to have no such cultural incidence.[25] Peter Waite has said that by "the federal principle" the Fathers of Confederation did not mean the distribution of legislative powers at all, but rather the structure of Parliament and in particular the relation between the Senate and the House of Commons.[26]

The formula for the distribution of legislative authority in the British North America Act assigned the residual powers to the Dominion. Section 92 enumerated fifteen classes of subjects about which the provinces exclusively might make laws, along with a sixteenth category, "Generally all Matters of a merely local or private Nature in the Province." Section 93 provided for exclusive provincial jurisdiction over education, with safeguards for the rights of denominational schools as these rights existed by law at the time of union, or were subsequently so established. Section 95 enacted that both Parliament and the provinces might make laws in respect to agriculture and immigration, with the proviso that those of the Dominion would prevail in the event of a conflict. These were, then, the legislative powers of the provinces. The opening words of Section 91 enacted: "It shall be lawful for the Queen, by and with the Advice and Consent of the Senate and House of Commons to make Laws for the Peace, Order, and Good Government of Canada, in relation to all Matters not coming within the Classes of Subjects by this Act assigned exclusively to the Legislatures of the Provinces." If the Act had not gone on to elaborate this general grant of law-making power, the subsequent judicial interpretation of the Canadian constitution would have been very different from what it turned out to be. In passing on the validity of an enactment of Parliament the courts would have had no alternative to ascertaining whether or not it encroached on provincial legislation as specified in Sections 92 and 93, and any provincial enactment would have had to be justified as coming within one of these Sections or Section 95. However, Section 91 went on to enact "and for greater Certainty, but not so as to restrict the Generality of the foregoing Terms of this Section, it is hereby declared that . . . the exclusive Legislative Authority of the Parliament of Canada extends to all Matters coming within the Classes of Subjects next herein enumerated . . .." There were then listed twenty-nine classes of subjects. There has never been a satisfactory explanation of why the framers of the Act resorted to such an enumeration. As we shall see, judicial interpretation from the late nineteenth century onward came to find the peacetime legislative powers of Parliament not in the authority to enact laws for the "Peace, Order, and Good Government of Canada," but rather in the enumerated headings of Section 91.

In terms of substance, most of the powers of the provinces can be subsumed under one or both of these classes of subjects: (1) those matters where the traditions of the English- and French-speaking communities of the former province of Canada differed significantly; (2) those matters which in British North America of the 1860s were usually the responsibility of local governments. Thus were included jurisdiction over education, what we would now call health and welfare matters, the control of provincial Crown lands and natural resources, municipal institutions, and the administration of justice in the province, as well as concurrent powers with the Dominion over agriculture and immigration. The provinces were also given exclusive powers to legislate in respect to "Property and Civil Rights in the Province." From the Quebec Act of 1774 onward, Quebec had been given the right to carry on the system of private law derived from France, and thus the provinces were given jurisdiction over property and civil rights, so that the civil law traditions might continue in Quebec and the common law traditions in provinces with English-speaking majorities.[27]

The powers conferred on the Dominion were deemed necessary to secure military defence, the eventual inclusion of all remaining British territories in North America within Canada, and the establishment of an integrated national economy. Under the enumerated headings of Section 91 were included powers over trade and commerce; the various aspects of inter-provincial transportation and communication; banking, currency, interest, and legal tender; and patents and copyrights. As we have seen, Section 95 conferred concurrent powers on the Dominion and the provinces in respect to agriculture and immigration, with the proviso that federal laws should prevail in the event of a clash. Several sections of the Act provided for the federal authorities taking action to include remaining British possessions in North America in the Dominion, e.g. Newfoundland, and the western territories still under the control of the Hudson's Bay Company. Parliament received the exclusive power to give legislative implementation to British treaties in Canada. The national authorities were to have exclusive powers over defence. Along with these nation-building and nation-maintaining powers, the exclusive authority to legislate in respect to the criminal law and to procedures in criminal matters was conferred on the Dominion, and the central government was given crucial responsibilities in respect to a unified judicial system.

In conferring what were then the most costly functions of government on the Dominion, the framers of the Confederation settlement provided that Parliament might raise monies by "any Mode or System of Taxation" while the provinces were limited to direct taxes. The effect was to give the Dominion exclusive access to customs and excise duties, the sources of most public revenues at the time, while the provinces would be confined to taxes on real property, proceeds from the sale of Crown lands and the exploitation of natural resources and to incidental fees and revenues. The provinces were also to receive annual subsidies from the Dominion according to a schedule provided for in the British North America Act.

The BNA Act provided for a single judicial system in Canada rather

than, as in the United States, a dual system of courts dealing with national and state matters respectively. Although the Act seemed to contemplate that for the most part the Dominion and the provinces would
carry on their respective legislative and administrative responsibilities
in relative independence of one another, the judicial system was
clearly expected to operate through cooperation between the two
levels. The provinces were given exclusive jurisdiction over "The Administration of Justice in the province, including the "Constitution,
Maintenance, and Organization of Provincial Courts, both of Civil and
Criminal Jurisdiction, and including Procedure in Civil Matters in
these Courts." However, the Governor-General—in effect the federal
cabinet—was to appoint the judges of the superior, district and county
courts in each province; these judges were to be paid by the Dominion
and were to serve during good behaviour, subject to removal by the
Governor-General on an address from the Senate and House of Commons. Parliament was given exclusive authority to legislate in respect
to the criminal law and to procedures in criminal matters. It was further
provided in Section 101: "The Parliament of Canada may . . . provide
for the Constitution, Maintenance, and Organization of a General Court
of Appeal for Canada, and for the Establishment of any additional
courts for the better Administration of the Laws of Canada."

Quasi-Unitary Features of the Canadian Constitutional System

Sections 91, 92, 93 and 95 of the British North America Act distribute
legislative powers between Parliament and the provinces. However,
under the explicit terms of the Act and its subsequent judicial interpretation, there are several ways by which the federal authorities may by
unilateral action trespass on, modify, displace or influence the exercise
by the provinces of the latters' legislative jurisdiction.

There were four quasi-unitary provisions in the terms of the British
North America Act of 1867:

(1) Under Sections 55 and 90 the provinces were put in a position of
   colonial subordination to the Dominion (as were the Dominion authorities in relation to the United Kingdom).[28] The Lieutenant Governor of a province, a Dominion officer, had the power to "reserve"
   a provincial bill and when he did so the bill did not become law unless the federal cabinet so decided. Whether reserved or not, any
   provincial bill might be vetoed—"disallowed"—by the federal cabinet within a year of its enactment.

(2) Section 132 read:

The Parliament and Government of Canada shall have all Powers necessary or proper for performing the Obligations of Canada or of any Province thereof, as Part of the British Empire, towards Foreign Countries.

At the time of Confederation, of course, the government of the United Kingdom bound Canada and other parts of the Empire in international affairs. Section 132 permitted the Dominion authorities to carry out such Imperial obligations, even if this required action within fields of jurisdiction otherwise conferred on the provinces.

(3) Under Section 93 the federal cabinet and Parliament were made the guarantors of the educational rights of denominational minorities against provincial encroachments. If, in its judgment, the cabinet decided such rights had been overridden by a province, the cabinet might intervene, but if this proved ineffective in restoring these rights, Parliament might enact "remedial" legislation.

(4) Under Section 92:10(c), Parliament was given the power to bring "Works" otherwise within provincial jurisdiction under federal control.

None of these quasi-unitary devices has recently been used to strengthen the power of Ottawa against the provinces:

(1) The last exercise of the power of disallowance was in 1943. The last time reservation was used was in 1961, when the Lieutenant-Governor of Saskatchewan refused his assent to a bill passed by the Legislative Assembly of that province. However, this official had reserved the bill without seeking the prior advice of the federal cabinet, which subsequently approved the enactment.[29]

(2) Since the enactment of the Statute of Westminster by the Parliament of the United Kingdom in 1931, the U.K. authorities have not assumed international commitments on behalf of Canada or other sovereign nations of the Commonwealth. Section 132 is thus inoperative as a source of power by which the federal authorities might encroach on jurisdiction which is otherwise provincial, although Canada is still bound by certain international obligations incurred on her behalf as part of the British Empire prior to 1931.

(3) Parliament has never enacted remedial legislation in support of the educational rights of a provincial denominational minority.

(4) Parliament's "declaratory power" to bring "Works" under federal control has fallen into disuse and has not been exercised since 1961.[30]

A quasi-federal device which *has* been of very great importance in recent decades is the federal power to spend or lend the revenues at its disposal, and to attach almost any conditions it chooses to define eligibility for such largesse—whether the beneficiaries be provincial or local governments, private associations, or private individuals.[31]

This power provides a way in which the federal authorities can, as they wish, insert themselves in almost any matter within provincial jurisdiction where significantly large expenditures are involved. The spending power has been the legal basis for such varied federal programs as family allowances, assistance to the arts through the Canada Council, various schemes of loans and subsidies for housing, support of provincial schemes of medical and hospital insurance, grants to individuals to improve the insulation of their houses, and financial assistance to the provinces in providing education in their minority official languages. Most constitutional scholars find the legal justification for the spending power lies in Section 91:1(A), which gives Parliament the power to legislate in respect to "The Public Debt and Property," although others have defended this power by reference to "Peace, Order, and Good Government." Frank Scott has made yet another argument that it is justified on the basis of the prerogative power of the Crown to expend the monies at its disposal as it chooses, subject only to prior parliamentary approval.[32] There has been relatively little judicial determination of the limits of the spending power. There would appear to be only three such legal limitations, none of them of great practical consequence, in restricting federal encroachments on subjects within provincial legislative jurisdiction:

(1) So far as a matter within provincial jurisdiction is concerned, the failure of individuals or groups to conform to the conditions of eligibility for federal largesse cannot be made an offence in federal law.

(2) Parliament may not finance a program within provincial jurisdiction partly or wholly from the proceeds of a levy made for that specific purpose.

(3) The national authorities may not, under the guise of the spending power, set up what is in essence a regulatory scheme encroaching on provincial jurisdiction.

Another quasi-federal aspect of the BNA Act lies in the expansion of federal powers through "Peace, Order, and Good Government," what Peter Hogg has called for convenience "p.o.g.g." The subtleties of p.o.g.g. are immense, some of our finest legal minds have given a lifetime of study to these mysteries and little else, and the more sophisticated expressions of this dialectic—such as the opinion of Chief Justice Laskin in the Anti-Inflation Reference of 1976—are no more understandable to the Canadian layman than is, say, astrophysics. But at the risk of great over-simplification, something needs to be said about the ways in which federal powers have been extended by resort to "p.o.g.g." beyond the enumerated headings of Section 91.[33]

The first kind of situation in which federal powers have been extended through resort to "p.o.g.g." relates to emergencies. In a later section of this chapter, there will be some discussion of emergency powers under the War Measures Act to meet conditions of "war, invasion or insurrection, real or apprehended." During the 1930s the Judicial Committee of the Privy Council invalidated several social measures of the Bennett "New Deal" which the federal government had defended as necessary to meet the exigencies of the Great Depression.[34] However, in 1976 a majority of the Supreme Court of Canada upheld the federal anti-inflation legislation of the previous year as a valid exercise of emergency powers, even though the enactment under review did not explicitly refer to the existence of an emergency.[35] The major restriction on the power is that it cannot be used in this context to deal with other than a temporary matter. Apart from this limitation, the 1976 decision appears to open the door to the federal authorities extending their powers almost at will to meet a peacetime economic emergency.[36]

The second class of circumstance in which Parliament's powers have been extended beyond the explicit enumerated headings of Section 91 relates to some matter becoming of national concern or having a "national dimension." In *Russell v. the Queen*, decided in 1882, the Judicial Committee upheld Dominion legislation regulating the sale of alcoholic beverages on the grounds that this matter was of "general concern to the Dominion" and that uniform legislation which only Parliament could enact was necessary to deal with this.[37] Lord Watson speaking for the Judicial Committee enunciated the national-dimensions test in the *Local Prohibition* case of 1896. "Their Lordships do not doubt that some matters, in their origin local and provincial, might attain such dimensions as to affect the body politic of the Dominion, and to justify the Canadian Parliament in passing laws for their regulation or abolition in the interests of the Dominion."[38] In this century the national-dimensions test has been used to uphold federal legislation related to the control of aeronautics and of broadcasting, the regulation of the National Capital District, and the production of uranium.

The federal spending power and p.o.g.g. offer the federal authorities considerable opportunities to extend their activities beyond the enumerated headings of Sections 91 and 95. There are no comparable provisions for the expansion of provincial authority. So far as the spending power is concerned, the crucial limitations on federal action are financial and political rather than legal, and relate to the availability of federal revenues, the urgency Ottawa has about influencing matters within provincial jurisdiction, and how much opposition from the provinces it is willing to tolerate in so doing. In respect to p.o.g.g., the judiciary, most importantly of course the Supreme Court of Canada, has a very wide discretion to decide what may be justified under this general power. Almost inevitably in such cases, the courts will have to make judgments of a broadly social or economic nature about whether an emergency exists or whether a matter otherwise provincial has acquired a national dimension.

A last quasi-unitary aspect of the Canadian constitution relates to judicial organization. Unlike the United States with its dual system of courts which interpret the laws enacted by the national and state authorities respectively, Canada has essentially a unified judicial system. Under Section 92(14) the provinces have exclusive authority to enact legislation respecting "The Administration of Justice in the Province, including the Constitution, Maintenance and Organization of Provincial Courts, both of Civil and Criminal Jurisdiction, and excluding Procedure in Civil Matters in these Courts." (Procedure in criminal matters is within federal jurisdiction under Section 91(27) related to "Criminal Law."). However, under Section 96 the Governor General, in effect the federal cabinet, appoints the members of the "Superior, District and County Courts of each Province." The salaries and pensions of these judges are paid for from federal funds and they are removable only by an address of the Senate and House of Commons on the motion of the government.

Despite the elements of a unified judicial system under the shared control of the federal and provincial authorities under the provisions outlined above, other Sections of the British North America Act allow Parliament to move towards duality in judicial organization. Section 101 enacts, "The Parliament of Canada may, notwithstanding anything in this Act, from Time to Time provide for the Constitution, Maintenance and Organization of a General Court of Appeal for Canada, and for the Establishment of any additional Courts for the better Administration of the Laws of Canada." In 1875 under this authority the Supreme Court of Canada was established as a general court of appeal. In 1949 Parliament made the Court the final judicial authority in Canadian constitutional cases. The jurisdiction of the Court is determined by federal law and its size and personnel by the federal authorities. Section 101 is also quasi-unitary in that it gives the federal government the authority to confer on federal courts the power to deal with any of the laws enacted by the Parliament of Canada and thus to remove these from the jurisdiction of the provincial courts. This Section was the legal basis of Ottawa's action in 1971 in expanding the jurisdiction of the newly established Federal Court of Canada beyond that of its predecessor, the Exchequer Court, to include the review of the decisions of federal administrative tribunals and to include certain suits between citizens involving federal law. It may be noted in conclusion that there are no corresponding constitutional provisions permitting the provinces to press the judicial system in the direction of a dual judicial system, and Section 96 providing for the appointment by the Governor in Council of the members of the superior, district and county courts of each province has been interpreted to forestall the provinces from conferring judicial functions on provincial administrative tribunals.[39]

The Amendment of the British North America Act

The amendment of a codified constitution is the most fundamental of political processes. Formal amendment is only one of the procedures of constitutional change, but as William S. Livingston points out, "It differs from the others in that it is superior to them and may be employed to transcend or repudiate any change that may be brought about by other means."[40] The failure of Canadians to agree on an amending procedure is the most obvious failure of their constitutional experience.

The British North America Act of 1867 did not specify an explicit procedure for its own amendment and the matter was mentioned only once in the Confederation Debates. It was undoubtedly taken for granted that the United Kingdom Parliament would be the amending authority but probably also, in the light of Canadian experience under the Act of Union, that no amendment would be enacted without the request or consent of the Dominion. The procedure by which Canadian initiative would take place was not specified, perhaps because the Fathers of Confederation believed it unlikely they could come to agreement on such a procedure.

From Confederation until the period after the First World War, the British North America Act was amended on several occasions by the Imperial Parliament at the request of Canada. However, no settled conventions developed to regulate the procedures within the Dominion for making such a request. Serious and protracted debates about a domestic amending procedure began only in the 1920s when Canada along with the other Dominions was on the verge of attaining full legal recognition of its self-governing status. However, when this development culminated in the enactment by the United Kingdom Parliament of the Statute of Westminster in 1931, it was provided at the request of the Canadian government that "Nothing in this Act shall be deemed to apply to the repeal, amendment or alteration of the British North America Acts, 1867 to 1930, or to any order, rule or regulation made thereunder." The federal and provincial governments had been unable to agree on an amending procedure.

A Dominion-Provincial Conference was called in 1935 and a subcommittee appointed to deal with a procedure for constitutional amendment. The Dominion and all the provinces except New Brunswick agreed that Canada should have the power to amend the constitution if a method satisfactory to all parties could be worked out. The desperate circumstances of the Great Depression soon halted even a desultory attempt to reach agreement. When the Royal Commission on Dominion-Provincial Relations was appointed in 1936, its terms of reference were limited to financial matters and did not include recommendations for an amending procedure.

In 1949 at the request of the Parliament of Canada the United Kingdom Parliament amended the British North America Act to provide the following:

> 1. The amendment from time to time of the Constitution of Canada, except as regards matters coming within the classes of subjects by this Act assigned exclusively to the Legislatures of the provinces, or as regards rights or privileges by this or any other Constitutional Act granted or secured to the Legislature or the Government of a province, or to any class of persons with respect to schools or as regards the use of the English or the French language or as regards the requirements that there shall be a session of the Parliament of Canada at least once each year, and that no House of Commons shall continue for more than five years from the day of the return of the Writs for choosing the House: provided, however, that a House of Commons may in time of real or apprehended war, invasion or insurrection be continued by the Parliament of Canada if such continuation is not opposed by the votes of more than one-third of the members of such House.

The procedure established in 1949 still governs amendment of the British North America Acts. Subsequent attempts to patriate the constitution and to bring into operation a procedure which would explicitly determine the roles of Parliament and the provinces in constitutional amendment will be discussed in the next chapter.

Since 1949 there have been three amendments enacted by the Parliament of the United Kingdom on Joint Address from the Senate and House of Commons and with the consent of all the provinces:

—an amendment of 1951 enabled the Parliament of Canada to make laws in respect to old-age pensions, with such laws to give way if they conflicted with provincial legislation on the same subject.

—an amendment of 1960 required subsequent appointees to provincial superior courts to retire at age 75.

—an amendment of 1964 provided that Parliament might enact laws in respect to supplementary benefits to old-age pensions, along with survivors' and disability benefits, with the provision of provincial paramountcy as in the 1951 amendment.

There have also been five amendments enacted by the Parliament of Canada alone by virtue of its jurisdiction under the 1949 amending procedure. Two of these (1952, 1974) provided for general readjustments of representation in the House of Commons. A 1965 amendment provided for the compulsory retirements of subsequently-appointed Senators at age 75. Two amendments in 1975 altered the representation of the Yukon and Northwest Territories in the House of Commons and Senate.

The principle usages surrounding constitutional amendment which have emerged from past practices were outlined in a document *The Amendment of the Constitution of Canada* issued under the name of the federal Minister of Justice in 1965:

> *The first general principle* . . . is that although an enactment by the United Kingdom is necessary to amend the British North America Act, such action is taken only upon formal request from Canada. No Act of the United Kingdom Parliament affecting Canada is therefore passed unless it is requested and consented to by Canada. Conversely, every amendment requested by Canada in the past has been enacted.
>
> *The second general principle* is that the sanction of Parliament is required for a request to the British Parliament for an amendment to the British North America Act. This principle was established early in the history of Canada's constitutional amendments, and has not been violated since 1895. The procedure invariably is to seek amendments by a joint Address of the Canadian House of Commons and Senate to the Crown.
>
> *The third general principle* is that no amendment to Canada's Constitution will be made by the British Parliament merely upon the request of a Canadian province. A number of attempts to secure such amendments have been made, but none has been successful. The first such attempt was made as early as 1868, by a province which was at that time dissatisfied with the terms of Confederation. This was followed by other attempts in 1869, 1874 and 1887. The British Government refused in all cases to act on provincial government representations on the grounds that it should not intervene in the affairs of Canada except at the request of the federal government representing all of Canada.
>
> *The fourth general principle* is that the Canadian Parliament will not request an amendment directly affecting federal-provincial relationships without prior consultation and agreement with the provinces. This principle did not emerge as early as others but since 1907, and particularly since 1930, has gained increasing recognition and acceptance. The nature and the degree of provincial participation in the amending process, however, have not lent themselves to easy definition.[41]

The existing law and conventions of constitutional amendment in Canada leave three major questions unanswered.

First, are there any conceivable circumstances under which the United Kingdom authorities would refuse to enact an amendment requested in the normal form of a Joint Address of the Senate and House of Commons of Canada? W. R. Lederman has argued that if such a request involved the distribution of legislative powers between Parliament and the provinces the British authorities would uphold what he regards as the binding convention of unanimous provincial consent and under such circumstances, "in the face of any provincial dissent, I think the present convention requires that the British government and Parliament do nothing, simply regarding the request from the Canadian Parliament . . . as improper, that is, unconstitutional and illegal."[42] Peter Hogg has taken the contrary and, in my opinion, now more defensible view.[43] Neither before nor after 1949 has there been an instance in which the United Kingdom authorities inquired into whether or not the Canadian authorities had sought or secured provincial consent for a proposed amendment. And, as Hogg argues, such action would be "an objectionable interference in Canadian domestic affairs" which British politicians in almost any conceivable circumstance would avoid.

Second, is unanimous provincial consent required before the Parliament of Canada requests the U.K. authorities to amend those parts of the constitution excepted from unilateral control of the Canadian Parliament by the 1949 provisions? As we have seen, such consent was secured for the amendments of 1951 and 1964 changing the division of legislative power, and in 1940 there was also provincial unanimity for an amendment conferring exclusive jurisdiction over unemployment insurance on the Dominion. There was also unanimous provincial consent for the 1960 amendment providing for the retirement of judges of provincial superior courts at age 75, although it can plausibly be argued that under Section 99 of the British North America Act of 1867 and the 1949 provisions the Parliament of Canada might have effected this amendment without recourse either to the Parliament of the United Kingdom or to the provinces. There have thus been relatively few amendments altering the distribution of legislative powers and because of this one can plausibly argue that unanimous provincial consent is not a binding convention, particularly if only one in perhaps two of the smaller provinces refused assent to an amendment agreed upon by the others.

Third, what is the scope of Parliament's power to amend the constitution by unilateral action? In sponsoring the 1949 provision, Prime Minister St. Laurent argued that the power which was given to Parliament to determine the structure and procedures of the government of Canada was analogous to the power of the provinces to amend their respective constitutions, except for the office of the Lieutenant Governor, under Section 92(1). Does the 1949 procedure confer on Parliament powers extensive enough to abolish the monarchy or to abolish the Senate or radically change its composition and powers? Acting in response to a motion of the Special Joint Committee of the Senate and House of Commons on the Constitution of Canada, the federal government in late 1978 submitted to the Supreme Court of Canada a reference requesting a determination of Parliament's powers in respect to changes in the powers and composition of the Senate and a clarification of this matter is expected soon.*

The law and conventions of the Canadian constitution provide few opportunities for popular or even legislative participation in constitutional amendments. The convention that the most crucial amendments are effected by way of a Joint Address of Parliament and the House of Commons provides for parliamentary debate on such proposed changes. However, the circumstance that this debate takes place *after* the consent of the provinces has been obtained means that Parliament can only assent to or respect the proposed amendment but cannot cause its terms to be altered. So far as the provinces are concerned, the prevailing conventions dictate that the consent of governments only is required with no necessary involvement of their respective legislatures. While the cabinet of any province is of course free to submit a proposed amendment to its legislature, of the amendments of 1940, 1951, 1960 and 1964, the first was enacted without being referred to any provincial legislature, the second involved the legislative assemblies of Quebec, Saskatchewan and Manitoba, and the latter two only the legislature of Quebec.[44] As we shall see in the next chapter, the federal and provincial governments come very close to agreement on the terms of the Victoria Charter in 1971. If such changes had been agreed upon by Quebec, very significant changes in the constitutional system might well have been effected with only perfunctory debate by Parliament and perhaps none at all in some of the provincial legislatures. In general terms, formal constitutional amendment in Canada is recognized as being primarily the business of governments rather than of legislatures or the wider public.

Judicial Review of the Canadian Constitution

The British North America Act of 1867 did not provide explicitly for judicial review, i.e., the procedure by which judicial bodies determine the validity of legislative enactments or executive acts in terms of their compatibility or otherwise with the terms of a codified constitution. The domestic constitutional system of the United Kingdom did not include such a procedure since the Crown in Parliament was sovereign and there could be no legal challenge to its will. From the early days of the British Empire, however, it had been customary to allow appeals to the Crown against enactments of colonial legislatures and the procedures for such appeals had been formalized with the recognition by Imperial statute of the Judicial Committee of the Privy Council in 1833.[45]

---

*In its decision in late 1979 and as yet unreported the Supreme Court denied Parliament's power to change the powers and composition of the Senate.

As Peter Russell has pointed out, the power of the courts to pass on the validity of Canadian legislation in the early years of Confederation "might have been as much a corollary of imperialism as of federalism."[46] The British North America Act was an Imperial statute and according to the Colonial Laws Validity Act of 1865 enactments of colonial legislatures were invalid if they conflicted with those of the United Kingdom. However, as it happened, judicial review of the British North America Act did not evolve as an instrument for securing Imperial influence in Canadian affairs, but rather as a practical device for delineating the respective legislative powers of Parliament and the provinces.

Until the abolition of appeals to this body by an act of the Canadian Parliament in 1949, the Judicial Committee of the Privy Council was the final appellate authority in interpreting the Canadian constitution. The Judicial Committee was composed of members of the House of Lords usually named to the Committee because of their distinguished judicial backgrounds.

There is a vast literature of analysis and criticism of the work of the Judicial Committee in reviewing the British North America Act[47] and its general directions in interpreting the Act are here summarized in very brief form. After the mid-1890s the dominant trends of judicial interpretation by the Committee worked in the following directions:

—the general power of Parliament to legislate for the "Peace, Order, and Good Government of Canada" was interpreted restrictively. Thus in most circumstances federal enactments had to be justified as coming within one of the enumerated powers of Section 91.

—the power of Parliament to legislate in respect to "Trade and Commerce" was interpreted restrictively. The United States Supreme Court has found in the power of Congress to regulate interstate commerce a very wide scope for national control over economic matters, but the dominant Canadian tradition of interpreting the trade and commerce power has been otherwise.

—the exclusive power of the provinces to legislate in respect to "Property and Civil Rights" was interpreted broadly. In respect to economic matters this became the *de facto* residual power of the constitution.

In *Re Regulation and Control of Aeronautics* in 1932, Lord Sankey speaking for the Judicial Committee thus summarized "four propositions" about the division of legislative powers which had been developed through previous decisions of that body:

> (1) The legislation of the Parliament of the Dominion, so long as it strictly relates to subjects of legislation expressly enumerated in Section 91, is of paramount authority, even though it trenches upon matters assigned to the provincial legislatures by Section 92.

(2) The general power of legislation conferred upon the Parliament of the Dominion by Section 91 of the Act in supplement of the power to legislate upon the subjects expressly enumerated must be strictly confined to such matters as are unquestionably of national interest and importance, and must not trench on any of the subjects enumerated in Section 92, as within the scope of provincial legislation, unless these matters have attained such dimensions as to affect the body politic of the Dominion.

(3) It is within the competence of the Dominion Parliament to provide for matters which, though otherwise within the competence of the Provincial Legislature, are necessarily incidental to effective legislation by the Parliament of the Dominion upon a subject of legislation expressly enumerated in Section 91.

(4) There can be a domain in which Provincial and Dominion legislation may overlap, in which neither legislation will be *ultra vires* if the field is clear, but if the field is not clear and the two legislations meet, the Dominion legislation must prevail.[48]

Three decisions by the Judicial Committee in 1937 denied the federal government the powers which many thoughtful Canadians believed necessary to deal with the social and economic circumstances of the Great Depression:

—three enactments of Parliament in 1935 dealing with minimum wages, the limitations of working hours and a weekly day of rest in industrial undertakings were declared invalid. This legislation was declared to be within provincial jurisdiction over property and civil rights.[49] In justifying this legislation the federal authorities had asserted that it was in fulfillment of international obligations accepted by Canada as a member of the International Labour Organization. The Judicial Committee denied this claim, and asserted the important principle that Parliament did not acquire any legislative power it would not otherwise have had by virtue of Canada as such incurring an international obligation.

—the Judicial Committee declared *ultra vires* federal legislation providing for the regulation of the marketing of natural products through a national board.[50] The Committee found the legislation to be an encroachment on property and civil rights because it dealt in part with intra-provincial trade in natural products.

—the Judicial Committee struck down a national scheme of unemployment insurance.[51] Again the major grounds were that federal legislation encroached on provincial jurisdiction over property and civil rights.

There was what one might call a counter-tradition of interpretation by the Judicial Committee which found in Parliament's power to legislate for the "Peace, Order, and Good Government of Canada" an independent source of legislative authority.[52] Although from the mid-1890s onward this was not the prevailing tradition, from time to time it did allow Dominion legislation to be upheld on the grounds that some matter could be dealt with only by the national government. By reliance on the general power, Parliament and the federal cabinet were permitted to override the legislative jurisdiction of the provinces in the two World Wars and to deal with the economic and other dislocations occasioned by international conflict after hostilities had ended. In other circumstances the Judicial Committee was able to find justification in the general power for federal legislation regulating the sale of alcoholic beverages and broadcasting and for the incorporation of companies with Dominion objects.

Until the past few years at least it has been the conventional wisdom in English Canada to be critical of the work of the Judicial Committee in interpreting the Canadian constitution. There have been two currents of criticism. The first asserts that, according to the rules of statutory interpretation accepted in the Anglo-Canadian tradition, the Judicial Committee misinterpreted the clear meaning of the British North America Act. The most exhaustive argument along these lines was made in a Report of the Parliamentary Counsel of the Senate, William F. O'Connor, published in 1939.[53] On the basis of a thorough review of Canadian constitutional experience up to and including the events surrounding Confederation, O'Connor concluded that the framers of the British North America Act had clearly embodied a scheme for the distribution of legislative powers in its terms. However, from 1896 onward this scheme had been repealed by "judicial legislation." O'Connor proposed that this situation be righted by a constitutional amendment which would in effect direct the judicial authorities to interpret the BNA Act by the normal legal rules. The second line of criticism has come from the judicial activists.[54] According to this kind of argument, the normal rules of statutory interpretation are not in themselves adequate guides to courts in reviewing a constitution. Judicial review is inevitably a policy-making role, and in performing it judges should explicitly take into account their own considered views of the basic nature of the polity and its needs, and the social and other contexts of the matters before them. Within this formulation, the tradition of "black letter" statutory interpretation followed by the Judicial Committee was inadequate in resolving some of the basic problems of Canadian life. The criticisms based on technical standards of statutory interpretation and on the perspectives of the judicial activists were in a logical sense contradictory, although some detractors of the Privy Council supported both at once. The two streams of criticism were in agreement, however, in their general conclusion that the powers of the Dominion had been unduly restricted and those of the provinces unduly expanded by the Judicial Committee.[55]

The Judicial Committee has of course had its supporters. Using a highly technical approach, a 1967 book by G. P. Browne has attempted a refutation of the O'Connor argument that the Judicial Committee deviated from the normal rules of statutory interpretation in review of the British North America Act.[56] Among French-speaking scholars it has been argued that the result of the Judicial Committee's work was to recognize in a prudent and basically statesmanlike way the pervasive cultural and other particularisms of Canadian life. In a 1951 article Louis-Phillipe Pigeon, now Mr. Justice Pigeon of the Supreme Court of Canada, defended the way the BNA Act has been interpreted in these terms:

> A great volume of criticism has been heaped upon the Privy Council and the Supreme Court on the ground that their decisions rest on a narrow and technical construction of the B.N.A. Act. This contention is ill-founded. The decisions on the whole proceed from a much higher view. As appears from passages I have quoted, they recognize the implicit fluidity of any constitution by allowing for emergencies and by resting distinctions on matters of degree. At the same time they firmly uphold the fundamental principle of provincial autonomy: they staunchly refuse to let our federal constitution be changed gradually, by one device or another, to a legislative union. In doing so they are preserving the essential condition of the Canadian confederation.[57]

Pierre Elliott Trudeau put the same view pithily in 1964. "It has long been a custom in English Canada to denounce the Privy Council for its provincial bias; but it should perhaps be considered that if the law lords had not moved in this direction, Quebec separatism might not be a threat today: it might be an accomplished fact."[58] An English-Canadian scholar of the constitution. G. F. G. Stanley, assented to the Pigeon-Trudeau viewpoint in 1969:

> The decisions handed down by their Lordships of the Judicial Committee set the pattern of our constitution for over seventy years. Uninfluenced by local sympathies or party affiliations they set out conscientiously to maintain the true federal character of Canada and to resist the encroachments of the Federal Parliament upon the powers of the Provincial Legislature and *vice versa*. The Judicial Committee, by its careful and unprejudiced approach to Canadian problems, lessened the political dangers of excessive centralization and preserved that federalism which is the distinctive feature of our country.[59]

Both critics and supporters of the Judicial Committee appear to have exaggerated its importance in determining the shape of Canadian federalism. By the end of the nineteenth century several important developments other than judicial review had worked toward enhancing the strength and independence of the provinces—the parliamentary enactment of 1873 ending joint membership in Parliament and the provincial legislatures; the emergence of strong provincial leaders and parties able and willing to challenge the dominance of the Dominion; the adverse economic circumstances of 1873 onward, which denied the federal government some of the legitimacy it might otherwise have had;

the failure of the Dominion authorities to give effective aid to the educational minorities in the provinces when the privileges of these minorities were challenged by provincial action; and the election in 1873 and again in 1896 of federal Liberal governments more sympathetic to provincial sensibilities than the Conservatives they displaced. Thus it can plausibly be argued that the Judicial Committee's decisions in 1896 and soon after did little more than give retroactive recognition to the underlying particularisms of Canadian life which the framers of the Confederation settlement had too sanguinely believed would yield to the integrative thrust of the Dominion power.

The context of the Privy Council decisions of the 1930s restricting federal jurisdiction is perhaps more complex, and the most vigorous line of Canadian criticism of the Judicial Committee appears to date from this decade rather than before. Critics of the Judicial Committee's work during this decade have sometimes argued as if all right-thinking Canadians recognized the need for a significant extension of federal powers to meet the desperate circumstances of the Great Depression. The Canadian electorate, however, seems to have been more divided on the relative powers appropriate to the federal and provincial authorities. The Bennett government, whose major "New Deal" reforms were overturned by the Judicial Committee, sustained one of the most decisive defeats in Canadian history in the general election of 1935, dropping from the 1930 results of 137 to 40 seats in the House of Commons and from 48.8 per cent to 29.6 per cent of the popular vote. The incoming Liberal government was significantly more hesitant than its predecessor in asserting federal power. Also, the 1930s brought into office strong provincial leaders devoted to provincial autonomy—Aberhart in Alberta, Duplessis in Quebec, Hepburn in Ontario, MacDonald in Nova Scotia, and Pattullo in British Columbia. J. R. Mallory argued in a book published in 1954 that throughout the history of judicial review of the Canadian constitution the courts, and of course the Judicial Committee, had stood against the public regulation of economic activity by both the Dominion *and* the provinces.[60] Thus, "The plea of *ultra vires* has become the automatic litigious response to attempts by governments to regulate economic life, just as the due process clause was employed for a similar purpose in the United States."[61] Mallory described the 1920s and 1930s this way: "The paralyzing effect of judicial interpretation on the Canadian constitution in the years between the wars was a reflection of the continuing indecision of the Canadian people. For much as an increase in the activity of the state was demanded by a large section of the population, the same measure was bitterly contested by other groups who stood to gain more by the old equilibrium than by the new. Thus every halting step in the direction of satisfying collective wants was transferred into a debate on constitutional first principles."[62]

As Alan Cairns has pointed out, the Judicial Committee had several weaknesses as the final appellate body in Canadian constitutional cases.[63] It was isolated "from the scene in which its judgments applied." There was the absence in Canada of a sophisticated tradition of critical jurisprudence. The Judicial Committee's decisions were expressed as single opinions and the absence of dissents "hindered the development of a dialogue over the quality of its judgments." But its most important weakness in Cairns' view was the legal doctrine which ostensibly guided its decisions. This doctrine directed the judicial authorities to "eschew considerations of policy and to analyze the BNA Act by the standard canons for the technical construction of other statutes." However, "it is self evident that no technical analysis of an increasingly ancient constitutional document can find answers to questions undreamt of by the Fathers."[64] The result was the concealment of the real grounds for many of the Judicial Committee's most important decisions and the masking of the actual policy choices it made "behind the obfuscating language and precedents of statutory interpretation."

Until 1949 the Supreme Court of Canada was very much subordinate to the Privy Council in judicial review of the constitution. A large number of cases from provincial courts went directly on appeal to the latter body and bypassed the Supreme Court: in 1938 such appeals had outnumbered those from the Supreme Court by 329 to 198.[65] The Supreme Court also believed itself rigidly bound by the precedents of the Judicial Committee. As Bora Laskin wrote, "As Privy Council decisions multiplied, the Supreme Court became engrossed in merely expanding the authoritative pronouncements of its superior. The task of the Supreme Court was not to interpret the constitution but rather to interpret what the Privy Council said the constitution meant."[66]

In December 1949 the Supreme Court of Canada became Canada's final appellate court. This change was effected by an enactment of Parliament. The constitutional validity of the reform had been affirmed in advance by a decision of the Judicial Committee of the Privy Council itself in 1947.[67]

So far as the delineation of the respective jurisdictions of Parliament and the provinces was concerned, judicial review in the two decades after 1949 played a less crucial and contentious role in shaping Canadian federalism than in certain periods in the past—certainly less than in the 1930s. Frank Scott in 1961 pointed to the importance in post-war Canada of fiscal and monetary policy as economic regulators and asserted that the question of legislative jurisdiction seemed to have been bypassed, "the lawyers are moving out and the economists are moving in."[68] From 1960 onward came a series of attacks from Quebec scholars and from the Quebec government on the legitimacy of the Supreme Court of Canada as the final appellate tribunal in constitutional matters. The general argument here was that because the Court operated under federal law and because its members were appointed by the fed-

eral government, a neutral and objective interpretation of the constitution was impossible. However, after an exhaustive review of this kind
of criticism Peter Russell concluded, "this viewpoint . . . has been sustained, not by any tangible evidence that members of the Supreme
Court are biased in favour of the level of government which appointed
them, but by an objection in principle to the constitutional arbitration
by a tribunal which is organically part of the federal level of government."[69]

Despite its relatively restricted role in shaping the federal balance
during its first two decades as the final appellate tribunal, the Supreme
Court of Canada did embark in a direction which both enhanced federal
power and provided a better basis than before for federal-provincial co-
operation through the device of delegation:

—in the case of *Johannesson v. West St. Paul* decided in 1952 the Court
upheld federal jurisdiction over aeronautics on the basis of the
"national importance" test.[70] The restrictive interpretation of "Peace,
Order, and Good Government" had limited this to emergency situations; the more expansive interpretation had asserted that Parliament
might enact legislation in respect to matters which were deemed to
be of national significance. Both tests had been applied by the Judicial Committee and in *Johannesson* the majority of the Supreme
Court chose to rely on the more expansive view of legitimate federal
powers.

—the Court gave a somewhat more generous interpretation to the
powers of Parliament to legislate in respect to "Trade and Commerce." One of the most common arguments of critics of the Judicial
Committee was that this body had emasculated "Trade and Commerce" as a source of federal power to undertake national economic
regulation. In a relatively small number of cases the Supreme Court
gave a somewhat more expansive interpretation to this power than
had the Judicial Committee.[71]

—in *P.E.I. Potato Marketing Board v. H. B. Willis Inc.* decided in 1952[72]
the Court upheld the validity of federal legislation delegating powers
to regulate inter-provincial and export trade to provincial marketing
boards. The previous year the Court had declared unconstitutional an
attempt of the Nova Scotia legislature to delegate a part of its jurisdiction over labour matters to the Parliament of Canada.[73] In the Willis
case the Court provided the legal sanction for a technique of delegation which might if used by the federal and provincial governments
overcome some of the difficulties of regulating an interdependent national economy by the two levels of jurisdiction.

As it assumed its role as Canada's final appellate tribunal the Court
showed some tendency to modify the positivistic tradition of constitutional interpretation which characterized the Judicial Committee. W. R.
Lederman has lucidly summarized the different ways in which courts
may approach judicial review: "there are principally two types of inter-

pretation—literal or grammatical interpretation emphasizing the words found in statutes and constitutional documents—and sociological, which insists that constitutional words and statutory words must be carefully linked by judicially noticed knowledge and by evidence to the ongoing life of society."[74] Judicial review of the Canadian constitution has been predominantly in the first tradition, but in a somewhat tentative way the Supreme Court since 1949 has come to accept some of the perspectives of the second.

From the late 1960s onward the Supreme Court of Canada made a series of decisions which both enhanced federal powers and gave rise to provincial pressures for changes in the position of the Court under the existing constitutional system and for provincial participation in the choice of members of the Court:

—in a number of decisions the Court challenged what the provinces regarded as their ownership rights over natural resources. The *Off-Shore Minerals Reference* of 1967 declared the mineral resources past the shoreline of British Columbia to be federal.[75] The *Canadian Industrial Gas and Oil v. Government of Saskatchewan* case decided in 1977, declared a Saskatchewan taxing statute invalid as an encroachment on the federal power to regulate trade.[76] The *Central Canada Potash* decision of 1978 overturned a Saskatchewan program of prorationing the production of potash.[77]

—in the contentious area of telecommunications, the Court upheld the exclusive power of the Parliament of Canada to licence cablevision systems and the programs of these systems where the latter involved the interception of broadcast signals.

—in the *Reference re Anti-Inflation Act* of 1976, as we have seen, the Supreme Court upheld the 1975 enactment giving Parliament control over profits, prices, wages and dividends for a three-year period under Parliament's general power to legislate for the "Peace, Order, and Good Government of Canada." This is undoubtedly the most important constitutional decision made by the Court since 1949.[78] Although the majority decision was based on very complex legal reasoning, its general import was to give an expansive interpretation of Parliament's powers to override provincial jurisdiction to meet a peacetime economic emergency, despite the fact that the enactment under review did not explicitly declare that the inflationary conditions of the time constituted an emergency.

In the cases noted above and in other decisions during the past decade, the Court has broadened the scope of federal powers which may be justified under "Peace, Order, and Good Government" and "Trade and Commerce," and has narrowed provincial powers in respect to the marketing of natural products, the ownership of natural resources, telecommunications and direct taxation. According to Peter Russell's calculations on the period from 1950 to 1972 no federal law was judged invalid while 20 provincial enactments were so declared.[79] In three subsequent decisions the Court pronounced against federal power, but in only one of these—*Macdonald v. Vapor Canada Ltd.* in 1976[80]—was there a direct challenge to an important aspect of federal legislative jurisdiction.

The Supreme Court of Canada has come to play a more crucial and contentious role in the Canadian political system than at any previous time. As we shall see in the next chapter, from the Victoria Conference onward most of the proposals for comprehensive constitutional reform have recommended that provincial/regional representation in the Court as well as its jurisdiction be entrenched in the constitution and that the provinces be associated in choosing members of the Court. Saskatchewan more than any has borne the brunt of recent decisions restricting provincial powers, and Premier Allan Blakeney introduced a brief into the First Minister's Conference of October 30-November 1, 1978 which reviewed the Court's constitutional decisions over the past five years and asserted "Recent decisions of the Supreme Court of Canada reveal two striking features (i) absence of effective limits on federal powers (ii) serious erosion of provincial powers. They go a long way towards undermining the concept of a balanced federalism developed by the Privy Council."[81] In his controversial book *In the Last Resort: A Study of the Supreme Court of Canada* published in 1974, Paul Weiler presented an argument that the Court has not played and cannot play a useful role as "the umpire of the federal system."[82] In Weiler's view the kinds of cases which come before the courts in judicial review of the constitution are essentially economic, social and political in nature, and because of this cannot appropriately be resolved by the normal processes of statutory interpretation. Such matters are better resolved by federal-provincial negotiation and in using the analogy of industrial relations Weiler argued that genuine bargaining is frustrated when the parties have final resort to arbitration. He argued also that no private litigant should have the right to mount a challenge in the courts on the grounds that a federal or provincial law encroached on the jurisdiction of the other level of government. There would be a few circumstances, presumably rare, where federal and provincial enactments imposed contradictory obligations on individuals or groups. However, even in these situations judicial discretion would be removed by resort to the paramountcy role that federal legislation should prevail.

Has the Supreme Court of Canada as final appellate tribunal in constitutional cases shown a bias in favour of federal power? Such a judgment could responsibly be made only after an exhaustive reading of all the Court's constitutional decisions since 1949, measured against some standard, almost impossible to formulate satisfactorily, of what an "objective" interpretation of the constitution would be. Gilbert L. Écuyer made a very detailed study *La cour suprême du Canada et les partages des compétences 1949-1978* under the auspices of the Quebec Department of Inter-governmental Affairs. L'Écuyer's conclusion was that the Court had been more favourable to federal power than was the Judicial Committee. In general, the former's interpretation was judged to be both in harmony with the text of Articles 91 and 92 and with the spirit of the Fathers of Confederation. The Canadian constitution, in fact, argues L'Écuyer, embodies both in its text and in its spirit "une vision centralisatrice." Interestingly, this document has been widely quoted by the government of Saskatchewan in some of its criticisms of recent Supreme Court decisions. From another perspective, Peter Hogg has argued that the general thrust of the Court's decisions has been in the direction of "a presumption of constitutionality" which he defines as "the idea that a burden of demonstration lies upon those who would challenge the validity of a statute that has emerged from the democratic process."[83] The statement is made that the Supreme Court "has been more restrained in judicial review than was the Privy Council, and its practice may perhaps be regarded as consistent with a presumption of constitutionality."[84] According to Russell's calculation, in the 1950-72 period the Court upheld the constitutionality of federal and provincial laws in 54 decisions as against 20 decisions in which provincial laws were invalidated.[85]

Legislation enacted by Parliament in 1974 clearly contemplates a more important role for the Supreme Court of Canada in shaping Canadian law. One of these amendments removed the automatic right of litigants to appeal to the Court in civil cases where the amount in issue was more than $10,000. Another gave the Court wide discretion to hear appeals from other courts when in the opinion of the former body important issues of law or fact are involved.

Along with the 1974 changes in the jurisdiction of the Court there are other factors which go to make that body increasingly important as umpire of the federal system. G. Bruce Doern and V. Seymour Wilson have suggested that the increasing importance of "regulatory issues and regulatory legislation" in federal-provincial relations as against fiscal matters and "big-spending joint programmes" may "involve the courts relatively more often than we have been accustomed to in the recent past."[86] It is also at least possible that the courts themselves will remove some of the present limitations on judicial standing and thus make it easier for private persons and groups to establish themselves as litigants or intervenors in constitutional and other cases. Further, the expanding scope and increasing virulence of federal-provincial conflict and the decreasing capacity of governments to resolve their differences by negotiation appear to be leading these governments more than in the past to seek judicial arbitration through the reference procedure.

Human and Linguistic Rights and the Federal Dimension of the Canadian Constitution

The protection of human and linguistic rights in Canada is related directly to federalism because jurisdiction over such rights is divided by the British North America Act between Parliament and the provincial legislatures. Judicial decision has left several crucial aspects of this division unclear. The protection of human rights has also been a major focus in recent discussion for reform of the Canadian constitution.

The British North America Act of 1867 gave explicit protection to human rights only in respect to circumstances where a linguistic or religious group was in a minority position:

(1) Section 93 restricted the rights of provinces to encroach on the privileges of separate Roman Catholic and Protestant schools existing "by Law" at the time of union, or subsequently so established.

(2) Section 133 provided that:

> Either the English or the French Language may be used by any Person in the Debates of the Houses of the Parliament of Canada and of the Houses of the Legislature of Quebec; and both those Languages shall be used in the respective Records and Journals of those Houses; and either of those Languages may be used by any Person or in any Pleading or Process in or issuing from any Court of Canada established under this Act, and in or from all or any of the Courts of Quebec.
>
> The Acts of the Parliament of Canada and of the Legislature of Quebec shall be printed and published in both those Languages.

(3) Various Sections protected the representation of the English-speaking minority in Quebec in Parliament and the Legislature of that province.[87]

Beyond these explicit recognitions of minority rights, the British North America Act was based on the principle of parliamentary supremacy qualified by a constitutional division of legislative powers. The protection of human rights was to rest on the traditional safeguards of the civil and common law systems as these safeguards were from time to time modified by enactments of Parliament and the provincial legislatures. Although there was a restricted entrenchment of human rights as such, there were significant constitutional prescriptions concerning the legislative bodies which would enact laws in respect to human rights and other matters.[88]

Judicial review of the Canadian constitution in respect to human rights has been dominated by what two writers of a recent text on constitutional law have called "the division of powers approach."[89] In this approach, what are variously regarded as human rights do not possess any independent constitutional value and when any federal or provincial enactment allegedly overriding such rights is subjected to judicial review, the only relevant question to be decided by the courts is whether Parliament or the provincial legislature has trespassed on the powers of the other level. If it is determined that it did not, the legislation is valid even if it overrides the most fundamental of human rights.

The constitutional division of legislative powers over human and linguistic rights is a complex matter whose elements are given in only a summary form here.[90] Some of the most important of rights relating to arrest, detention and trials are squarely within Parliament's exclusive jurisdiction over the criminal law and criminal procedure, although in practice such rights depend in particular circumstances on the actions of the provinces and their constituent municipalities in the processes of law enforcement, and the administration of justice. The national and provincial authorities are free to protect egalitarian rights as they wish by enjoining discrimination on the basis of sex, race, national origin, religion or other individual characteristics, as these relate to matters within federal and provincial legislative jurisdiction respectively. In *Jones v. A.G.N.B.*, decided in 1974[91] the Supreme Court of Canada upheld the validity of the federal Official Languages Act of 1969. It appears constitutionally valid for Parliament and the provincial legislatures to enact laws in respect to language rights as they wish—of course as such laws relate to subjects within their respective jurisdictions—so long as the minimum standards provided for under Section 133 of the BNA Act are not restricted.[92] The most contentious area of rights relates to what Bora Laskin (now Mr. Chief Justice Laskin of the Supreme Court of Canada) in a 1959 article called "political civil liberty," the substance of which is "freedom of association, freedom of assembly, freedom of utterance, freedom of the press [or the use of other media for dissemination of news and opinion] and freedom of conscience and religion."[93] Laskin argued that these freedoms "are embraced by federal power to make laws for the peace, order, and good government of Canada, which includes power to legislate in relation to the criminal law." The contrary viewpoint is that, in large part, these liberties are within provincial jurisdiction over "property and civil rights," although Laskin's position has been in the main accepted by the Canadian courts in the past generation.

From time to time some Canadian judges have attempted to break out of the seeming rigidities of the division-of-powers approach, and to erect other barriers to governments encroaching on human rights than one level encroaching on the jurisdiction of the other. The most important attempt in this direction has found in the preamble to the British North America Act an implied bill of rights. In *Reference re Alberta Statutes* of 1938, an Alberta enactment restricting the freedom of the press was invalidated by the Supreme Court of Canada.[94] In their opinions, Duff, C. J. and Cannon, J. advanced the wholly unprecedented principle that because the preamble to the BNA Act stated that the colonies wished to be united with "a Constitution similar in Principle to that of the United Kingdom," provincial restrictions on rights essential to the workings of parliamentary government were invalid. In the next twenty-five years this argument was used in several subsequent Supreme Court decisions striking down provincial legislation, and in his *obiter* in the *Switzman* case in 1954, Abbott J. argued that the preamble imposed similar restrictions on Parliament.[95] The notion of the inherent rights of Canadian citizenship stemming from the Confederation settlement of 1867 was most persuasively argued by Mr. Justice Rand of the Supreme Court of Canada in several of his opinions in the 1950s and 1960s. However, such a view has not recently been supported by members of the Court, and in general Parliament's power over the criminal law has been the major barrier to provincial encroachment on political civil liberties.

Since the end of the Second World War Parliament and all the provinces have enacted legislation for the protection of human rights. The most important of these statutes is the Canadian Bill of Rights enacted by Parliament in 1960. Throughout his adult life, Prime Minister Diefenbaker had been committed to the more effective protection of human rights and would clearly have preferred the entrenchment of such rights by a constitutional amendment binding on all governments in Canada. However, it appears to have been the judgment of Mr. Diefenbaker and his colleagues that unanimous provincial consent for such an amendment could not be secured, and the 1960 Bill of Rights applies only to matters otherwise within federal jurisdiction and can be altered or amended by the same procedures as apply to other enactments of Parliament. The Bill of Rights affirms the existence of the traditional rights of religion, speech, assembly and the press; legal rights relating to arrest, trial and detention; and the right not to be discriminated against "by reason of race, national origin, colour, religion or sex."

There were two contradictory directions in which the courts, most crucially of course the Supreme Court of Canada, could move in interpreting the meaning and effect of the Bill of Rights. The first was to regard it as only a guide to the interpretation of federal statutes which would not invalidate any enactment of Parliament unambiguously contrary to its terms, the other to see the Bill as overriding any federal law or executive act which contravened its provisions. For almost a decade, the first interpretation appeared to be the one accepted as authoritative by the Supreme Court. However in 1969 the Court by a 6-3 majority invalidated Section 94(b) of the Indian Act, which provided a harsher penalty for an Indian in the Northwest Territories being intoxicated in a public place than for other citizens.[96] It was thus established that the Bill of Rights was a constitutional statute by whose provisions other federal enactments were to be measured and, if found wanting, nullified. Subsequent to the *Drybones* decision of 1969 the Court has, however, shown little disposition to challenge federal laws or executive acts as being contrary to the Bill of Rights.

For a generation there has been a strong current of influence pressing for the "entrenchment" of human rights in Canada, i.e., giving constitutional recognition of human rights in those parts of the constitution most difficult of subsequent amendment. In the decade immediately after the Second World War, this argument was often advanced in terms of Canada's alleged inability to fulfil its international obligations as a member of the United Nations.[97] This position is now uncommon. At the first Federal-Provincial Constitutional Conference of February 1968, the federal government presented a proposal for a constitutionally-entrenched Charter of what were classified as political, egalitarian, legal and linguistic rights.[98] In Ottawa's view, such a Charter would not only safeguard rights more effectively but would at one stroke remove the ambiguities of the division of legislative powers related to human rights. Subsequent discussions with the provinces soon made it apparent that no agreement was possible on entrenchment as extensive as that desired by the federal authorities, and the Charter issuing from the Victoria Conference of 1971 provided for much more limited safeguards. The Draft Constitutional Amendment Bill proposed by the Trudeau government in mid-1978 also contained a Canadian Charter of Human Rights and Freedoms by which the federal government would be bound from the first and would bind each province which subsequently opted into this arrangement.

Despite the rhetoric of the supporters of an entrenched Bill of Rights about "guaranteeing" human rights, the basic question here is the extent to which courts will—and should—challenge the will of legislative assemblies and of elected and appointed executive officials. As we have seen, the Supreme Court of Canada has not been very bold in doing so by reference to the Diefenbaker Bill of Rights. But would the judiciary be more aggressive if there were a constitutionally-entrenched Charter removing once and for all the doubt about whether the 1960 Bill should properly be interpreted as a constitutional statute or, alternatively, no more than an interpretive guide? While it is possible to suggest that entrenchment would be a directive to the courts to invalidate statutes or executive acts found to be contrary to its provisions, one could make the contrary argument that the effect might be to make the judiciary even less willing than now to challenge legislative assemblies and governments. Under the existing circumstances an elected majority in Parliament might counter a judicial decision invalidating one of its measures either by amending the Bill of Rights itself or, more probably, by re-enacting the law declaring the legislation to be valid notwithstanding the Bill of Rights. Thus in mounting a challenge to a government under the existing arrangements the courts are aware that their decision is not irrevocable. It would be otherwise under entrenchment and this in itself might lead judges in the direction of extreme caution.

For the next two decades or so I would expect Canadian judges not to be aggressive in the safeguard of human rights, whether there is constitutional entrenchment or not. As Peter Hogg suggests, there is a general disposition of the Supreme Court of Canada toward a "presumption of constitutionality," and such a disposition seems inherent in the tradition of British parliamentary sovereignty, according to which the judiciary has no authority to challenge Parliament's will. However, there are contrary currents of thought in some of Canada's law schools, and it is possible that when some of the exponents of judicial activism come to the bench there will be more willingness to challenge elective majorities. The 1970 casebook of J. Noel Lyon and Ronald L. Atkey, *Canadian Constitutional Law in Modern Perspective*, makes the case for judicial activism in its most undiluted form. These writers are impatient with the division-of-powers approach to judicial review where human rights are involved, and give this prescription: "If a fundamental rights issue is clearly perceived, a court should attempt to meet the issue head-on, and should be loath to allow *any* level of government to deny this right through claims that it is merely acting within its proper sphere of legislative jurisdiction."[99] Not surprisingly, Lyon and Atkey are severely critical of what they call "the English notion of legislative supremacy" and the resort to this "notion" by Canadian judges to deal with human rights questions within a division-of-powers framework, and thus their refusal to assign constitutional rights any independent constitutional value. This is probably a minority view, even among legal scholars in Canada, and unless and until it comes to prevail among members of the Canadian judiciary the courts will remain somewhat unaggressive in imposing their own definitions of human rights on governments and elected legislative assemblies.[100]

The Constitution and External Relations[101]

Up until the period after the end of the First World War, international relations comprised for the most part matters of peace and war, trade, and the negotiation and implementation of treaties of a general nature. So far as federal nations were concerned, these were matters of concern to the central governments alone, and did not engage in any direct way the jurisdiction of their constituent states or provinces. Today there is a steadily increasing range of international interactions covering nearly every matter with which public policy is involved—labour conditions, human rights, health, environmental pollution, education, cultural development, telecommunications, various forms of public control over economic affairs, and so on. In Canada as in other federations, many of these newer matters of international intercourse are wholly or partly within the jurisdiction of the provinces.

As we have seen, Section 132 of the British North America Act of 1867 gave the "Parliament and Government of Canada" plenary powers to implement Canadian obligations incurred on the Dominion's behalf as a part of the British Empire. Thus in the first half-century after Confederation, the respective roles of the federal and provincial authorities in international affairs was not a matter of particular constitutional significance, although Ontario and Quebec had London offices from 1908 and 1911 respectively, while the same official represented both Dominion and Quebec interests in Paris from 1882 to 1912, and Quebec in 1915 opened an office in Brussels.[102]

So far as federalism and Canadian international relations are concerned, the leading judicial decision is the *Labour Conventions* reference decided by the Judicial Committee of the Privy Council in 1937.[103] At issue was the constitutional validity of three pieces of social legislation enacted by Parliament in 1935 as part of Prime Minister Bennett's "New Deal." The essential argument of the lawyers for the Dominion was that the legislation was enacted in fulfilment of Canada's obligations as part of the British Empire under the Treaty of Versailles, and was thus justified under Section 132, although the matters were otherwise within provincial jurisdiction according to Section 92 of the British North America Act. The Judicial Committee denied this claim by stating: "The obligations are not obligations of Canada as part of the British Empire, but of Canada, by virtue of her new status as an international person . . ." But the most significant part of the decision was its assertion that the Parliament of Canada did not acquire any legislative powers it would not otherwise have by virtue of the Canadian government incurring an international obligation by way of a treaty or otherwise. Thus, "For the purposes of ss. 91 and 92, i.e., the distribution of legislative powers between the Dominion and the Provinces, there is no such thing as treaty legislation as such. The distribution is based on classes of subjects; and as a treaty deals with a particular class of subjects so will the legislative power of performing it be ascertained." The Judicial Committee deliberately refused to give an opinion on the executive power to conclude treaties and other international obligations binding Canada, i.e., whether these might be made by the federal government even though Parliament did not have the power to implement such obligations or, alternatively, whether such agreements might be made only by the authority which had legislative jurisdiction to implement them.

The late 1960s saw a vigorous and impassioned debate between the federal and Quebec governments concerning the respective roles of these governments in international affairs. As a manifestation of "épanouissement" the new Quebec vastly extended its international activities, particularly with France and the former French colonies in Africa. In this drive for international status, Quebec was assisted by the De Gaulle government and France's African allies of La Francophonie. For its part the federal authorities came to believe, and with some justification, that France was mischievously involving itself in Canadian domestic affairs with the eventual object of breaking up the Canadian federation.

So far as the Quebec-Ottawa struggle was conducted in terms of legal and constitutional argument, the contestants based their cases on conflicting claims to conclude international agreements,[104] a matter which, as we have seen, was left unresolved by the Judicial Committee in the *Labour Conventions* reference. The Quebec assertion was that the prerogative power to conclude such agreements followed the division of legislative powers in the BNA Act. The implication was that so far as matters within provincial legislative jurisdiction were concerned, Quebec might assume any international status that other nations were willing to confer on her. Ottawa's case was that the prerogative power to enter into international arrangements and to conclude agreements binding in public international law resided in the federal executive alone. However, because in many circumstances the subject-matter of international relations was partly or wholly within provincial legislative jurisdiction, the provinces could and should play an important role in international affairs so long as they did not do this independently of the federal government. Thus, in constituting the Canadian delegations to international conferences dealing with provincial matters the federal authorities would normally choose provincial ministers or appointed officials. The federal authorities made much of the point that Canada had a single international personality and that the United Nations and its specialized agencies, as well as other international associations and international law, drew a very sharp line between jurisdictions which were sovereign states and those which were not. The general case was made that "foreign policy is indivisible," although in the Canadian circumstances this did not preclude the provinces in co-operation with the federal government being involved in international affairs.

The constitutional issue of the respective roles of the federal and provincial governments in international affairs remains unresolved and the efforts to effect a comprehensive reform of the constitution from 1967 onward have not had this issue on the agenda. In recent years the provinces other than Quebec have vastly extended their activities outside Canada—at present Ontario operates some 15 offices abroad—yet

none of these provinces has been disposed to challenge federal jurisdiction over international relations in any direct way. The extension of
federal legislative powers to include all matters of international intercourse would result in an intolerable centralization. Yet the dominant
legal opinion appears to be that only the government of Canada is a
recognized actor in public international law—in contrast with private
international law regulating the relations of individuals and non-sover-
eign entities across national boundaries—and that Canada incurs the
sole responsibility for carrying out treaties and other international
agreements, whether or not the federal authorities have the domestic
jurisdiction to enact legislation implementing such obligations. Thus if
Canada is to be an effective participant in the host of international and
transnational dealings involving matters wholly or partly within provincial legislative jurisdiction, the cooperation of the two orders is required.

Canada's Other Constitution: Emergency Powers[105]

The complex division of legislative powers between two levels of government which characterizes federalism is obviously inappropriate in
times of domestic and international crisis. Contemporary federations
make constitutional provisions for such emergencies in very different
ways.[106] The Constitution of the United States contains very few and
relatively specific provisions respecting emergencies, and the late Clinton Rossiter has written of the American constitutional tradition in this
respect: "The traditional theory of the Constitution is clearly hostile to
the establishment of crisis institutions and procedures. It is constitutional dogma that this document foresees any and every emergency,
and that no departure from its solemn injunctions could possibly be
necessary."[107] At the other end of the spectrum, the Constitution of
India adopted in 1949 gave the federal executive sweeping powers to
override the normal legislative powers of the states in cases of emergency caused by war, internal disturbances, the perceived inability of a
state government to carry on its affairs in accordance with the Constitution, and financial instability. These powers have been used by the national authorities on several occasions.

To return to the Canadian situation, the War Measures Act was enacted in August 1914, and has since remained as a federal statute subject to being brought into effect by proclamation of the Governor-in-
Council when, in his judgment, there exists "war, invasion, or
insurrection, real or apprehended." The Act gives the federal cabinet
discretion not only to declare the coming into being of such an emer-

gency but also its passing. When the Act is proclaimed in force, the cabinet is given almost unlimited powers to cope with the situation, to give effect to its will through orders and regulations, and to prescribe penalties for violations of such orders and regulations, with the limitation that no such penalty shall exceed a fine of five thousand dollars or imprisonment for five years or both fine and imprisonment. When the Canadian Bill of Rights was enacted in 1960 there were provisions to associate Parliament with the cabinet in respect to War Measures Act powers. Under the 1960 legislation the cabinet is required to lay a proclamation declaring an emergency before Parliament "forthwith" or "if Parliament is then not sitting, within the first fifteen days next thereafter that Parliament is sitting." Further, when a proclamation is laid before Parliament any ten members of either House can force a debate that the proclamation be revoked and if both Houses so decide, actions of the cabinet taken under the Act cease to have future effect. Thus under emergency conditions as determined by the federal cabinet Canada becomes what Rossiter has called a "constitutional dictatorship," with the federal cabinet assuming many of the most important functions of Parliament and overriding the normal legislative jurisdiction of the provinces.

As interpreted by the courts, the constitutional justification of emergency powers lies in the general authority of Parliament to legislate for the "Peace, Order, and Good Government of Canada."[108] The national authorities may override provincial powers not only when international hostilities are in progress, but also for a time after in dealing with the economic and other dislocations occasioned by the war. Further, "The length of time that an emergency may exist and hence relevant Dominion legislation may be upheld on emergency grounds is uncertain; but the question is essentially a political one and the courts are therefore very loath to question the decision of the Dominion Parliament on the length of the emergency period."[109] Canada was governed under the War Measures Act during the First and Second World Wars, and after the phasing out of the Act after 1945, under emergency enactments of more limited scope until 1954.

Although the War Measures Act mentions insurrection, until the Quebec crisis of 1970 most Canadians had regarded the Act almost entirely within the context of the country's involvement in international conflict. However, in the early hours of the morning of October 16 of that year, the Act was proclaimed in force and the Public Order Regulations issued under its authority. The Regulations declared to be illegal Le Front du Libération du Québec, any successor organization or any group advocating force or crime as a means of effecting governmental changes in Canada. There was specified a list of indictable offenses for individuals who belonged to unlawful political associations, advocated force or crime to bring about political change, or gave assistance to such unlawful activities. Peace officers, including members of the armed forces, were given sweeping powers of search and arrest without warrants, and at the discretion of the Attorney-General of a province a person might be detained up to twenty-one days before being charged with a specific offence under the Regulations. The Regulations were replaced by the Public Order Temporary Measures Act on December 3, 1970. The latter enactment shortened the period and required stronger proof of adherence to an unlawful political organization. The Act lapsed on April 30, 1971.

The 1970 crisis was unique in Canadian constitutional theory and practice. Previously, emergency legislation in Canada had come into existence at the initiative of the federal government alone and had had the effect of overriding the normal legislative jurisdiction of the provinces. However, in 1970 the proclamation of the War Measures Act appears to have resulted from a common perception of the crisis by the federal, Quebec, and Montreal governments, and the Public Order Regulations enhanced the powers of the law enforcement authorities under the immediate control of the Attorney-General of Quebec. During the debates of the House of Commons, Prime Minister Trudeau and his colleagues asserted again and again the exclusive responsibility of the Quebec government for the administration of justice in the province and refused to intervene in these matters. However, in their refusal to renew the Public Order Temporary Measures Act when it expired in 1971 the federal authorities in a sense reasserted their power to determine what legislative powers were necessary for the effective control of subversion in Quebec.

The War Measures Act gives the federal cabinet sweeping powers to declare an emergency, to take the actions it chooses to deal with such circumstances and to decide to end the state of emergency. So far as the proclamation is concerned Section 2 of the Act states:

> The issue of a proclamation by Her Majesty, or under the authority of the Governor in Council shall be conclusive evidence that war, invasion, or insurrection, real or apprehended, exists and has existed for any period of time therein stated, and of its continuance, until, by the issue of a further proclamation it is declared that war, invasion or insurrection no longer exists.

The impact of this Section would seem to be to preclude any judicial challenge of the cabinet in declaring an emergency to exist and in determining the duration of the emergency. Courts in the Anglo-Canadian tradition are disposed not to recognize such "privative clauses" as valid. However, in practical terms it seems unlikely that any senior Canadian court would decide to substitute its own judgment for that of the federal cabinet under these circumstances. When a proclamation under the Act is in effect the Canadian system of government ceases to

be either parliamentary or federal—the cabinet is permitted to proceed
by order and regulation where otherwise legislation would be required,
including the prescription of penalties for violation of such orders and
regulations, and to wield powers which are otherwise within provincial jurisdiction.

The Flexible Constitution

The Canadian constitution has proved to be a flexible instrument of
government, and if this were not so Canadians would not have had 113
years of constitutional experience without a break with the past. The
constitution has permitted and in some cases facilitated new balances
to be struck in federal and provincial powers as the relative vigor and
effectiveness of the two orders of governments shifted and as the importance of the responsibilities assigned to them by the constitution
changed. In this ongoing process explicit constitutional amendments
and new delineations of federal and provincial powers through judicial
review have been much less important than the interactions among
governments which I shall designate in Chapter 4 as "executive federalism."

Several elements of this constitutional flexibility may be mentioned:

—the exercise of the federal spending power has permitted Ottawa to
  involve itself in matters within the legislative jurisdiction of the
  provinces. The constitutional distribution of responsibilities is somewhat resistant to change through amendment or evolving patterns of
  judicial review. Thus the spending power has facilitated a response
  to these rigidities where the federal government has wished to pursue some national interest in respect to matters within provincial
  legislative jurisdiction.

—the power of Parliament to enact laws for the "Peace, Order, and
  Good Government of Canada" permits a progressive redefinition by
  the courts of matters within federal jurisdiction according to the
  emergency and national-dimensions tests. Of particular recent importance here has been the judgment of the Supreme Court of Canada
  in the Anti-Inflation Reference of 1976 establishing the power of Parliament to enact legislation in respect to a peacetime economic emergency.

—the inter-delegation of powers between the federal and provincial
  governments is permitted. In 1950 the Supreme Court of Canada denied the constitutionality of a proposed Nova Scotia enactment providing that the province might delegate its legislative powers over labour relations to the Parliament of Canada. However, in 1952 the
  Court decided that it was permissible for one level to delegate its

powers to an administrative agency established by and operating under the legislative authority of the other. As the spending power provides a measure of constitutional flexibility where large public expenditures are involved, so delegation mitigates the rigidities of the division of legislative powers in respect to public regulation. This device has been used in the regulation of the marketing of natural products, interprovincial motor transport, and fish inspection.

—the concurrency of federal and provincial powers permits the order of government which develops more urgency than the other about particular aspects of public policy to take action in such matters. The most explicit of procedures here is for the constitution to vest powers over some matters in both orders of government, with provisions determining which is to prevail in the event of a clash. Under the Canadian constitution such concurrency as specifically embodied in the BNA Act is limited to agriculture, immigration and old age pensions, and both Parliament and the provinces may levy direct taxes. However, there are several other areas of jurisdiction which are *de facto* concurrent in the sense that both orders may find jurisdiction to act when this is deemed expedient.[110] This is so in a sense in respect to the exercise of the spending power. *De facto* concurrency also prevails in a very large number of matters within the field of public regulation-environmental pollution, credit-granting institutions, insurance, driving offences, consumer protection and the sale of securities. The exercise of the criminal law power has proved to be an effective device by which the federal government can involve itself in regulatory activities otherwise wholly or partly within provincial legislative jurisdiction. Under this justification Parliament has already enacted legislation prohibiting the adulteration of food products, certain actions which pollute the natural environment, various kinds of practices in labour relations, and actions restraining competition.

There are prices to be paid for constitutional flexibility. It weakens the accountability of governments to their respective legislatures and electorates and gives politicians plausible constitutional justifications for their failure to act when public action is clearly required. Provinces or regions which are, or believe themselves to be, in a permanent minority position in national affairs can be expected to be anxious when in relation to many important matters their actual position is determined not so much by the constitution as judicially interpreted but by their own political bargaining power—and in relative terms the procedures of flexibility give Ottawa more scope for encroaching on provincial responsibilities than the reverse. Before he entered elective politics, Pierre Elliott Trudeau wrote the most trenchant criticism of flexibility in the Canadian federal system that has ever been made.[111] He said in 1961 that "whenever an important segment of the Canadian population needs something badly enough, it is eventually given to them by one level of government or the other, regardless of the constitution."[112] The main drawback of this circumstance according to Trudeau was that "it tends to develop paternalistic instincts in more enterprising governments, at the expense of democratic maturation in others."[113] Thus if one level finds that it cannot discharge its responsibilities, the better remedy is to seek an explicit transfer of jurisdiction through constitutional amendment. Although he and Trudeau were fundamentally opposed in their prescriptions for Canadian federalism, the late Daniel Johnson, while Leader of the Opposition in Quebec, also opposed the flexible nature of the Canadian federal system when he wrote in 1965:

> Au lieu d'une véritable constitution, nous avons un régime mouvant, qui est constamment en mutation et qui est le produit des accords formels ou tacites entre Ottawa et la majorité des provinces.[114]

In general terms, the fundamental defect of flexibility is, as Johnson pointed out, that the federal system is cut adrift from its constitutional base and becomes a regime shaped decisively by the bargaining powers of the federal and provincial government rather than by legal norms.

The Constitution in the Canadian System of Government

An attempt has been made to outline the basic elements of the Canadian constitution. But something needs to be said about the place of the constitution in the Canadian system of government with special emphasis on how Canadians have perceived this constitution.

Canadians have never been constitution-worshippers and the existing constitution has never been a symbolic focus of loyalty to the political community. This can be explained in terms of both the circumstances of the Confederation settlement itself and the continuing tradition of English law. In constitutional terms, the settlement of 1864-1867 was conservative in its disposition to preserve the well-understood principles of British parliamentary government and, unlike the Americans some 80 years before, the British North American politicians had neither the need nor the desire to establish new foundations for political authority or to debate fundamental political principles. The legal embodiment of the Confederation settlement in the British North America Act of 1867 thus was not perceived to be a symbol of Canadian unity. As we have seen, the Act made no mention of some of the most fundamental principles of the constitution. It contained not only provisions which were of basic constitutional importance—most crucially of course the division of legislative powers between Parliament and the provinces—but transitional provisions which were soon "spent," and the constitutions of Ontario and Quebec which could be and were amended by the legislatures of these provinces. The BNA Act of 1867 and the later amendments to it are written in the prosaic and often turgid language of legal draftsmen in the positivist tradition whose audience has been lawyers and judges rather than ordinary citizens.

Despite what has been said above, in the period prior to the last two decades, most Canadians had, and were instructed in, a decent respect for their constitution and made important claims and counter-claims against one another by reference to that constitution:

—the various formulations of the contract or compact theory of Confederation which were central to constitutional debate during much of Canadian history were based on the legitimacy of the Constitution.[115] There were two major variants of this theory, one arguing from a compact among provinces—or at least the original ones—and the other between French and English. Both versions argued that the terms of the original compact, contract or treaty could not be changed without the consent of the partners to it, and both rested on the premise that the constitution as an embodiment of this original agreement was legitimate. It may be mentioned too that even groups who felt most aggrieved did not assert the basic legal principle to the effect that when one party to a contract does not carry out his obligations the other party is relieved from his responsibilities and the contract itself is voided. I can find only one such expression and that in the book of a Quebec separatist, Raymond Barbeau, published in 1961 "Les conditions essentielles du pacte fédéral . . . ont été violées. . . . Par conséquent, les souverainistes sont parfaitment justifiés de la considérer comme nul, arbitraire et dénués de tout intérêt."[116] In contrast with this legitimism of Canadian constitutional thought, there has been in the United States a recurrent appearance of the doctrine of "interposition and nullification" by which states have asserted the right to "interpose" themselves between the national government and citizens when the state authorities judged that the former has exceeded its constitutional powers. This doctrine was asserted as recently as the late 1950s by the legislatures of several southern states in reaction to decisions of the Supreme Court outlawing racial discrimination in schools.[117]

—the criticisms of the provincialist interpretations of the BNA Act by the Judicial Committee of the Privy Council asserted the legitimacy of the constitution as such critics understood the true meaning of the constitution to be. The positivists argued that according to the rules of statutory interpretation derived from the English legal tradition the Judicial Committee had botched the job. The other line of attack took the view that the underlying spirit of the Confederation settle-

ment was in the direction of a centralized federation and the Judicial
Committee had subverted this purpose. These formulations could be
reconciled at least in part by the argument that the intentions of the
Fathers had been embodied in a fairly explicit way in the terms of the
BNA Act and that the Act had subsequently been misinterpreted by
judicial review. Such views, which were the conventional wisdom in
English-speaking Canada from the 1930s through the 1950s, im-
plicitly accepted the legitimacy of the constitution.

From the early 1960s onward the Canadian constitution has been
denigrated. It would be tedious to do more than to give a few examples
of such denigration from a wide variety of sources. In his elaboration of
a new Canadian constitution in 1964 Peter J. T. OHearn spoke of the urgency of replacing "the debris of Imperial Statutes, Royal Instructions,
Orders in Council and the battered hulk of the British North America
Act and its train of amendments"[118] T. C. Douglas as leader of the New
Democratic Party said in 1966 "The time has come for Canadians to free
themselves from the dead hand of the past and forge a constitution that
will enable Canada to keep its rendezvous with destiny . . . I do not
think that the dead hand of the past should be allowed to stay the onward march of progress. Human rights are sacred but constitutions are
not."[119] In his opening statement to the Confederation of Tomorrow
Conference in 1967, Premier Daniel Johnson of Quebec spoke of the
"impotent" Constitution "which no longer in any sense conforms to
Canadian reality."[120] The Report of the Special Joint Committee of the
Senate and House of Commons on the Constitution of Canada published in 1972 asserted "The measure of the inadequacy of the British
North America Act is that it does not serve Canadians fully as an in-
spirational ideal."[121] The document *A Time for Action,* issued over the
signature of Prime Minister Trudeau in June 1978 as a prelude to the
federal government's constitutional proposals, had a long dossier of
criticisms of the existing constitution—among them its lack of "educa-
tive value," its "obscure and anachronistic language," its inexplicit-
ness in the division of legislative powers, its lack of a bill of rights.[122]

In an article published in 1971 Alan Cairns spoke of the "detached,
unappreciative Canadian attitudes to one of the most durable and successful constitutions in the world." His basic explanation was that
Canadians had failed to understand the nature of a "living constitution."[123] To Cairns, the intentions of the Fathers of Confederation are irrelevant to our present circumstances. The constitution of today is not
that of 1867; it has shown a remarkable capacity for adaptation and
constitutions are "like wine—much better when aged."

Concomitant with the explicit denigration of the existing constitution has come a tendency for governments to press their interests and
frame their policies with almost no reference to the constitution. Two
examples of this can be given.

First, federal and provincial claims and counter-claims about involvement in activities which are in a broad sense educational are characteristically made with little reference to constitutional principle.[124] When the Fathers of Confederation conferred exclusive legislative jurisdiction over education on the provinces they were thinking in terms of publicly-supported elementary schools, to a lesser degree secondary schools and universities, and of course not of the array of such public activities as educational broadcasting, manpower training, research, training in the minority official language of a province, aids to various forms of cultural activity and so on. Apart from the educational rights of denominational minorities there has been almost no clarification by the courts of the respective roles of the federal and provincial governments in activities which are broadly speaking educational. In justifying federal involvement in such activities, many claims have been made that rest on principles other than constitutional ones—for example, that universities are in some sense national institutions, that research is inherently a national function, that the federal authorities cannot carry out effective full employment policies without involvement in manpower training, that the federal authorities have generalized responsibilities for cultural development, that Ottawa has specific responsibilities for ensuring access to education for official-language minorities, etc. Provincial counter-claims made more often than not by Quebec spokesmen assert an exclusive jurisdiction for the provinces over such matters in terms which have no constitutional justification in the narrow sense.

Secondly, the composition of the two chambers of the Parliament of Canada is now dealt with outside the framework of constitutional principle. The most crucial element of the constitutional bargain hammered out in 1864 was that there should be representation by population in the House of Commons and the equal representation of each of the regions in the Senate—the composition of this latter body, rather than the division of legislative powers, was the most contentious issue resolved by the Fathers. Yet the various proposals which have recently been advanced for replacing the existing Senate by a House of the Provinces or House of the Federation diverge widely from this principle of equal regional representation in the second chamber and make no reference to this principle. More surprisingly, parliamentarians in this decade have dealt with the membership of the House of Commons outside the framework of the original Confederation bargain. As described in an article by J. R. Mallory "Amending the Constitution by Stealth," Parliament has determined representation in the House of Commons by the Representation Act of 1974, apparently oblivious to the fact that it was affecting a constitutional change of some importance which had on previous occasions been accomplished through explicit amendments to the BNA Act.[125] There were two conflicting principles here in respect to membership in the House, the principle of representation by population and the principle of "equitable" representation which would sustain the positions of provinces whose populations were in decline relative to that of Canada as a whole. Yet as Mallory describes the situation, the pragmatic resolution of the matter embodied in the 1974 Act was arrived at without debate on these principles being clearly joined and with little reference to the original Confederation settlement.

There has thus been a steadily declining respect for the Canadian constitution without the federal and provincial governments having been able to agree on an allegedly better constitutional system. This declining legitimacy of the constitution comes at the same time that judicial review is playing a more crucial and contentious role in the federal system than has been the case since the 1930s. Justifiably or otherwise, the provincial governments have ceased to regard the Supreme Court of Canada as a neutral arbiter of constitutional questions. Along with these developments there is a wide-spread disposition among informed Canadians to take a more critical view than hitherto of the exercise of power by the courts in judicial review of the constitution and their other functions. Canadians have held, and hold, their courts in high regard, and until very recently the judiciary has for the most part been free from the ongoing criticism to which the other branches of government have been exposed. Yet this respect was in large measure based on the fallacious assumption that judicial decisions were in a mechanical way deduced from rules of law—an assumption which it is not unfair to charge lawyers and judges with perpetuating, knowingly or otherwise. However, this perception is changing and as Peter Russell points out, "It is unlikely that as the public becomes more sophisticated about the realities of the judicial process, judicial power can continue to hide behind the mask of an ideology which denies the very existence of that power."[126] A critical problem remains: as judicial review of the constitution is increasingly perceived to be something more than the application of established law to particular circumstances, on what sources of legitimacy will the courts draw in playing this contentious role? The difficulty is compounded when the legitimacy of the constitution itself is in decline.

Notes

1. See R. L. Watts, *New Federations: Experiments in the Commonwealth*, Oxford: Oxford University Press, 1966.
2. A. V. Dicey, *Law of the Constitution*, Seventh Edition, London: Macmillan and Company, 1908, p. 140.

3. Clinton Rossiter, *1787: the Grand Convention*, New York: Mentor Books, 1968, p. 20.

4. For modern accounts see Rossiter, *op. cit*; Catherine Drinker Bowen, *Miracle at Philadelphia*, Toronto: Bantam Books of Canada, 1966; and Carl Van Doren *The Great Rehearsal*, New York: Viking Press, 1948. For detailed analysis of the intellectual dimensions of the American Revolution and the framing of the Constitution see Gordon S. Wood, *The Creation of the American Republic 1776-1787*, New York: W. W. Norton, 1969, and Bernard Bailyn, *The Ideological Origins of the American Revolution*, Cambridge, Mass.: The Belknap Press of Harvard University Press, 1967.

5. For John A. Macdonald's analysis as expressed at the Quebec Conference in 1864, see G. P. Browne, ed., *Documents on the Confederation of British North America*, Carleton Library, Toronto: McClelland and Stewart, 1969, pp. 94-95. He said "The various states of the adjoining Republic had always acted as separate sovereignties. . . . The primary error in the formation of their constitution was that each state reserved to itself all sovereign rights, save the small portion delegated. We must reverse this process by strengthening the General Government and conferring on the Provincial bodies only such powers as may be required for local purposes."

6. Quoted in J. Murray Beck, *Joseph Howe: Voice of Nova Scotia*, Carleton Library, Toronto: McClelland and Stewart, 1964, pp. 173-174.

7. Ibid., pp. 161-162.

8. Ibid., p. 38.

9. For a discussion of these "exceptions to exhaustive distribution," see Peter W. Hogg, *Constitutional Law of Canada*, Toronto: Carswell, 1977, pp. 198-200.

10. Thomas A. Hockin, *Government in Canada*, Toronto: McGraw-Hill Ryerson, 1976, p. 7.

11. For a thoughtful but pessimistic argument that the effective accountability of governments is impossible because of the present scope of public activity, see Robert L. Stanfield, "The Present State of the Legislative Process in Canada: Myths and Realities," in W. A. W. Neilson and J. C. MacPherson, eds., *The Legislative Process in Canada*, Montreal: Institute for Research on Public Policy, 1978, pp. 39-50.

12. Compiled from table in John Stewart, *The Canadian House of Commons: Procedure and Reform*, Montreal: McGill-Queen's University Press, and London 1977, pp. 200-201.

13. Ibid., p. 14.

14. Ibid., p. 16.

15. Ibid., p. 30.

16. For a more extensive discussion see Donald V. Smiley, "Federalism and the Legislative Process in Canada," in Neilson and MacPherson, *op. cit.*, pp. 73-87.

17. In 1919 the Judicial Committee of the Privy Council invalidated the Manitoba Initiative and Referendum Act on the general grounds that it interfered with the Lieutenant Governor's powers by requiring this official to submit to the voters a proposed law and would have denied his power to prevent such a proposal from becoming law if approved by these voters. (1919,) A.C., 670.

18. See Hogg, *op. cit.* Chapter 1.
19. The Honourable Guy Favreau, *The Amendment of the Constitution of Canada*, Ottawa: Queen's Printer, 1965, p. 13.
20. A useful collection here is Maurice Ollivier, ed., *British North America Act and Selected Statutes, 1867-1962*, Ottawa: Queen's Printer, 1962. However, the compiler gave no indication of his principles of selection for constitutional statutes.
21. The opening words of Stewart's book are these "The procedures by which the House of Commons does its work are in a sense part of Canada's constitution." Stewart, *op. cit.*, p. 1.
22. Ibid., pp. 4-5.
23. Respectively Bora Laskin, *Canadian Constitutional Law*, Toronto: Carswell, 1966, and J. D. Whyte and W. B. Lederman, *Canadian Constitutional Law*, Second Edition, Toronto: Butterworths, 1977.
24. Donald Creighton, *British North America at Confederation*, A Study Prepared for the Royal Commission on Dominion-Provincial Relations, King's Printer: Ottawa, 1939, Section IX "The Division of Economic Powers at Confederation."
25. *The Report of the Quebec Royal Commission on Constitutional Problems*, Quebec: Queen's Printer, 1956, Volume I, First Part, Chapter III "The Political Work of the Fathers of Confederation and the Spirit of the Federative Pact."
26. Peter Waite, *The Life and Times of Confederation, 1864-1867*, Toronto: University of Toronto Press, 1962, Chapter VIII, "Confederation and the Federal Principle."
27. Section 94 contemplated an early assimilation of the private law of the common law provinces into a single code under Dominion jurisdiction. This Section never became operative.
28. See G. V. La Forest, *Disallowance and Reservation of Provincial Legislation*, Ottawa: Queen's Printer, 1955, reprinted 1965.
29. For an account of this incident, see J. R. Mallory "The Lieutenant Governor's Discretionary Powers: The Reservation of Bill 56 in Saskatchewan," *Canadian Journal of Economics and Political Science* 28, Nov. 1961, pp. 518-522.
30. Hogg, *op. cit.*, p. 41 n.
31. For analysis of the constitutional nature of the spending power see Hogg, *op. cit.*, pp. 68-72, and Gerald V. La Forest, *The Allocation of Taxing Power Under the Canadian Constitution*, Toronto: Canadian Tax Foundation, 1967, pp. 36-44.
32. Frank R. Scott, "The Constitutional Basis of the Taxation Agreements" in Frank R. Scott, *Essays on the Constitution*, Toronto: University of Toronto Press, 1977, p. 296.
33. Hogg's analysis of this complicated subject is the most lucid one I know. Hogg, *op. cit.*, Chapter 14. See also Bora Laskin, "Peace, Order, and Good Government Re-examined" in W. R. Lederman, ed., *The Courts and the Canadian Constitution*, Carleton Library, Toronto: McClelland and Stewart, 1964, pp. 66-104.
34. *A.G. Can. v. A.G. Ontario* (1937) A.C. 355. Hogg believes "that it was also a

relevant factor that the new deal legislation was permanent rather than temporary." Hogg, *op. cit.*, p. 250 n.

35. *Re Anti-Inflation Act*, (1976), 2 S.C.R., 378.
36. The actions taken by the Organization of Petroleum Exporting Countries in late 1973 led Parliament to enact the Energy Supplies Allocation Act in early 1974. The Act empowered the Governor in Council to declare a national emergency in the event of an actual or anticipated shortage of petroleum and to allocate petroleum at the wholesale level. This Act expired in 1976 and in the wake of events in Iran similar stand-by legislation, the Energy Supplies Emergency Act, was enacted in late March 1979.
37. 1881-827 (A.C.) 473.
38. 1896 (A.C.) at p. 361. Somewhat paradoxically this statement was made within the context of a decision restricting Parliament's powers to legislate in respect to alcohol consumption which in effect reversed *Russell v. the Queen*.
39. Hogg, *op. cit.*, pp. 134-137.
40. *Federalism and Constitutional Change*, Oxford University Press, Oxford 1955, p. 13.
41. The Honourable Guy Favreau, *The Amendment of the Constitution of Canada*, Ottawa: Queen's Printer, 1965, p. 15. Reproduced by permission of the Minister of Supply and Services, Canada.
42. Quoted in Hogg, *op. cit.*, pp. 20-21.
43. Ibid., p. 21.
44. Favreau, *op. cit.* pp. 13-14. Reproduced by permission of the Minister of Supply and Services Canada.
45. See Lord Sankey's short account of the history of the Judicial Committee of the Privy Council in *British Coal Corporation v. The King* (1935) A.C. 500 at pp. 510-512. This is reprinted in W. R. Lederman, ed., *The Courts and the Canadian Constitution*, Carleton Library, Toronto: McClelland and Stewart, 1964, pp. 63-65.
46. Peter H. Russell, "Introduction," in Peter H. Russell, ed., *Leading Constitutional Decisions*, Carleton Library, Toronto: McClelland and Stewart, 1965, p. xi.
47. See particularly the *O'Connor Report*, in G. P. Browne, *The Judicial Committee and the British North America Act*, Toronto: University of Toronto Press, 1967; and, more generally, Edward McWhinney, *Judicial Review in the English-Speaking World*, Fourth Edition, Toronto: University of Toronto Press, 1969. See also Alan C. Cairns' brilliant article "The Judicial Committee and Its Critics," *Canadian Journal of Political Science* IV, (September 1971), pp. 301-345.
48. (1932) A.C., 54 at pp. 71-72. By permission of Information Canada.
49. *A.-G. Can. v. A.-G. Ont.* (1937) A.C. 326.
50. *A.-G. B.C. v. A.-G. Can.* (1937) A.C. 377.
51. *A.G. Can. v. A.-G. Ont.* (1937) A.C. 355.
52. For a comprehensive review of the Judicial Committee's treatment of the general power, see Bora Laskin, " 'Peace, Order and Good Government' Reexamined" in Lederman, *op. cit.*, pp. 66-104.
53. *O'Connor Report*, in Browne, *op. cit.*

54. For one of a number of articles on this general line see Vincent C. MacDonald, "The Privy Council and the Canadian Constitution," *Canadian Bar Review* XXVI, 1948, pp. 1021ff.
55. See Cairns' article cited in n. 47.
56. Browne, *op. cit.*
57. Louis-Phillipe Pigeon, "The Meaning of Provincial Autonomy" *Canadian Bar Review* 29 (1951). By permission of the author and the *Canadian Bar Review*.
58. Pierre Elliott Trudeau, "Federalism, Nationalism, and Reason," in Pierre Elliott Trudeau, *Federalism and the French Canadians*, Toronto: Macmillan of Canada, 1968, p. 198.
59. G. F. G. Stanley, *A Short History of the Canadian Constitution*, Toronto: Ryerson Press, 1969, p. 142.
60. J. R. Mallory, *Social Credit and the Federal Power in Canada*, Toronto: University of Toronto Press, 1959, Chapters 3 and 4.
61. *Ibid.*, p. 54.
62. *Ibid.*, p. 56.
63. Cairns, *op. cit.*, pp. 327-332.
64. *Ibid.*, p. 327.
65. Peter H. Russell, *The Supreme Court of Canada as a Bilingual and Bicultural Institution*, Documents of the Royal Commission on Bilingualism and Biculturalism, Ottawa: Queen's Printer, 1969, p. 26.
66. Bora Laskin, "The Supreme Court of Canada: A Final Court of and for Canadians," Lederman, *op. cit.*, p. 143. Laskin's 1951 article at pp. 125-151 is an excellent analysis of the previous status and future prospects of the Court written near to the time when it became the final appellate tribunal for Canadian cases.
67. *A.G. Ont. v. A.G. Can.* (1947) A.C. 127.
68. Frank Scott, "Our Changing Constitution," in Lederman, *op. cit.* p. 27.
69. Peter H. Russell, "The Supreme Court of Canada," in Russell, *op. cit.* p. 37. For one Quebec argument on comparative lines see Jacques Brossard, *La Cour Suprême et la Constitution*, Montréal: Les presses de l'université de Montréal, 1968.
70. 1 S.C.R. 292.
71. Hogg, *op. cit.*, pp. 271-275.
72. 2 S.C.R., 392.
73. *A.G.N.S. v. A.G. Canada* (1951) S.C.R. 31.
74. W. R. Lederman, "Thoughts on Reform of the Supreme Court of Canada," *The Confederation Challenge*, Ontario Advisory Committee on Confederation, Vol. II, Toronto: Queen's Printer, 1970, p. 295.
75. (1967) S.C.R. 792.
76. *Central Canada Potash et al. v. Government of Saskatchewan.*
77. As yet unreported.
78. For an excellent article on the dynamics of this decision and its consequences, see Peter Russell, "The Anti-inflation case: the Anatomy of a Constitutional Decision," *Canadian Public Administration* 20, Winter 1977, pp. 632-665.
79. Peter Russell, "The Supreme Court since 1960," in Paul Fox, Editor, *Politics Canada*, Fourth Edition, Toronto: McGraw-Hill Ryerson, 1977, p. 541.

80. (1976) 66 D.L.R. (3d.), 1.

81. See also Premier Blakeney's letter to Prime Minister Trudeau on the same matter dated October 10, 1978 and reprinted in *Proposals on the Constitution, 1971-1978,* Collated by the Canadian Intergovernmental Conference Secretariat, Ottawa, 1978, pp. 244-259.

82. Paul Weiler, *In the Last Resort: A Study of the Supreme Court of Canada,* Toronto: Carswell, 1974.

83. Ibid., p. 88.

84. Ibid.

85. Peter Russell, "The Supreme Court since 1960," in Fox, *op. cit.,* p. 541.

86. G. Bruce Doern and V. Seymour Wilson, "Conclusions and Observations," in G. Bruce Doern and V. Seymour Wilson, eds., *Issues in Canadian Public Policy,* Toronto: Macmillan of Canada, 1974, p. 31.

87. Section 22 and Section 23(6) (Senate of Canada), Section 40 (House of Commons), Section 72 (Legislative Council of Quebec) and Section 80 (Legislative Assembly of Quebec).

88. Section 20 (annual sessions of Parliament), Section 39 (no joint membership in Senate and House of Commons), Sections 44-47 (Office of the Speaker of the House of Commons), Section 51 (basis of representation in the House of Commons), Sections 53-54 (money bills).

89. Noel Lyon and Ronald G. Atkey, *Canadian Constitutional Law in a Modern Perspective,* Toronto: University of Toronto Press, 1970, p. 375.

90. For extended discussions see D. A. Schmeiser, *Civil Liberties in Canada,* Toronto: Oxford University Press, 1964, and Walter Surma Tarnopolsky, *The Canadian Bill of Rights,* Second, Revised Edition, Carleton Library, Toronto: McClelland and Stewart, 1975.

91. (1975) 2 S.C.R. 127.

92. For an exhaustive account of the law of languages in Canada, see Claude-Armand Sheppard *The Law of Languages in Canada,* Studies of the Royal Commission on Bilingualism and Biculturalism, Ottawa: Queen's Printer, 1971.

93. "An Inquiry into the Diefenbaker Bill of Rights," XXXVII *Canadian Bar Review,* March 1959, p. 80.

94. (1938 S.C.R.) 100.

95. *Switzman v. Elbing* (1957) S.C.R. at 328.

96. *R. v. Drybones,* (1970), S.C.R. 282.

97. See for example Frank R. Scott, "Dominion Jurisdiction over Human Rights and Fundamental Freedoms," in Scott, *op. cit.,* pp. 209-212.

98. The Honourable Pierre Elliott Trudeau, *A Canadian Charter of Human Rights,* Ottawa: Queen's Printer, 1968.

99. Lyon and Atkey, *op. cit.,* p. 377. For a critique of this argument see my review of this book in *Canadian Bar Review,* March 1972, pp. 139-148.

100. The most sophisticated argument available against the constitutional entrenchment of human rights in Canada is contained in the *Report* of the (Ontario) Royal Commission of Inquiry into Civil Rights, Toronto: Queen's Printer, 1969, Volume 4, Section 3.

101. For a useful collection of documents, see Howard A. Leeson and Wilfred Vanderelst, eds., *External Affairs and Canadian Federalism,* Toronto: Holt, Rinehart and Winston of Canada, 1973.

102. Ibid., pp. 48-49.

103. *Attorney-General of Canada v. Attorney-General for Ontario and others,* A.C. (1937), 328.

104. For the Quebec position, see *Working Paper on Foreign Relations,* prepared by the Quebec delegation for the Continuing Committee of Officials of the Constitutional Conference, Quebec, February 5, 1969 (mimeo.). The federal view at that time was contained in Honourable Paul Martin, *Federalism and International Relations,* Ottawa: Queen's Printer, 1968. Section V of Leeson and Vanderelst, *op. cit.,* gives a selection of documents on this controversy.

105. For an excellent analysis of the relation between constitutionalism and emergency powers, see Clinton Rossiter, *Constitutional Dictatorship: Crisis Government in the Modern Democracies,* Second Edition, New York, 1963. On the constitutional aspects of the Canadian War Measures Act, see Walter Surma Tarnopolsky, *The Canadian Bill of Rights,* Second Revised Edition, Carleton Library, Toronto: McClelland and Stewart, 1975, Chapter IX.

106. The newer federations in the Commonwealth have provided more explicitly for emergency powers than do the constitutions of the older federations. See R. L. Watts, *New Federations: Experiments in the Commonwealth,* Oxford University Press, 1966, pp. 315-319.

107. Rossiter, *op. cit.,* p. 212.

108. The leading case here is *Fort Frances Pulp and Paper Co. v. Manitoba Free Press,* (1923), A.C. 695.

109. R. MacGregor Dawson, *The Government of Canada,* Fifth Edition, Revised by Norman Ward, Toronto: University of Toronto Press, 1970, p. 92.

110. See generally Barry Strayer, "The Flexibility of the BNA Act," in Trevor Lloyd and Jack McLeod, eds., *Agenda 1970: Proposals for Creative Politics,* Toronto: University of Toronto Press, 1968, pp. 197-216.

111. Pierre Elliott Trudeau, "Federal Grants to Universities," in Trudeau, *Federalism and the French Canadians,* pp. 79-102. His argument went much beyond university grants in its implications.

112. Ibid., p. 138.

113. Ibid., p. 138.

114. Daniel Johnson, *Égalité ou Indépendance,* Montréal: Éditions Renaissance, 1965, p. 73.

115. See Ramsay Cook, *Provincial Autonomy, Minority Rights and the Compact Theory 1867-1921,* Studies of the Royal Commission on Bilingualism and Biculturalism, Ottawa: Queen's Printer, 1969, and R. Arès, S.J. *Dossier sur le pacte fédératif de 1867,* Montréal: Les éditions Bellarmin, 1967.

116. Raymond Barbeau, *J'ai choisi l'indépendance,* Ottawa: Les éditions de l'homme, 1961, p. 82.

117. Charles S. Hyneman, *The Supreme Court on Trial,* New York: Atherton Press, 1963, pp. 20-22.

118. Peter T. J. OHearn, *Peace, Order and Good Government: A New Constitution for Canada,* Toronto: Macmillan of Canada, 1964, p. 6.

119. *Globe and Mail,* Toronto, April 13, 1966, p. 7.

120. Daniel Johnson, *The Government of Québec and the Constitution,* Québec: L'Office D'Information et de Publicité du Québec, 1969(?), p. 30.
121. *Final Report,* Ottawa: Information Canada, 1972, p. 6.
122. The Right Honourable Pierre Elliott Trudeau, *A Time For Action,* Ottawa: Ministry of Supply and Services, 1978, pp. 19-21.
123. Alan C. Cairns, "The Living Canadian Constitution," reprinted in J. Peter Meekison, ed., *Canadian Federalism: Myth or Reality?* Third Edition, Toronto: Methuen of Canada, 1977, pp. 86-99.
124. For a more extensive outline of these claims, see Donald V. Smiley, *Canada in Question,* Second Edition, Toronto: McGraw-Hill Ryerson, 1976, pp. 30-34.
125. J. R. Mallory, "Amending the Constitution by Stealth," Queen's Quarterly LXXXII, Autumn 1975, pp. 394-401.
126. Peter Russell, "Judicial Power in Canada's Political Culture," in Martin L. Friedland, ed., *Courts and Trials: A Multidisciplinary Approach,* Toronto: University of Toronto Press, 1975, p. 79.

CHAPTER 3

EXPLICIT CONSTITUTIONAL REFORM

Prior to the 1960s there was relatively little discussion of comprehensive constitutional reform in Canada. In 1887 it is true the newly-elected premier of Quebec, the nationalist Honoré Mercier, convened an interprovincial conference which was attended by representatives of the governments of all the provinces except British Columbia, and which adopted a series of resolutions in opposition to the centralist tendencies of John A. Macdonald's brand of Conservatism, including recommendations that the power of disallowance be abolished and that the provincial governments appoint members of the Senate.[1] Interestingly, however, when the premiers came back to their own provinces the resolutions adopted by the conference were defeated in the upper chambers of the Nova Scotia and New Brunswick legislatures and were never put before the Legislative Council of Quebec. The Liberal opposition in Parliament failed to take up the provincialist cause and the first concerted effort to change the constitutional settlement of 1864-1867 soon lapsed.

During the period between the First and Second World Wars there was considerable debate about a domestic amending formula for the British North America Act.[2] A Dominion-Provincial conference was held on this subject in 1927, but this and subsequent discussions between the federal and provincial governments failed to find agreement on such a formula. Because of this disagreement and at the request of the government of Canada, the Statute of Westminster enacted by the Parliament of the United Kingdom which recognized the legal independence of Canada and the other Dominions contained this provision:

"Nothing in this Act shall be deemed to apply to the repeal, amendment or alteration of the British North America Acts, 1867 to 1930, or to any order, rule or regulation made thereunder." A subsequent Dominion-Provincial Conference in 1935 again failed to agree on patriation and an amending formula.

The 1930s also saw a vigorous debate on the patterns of interpretation of the British North America Act by the Judicial Committee of the Privy Council.[3] Among many constitutional reformers this question was linked with the amending procedure to the general effect that substantive amendments to the constitution were necessary to undo the damage allegedly done by the Judicial Committee and to give the Dominion what were regarded as the appropriate powers to meet both domestic needs and the imperatives of effective Canadian action in international affairs. Such reformers also promoted the suggestion that the Supreme Court of Canada be made the final appellate tribunal in constitutional questions so that constitutional interpretation be made by a body in harmony with Canadian needs. One of the most searching and scathing critiques of the record of the Judicial Committee, the "O'Connor Report," did not, however, recommend the displacement of this body but rather that there be an amendment to the constitution which would in effect direct the judicial authorities to interpret the constitution properly,[4] i.e., in accord with its own explicit terms and the accepted British practices of statutory interpretation.

As we saw in the last chapter, the federal government in 1949 caused the British North America Act to be amended by including in it the amending procedure now in effect. This change was brought about without the advice or consent of the provinces. With the new amending procedure in place, the federal government convened a Dominion-Provincial conference in 1950 to see if agreement on patriation and a procedure for amendment could be reached, but again there was failure.

Constitutional Reform 1960—1966: The New Quebec and the Fulton-Favreau Formula

The autonomist pressures from Quebec which followed the election of the Lesage Liberals to power in that province in June 1960 began the challenge to the Canadian constitutional system which still persists. During its period in office from 1960 to 1966 the Lesage government did not, however, evolve a coherent position in respect to explicit constitutional change.[5] In part no doubt this was a result of unresolved differences within the government itself, in part a result of the circumstance that the administration was experiencing a relatively high

degree of success in extending its range of discretion within the existing constitutional framework. During their last years in power Premier
Lesage and his chief constitutional adviser, Paul Gérin-Lajoie who was
Minister of Education, came to speak of Quebec's needs for a special
status in Confederation. However, it was never entirely clear whether
they believed such a status required explicit changes in the constitution or, alternatively, whether it could be obtained by adjustments
within the existing distribution of legislative powers.[6]

In the debate on the Speech from the Throne on January 18, 1960
Prime Minister Diefenbaker announced that his government would undertake a renewed effort to secure the agreement of the provinces on a
domestic amending formula. A Dominion-Provincial Conference in
July of that year took up the matter and discussions were continued
under the Pearson government which came to power as a result of the
general election of April 1963. At the end of the Federal-Provincial
conference held in Charlottetown on September 1-2, 1964, the first
ministers announced in a press communiqué that they had "affirmed
their unanimous decision to conclude the repatriation of the BNA Act
without delay."[7] A conference of attorneys-general met the next month
to work out the final details of patriation and a new amending formula.
The conclusions of this group were unanimously accepted by another
first ministers' conference on October 14, 1964, and came to be known
as the Fulton-Favreau Formula in recognition of the two successive
federal Ministers of Justice who had presided over the negotiations
from 1960 to 1964.

The basic elements of the Fulton-Favreau Formula were these:
(1) There was a "sign-off" provision by which no future statute of the
    United Kingdom would apply to Canada.
(2) The most crucial elements of the constitution were to be amendable
    only with the consent of Parliament and all the provincial legisla-
    tures. These elements were provincial legislative powers, the use of
    the English and French languages, denominational rights in educa-
    tion, and the provisions of Section 51 A of the BNA Act determin-
    ing that a province would always have at least as many members of
    the House of Commons as Senators.
(3) Certain basic aspects of the structure and functioning of the Gov-
    ernment of Canada required the concurrence of at least two-thirds
    of the provinces having together at least half the Canadian popula-
    tion. This category included provisions related to the Crown and its
    Canadian representative, the five-year limit on the duration of each
    House of Commons, the number of members from each province in
    the Senate, and representation of the provinces proportionate to
    their respective populations in the House of Commons. Apart from
    these exceptions, Parliament had the exclusive authority to amend
    the constitution in respect to "the executive government of Canada,
    and the Senate and House of Commons."

(4) The rigidities of the proposed amending formula as these related to the distribution of legislative powers were somewhat tempered by provision for the delegation of powers between the two levels by mutual consent. Any of the powers of Parliament might be delegated to the provinces providing Parliament and at least four provincial legislatures enacted similar laws in respect to these powers. Provincial powers over prison and reform institutions, local works and undertakings, property and civil rights, and "Matters of a merely local or private Nature" might be delegated to Parliament so long as at least four provinces had so consented or all the provinces had been consulted and Parliament had declared that the matter was of concern to fewer than four.

It thus seemed by the mid-1960s that Canada was on the verge of adopting a wholly domestic procedure for constitutional amendment. However, in January, 1966, Premier Lesage of Quebec informed Prime Minister Pearson that "the government of Quebec has decided to delay indefinitely the proposal for constitutional amendment."[8] He gave as the reasons for this action conflicting interpretations within the province about the meaning and effect of the proposed procedure and the view that its adoption would make impossible the abolition of the Quebec Legislative Council or the curtailment of its powers without the consent of that body. The more important reason for the Quebec action was undoubtedly the political storm the Fulton-Favreau Formula had raised in the province, including the challenge of the opposition Union Nationale to fight an election on the issue. Quebec governments in the past had always insisted on a rigid amending procedure and Premier Lesage and his colleagues had made as their major defence of the proposed procedure that Ottawa and the provinces had never previously been willing to accept unanimous provincial consent for amendments involving the distribution of legislative powers. However, by the mid-1960s the prevailing currents of thought and policy in Quebec had come to reject constitutional conservatism and to assert that the province's interests required radical constitutional changes. From this latter perspective, the rigidities of the proposed amending procedure became for Quebec what the Leader of the Opposition in the province called "une camisole de force," a straight-jacket, in the sense that even the smallest of the provinces could frustrate Quebec's aspirations for change.

The Attempt of Comprehensive Reform 1967-'71[9]

The interprovincial Confederation for Tomorrow Conference convened by the government of Ontario in November 1967 began the first attempt made by the federal and provincial jurisdictions to review the Canadian constitution in a comprehensive way.

The Confederation for Tomorrow Conference was an Ontario initiative directed toward commencing—or resuming—a dialogue on the future shape of Canadian federalism and in particular on the place of Quebec in Confederation. From the Ontario perspective the situation, as it had developed when planning for the Conference began early in 1967, must indeed have appeared critical and unsatisfactory. The Quebec general election of June, 1966, had brought to power a government committed to urgent and early reform of the constitution on binational lines. The emerging attitudes in Ottawa toward the provinces, and in particular toward Quebec, had become increasingly less conciliatory and the growing influence of Pierre Elliott Trudeau and the Liberal "new guard" from Quebec over federal policies combined both a personal distrust of the Union Nationale leaders and an inflexibility toward Quebec's continuing demands for an increased scope of autonomy. From the Ontario point of view, the mutual isolation of Ottawa and Quebec posed grave challenges both to national unity and to the role in national reconciliation that the province, and in particular Premier John Robarts, had assumed. A polarization between the federal and Quebec governments would in the long run give Ontario only the unpalatable options of siding with one of these contenders or of standing aside and leaving some of the most critical issues of the Canadian federation to be resolved without significant Ontario influence on the outcome. Further, there seems to have been some anxiety in the Ontario government that during the past few years many important but piecemeal changes had been effected in federal-provincial relations without adequate consideration of the cumulative impact on the federal system.

The 1967 Conference consisted of a frank and general discussion of the views of the provincial leaders on Confederation with of course a focus on the place and demands of Quebec. No formal resolutions were put forward and the crucial matter of federal-provincial financial relations was excluded from the agenda. At the end of the meeting a committee of four Premiers—those of Alberta, Ontario, Quebec and Nova Scotia—was established to analyze the results of the Conference and to "explore the subjects and form of future discussion."[10] The final communique isolated these broad subjects for subsequent consideration— "constitutional change; regional disparities; language practices and rights."

The reaction of the federal government to the Ontario initiative was cool, although four federal officials attended the meetings as observers. Prime Minister Pearson and his colleagues resented such an initiative being taken by a province, despite the assurances that they had been able to secure from Premier Robarts that the conference would not undertake to make decisions or indulge in constitutional drafting but rather would be a forum for free and wide-ranging discussions unfettered by the procedures which had come to be used in federal-provincial meetings. Prime Minister Trudeau in his press conference of July 27, 1971 reconstructed the federal view of late 1967.[11] It was that revising the constitution was not an urgent priority. The comprehensive reform of the constitution was more complex and more difficult to effect than many of the enthusiasts for such reform supposed. The existing constitution had proved itself to be a flexible instrument and under it there had been in recent years a shift in power to the provinces. However, in Ottawa's view, once the provinces had initiated what amounted to a process of constitutional review it would be irresponsible for the federal government to stand aside. Thus late in 1967 it was announced that the terms of reference of a federal-provincial conference called for early 1968 to discuss the more effective protection of human rights, including linguistic rights, would be broadened to include a comprehensive review of the Canadian constitution.

At the first Constitutional Conference of February, 1968, the federal government presented its plan for reviewing the constitution.[12] The process as suggested would proceed in three stages. First there would be discussion of the more effective protection of human rights through their constitutional entrenchment. Then there would be consideration of "the central institutions of Canadian federalism"—specifically, Parliament, the Supreme Court of Canada, the federal public service and the national capital—in order to make these more representative of the "federal character of the country." At the end of the process the federal and provincial governments would turn their attention to the division of powers between the two levels. The rationale for this sequence seems to have been that if individual rights and cultural and provincial particularisms were more effectively protected by constitutional entrenchment and by restructuring certain institutions of the federal government, there would be less pressure than otherwise for safeguarding these rights by an extension of provincial powers.[13] It was also decided by Ottawa that constitutional review should be comprehensive rather than piecemeal, in effect that the governments would not commit themselves to particular changes as the review proceeded but rather would await the eventual negotiation of a new constitutional package.

The federal plan was based on the assumption that rationality in the review procedure required the governments first to discuss and, it was hoped, agree on general principles about the nature of the Canadian community and then to embody these principles in concrete constitutional changes.[14] Such general statements would be enacted as a preamble to the new constitution, and the federal emphasis on the entrenchment of human rights seems to have been based partly on the conviction that such individual rights rather than the older and more collectively oriented purpose of "Peace, Order, and Good Government" had become the primary objective of the Canadian political community. For reasons that were never explained, the federal government felt with some urgency that the new constitution would be—as the existing one had never been—a symbolic focus of Canadian political allegiance.[15] The federal approach reflected very directly the views of Pierre Elliott Trudeau, who throughout his adult life had been deeply concerned with constitutional matters.

Most of the first Constitutional Conference of February, 1968 was devoted to a consideration of what most if not all of the participating governments agreed were the two most pressing substantive problems of the Canadian federation—regional economic disparities and language rights.[16] On the second matter there was a prevailing disposition among all the governments that there should be an extension of the recognition of the French language, and the leaders of all the governments except that of Quebec gave an account of what his administration was doing and proposed to do in this respect. At the end of the Conference a "consensus on language rights" was accepted in terms of a recognition that "French-speaking Canadians outside of Quebec should have the same rights as English-speaking Canadians in Quebec."[17] There were, however, deep disagreements among the governments in respect to linguistic matters. The so-called "consensus" had been reached after the Premiers of Alberta and British Columbia had left the meeting, and throughout the previous discussions Alberta, with some support from Saskatchewan and British Columbia, had argued against the "constitutional and legalistic approach to linguistic matters" and in particular against the constitutional entrenchment of linguistic rights. The federal government and those of several of the other provinces were favourably disposed or at least open-minded to such entrenchment as had recently been recommended by a Report of the Royal Commission on Bilingualism and Biculturalism.[18] The Quebec position was that the division of powers rather than linguistic rights was the matter of urgency, and that a more extensive recognition of such rights should be imposed neither by the Conference nor the federal government.

From the beginning, the provinces showed various degrees of commitment to the process of constitutional review. In one of his first policy statements after the 1968 general election Prime Minister Trudeau was critical of some provinces, which he did not name, for their reluctance about the review process.[19] It is broadly accurate to say that apart perhaps from an amending procedure, a matter absent from the 1968 federal plan for constitutional revision, neither Ottawa nor the governments of any of the provinces with English-speaking majorities felt any urgency about substantive change in the constitution except as such changes might provide for some form of "great new act of accommodation" between the English and French communities as foreseen by Prime Minister Pearson in his opening address to the Conference of February 1968.[20] The governments of the western provinces were generally conservative about constitutional matters, although from time to time the Premier of British Columbia indulged his highly developed talents for obstruction by introducing into discussion daring proposals quite impossible for the other governments to take seriously.[21] As a price for their continuing participation in the review process, all the provinces from time to time insisted on raising issues which were only in a tangential way if at all constitutional, particularly matters of financial relations with Ottawa. At the Conference of February, 1970, for example, there was no discussion of constitutional review at all but rather consideration of substantive problems facing the two levels—inflation, western agriculture, environmental pollution and the administration of shared-cost programs.

Between the first of the Conferences in 1968 and the proceedings leading up to those of February and June, 1971, the process of review was rather diffuse. The sequence for discussion suggested by Ottawa in the first meeting was soon put aside, and the governments encouraged to put forward "propositions" related to constitutional reform. The status of such recommendations was thus defined in a federal document of February, 1969:

> The propositions submitted by the Government of Canada, like those of other governments, are for discussion purposes only and are in no sense final. Nor are they intended as proposed drafts of constitutional articles. Propositions may be withdrawn, altered or replaced as discussions continue.[22]

At this Conference Ottawa presented a series of detailed proposals related to individual rights and the restructuring of several of the institutions of the federal government. Quebec throughout pressed its plans for a radical reform of the constitution on bi-national lines.[23] The other provinces responded to the call for propositions with widely varying degrees of seriousness and urgency. Under these circumstances it was impossible for discussion to be focused, and from about the middle of 1969 onward the emphasis appears to have shifted for a time to a consideration of several federal position papers related to the division of taxing[24] and spending powers and the respective responsibilities of the two levels of government for income security and social services.

By the fall of 1970 it seemed that the process of constitutional review had almost broken down. The Federal-Provincial Conference of September of that year, like the one held in the preceding February, dealt entirely with inter-governmental problems other than those directly related to the constitution, although in a formal sense both were constitutional conferences. In a position paper published in June, 1970, the Premier of Alberta analyzed the lack of progress that had been made and concluded "the process of constitutional review has not in any meaningful way reduced the inherent conflicts in the federal system, nor has it facilitated changes in the federal bargain."[25] The Alberta position was basically critical of the "holistic" approach to constitutional review and suggested that more progress could be made if problems narrower in scope could be considered. Other governments than that of Alberta were undoubtedly dissatisfied with the way in which reform of the constitution was proceeding, and so far as public expectations of change had been aroused, the process was losing its credibility.

Sometime late in 1970 there was a renewed effort to focus constitutional review and bring it to some kind of conclusion. The hopeful new element in the situation was the election of the Bourassa Liberals in the Quebec general election of April, 1970, on a straightforwardly federalist platform. Unlike its predecessor, the new government was not disposed to advance the Quebec position through nationalist rhetoric or abstract and doctrinaire statements of principle. Perhaps here there appeared the elements of a possible constitutional accommodation in which Quebec would trade its support for a new amending formula, the first priority in constitutional change for most if not all of the other governments, in exchange for extended provincial powers over social policy. The Constitutional Conference of February, 1971, gave its attention to "the questions of an amending formula and an early patriation of the Canadian Constitution" and published a proposed amending procedure which the "First Ministers agreed . . . was a feasible approach." Consideration was also given to the constitutional entrenchment of human rights, Quebec's demands in the field of social policy and other matters which in a refined form finally appeared in the Victoria Charter.

Between the February Conference and the one held in Victoria the succeeding June there were intensive constitutional discussions between Ottawa and the individual provinces. The federal government appears to have been determined to achieve *some* conclusion from the review process, and in particular to focus discussion on constitutional matters exclusively without the previous diversions to other aspects of federal-provincial relations.[26]

The most difficult substantive problem to be dealt with in the constitutional discussions was in respect to social security.[27] The basic elements of the Quebec proposal were these:

(1) Subject to the important qualifications outlined below, the Parliament of Canada would have the power to legislate in respect to the major areas of income-maintenance where it is now active—family allowances, manpower training allowances, guaranteed old-age income supplement, youth and social allowances, unemployment insurance, old-age pensions and supplementary benefits to survivors and disabled persons regardless of age.

(2) In respect to family and manpower training allowances and to the old-age income supplement, any province might enact to the effect

that federal law would prevail within the province only to the extent the province so decided. When such action was taken, the non-participating province would receive from the federal government the fiscal equivalent of what otherwise would have been disbursed in the province had the federal law applied. The same provision would apply to new federal income-security schemes.

(3) In respect to youth and social allowances, unemployment insurance and old age pensions and survivors' benefits, no federal law would affect the operation of any present or future provincial enactment. These fields would be concurrent with provincial paramountcy.

The Quebec government argued for its proposal largely in terms of rationalization and efficiency in designing and implementing income-maintenance policies and of the benefits of integrating all aspects of social policy under one level of government.

The net effect of the Quebec proposal would have been to place existing and future federal powers in the income-security field at the discretion of the provinces and this contradicted squarely Ottawa's position that the central government could not responsibly give up its role in equalizing incomes among individuals throughout Canada. Prime Minister Trudeau thus summarized the federal position in his opening statement to the Victoria Conference:

Quebec's proposal that provincial legislatures should have the power to limit the authority of Parliament to make income security payments such as old age pensions and family allowances within their province is one of the important issues before this conference. By the present system of income security, Parliament transfers billions of dollars a year to the old, the poor, the unemployed and families with children, from taxpayers and contributors who have the ability to pay. This federal redistribution is particularly important to poor people in those parts of Canada where opportunities and incomes are less than average—and that includes seven of our ten provinces. If, as the government of Quebec proposes, provincial laws could nullify federal income security laws in a province, and divert the federal revenue through the provincial treasury to be spent as the provincial government decided, then provincial governments would have a strong inducement to have such laws. But in those circumstances Parliament would be less likely to impose taxes on Canadians generally to make payments to provincial governments than it would to make payments directly to the needy old people and families with children. Taxpayers themselves would be less prepared to pay taxes to the federal government for programmes controlled by provincial governments other than their own, than to support programmes of the federal parliament which they themselves elect. Consequently, the constitutional change proposed by Quebec would, over the years, lead to an erosion of federal income security programmes and their replacement by purely

provincial plans. In the latter case, the old and the poor in the wealth-
ier provinces might do as well as if the federal government were making the payments, but in the other provinces including Quebec, the tax
base would not support as good income security payments as Parliament could provide.[28]

The so-called "Victoria Charter" emerging from the June Conference
in 1971 had the following elements:

(1) There was a formula for the patriation and amendment of the Canadian constitution. This formula was outlined in the previous
chapter.

(2) There was to be constitutional entrenchment of certain human
rights in three categories:

(a) No federal or provincial law was to abrogate "freedom of
thought, conscience and religion; freedom of opinion and expression
and freedom of peaceful assembly and association." However there was
this qualification:

> Art. 3. Nothing in this Part shall be construed as preventing such limi-
> tations on the exercise of the fundamental freedoms as are reasonably
> justifiable in a democratic society in the interests of public safety,
> order, health or morals, of national security, or of the rights and free-
> doms of others, whether imposed by the Parliament of Canada or the
> Legislature of a Province, within the limits of their respective legisla-
> tive powers, or by the construction or application of any law.

(b) Universal suffrage and free elections were declared to be fundamental principles of the constitution. There should be no discrimination against citizens voting or holding elective office because of "national origin, colour, religion or sex." Parliament and each provincial
legislature had a maximum life of five years, except under emergency
conditions as determined by the federal cabinet when such period
might be extended if not opposed by more than one-third of the
members of such bodies. There were to be annual legislative sessions.

(c) In terms of linguistic rights, both English and French might be
used in the Parliament of Canada and all the provincial legislatures except those of Saskatchewan, Alberta and British Columbia. Statutes,
records and journals of Parliament were to be published in both languages. The statutes of each province were to be published in English
and French. Both languages could be used in the courts established by
Parliament and in the courts of Quebec, New Brunswick and Newfoundland. An individual had the right to use either language in com-
municating with the head offices of any agency of the government of
Canada or the governments of Ontario, Quebec, New Brunswick, Prince
Edward Island and Newfoundland. If any province subsequently extended the rights of the two languages beyond those contained in the
constitution such privileges could be revoked only by an amendment
to the constitution of Canada.

(3) Certain changes were to be made in the Supreme Court of Canada. Of the nine judges, three were to be chosen from the Bar of Quebec. The Governor in Council was to continue to appoint judges but there was a complex procedure for consulting with the provinces in making such appointments. When cases involving the Quebec civil law were before the Court, there were safeguards that these would be heard by judges of whom a majority were trained in the civil tradition of Quebec.

(4) Parliament might make laws in respect to old age pensions and supplementary benefits and to family, youth and occupational allowances, but such legislation was not to "affect the operation of any law present or future of a Provincial Legislature in relation to any such matter." Enactments could be made only after the provinces had been consulted.

(5) There was to be a conference of Prime Ministers and Premiers each year unless a majority of the heads of government decided otherwise.

(6) The existing provisions providing for the reservation and disallowance of provincial legislation were to be repealed.

It is significant that the Victoria Charter did not include several matters which had been the subject of previous discussion between Ottawa and the provinces and others which might have been expected to come to resolution in a review of the constitution which purported to be comprehensive. In terms of the entrenchment of rights, the Charter omitted entirely traditional rights connected with arrest and trial and linguistic rights in education, and in a sense the Charter was a retreat from the protection of denominational minorities in the existing constitution. Apart from the Supreme Court of Canada, there were no changes in the structure and functioning of the institutions of the central government. With the exception of limited fields of social security there was no change or clarification in respect to the division of legislative powers and the relation between the two levels of government in regard to such matters as taxing and spending, external relations, etc. There was here a very small constitutional package.

Before the first Ministers left Victoria it was agreed that within eleven days each would notify the Secretary of the Constitutional Conference whether or not his government was willing to recommend the adoption of the Charter to the respective legislature. This procedure has been the subject of conflicting interpretations. To some observers, it has been viewed as an ultimatum to Quebec, an indication to the province that the Charter was all that the other governments were willing to give. The federal Minister of Justice denied the validity of this interpretation.[29] According to Mr. Turner, the eleven-day waiting period was requested by the provinces. Reports of the Victoria meeting indicate that of all the heads of government Premier Bourassa was alone in being unable or unwilling to commit his administration to a particular solution at the Conference, and among the other leaders there was apparently a good deal of annoyance at this apparent vacillation.

On June 23, five days before the eleven-day limit expired, Premier Bourassa announced that his government would not accept the Charter in the form that had issued from Victoria. The operative part of the public announcement stated:

> This decision arises from the necessity to agree to as great an extent as possible on clear and precise constitutional texts, thus avoiding to transfer to the judiciary *(sic)* authority a responsibility which belongs first and foremost to the political authority, that is to those elected by the people. The texts dealing with income security have an uncertainty that meshes badly with the objectives inherent in any idea of constitutional revision. If this uncertainty were eliminated, our conclusion could be different.[30]

The Premier's statement reiterated the general commitment of the Quebec government and people to the federal option and suggested by implication that constitutional review should continue despite Quebec's rejection of the Charter.

What was behind Premier Bourassa's statement, "If this uncertainty were eliminated, our conclusion could be different"? Was only textual ambiguity in the way of Prime Minister Pearson's 1968 hope of a "great new act of accommodation" among Canadians? It is undeniable that the meaning and effect of the terms of the Charter relating to social security were not very clear. The proposal that in the defined areas of income-security no federal law "shall effect the operation of any law present or future of a province" comes from the existing provisions of Section 94A of the BNA Act relating to old age pensions and the courts have never had the occasion to clarify what this provision means. If, under the terms of the Victoria Charter, a province enacted a scheme of family allowances, would this action cause the federal family allowance plan to be terminated within the province? In such circumstances would the provincial government or citizens eligible for benefits establish a valid legal claim for financial compensation by the federal authorities? The constitutional vesting of concurrent powers in both Parliament and the provinces with one or the other having priority in the event of a conflict has a reasonably precise application so far as regulatory activities are concerned. For example, although this seems not to have happened, any clash between Ottawa and a province about those eligible for entry to Canada as immigrants would be resolved in favour of the federal authorities. The situation is much less clear in regard to the service-providing activities of government.

It is reasonable to suppose that Quebec's objections to the Charter were based on more fundamental grounds than its textual ambiguity, and it is significant to remember that Premier Lesage advanced the same reason of ambiguity for his repudiation of the Fulton-Favreau formula in 1966. Various nationalist groups in Quebec mobilized opposition to the Charter very quickly after the end of the Victoria meeting and the Premier was undoubtedly responding to this pressure.[31] Within Quebec there are continuing objections to any amending formula which would put Quebec's future constitutional position at the discretion of the other provinces. One can only conjecture whether the present or any future Quebec government will be able or willing to support such an amending procedure, regardless of other concessions it is able to gain for such support. In general, the proposals relating to income security as these emerged from the Victoria meeting were quite obviously the reflection of deep and unresolved differences among the participating governments rather than inexpert legal draftsmanship.

New Attempts at Constitutional Reform from 1974 Onward[32]

With the rejection of the Victoria Charter by Quebec the efforts directed towards constitutional reform lapsed. Soon after the Victoria Conference ended there began a series of intensive discussions between the federal and Quebec governments about the powers of the two levels in respect to income-maintenance programs. The resulting bargain about family allowances which was embodied in legislation enacted by Parliament in late 1973 was a significant victory for Quebec. Under this legislation each province was to have considerable discretion in allocating the global sums distributed by Ottawa within its boundaries in terms of the age of the children and the number of children in each family. This was a retreat from the federal position on income-maintenance programs defended before and during the Victoria Conference and demonstrated again the success of Quebec in its piecemeal quest for autonomy within the existing constitutional framework.

In the Speech from the Throne debate in the House of Commons on October 2, 1974 Prime Minister Trudeau declared the intention of his government to reactivate the process of constitutional review. However, the new federal strategy was to confine this to patriation and a new procedure for constitutional amendment along the lines of the Victoria Charter. The almost immediate response from Quebec was that its government would not agree on an amending formula unless this was linked to a new division of legislative powers.[33] Ontario in a somewhat similar vein linked discussion on an amending formula to the resolution of outstanding fiscal issues between the federal government and the provinces.[34]

At the first ministers' conference held to deal with petroleum prices in April, 1975 Prime Minister Trudeau raised the matter of patriation and an amending formula along the lines of the Victoria Charter. In a letter to all ten of the provinces ten days after the conference adjourned, Mr. Trudeau proposed that such reforms proceed in three steps: (1) approval by the legislatures of the provinces and both Houses of Parliament; (2) legislation by the United Kingdom giving legal validity to the measure; (3) a proclamation by the Governor General bringing the new arrangements into effect.[35] Subsequent to this there were intensive consultations between Gordon Robertson, Advisor to the Cabinet on Federal-Provincial Relations, and the premiers of each of the provinces.

It soon became clear that the provinces were unwilling to consider patriation and a new amending formula otherwise than within the framework of a wider review of constitutional matters. The conference of provincial premiers held in St. John's in August 1975 discussed the subject and the chairman of the meeting, Premier Frank Moores, conveyed this message to Prime Minister Trudeau on August 19: "While all the Premiers agreed that . . . patriation was a desirable objective, it was generally felt that this issue should be dealt with in the context of a more general review of such aspects as the distribution of powers, control of resources and other related matters." In a more explicit sense the Bourassa government declared its unwillingness to agree to patriation without more specific guarantees of the French language and culture than were in the extant constitution. Ottawa's attempts to meet Quebec's requirements were contained in a proposed Draft Proclamation submitted for the discussion of the other provinces. The essential elements of the Draft Proclamation as presented on April 19, 1976 were the following: (1) the Victoria Charter amending formula along with provisions of the Charter related to the Supreme Court of Canada; (2) the constitutional entrenchment of the rights of the French and English languages so far as federal jurisdiction was concerned, along with a provision that any province might subsequently entrench language rights if it so chose; (3) a general provision to the effect that neither the government nor the Parliament of Canada "in the exercise of their respective powers, shall act in a manner that will adversely affect the preservation and development of the French language and the culture based on it."[36]

The 1976 Premier's conference held in August in Edmonton gave attention to patriation and the matter received further discussion at a meeting in Toronto in October. The results of these meetings were communicated to Mr. Trudeau by Premier Lougheed of Alberta on October 16.[37] The provinces reiterated their position of the previous year that although patriation was indeed desirable it should be accompanied by an expansion of provincial jurisdiction and involvement in cultural matters, immigration, communications and the taxation of natural re-sources, a limitation of the federal declaratory and spending powers, and a provision that the creation of new provinces should be subject to the general amending formula. In his response to Premier Lougheed's communication dated January 19, 1977[38] Prime Minister Trudeau crit-icized the provincial proposals as being "either too much or too little." On the basis of the experience in 1968-1971, Ottawa would very much prefer to proceed for the time being by limiting discussions to pa-triation and an amending formula. However, if the context were to be broadened the federal position was that this must include a much more comprehensive list of matters of constitutional concern than that sug-gested by the premiers.

By the end of 1976 the situation had been further complicated by the two westernmost provinces espousing a more rigid amending formula than that provided for by the Victoria Charter. The British Columbia government was now demanding that that province be recognized as a fifth region whose consent would be necessary for amendments.[39] The Alberta position was now that an acceptable amending formula must provide for unanimous provincial consent.

So far as the federal government was concerned there was little ini-tiative in constitutional reform for 18 months after the Quebec election of November, 1976. This election resulted, however, in more constitu-tional discussion among other Canadians than at any time in the country's history and in the early months of 1978 three comprehensive studies for reform made by other groups were published—that of a committee of the Canadian Bar Association,[40] that commissioned by the Canada West Foundation,[41] and that of the Ontario Advisory Com-mittee on Confederation.[42]

In June, 1978 the federal government made public the Constitutional Amendment Bill which contained a comprehensive set of proposals for constitutional reform.[43] What came to be known as Bill C-60 divided the constitution into those aspects which might be amended by the ac-tion of Parliament alone (Phase I) and those where change required the involvement of the U.K. authorities and the provinces (Phase II). Ac-cording to Ottawa's timetable, Phase I was to be implemented by July 1, 1979 and those of Phase II by 1981—the latter the 50th anniversary of Canada's accession to independence by the Statute of Westminster.

The major elements of Bill C-60 were these:
—there was a lengthy preamble, a Statement of Aims of the Canadian Federation, and a Canadian Charter of Rights and Freedoms, the lat-ter including rights related to the French and English languages. Par-liament would enact this part of the new constitution, thereby bind-ing federal institutions and, after the individual provinces had adopted such reforms, they would be entrenched in the constitu-tion.

—the Senate was to be replaced by a House of the Federation of 118 members, half chosen by the House of Commons and half by the provincial legislatures with provisions also for the representation of the Yukon and the Northwest Territories. In effect, members of this new second chamber were to be chosen by the party leaders in the House of Commons and the provincial legislative assemblies in proportion to their parties' share of the popular vote in the last federal or provincial election. The House of the Federation would have, with important exceptions, a two-months suspensive veto over bills enacted by the House of Commons and it would have to approve the appointment of Supreme Court judges and of the heads of certain federal agencies and crown corporations. The House would also be the guardian of the protection of the French and English languages and before any measure of "special linguistic significance" could be enacted by Parliament the agreement of majorities of French-speaking and English-speaking members of the House would be needed.

—the jurisdiction of the Supreme Court of Canada was to be entrenched in the Constitution. The constitution would also provide for provincial/regional representation in the Court—including four from Quebec and at least one each from the Atlantic provinces, Ontario, the prairie provinces and British Columbia—along with complex provisions for the cooperation of the requisite provinces with the federal authorities in the appointment of Supreme Court judges.

—there was to be a clarification of certain elements of the constitution related to the federal executive. These included a delineation of the respective powers of the Monarch and the Governor-General, a constitutional delineation of the powers of the cabinet, and the relations between the cabinet and the House of Commons.

Significantly, Bill C-60 did not contain provisions related to patriation and an amending formula nor did it deal with changes in the distribution of legislative powers between Parliament and the provinces.

There was intensive constitutional debate both within Parliament and between the federal government and the provinces subsequent to the presentation of Bill C-60. A First Ministers' conference on the constitution was held in early November 1978. The provinces failed to agree on whether it was appropriate to entrench human and linguistic rights in the constitution. However, the federal authority broke the logjam so to speak by suggesting the discussion of an enumerated list of suggested changes in the division of powers between the two orders of government. These matters were turned over to a committee of the attorneys-general and ministers of intergovernmental affairs and the first ministers reassembled in early 1979. At this Conference the major matters under discussion were (1) resource ownership and interprovincial trade (2) indirect taxation (3) the Supreme Court (4) family law (5) equalization and regional development (6) the spending power and (7) the declaratory power. There appears to have been agreement only on the transfers of powers on the validity of marriage to the provinces and limitations on the power of Parliament to declare "Works" otherwise provincial within federal jurisdiction.

The context of the current constitutional negotiations differs from that of the 1968-1971 period in two significant ways.

First, the process is now less centred on Quebec's interests and grievances. It is broadly accurate to state that in the discussions which ended with the Victoria Conference the governments of Canada and of the provinces with English-speaking majorities had little urgency about constitutional reform apart from such reform leading to a new accommodation with Quebec. To widely varying degrees, the provinces other than Quebec manifest an increasing dissatisfaction with the workings of the existing constitutional system and this dissatisfaction is most profound in the three westernmost provinces. The relation of Quebec to this process is complex and ambiguous. The PQ government is dedicated of course to ending Confederation so far as Quebec is concerned while reaping what benefits for that province it can while the existing system continues. The Lévesque administration has thus taken no initiatives in these discussions. So far as the other governments are concerned, there are undoubtedly widely divergent estimates of the relation between the process of constitutional review and the success of attempts to retain Quebec in Canada. Most of these governments appeared at the conference held early in 1979 to be willing to put aside objections to particular constitutional reforms with the objective of arriving at agreement on a comprehensive package of changes. Other administrations, including those of Alberta and less certainly Manitoba and British Columbia, were less flexible.

Second, there is a consensus that the institutions of the federal government should be reformed to make these more representative of regional and provincial interests. During the earlier period reforms in the federal system were seen almost entirely in terms of changes in the division of powers between Ottawa and the provinces. The federal government's plan for review as presented in 1968 included, it is true, suggestions that there be discussion of changes in the "central institutions of Canadian federalism" including Parliament, the Supreme Court, the federal public service and the national capital.[44] However, this general proposal was focussed almost entirely on the French-English dimension of representivity and at any rate was soon forgotten in the ensuing constitutional discussions. The newer conventional wisdom is that the institutions of the federal government itself must be reformed to make them more representative of and more sensitive to provincial and regional particularisms. This is of course the assumption behind such proposals as those for replacing the Senate by a House of the Federation or House of the Provinces and for allowing the participation of the provinces in the appointment of judges of the Supreme Court of Canada.

Substantive Issues of Constitutional Reform

Although the process of constitutional review from the Confederation for Tomorrow Conference of 1967 onward has been very diffuse it is possible to isolate a number of substantive issues which have arisen:

1. The constitution as a symbolic focus of allegiance to Canada

As we saw at the end of Chapter 2, there is now a common disposition to assert that the existing constitution is an inadequate symbol of Canadian nationhood and that this should be remedied in any new constitutional document. This disposition was expressed in Bill C-60 by a lengthy preamble and by a Statement of Aims of the Canadian Federation. Such constitutional provisions would presumably have two objectives. First, they would give guidance to judges and courts in interpreting the more explicit clauses of the constitution. Second, they would aid in the constitution becoming a focus of national allegiance for all Canadians. There has been little discussion of whether these two aims are fully compatible. If the constitution is primarily or exclusively regarded as a legal document, its audience so to speak is lawyers and judges and from this perspective its terms should be as explicit and unequivocal as it is possible to frame them. On the other hand, if the constitution is to be a national creed it will be evocative of the historical memories and moral commitments of the Canadian people. It is by no means self-evident that good law and good rhetoric are fully reconcilable—the turgid language of Bill C-60 fails in my view to meet either test. A possible result of a lengthy preamble or statement of aims would be to confer on courts more discretion than they would otherwise have in interpreting the constitution's more explicit provisions, and from this perspective the effect of a preamble would be to enhance the powers of the judiciary rather than to guide and channel them.

2. Patriation and an amending procedure

Some of the issues surrounding patriation and an amending procedure were discussed in the previous chapter. It appears unlikely that the provinces can be brought to agreement among themselves on such a procedure and if such did come about it seems likely that the federal government would accept the result. The Trudeau government, and more specifically the Prime Minister himself, regarded the resolution of this matter as of great urgency and reiterated frequently their determination to proceed to effect change even without the unanimous consent of the provinces. If the federal Liberals had been returned in the 1979 general election, patriation and a new amending formula might have been achieved, perhaps after one more first ministers' conference dealing with this issue. The new Clark government appears less urgent about constitutional reform.

3. The entrenchment of human and linguistic rights

The essential issue in the constitutional entrenchment of human and linguistic rights is the relative roles of courts and legislatures in the definition and ranking of such rights. Along with patriation and an amending formula, entrenchment became a matter of great urgency for Prime Minister Trudeau and his government. It is possible even under the Clark government that within the short-term future human and linguistic rights so far as these relate to federal jurisdiction alone will be specified in the constitution by the action of Parliament alone. Under the existing procedure of constitutional amendment this would not be entrenchment as this term is commonly used because such rights could subsequently be modified or abolished by enactment of Parliament. Three of the provinces—Manitoba, Alberta and British Columbia—are forthrightly opposed to entrenchment and it seems unlikely that agreement on this matter will be achieved in the forseeable future, although Bill C-60 provides a way in which individual provinces might opt into such arrangements.

4. The replacement of the Senate

The proposal of a House of the Federation as proposed in Bill C-60 has received little support and is likely to be soon forgotten. A more popular recommendation which has come from several quarters is a House of the Provinces whose members would be appointed by the provincial governments and who would act as delegates of these governments.[45] The reform of the second chamber has not yet been discussed by the federal and provincial authorities and there would appear to be several difficulties to be overcome before such a reform could be effected, at least if it were believed necessary to get the agreement of the provinces. The consent of a majority of the Senate as it is now constituted would of course be necessary and one can only speculate about the incentives which would be required to induce Senators to co-operate in their own displacement. It is almost inevitable that there would be contention about the formula for dividing representation among the provinces in the new body. It would also be necessary to decide on the powers of this reformed second chamber—the nature of its vetoes over the House of Commons and, more specifically, the kinds of legislation which could be enacted by that House alone without recourse to the approval of the House of the Provinces. Furthermore, no one, it seems, has thought through carefully the relation between the new second chamber and the ongoing processes of executive federalism.

5. A restriction of federal powers of unilateral decisions

If constitutional reform of a comprehensive nature is achieved, it is likely that there will be constitutional restrictions on powers which the federal government can now exercise unilaterally:

—the *federal spending power*. In 1969 Prime Minister Trudeau introduced into the Federal-Provincial Conference a proposal for constitutional restriction on the power of the federal government to undertake shared-cost programs on matters within provincial legislative jurisdiction and it seems likely that some form of this proposal will be reactivated in future constitutional discussions.[46] Under the federal plan, shared-cost programs could be established only after a "national consensus" had been secured, a consensus which would consist of the approval of a majority of the governments in each of Canada's four Senate regions—the Maritime region, Quebec, Ontario, and the western provinces. When a province did not participate in such an arrangement there would be federal payments to its residents equal to the amount that the province would have received had it participated.

—the *federal declaratory power*. There is likely to be some constitutional restriction on the existing power of Parliament to declare "Works" otherwise within provincial jurisdiction to be "for the general Advantage of Canada or for the Advantage of Two or more of the Provinces." The alternatives here would seem to be either that this power could not be exercised without the consent of the province(s) where these "Works" were located or some provision for federal-provincial consultation before such a declaration by Parliament might be made.

—the *termination of federal payments to the provinces*. Section 99 of Bill C-60 provided that the federal government would be constitutionally bound to make payments to the provinces under arrangements it had entered into with the latter and that such payments might not be unilaterally abrogated by Parliament.

6. The division of legislative powers

The past decade has amply demonstrated that the provinces will participate in constitutional discussions only if the division of legislative powers is made the subject of central concern. The matters on which early federal-provincial agreement is most likely relate to an extension of provincial powers in respect to family law and provisions that the provinces might levy certain forms of indirect taxation, although in respect to the latter there are complications to ensure that such provincial taxes would not act as barriers to interprovincial or international trade or result in the double taxation of persons or businesses. There are a very large number of other fields of jurisdiction in dispute—among them, the marketing of natural products, fisheries, the ownership of off-shore resources, telecommunications, cultural policy and immigration. At the present the most contentious issue is the ownership and control of natural resources, particularly in the context of the vigorous objection of the western provinces to the expanded interpretation given by the Supreme Court of Canada to federal powers over trade and commerce.

7. The Supreme Court of Canada

There seems to be almost no objection to the general principle that the jurisdiction of the Supreme Court of Canada should be entrenched in the constitution. However, there appears to have been no federal-provincial discussion of what the jurisdiction of the Court should be—whether, most crucially, it should continue to be a general court of appeal or, alternatively, whether its powers should be wholly or for the most part restricted to what were defined as constitutional matters. There is also it appears general agreement that the constitution define provincial/regional balances in the Court and that the requisite provincial governments be given some participation in appointments to it. This latter reform would not perhaps politicize the Court in a partisan sense, and because in many if not most cases the appointees would have to have the approval of governments of different partisan complexions, the previous affiliation of an aspirant with a particular party might be a disadvantage. However, particularly in the context of the increasingly contentious position of the Court in judicial review of the constitution, more explicit attention might then be paid to the jurisprudential philosophy of prospective judges as this relates to the division of powers and human rights.

The Prospects for Comprehensive Constitutional Reform

The various attempts to review and reform the Canadian constitution in an explicit way have failed. The high point of this process appears to have been the Victoria Conference of 1971 when all the provinces except Quebec were brought to agreement on a package of significant constitutional changes; no similar amount of consensus has subsequently been attained. As I suggested in the last chapter, the process of debate over the past decade has weakened the legitimacy of the existing constitution without replacing it with something allegedly better and the federal and provincial governments increasingly press their claims with little or no reference to constitutional norms. The quality of this debate has been on the whole of abysmally low quality; our unbroken constitutional development has not forced on Canadians the necessity of discussing the first principles of the constitutional order as did the English in the seventeenth century and the Americans in the eighteenth.

Why then has constitutional review failed? The following suggestions must be made tentatively.

First, and most obviously, successive governments of Quebec have not agreed on changes acceptable to Ottawa and the other provinces. The process of reform has thus been obstructed by the unresolved differences among the Quebec political elites—including of course those of the federal government—about what constitutional changes, if any, are sufficient to retain Quebec's continued adherence to Confederation. The situation has been further complicated by the election of the PQ government whose position in matters of constitutional reform must almost inevitably be obstructive. Furthermore, as of late 1979, the provincial Liberals, who would be carrying the burden of the federalist cause in the forthcoming referendum, had not yet promulgated their constitutional program in an explicit and authoritative way.*

Secondly, the governments have not been brought to agreement on the appropriate scope of constitutional review. At the beginning of the review process in 1968, Ottawa opted for comprehensive discussions in which agreement on specific changes would be put by in anticipation of the eventual negotiation of a package of reforms. As we have seen, the Trudeau government adopted a contrary strategy in 1974-1976 in its search for consensus on patriation and a new amending formula but the provinces insisted on a discussion of the distribution of legislative powers. One can thus say that there are continuing and unresolved differences about what items are properly on the agenda of constitutional review, although as I have indicated earlier the prolonged debate has focussed the attention of governments on a range of constitutional issues.

Third, the federal and provincial governments have apparently not regarded the penalties of failure to agree on constitutional change to be very high. The group of politicians who assembled in Philadelphia in 1787 and those who gathered in Charlottetown and Quebec in 1864 were united by a common sense of urgency, widely varying in its degrees of course, and a perception that the failure to agree would have most unfortunate if not calamitous consequences. In a purely intellectual sense, most if not all of the participants in the recent federal-provincial discussions might assent to the general proposition that constitutional reform is necessary if Confederation is to be preserved. However, such positions had not been translated into action by late 1979.

* In early 1980 these proposals were presented in the document *A New Canadian Federation. The Constitutional Federation of the Quebec Liberal Party,* Montreal. These proposals were accepted by the party with few changes at its convention in February 1980.

Notes

1. P. B. Waite, *Canada 1874-1896: Arduous Destiny*, Toronto: McClelland and Stewart, 1971, pp. 194-195.
2. For general accounts of a history of the search for an amending procedure, see Paul Gérin-Lajoie, *Constitutional Amendment in Canada*, Toronto: University of Toronto Press, 1950, and W. S. Livingston, *Federalism and Constitutional Change*, Oxford: Clarendon Press, 1956, Chapter 2.
3. Alan C. Cairns, "The Judicial Committee and Its Critics," *Canadian Journal of Political Science* IV, September 1971, pp. 301-345.
4. Senate of Canada, Session of 1939, *Report Pursuant to Resolution of the Senate to the Honourable the Speaker by The Parliamentary Counsel Relating to the Enactment of the British North America Act, 1867, any lack of consonance between its terms and judicial construction of them and cognate matters*, p. 13.
5. Donald V. Smiley, *The Canadian Political Nationality*, Toronto: Methuen, 1967, pp. 78-86.
6. After the Quebec Liberal government was defeated in the election of 1966 the constitutional debate within its ranks was joined. Don Murray et Vera Murray, *De Bourassa à Lévesque*, Montréal: Éditions Quinze, 1978, pp. 49-67.
7. The Honourable Guy Favreau, *The Amendment of the Constitution of Canada*, Ottawa: Queen's Printer, 1965, p. 30.
8. Ibid., chapter 4.
9. *The Constitutional Review, 1968-1971*, Secretary's Report, Canadian Intergovernmental Affairs Secretariat, Ottawa: Information Canada, 1974.
10. This committee did not become operative, as the process of constitutional review under Ottawa's leadership made it redundant.
11. *Transcript* (mimeo) from the Prime Minister's Office.
12. The Right Honourable Lester B. Pearson, *Federalism for the Future*, Ottawa: Queen's Printer, 1968.
13. Ibid., pp. 34-36.
14. For a justification of the comprehensive approach see The Right Honourable Pierre Elliott Trudeau, *The Constitution and the People of Canada*, Ottawa: Queen's Printer, 1969, p. 2.
15. See generally Ibid., pp. 4-22. "... the Constitution must express the purpose of Canadians in having become and resolving to remain associated together in a single country, and it must express as far as this is possible in a constitution what kind of country Canadians want, what values they cherish, and what objectives they seek." pp. 4-6.
16. *Proceedings*, Queen's Printer, Ottawa; 1968.
17. Ibid., p. 545.
18. *Report of the Royal Commission on Bilingualism and Biculturalism*, Book I, *The Official Languages*, Ottawa: Queen's Printer, 1967.
19. Speech to the Canadian Bar Association National Convention, Vancouver, September 5, 1968 (mimeo).
20. *Proceedings*, p. 5.
21. Such as those for ousting Ottawa completely from the direct tax fields, creating five provinces to replace the existing ten, and changing the federal

role from interprovincial equalization to equalization among individuals wherever they lived in Canada.

22. Trudeau, *op. cit.*, p. 46.

23. See a summary of the positions taken by Quebec under the Union Nationale government in *The Government of Quebec and the Constitution*, Québec: L'Office d'information et de publicité du Québec, 1969.

24. The Honourable E. J. Benson, *The Taxing Powers and the Constitution of Canada*, Ottawa: Queen's Printer, 1969.

25. The Honourable Harry E. Strom, *The Process of Constitutional Review: A Position Paper*, Edmonton: 1970, p. 15.

26. In particular, Ottawa resisted the pressures of Ontario and perhaps other provinces that the Victoria meeting should discuss fiscal matters.

27. *Outline of Quebec's Constitutional Proposals on Social Security*, Cabinet du Premier Ministre, June, 1971 (mimeo).

28. Prime Minister's Office, (mimeo), pp. 3-4.

29. Canadian Broadcasting Corporation Interview "Encounter," Transcript mimeo., July 1971.

30. Communiqué from Premier Bourassa's Office, June 23, 1971, (mimeo).

31. Prior to the Victoria Conference all three opposition parties in the Quebec National Assembly had expressed their hostility to what had come to be called the Trudeau-Turner formula for amendment. See Assemblée Nationale, *Journal des debats*, Commission permanente de la Constitution, 18 mai 1971, pp. BB16-1335.

32. The Canadian Intergovernmental Affairs Secretariat has collated the various proposals made by the federal and provincial governments from the Victoria Conference to the end of 1978. *Proposals on the Constitution 1971-78*, Ottawa, 1979. Hereafter cited as *Proposals*.

33. *Toronto Star*, March 28, 1972.

34. *Toronto Star*, March 29, 1972.

35. From Prime Minister's Office.

36. *Proposals*, p. 90, p. 372.

37. *Proposals*, pp. 229-230.

38. From Prime Minister's office.

39. *Proposals*, pp. 373-374.

40. *Towards a New Canada*, Canadian Bar Foudation.

41. David Elton, Frederick C. Engelmann and Peter McCormick, *Alternatives: Towards the Development of an Effective Federal System for Canada*, Calgary: Canada West Foundation, 1978.

42. *First Report*, Toronto: Ontario Advisory Committee on Confederation, 1978.

43. *The Constitutional Amendment Bill: Text and Explanatory Notes*.

44. Pearson, *op. cit.*, pp. 24-30.

45. This kind of proposal was made independently by the Canadian Bar Association, the Canada West Foundation, and the Ontario Advisory Committee as cited in notes 40-42 above as well as the Report of the Task Force on National Unity, *A Future Together*, Ottawa: 1979.

46. *Federal-Provincial Grants and the Spending Power of Parliament*, Ottawa: Government of Canada, 1969, pp. 38-50.

CHAPTER 4
EXECUTIVE FEDERALISM

Canada like other federations has moved away from "classical federalism" in which each level of government performed the responsibilities assigned to it by the constitution in relative isolation from the other.[1] In the period since the end of the Second World War constitutional amendment and judicial review have been somewhat unresponsive in re-delineating the respective roles of the federal and provincial governments as circumstances change, although as we saw in Chapter Two judicial review of the constitution has assumed a greater importance from the mid-1970s onward. Further, as the argument will be made in Chapter Five, the relations between the federal and provincial wings of the political parties are not very effective in giving authoritative resolution to the conflicts between centrifugal and centripetal tendencies in contemporary Canada. Thus in managing the ongoing federal system a very heavy load is borne by executive federalism, which may be defined as the relations between elected and appointed officials of the two orders of government in federal-provincial interactions and among the executives of the provinces in interprovincial interactions.

It must be emphasized that in the Canadian system of government the executive has a very wide scope of discretion—freedom from effective control of the elected legislature, of party organizations and, in most circumstances, of private interest groups. We saw in Chapter Two that the federal cabinet had sweeping powers under the War Measures Act to suspend both the parliamentary and federal elements of the Canadian constitution. This is, of course, the extreme case but even under normal circumstances the Canadian political system is characterized by "a collective central energizing executive as the key engine of the state"[2] and this characteristic applies to both federal and provincial governments.

Executive Federalism Prior to 1945

Relatively little has been written about executive federalism prior to the Second World War. In Sir John A. Macdonald's first cabinet there was a minister who was Secretary of State for the Provinces—this portfolio was abolished in 1873—who was the formal channel for relations between the Dominion and provincial governments according to the well-understood pattern of interactions between colonial and imperial authorities. However, as early as October 1868 there was a conference much like contemporary ones with the meetings of representatives of the Dominion, Ontario, Quebec and New Brunswick governments to sort out the respective responsibilities of the two levels over immigration, which had been made a subject of concurrent jurisdiction by Section 95 of the BNA Act.[3] J. A. Corry's monograph *Difficulties of Divided Jurisdiction*, prepared for the Rowell-Sirois Commission, gave a short account of Dominion-provincial relations as they had emerged by the late 1930s in respect to the marketing of natural products, the regulation of insurance, fisheries, conciliation in industrial disputes and conditional grants.[4] More intensive research on those interactions prior to the past generation would no doubt turn up many other executive interactions, but for the most part it is reasonable to suppose that in regard to most functions federal and provincial governments carried out their respective constitutional obligations in relative isolation from one another. In his history of the TransCanada Pipeline, William Kilbourn gives an example of this isolation perpetuated into the post-war period by noting that in 1952 Premier Leslie Frost of Ontario used the occasion of the opening of a new oil refinery at Sarnia to introduce the Premier of Alberta to the federal Minister of Trade and Commerce.[5] Such was the nature of federal-provincial relations in those days that Ernest Manning and C. D. Howe had never met, though each had been a powerful cabinet minister since 1935.

The Influences Leading to Executive Federalism

There are several interrelated factors at work to make the interaction between federal and provincial governments more frequent:
—the ever-broadening scope of public decision brings into being new circumstances where federal and provincial objectives must somehow be harmonized if public policy is to be effective. To take an im-

portant example, government responsibility for employment opportunities can be effectively discharged only through a plethora of measures relating to economic stabilization, regional economic development, vocational education and occupational retraining for adults, etc. Without minimal levels of co-operation federal and provincial governments will increasingly frustrate the policies of each other by inadvertence or even in some cases by deliberate design.

—nationalist and egalitarian sentiments propel the federal government into action directed toward establishing minimum Canada-wide standards in respect to such public services as are from time to time defined to be vital to the welfare of all citizens. These services are for the most part within the constitutional jurisdiction of the provinces. Gunnar Myrdal has argued that "the welfare state is nationalistic," a series of responses to the dislocations suffered by citizens through the progressive disintegration of the international economic order,[6] and at the successive Federal-Provincial Conferences he attended Premier Smallwood used his gifts of vivid exposition to call attention to the unequal opportunities lying ahead for a baby born in a Newfoundland outport compared with those available to a child born in the more favoured parts of Canada, and demanded that Ottawa take steps to remedy these inequalities.

—contemporary levels of taxation, along with the deliberate use of fiscal policy by the federal and provincial governments to secure employment, growth and price stability objectives, mean that there is an increasingly intense competition for tax sources and that the expenditure policies of each level have direct and indirect consequences for the other. These matters will be analyzed in Chapter 6.

—there is an increasing number of fields in which both levels of government are active. In their 1978 study commissioned by the Quebec Department of Intergovernmental Affairs Germain Julien and Marcel Proulx attempted to assign numerical weights to the "chevauchement" (overlapping) of federal and Quebec programs and discovered that there was federal participation in 61 per cent of the Quebec programs and Quebec involvement in 58 per cent of federal programs.[7] There are several circumstances behind such joint participation. In some circumstances Ottawa has involved itself in matters within provincial jurisdiction through the exercise of the federal spending power. In other cases, such as those related to culture and communications, the constitution as judicially interpreted does not clearly delineate the respective responsibilities of the two orders of government. In yet other cases—for example, the regulation of insurance, consumer protection, the development and sale of natural resources—the operative constitution is characterized by *de facto* federal-provincial concurrency.[8]

—the provincial governments have increasingly asserted the role of representing what they judge to be provincial interests in respect to matters which are within federal jurisdiction. Such matters include Ottawa's policies in banking, tariffs, transportation, broadcasting and monetary management. In part the rationale for such involvement is that federal policies bear directly on the way in which the provinces can carry out their responsibilities, in part that as governments the provinces are the most legitimate expression of the interests of residents of their respective provinces in respect even to matters within federal jurisdiction.

—as we shall see, there is an increasing disposition towards interprovincial interactions. Some of these involve groupings of contiguous provinces, others the collaboration of all ten provincial jurisdictions.

The Machinery of Executive Federalism

Gérard Veilleux of the federal Department of Finance has made an up-to-date listing of federal-provincial liaison agencies between 1957 and 1977.[9] In the former year there were 5 such groupings at the ministerial level and 59 at the administrative level, in 1977 some 31 ministerial groups and 158 involving appointed officials. The situation in 1977 was categorized by level and function in this fashion:

FUNCTION	MINISTERIAL LEVEL	ADMINISTRATIVE LEVEL
General Government Services	6	34
Protection of Persons and Property	5	7
Transportation and Communications	7	18
Health	1	10
Social Welfare		2
Recreation and Culture	2	6
Education	2	4
Natural Resources and Primary Industry	7	42
Commercial and Industrial Expansion	1	4

These 158 liaison bodies met 335 times.

Veilleux has also tabulated interprovincial liaison bodies in 1977.

FUNCTION	MINISTERIAL LEVEL	ADMINISTRATIVE LEVEL
General Government Services	6	7
Protection of Persons and Property		1
Transportation and Communication	2	1

Health	1	
Social Welfare	1	
Recreation and Culture	1	1
Education	1	
Natural Resources, and Primary		
Industry	3	2
Commercial and Industrial		
Expansion	2	1

These 30 groups met 37 times. However, although this tabulation includes liaison agencies involving all the provinces, regional groupings of provinces are omitted.

In the period between the end of the Second World War and the establishment of the Continuing Committee on Fiscal and Economic Matters in 1955, institutionalized federal-provincial interaction was for the most part limited to two kinds of matters: (1) the periodic renegotiation of the tax arrangements, and (2) co-operation in respect to specific services and facilities, the latter often within the framework of shared-cost programs. There was relatively little integration of these two kinds of matters and the sharing of taxes and revenues was determined by finance and treasury departments who worked in relative isolation from officials and agencies of the two levels who were concerned with specific programs. Neither, as we shall see in Chapter 6, was there institutionalized collaboration in fiscal policy as an instrument of economic stabilization.

The establishment of the Continuing Committee on Fiscal and Economic Matters in 1955 was a breakthrough in the institutionalization of federal-provincial fiscal relations.[10] The press communiqué issued by the Conference of Prime Ministers and Premiers on October 3 of that year stated:

> By general agreement the Conference established a committee of federal and provincial officials to meet from time to time to exchange information and examine technical problems in the field of federal-provincial fiscal and economic relations. Representation on this committee will be designated by the Prime Minister or Premier of each government respectively and the chairman will be designated by the Prime Minister of Canada. The Committee will not take collective action but each of its members will report to his own government on the subjects discussed.[11]

It should be noted that the Committee was authorized only to share information and discuss technical matters and was to have no collective responsibility for either recommendation or action. It was made up of senior appointed officials. The Committee performed useful work in connection with the tax arrangements which came into effect in 1957 and acted as a Secretariat for several future Federal-Provincial Conferences. However, it was not until nine years later that more important progress was made in institutionalizing financial relations between the two levels.

The Federal-Provincial Conference of March 31-April 1, 1964 provided for the establishment of the Tax Structure Committee.[12] This new and more ambitious attempt to establish a machinery for fiscal cooperation came at one of the most turbulent of Conferences in recent times, at the end of which an angry Premier Lesage of Quebec issued his own dissenting communiqué and threatened to challenge in the courts Ottawa's alleged encroachments on provincial jurisdiction. The Tax Structure Committee was to consist of Ministers of Finance and Treasurers. It was given the collective responsibility to report on several important matters to the Federal-Provincial Conference of heads of government early in 1966. These matters included probable trends of public expenditure in the 1967-1972 period, general problems in shared-cost programs in this period, the joint occupancy of tax fields, equalization grants to the provinces, and "future intergovernmental liaison on fiscal and economic matters." The Continuing Committee on Fiscal and Economic Matters was in effect to be the staff agency of the Tax Structure Committee. It was also decided in 1964 that the Treasurers and Ministers of Finance should meet toward the end of each calendar year just prior to the time when each government's budget was being formulated to discuss the general economic and financial situation. This procedure was not regularized until nearly the end of the 1960s but is now in effect.

The beginning of constitutional review in 1968 brought into existence a Continuing Committee of Officials to supervise the process and a Federal-Provincial Constitutional Secretariat to serve the Committee and the Constitutional Conferences of First Ministers.

Along with the machinery relating to the most comprehensive concerns of the two levels, there is a vast and complex network of federal-provincial interactions dealing with more specific matters. These range in specificity from meetings related to the national inventory of historic buildings to the annual conference of ministers of health, labour, the environment, and so on. As a general rule, the more limited the scope of such interactions the more likely there is to be agreement—agreement based on the professional norms of engineers, foresters, social workers, public health specialists, and so on.[13] However, in their examination of federal-Ontario relations concerning adult occupational training in the late 1960s, J. Stefan Dupré and his colleagues told of the exacerbation of conflict based on the contradictory goals of officials from the two levels, with the federal concerns being related largely to manpower and employment considerations and those of the province to educational objectives.[14] In the past decade there has been a generalized trend toward subsuming federal-provincial relations at the middle and lower levels of the public services where under most circumstances professional and technical considerations are important, to machinery where ministers and their deputies are participants. The concerns of these latter officials are of course more directly related to broader policies and to partisan politics.

During the recent period there has been a rapid development of administrative machinery in the federal and provincial governments for dealing explicitly with intergovernmental affairs. Thus there has come into existence a new kind of official whom one might call the intergovernmental affairs manager, the official not involved directly with programs but rather with federal-provincial and interprovincial relations as such.

The first intergovernmental agency in Canada was the Quebec Department of Federal-Provincial Relations established by the Lesage government in 1961, and in 1967 reorganized as the Department of Intergovernmental Affairs. In its early years this portfolio was held by successive Premiers. Under the leadership of its Deputy Minister, Claude Morin, and with him a group of able young people with advanced training in law and political science, the Department played a crucial role in the agressive, sophisticated and single-minded pursuit of provincial autonomy by successive Quebec governments.

Because of the demonstrated effect of Quebec's sophistication in federal-provincial relations, Premier Robarts of Ontario in the mid-1960s caused to be established a Department of Treasury, Economics and Intergovernmental Affairs and recruited H. Ian Macdonald as the Deputy Minister of the new department. In 1978 the treasury and intergovernmental affairs functions were separated and a Department of Intergovernmental Affairs created. Unlike its counterparts in the other provinces, this latter Department is responsible for relations with the municipalities as well as with the federal and provincial governments. However, in contrast to the Quebec and Alberta departments it does not have control over Ontario's agencies outside Canada.

The newly-elected Lougheed government in Alberta created a Department of Federal and Intergovernmental Affairs in 1972 following the Quebec model closely.

Saskatchewan created a separate Department of Intergovernmental Affairs in 1978.

Under the Trudeau government there was a rapid development in the federal machinery for dealing with federal-provincial relations. In part this was a reflection of Trudeau's own preoccupation with questions relating to federalism, in part of his agressive concern with rationalizing the operations of government. The cabinet committee on Federal-Provincial Relations was one of the standing committees of cabinet until it was merged with the Priorities and Planning Committee. Ottawa's Federal-Provincial Relations Office was established as a separate department of government in 1975 under legislation enacted in the previous year. In their recent book on central agencies of the federal government, Colin Campbell and George J. Szablowski assert that "Since 1975 FPRO has acted as a full-fledged *second* cabinet secretariat developing policy-review capabilities in all substantive issue areas and in all geographic regions of the country."[15] From 1975 until the fall of 1979 Gordon Robertson, who had been Clerk of the Privy Council from 1963 onward, was Secretary of the FPRO and advisor to the cabinet on federal-provincial relations. In 1977 the post of Secretary of State for Federal-Provincial Relations was established and Marc Lalonde and later John Reid held this portfolio until the resignation of the Trudeau government as a result of the general election of May 22, 1979. This portfolio was continued in the Clark Cabinet which took office in June, 1979 and its incumbert, William Jarvis was a member of the "inner cabinet," and chaired the cabinet committee on federal-provincial relations, one of the five standing committees of cabinet.*

The First Ministers' Conference

The Federal-Provincial Conference of Prime Ministers and Premiers has come to be one of the most crucial institutions of Canadian federalism. Prior to the beginning of constitutional review in 1968 such conferences dealt almost exclusively with fiscal and economic matters and, from time to time, with attempts to agree on a formula for constitutional amendment. However, this range of discussions has come to be more extensive and such meetings are held with increasing frequency, at least twice each year.

The Federal-Provincial Conference very much needs detailed study. It is inaccurate to suggest, as some have done, that it has become the third level of government in Canada. Such an assertion ignores the important difference between the actual and potential powers of this emergent institution. In terms of potentiality, the Conference could prevail over even the constitution because the constitution could and would be amended in any direction on which the federal and all the provincial governments could agree. In fact, the capacity to reach agreement is very much circumscribed by the divergent policy and partisan political interests of its members. In the absence of further research, the following generalizations can be made about this emergent institution:

(1) The Conference has come to be a highly visible forum for the discussion of some of the most important issues facing Canada. The proceedings of the Confederation for Tomorrow Conference of November 1967 were nationally televised, as were those of the Constitutional Conferences of February 1968 and December 1969 and the conferences on energy in January 1974 and April 1975. Some if not

---

* In the Trudeau cabinet formed in 1980 there was no Secretary of State for Federal-Provincial Relations.

all of the participants dislike this degree of openness[16] and certainly none of the decisive processes of negotiation is going to be conducted before the television cameras. However, the increasing frequency of conferences and their extensive reportage by the media ensure the prominence of this institution in the consciousness of Canadians concerned with public affairs. At any rate, the very size of these gatherings makes any high degree of secrecy impossible—for example, at the Federal-Provincial First Ministers Conference on Energy held in January 1974 there were 57 ministers and 130 advisors officially accredited. Parliament and the provincial legislatures spend relatively little of their time with federal-provincial relations as such—there is not in Parliament or it seems in any of the provincial legislatures a committee dealing with these relations conforming to the more structured machinery on the executive side of government—and the publicity given to First Ministers' Conferences contributes to public awareness of these issues.

(2) Although up until the 1970s most of the discussions of the conferences centred on fiscal and constitutional matters, there has been a tendency to include other aspects of joint concern and to establish sub-committees, sometimes at the ministerial and sometimes at the official level, to report directly to the Conference. In the past five years there have been discussions about environmental pollution, Indian affairs, foreign investment, energy, the control of inflation, winter unemployment and other matters of mutual interest.

(3) During recent years there has been a vast improvement in the staff work of the conferences. Prior to the 1960s the provinces if not the federal government conducted themselves at such meetings in a somewhat amateurish way. This has now changed, although the variations among the provinces are very great. The improvement of the staff function came largely as a result of the work of the Continuing Committee on Fiscal and Economic Matters, the Tax Structure Committee and, during the 1968-1971 period, the Secretariat of the Constitutional Conference. With the breakdown in constitutional negotiations after the Victoria Conference the latter body became the Canadian Intergovernmental Conference Secretariat, among whose major duties is the provision of documentation for intergovernmental meetings. And of course the intergovernmental departments and agencies within particular jurisdictions contribute to the sophistication of the process.

(4) Federal-provincial relations at the First Ministers' level have not developed formalized and agreed-upon procedures. Despite the importance of these relations in the Canadian political system they have not been constitutionalized. Who has the authority to cause a conference to be called? How is the agenda to be determined? Are conferences to be open or closed? Should communiqués issued at the end of conferences make reference to unresolved differences among governments? Is it reasonable to expect first ministers to

commit their administrations at conferences or are there circumstances where such commitment can appropriately be delayed? Is it appropriate for governments, most crucially of course the federal government, to introduce new proposals into conferences without prior consultation with other jurisdictions? To what extent, if at all, is an incoming government bound by its predecessor? What are appropriate conditions of secrecy in federal-provincial relations? Because of the lack of firm conventions, relations have been conducted in a somewhat personalized way and participants in the intensive reactions of the 1960s spoke of the "clubby" atmosphere that had developed among elected and appointed officials. Yet more recently this informality has in a sense been challenged by the rapid turnover of personnel. At the political level there were changes in government in every jurisdiction but Ontario in the 1970s. And similar changes took place among appointed officials, although in Quebec the election of the PQ government saw the emergence as cabinet ministers of two persons—Claude Morin and Jacques Parizeau—who had been influential in federal-provincial relations in non-elective capacities under previous Quebec administrations.

(5) The First Ministers' Conference requires the Prime Minister of Canada to assume roles which may conflict. In this context he is at the same time chairman, the head of a government with interests to defend, and the leader of a national political party. Lester Pearson asserted that in federal-provincial conferences the Prime Minister "should often act more in a diplomatic capacity than in a political negotiating capacity."[17] In accord with this perspective Mr. Pearson made it a practice at such conferences to let one or another of his ministers put forward and defend the inevitably contentious positions of the federal government while he himself carried on negotiations in a more informal setting. The major aim of the Prime Minister was thus to preside over formal meetings of the conferences so as to facilitate harmony and constructive negotiation. His successor, Pierre Trudeau, had a style more oriented towards confrontation and towards a kind of discussion which sharpened points of disagreement. Mr. Trudeau had also a set of more firmly-held convictions about federalism and emphasized more his role as the defender of federal interests. It is as yet too early to judge how Prime Minister Clark will perform in this context.

A Digression: Regionalism or Provincialism?

The core of this chapter concerns territorially-based collaboration and conflict in Canada but the question remains as to whether the relevant units are provinces or regions. In contemporary Canadian debate the term "regionalism" has come to be used in a somewhat imprecise way. To take a prominent and recent example, the Report of the Task Force on Canadian Unity refers to regionalism and cultural duality as the two cleavages which are at the "heart of the present crisis."[18]

Murray Beck has pointed out that "social and natural scientists usually define a region according to ecological, climatological, physiographic, economic, political, or other criteria, the research problem dictating the definition that is used."[19] In governmental terms we sometimes use "region" in Canada to denote the administrative districts into which federal and provincial departments or agencies divide the territory under their control for their own convenience. In some provinces we use "region" in connection with units of local government more extensive than the rural or urban municipality. Among political scientists there are two commonly used definitions of region. The first relates to political culture, the common cognitive, evaluative and affective orientations toward political matters held by persons within an area and a sense among these persons that they are different from others in the society. The second definition of region was given by J. E. Hodgetts and applied to Canada in terms of systems analysis as "an identifiable area having sufficiently common interests that they can be articulated and aggregated and urged on the federal government as part of the demand inputs of our political system."[20] This latter definition is the one I shall use in this section.

Hodgetts argued that in Canada regions were not effective as aggregators and articulators of common interests. Regional interests do perform such a function in the American system because of the looseness of party discipline in the Congress and the procedures by which the President is chosen. However, the cohesiveness of the parties in the Canadian House of Commons "virtually eliminates the possibility of bloc voting in the name of the Prairies, the Maritimes, or any other region of transprovincial dimensions." Thus the provinces rather than the regions were the effective units for aggregating, articulating and pressing those interests confined to an area less extensive than Canada as a whole. Hodgetts explained the increasing attention being given to the region as "basically an artifice of administrators who . . . play a creative role in constructing regions appropriate to the functions entrusted to them." However, he saw the possibility that "once over the formative stage, the genuine need for a regional approach to policy-formation and implementation will in itself begin to create self-generating demand and support inputs which will no longer be bureaucratically inspired."[21]

Proceeding from a very different perspective than Hodgetts, Beck has challenged the notion that the Maritimes are a region.[22] His test was the definition given by Mildred Schwartz, "a region is made up of adjacent

areas, so that the entire region is distinguishable from others in that society, and can be treated as though it were a common political actor."[23]
There are, claims Beck, common characteristics of Maritime political
behaviour and attitudes—hereditary voting traditions, the continuing
support for the two-party system, the persistence of certain forms of patronage and electoral corruption, attitudes of cynicism and distrust
toward the political system, etc. But this traditionalism and conservatism does not result in a regional consciousness, but rather in deep
loyalties to the individual provinces and the three provinces have
shown little disposition to behave as "a common political actor."

As we shall see later in this chapter, there have been significant recent developments in interprovincial co-operation among the governments of the western and Atlantic provinces. However, the situation is
very far from one in which regional interests are articulated by a "common political actor." So far as effective political action is concerned,
the provinces rather than regions are the significant units.

Federal-Provincial Relations and the Regulatory Powers of Governments

In the mid and late 1970s much of the focus of conflict between the federal and provincial governments shifted from fiscal relations and
shared-cost programs to regulatory matters—telecommunications,
transportation, consumer protection, energy and the development of
natural resources, and the control of the natural environment. Circumstances specific to the regulatory function make such conflicts difficult
to resolve.

—constitutional jurisdiction is in most cases divided between the federal and provincial governments. In many situations also—most crucially perhaps in telecommunications—jurisdiction is not only
   divided but the constitution as interpreted by the courts has not
   clearly delineated the respective powers of Ottawa and the provinces.
—unlike the circumstances which prevail in respect to shared-cost programs, federal funds cannot be used to induce provincial compli-
   ance. So far as these programs are concerned, constitutional powers
   are usually provincial and Ottawa in a sense "buys" jurisdiction at a
   "price" arrived at through federal-provincial negotiation. This price
   is determined, on the federal side, by the urgency the central government feels in relation to matters in question and the availability of
   fiscal resources, and, on the provincial side, by the importance attached to the autonomy of these jurisdictions in respect to the service
   or facility for which federal funds are available. In the field of regula-

tion, such bargaining is usually impossible and the issues tend towards a zero-sum game which clearly creates winners and losers without solutions that would serve the interest of both orders of government.

—the most crucial and, so far as the provinces are concerned, the most contentious elements of the federal regulatory function are performed by agencies which have a significant degree of independence from the control of ministers and cabinets. This independence is usually justified in terms of the needs of these agencies to attract expertise which would not be available to departments of government, the imperatives of flexibility, and the desire to ensure the impartiality of the regulatory process by removing it from politics. However, the independence of these regulatory bodies from political control imposes barriers to federal-provincial bargaining and to the authoritative resolution of conflicts between the two orders of government by such bargaining.

Richard Schultz has studied the federal-provincial dimensions of the federal regulatory process more carefully than has any other person and in a recent study commissioned by the FPRO has recommended reforms along two general lines.[24]

First, the policy-making activities of federal regulatory agencies should be brought under direct and effective political control. The statutory powers of such agencies are characteristically framed in broad terms which confer on the regulatory body policy-making authority along with the adjudicative authority to apply statutory and agency rules to particular situations—and often the responsibility to advise the government on policy matters as well. The most important of Schultz' general recommendations to bring regulatory agencies under political control are these:

(1) All regulations of federal regulatory agencies should require either ministerial or Governor in Council approval before taking effect.

(2) All statutes creating federal regulatory agencies should contain a provision empowering the Governor in Council to issue, subject to statutory safeguards, policy directives to the agencies.

(3) Rules of procedure of all federal regulatory agencies should require Governor in Council or ministerial approval.[25]

If these recommendations were implemented, the existing statutory requirements governing most regulatory agencies which provides for appeals to ministers or the cabinet from agency decisions should, in Schultz's view, be abolished. The independence of regulatory agencies from political control needs to be safeguarded, but this independence should be confined to the adjudicative function.

Secondly, the provincial governments should be given a clearer and more explicit role in respect to federal regulatory agencies. These governments should be given the statutory right to participate in agency hearings—a privilege now under the discretion of the agencies themselves. There should also be provincial participation in the selection of members of regulatory agencies, particularly the Chairman and the Vice-Chairman. Members of the regulatory agencies should not be expected to act as the delegates of the governments which appointed them any more than do members of the judiciary but, as in the case of the Supreme Court of Canada, Schultz finds compelling reasons for involving the provinces in such appointments.

Schultz's proposals for enhancing the position of the provinces in the federal regulatory process involve a very fundamental perspective on the Canadian federal system. Provincial claims in these matters are justified on the general grounds that the exercise of federal regulatory powers impinges on the constitutional responsibilities of the provinces and that the provincial governments have a legitimate role in representing provincial interests. In respect to this latter argument, Schultz quotes a provincial official as saying:

> [One] cannot say that the Consumers' Association of Canada is representative of its constituency with any degree of confidence and this is also true of other groups. It is a different proposition as far as provincial governments are concerned. There is a different concept of representation that is involved with respect to governments as opposed to people. The assumption must always be made that a province does in fact represent its people.[26]

The reasoning of this official—particularly in the last sentence of his assertion—is questionable. It might reasonably be argued that the representative credentials of a provincial government extend only to matters within provincial legislative jurisdiction. This general question will be examined in more detail later in this chapter.

Interprovincial and Tri-Level Relations

At the Dominion-Provincial Conference held in late July 1960 the newly-elected Premier of Quebec, Jean Lesage, announced that he would soon invite his fellow premiers to an interprovincial conference.[27] Such a conference was convened in Quebec City the next month and since then the first ministers of provinces have gathered each August, with the various premiers acting as hosts in rotation and chairing the meeting.

In his presentation to the Federal-Provincial Conference of November 1963 Jean Lesage elaborated in more detail his government's views of the role interprovincial co-operation should play in a reformed federal system. Most crucially, such co-operation could help to forestall unilateral decisions by Ottawa encroaching on provincial ju-risdiction. In addition, all the provinces or groups of provinces might in respect to some matters design common policies "in which the fed-eral government would not have to participate unless such policies should have repercussion on it."[28]

During the 1960s relatively little progress was made in the direction of the Lesage goal of interprovincial co-operation. On both principled and pragmatic grounds it seems to have been the position of several of the provinces that it was inappropriate to deal with matters of federal-provincial concern in an interprovincial context, and in particular to form a provincial united front against Ottawa. By the end of the decade some of the provinces were beginning to absent themselves from the August meetings and in other cases the premiers were represented by cabinet colleagues.

The 1970s saw a resurgence of interprovincial collaboration involv-ing both all the provinces and regional groupings of provinces. In par-ticular, the provinces came to shed their former inhibitions about form-ing provincial united fronts against the federal government. At the Premiers' conference in August 1974 all the provinces protested the de-cisions of the federal government in its budget of the preceding May not to allow corporations to deduct provincial royalties from their in-come as taxable for federal purposes. In September 1974 the provincial ministers of health rejected Ottawa's proposal for a federal block grant in aid of health services. The provincial ministers of communications were able to agree in early 1975 on a common policy about the respec-tive roles of the two orders of government regarding broadcasting and telecommunications.[29] Just before the conclusion of the federal-provin-cial agreement leading up to the crucial 1977 legislation on fiscal ar-rangements there was formed a provincial united front on fiscal mat-ters. In conferences of the premiers in 1977 and 1978 the provinces were able to agree on the primacy of provincial jurisdiction in educa-tion as a response to federal efforts in the direction of entrenching the rights of official-language minorities.[30] Other examples of interprovin-cial agreement could be given.

During the past decade there has also been considerable develop-ment of co-operation among groupings of contiguous provinces.

The Council of Maritime Premiers was constituted in 1971, largely in response to the Report on Maritime Union (usually known as the Deutsch Report) which had recommended a legislative union of Nova Scotia, Prince Edward Island and New Brunswick.[31] Unlike other in-stances of inter-provincial co-operation, the Council is established by legislation of the participating jurisdictions. In specific initiatives the Council has brought into existence a Maritime Provinces Higher Edu-cation Commission, the Atlantic Provinces Policy Academy, and a

Land Registration and Information Service. The three provinces have on several occasions evolved a common regional position in respect to federal economic policies. In March 1976 the Council had a staff of 334 and in the 1976-1977 fiscal year a budget of $8.5 millions. Speaking after five years of its operation the Secretary of this body said in September 1976:

> . . . the Council has grown from a four-times-a-year discussion forum for three premiers with a secretary providing staff support, to an institution which comprises, in addition to the premiers' quarterly meetings, a substantial secretariat, four operating agencies, a Regional Treasury Board, and a complex and interrelated series of committees, agreements, contractual obligations, employees, codes, policies, budgets, cost-sharing formulae, labour relations, obligations, potentials and even that ultimate twentieth-century mark of institutionalization—its own logo.[32]

Collaboration among the governments of the western provinces is much less highly structured than is the case in the maritime region and there is no western secretariat.[33] As the Maritime Council of Premiers was triggered by the Deutsch Report, so western interprovincial collaboration came into existence largely as a result of the Western Economic Opportunities Conference of 1973. The Prairie Economic Council was formed in 1965 and met twice each year with the general objectives of reducing conflicts among the western provinces and resolving mutual problems of a relatively limited scope. However, it was not until the 1973 meeting that the governments of the prairie provinces—now joined by British Columbia—were impelled to formulate broad regional goals. The WEOC was convened by the federal government largely as a response to the very weak showing of the Trudeau Liberals in the western provinces in the 1972 general election. In Gartner's words,

> The onus was placed on the western provinces to determine, in the clearest possible terms, the direction in which they wanted western Canada to go in the future. This necessarily focused attention on the broader policy issues, and on integrating specific grievances within a broader framework. For the first time in history, the four western provinces joined together to present Ottawa with a single regional position.[34]

For the most part, western interprovincial co-operation has been based on economic matters and Gartner has pointed out that relatively little has been accomplished in such fields of social policy as those relating to bilingualism, corrections, education and native problems. Some of the collaboration in the economic field has been interprovincial in nature as in the cases of the Prairie Agricultural Machinery Institute, the

Western Canada Fertilizer Prices Review Panel, and a joint trade mission to Central and South America. Co-operation in other matters has resulted in a common stance by the western provinces *vis-à-vis* the federal government in such matters as tariff policies, transportation, the taxation of natural resources, and agricultural policy. One of the most important of these latter initiatives has taken place through the Western Premiers' Task Force on Constitutional Trends, formed in 1976, and including a minister from each of the provinces. At the annual conference of the premiers in April of that year, the heads of government "expressed their concern over the increasing tendency of the Government of Canada to legislate in subject areas which historically and constitutionally have been considered to be within the provincial sphere."[35] The Task Force has in its annual reports of 1977, 1978 and 1979 presented a detailed monitoring of federal actions affecting the provinces with an assessment of the impact on the western provinces, the degree and adequacy of Ottawa's consultation with the provinces prior to such actions being taken, the western position on the matter and—in the 1978 and 1979 Reports—the success or otherwise of provincial action to have the situation remedied.[36]

There is little institutional development of collaboration between the two central provinces of Ontario and Quebec.[37] In 1969 the Ontario-Quebec Permanent Commission was established under the terms of an Ontario-Quebec Agreement for Cooperation and Exchange in Cultural and Educational Matters and there have been several programs of educational and cultural exchanges. However, beyond this kind of collaboration there are, according to a recent study by Kenneth McRoberts, no major reciprocal agreements involving the joint formulation of Ontario-Quebec policies and no major instances of joint Ontario-Quebec projects.[38] In the immediate context it would appear that the prospects for constructive Ontario-Quebec co-operation are very much diminished because of the commitment of the government of the latter to sovereignty.

In the early 1970s there was discussion and some limited development towards associating the municipal governments with Ottawa and the provinces in social and economic policy, particularly as this related to the broad phenomenon of urbanization. In 1971 the federal government established the Ministry of State for Urban Affairs whose responsibilities, according to the proclamation setting up this agency, were to:

> formulate and develop policies for implementation through measures within fields of federal jurisdiction in respect of:
> (a) the most appropriate means by which the Government of Canada may have a beneficial influence on the process of urbanization in Canada;

(b) the integration of urban policy with other policies and programmes of the Government of Canada;

(c) the fostering of cooperative relationships in respect of urban affairs with the provinces and, through them, their municipalities,
and with public and private organizations.

So far as federal activities in regard to urbanization were concerned,
the Ministry was very much handicapped in that, according to David
M. Cameron's analysis, "Its only strength could derive from persuasion, persuasion aimed at a cabinet consisting primarily of operating
portfolios, or at a bureaucracy consisting primarily of operating agencies."[39] The basic rationale of MSUA was the perceived need for new
agencies without important operational responsibilities to formulate
and co-ordinate federal policies in emergent fields of concern. The
Ministry failed, however, to establish a position of decisive influence
in the face of the challenges offered by other federal agencies and by
the provinces, and Prime Minister Trudeau announced in 1978 that it
would be disbanded.

The first national tri-level conference was held in Toronto in November, 1972. Apart from Manitoba, which favoured direct contacts between the federal and municipal governments, all the provinces agreed
that contacts between Ottawa and the local authorities should be
through the provinces. At the 1972 Conference and subsequently, Ontario opposed tri-level consultations on a national basis, arguing that
the provinces alone were responsible for municipal development and
that what was desperately needed was more federal money granted un-
conditionally for urban development.[40] There are now tri-level consultations of a formal or informal variety in several of the provinces and
cities, and in Ontario each year federal representatives participate in
one of the quarterly meetings between the provinces and the representatives of Ontario municipalities.

In general terms, the aggressiveness of the provinces has inhibited
the kinds of direct federal-municipal relations which are common in
the United States. For several reasons Canadian municipalities have
been relatively ineffectual in influencing federal and provincial governments—perhaps because of the relative weakness, at least in comparison with the United States, of traditions of local democracy; because the Canadian Federation of Mayors and Municipalities has
lacked effective research and staff services and represents the divergent
interests of all kinds of municipalities; and because the CFMM in dealing with Ottawa and the provinces is a pressure group rather than a
government. Furthermore, the increasing sophistication of the provinces has led them to more comprehensive policies in such fields as
housing, urban transportation and metropolitan development, and thus
to resist more aggressively than before federal involvements in such
fields.

The Circumstances of Federal-Provincial Relations

I The Substance

In the period since the Second World War the scope of matters in which the two orders of government interact has vastly increased in scope. This section will in a broad-brush way outline the substantive nature of these interactions and the next will examine how federal-provincial relations have shaped and been shaped by the institutions and procedures by which such relations are conducted.

The centralized federal order which had been brought into existence during the Second World War was perpetuated until the late 1950s. There were two major instruments of this centralization. There was, first, the dominance of the federal government in fiscal matters, with its concomitant of Ottawa assuming the major responsibility for full employment through discretionary changes in fiscal policy. Secondly, there was the regime of conditional grants in which the federal authorities through the exercise of the spending power involved themselves in a large number of matters within provincial jurisdiction and influenced the range and quality of provincial services.

The way in which the centralized federal order which emerged out of the Second World War disintegrated will be examined in more detail in Chapter 6. From the ending of the tax-rental system in 1957 the provinces have become responsible for setting their own rates for the major direct taxes, and from 1966 Ottawa has pursued a fairly steady course of resisting provincial pressures for enhanced tax room in respect to these taxes. The regime of grants-in-aid was first brought under sustained attack by the provinces in the early 1960s and this process culminated in 1977 in federal legislation converting the three major programs related to medical insurance, hospital insurance and post-secondary education from conditional to unconditional financial assistance. Largely attendant on the failure of federal fiscal and monetary policies to bring about satisfactory conditions in respect to full employment, price stability and economic growth from the late 1950s onward, the provinces have become increasingly aggressive in economic matters.

Yet the pattern of federal-provincial relations in the past two decades is not a straightforward one of federal retreat. Although it is impossible to be precise about its origins, there was a counter-movement on the part of Ottawa to extend its involvement in respect to matters where it had previously been totally or almost completely inactive. From the mid-1960s there seems to have arisen in the higher ranks of the federal government an anxiety that with the increasing aggressiveness of the provinces the central authorities would be relegated to a role in which they had few significant contacts with citizens. The response to this anxiety was for Ottawa to put under way programs which would in fact give the federal government new constituencies—constituencies of women, environmentalists, native peoples, consumers, municipalities, cultural groups, persons involved in fitness and amateur sports, official-language minorities, ethnic groups, the scientific community, radical youth, and so on. A. D. Careless has said this of federal programs to narrow regional economic disparities:

> The federal government wanted a new constituency for its regional development schemes: one determined by the natural boundaries of commercial and economic activities and not those provincial boundaries into which most federal economic policies had artificially been squeezed. . . . The establishment of a virtually new constituency by Ottawa through direct spending, refusing the expansion of traditional transfers [to the provinces], and through elaborate provisions on DREE activities for the visible designation of all projects as clearly joint, constituted a new strategy in the assertion of federal power.[41]

The new kinds of initiatives to build sources of support for the federal government were undertaken for the most part in a period where the revenues of that government were elastic, i.e. at stable rates of taxation revenues increased proportionately more rapidly than GNP. Much of this elasticity was removed by the indexing of the personal income tax in 1972, and because of this and other fiscal restraints Ottawa has more recently refrained from attempting to create new dependencies and has in some cases cut back or even eliminated such dependencies. It might be mentioned almost parenthetically that few if any of the groups to which Ottawa showed itself in general more sensitive than the provinces have since shown any profound disposition to throw their influence behind federal power in the face of provincial efforts to weaken that power.

As we shall see in Chapter 6, the development and sale of natural resources has become from about 1973 onward the major focus of conflict between the federal and provincial government apart from the dramatic challenge posed by Quebec nationalism. Particularly in respect to Alberta and Saskatchewan these conflicts engage the most fundamental of provincial objectives.

The scope of matters discussed at the summit of federal-provincial interactions has consistently been extended. Prior to 1968, first ministers' meetings dealt almost exclusively with fiscal and/or constitutional matters. Although the 1968-1971 conferences on the constitution were in an explicit sense oriented around constitutional review, the price of the participation of some of the provinces in the review process caused these discussions to range over a wider range of policies, particularly in respect to economic affairs. As we have seen, there were intense interactions in the mid 1970s related to natural resources and the negotiation at the first ministers' level of the price at which domestic petroleum would be sold in Canada. However, in the first ministers' conferences of February and November 1978 there was a more comprehensive and structured approach to economic problems than ever before. At the earlier conference there was agreement on somewhat general medium-term objectives for economic policy and at the later meeting a reporting by the federal government of the actions which had been taken in furtherance of these objectives. This more comprehensive process involves not only the first ministers but also the program departments of their respective governments and in some cases private groups as well. It appears likely that in the future the heads of government will meet annually to review economic policy in its broadest sense.

II Processes and Institutions

The underlying question here is whether the thrust of these processes and institutions has been towards accommodation or conflict. It is a peculiarly difficult time to attempt such analysis because, as this is written (June 1979), a new federal government has just come to power and one can at best speculate about the administrative style of the Clark administration.

Federal-provincial relations in the recent period cannot be understood without reference to the ongoing movement of rationalization which has pervasively influenced the conduct of the federal administration and, to widely varying degrees, that of the provinces. Rationalization embodied three related imperatives.[42] First, the objectives and priorities of public policy should be explicitly formulated. Secondly, the aims of policy should be stated at a high level of generality and more specific aims controlled by broader ones. Thirdly, the effectiveness and efficiency of ongoing or projected programs should be evaluated with as much precision as possible, preferably in terms of quantitative measures. The characteristic devices of rationalization are cost-benefit analysis, management by objectives, the use of econometric models in economic forecasting, systems analysis, long-term program budgets, and Planning Programming and Budgeting System (PPBS).

The rationalization of the policy process appears to lead to increasingly intense conflicts between the federal and provincial governments. These following points might be made in support of such a judgment:

(1) G. Bruce Doern has written of the impact of Planning, Programming and budgeting procedures on federal-provincial relations:

> There is already a sense of competitiveness between the federal government and the Ontario government regarding the best way to intro-

duce PPB. It does not tax the imagination to see that we have reached a new era of analytical and bureaucratic competitiveness between the federal and provincial bureaucracies, especially between the big provincial bureaucracies of Ontario, Quebec and British Columbia.[43]

After the publication by the federal Minister of Finance of his White Paper on Tax Reform in 1969, there was a vigorous debate with the Ontario authorities. The substantive issue in dispute was whether Ottawa was concealing tax increases under the guise of tax reform. This debate about the validity of the federal projections of the tax yields consequent on its proposals could reasonably be regarded as a trial of bureaucratic competence between experts of the two governments.

(2) The conflicts in respect to conditional grants from 1960 onward can be explained partly in terms of the sharpening of federal and provincial objectives. The earlier grant-in-aid programs were begun in periods of buoyant federal revenues and of limited concern for the precise measurement of federal objectives. On the provincial side, "fifty-cent dollars" were more attractive than otherwise in the absence of precise program and budgetary goals. With relative financial stringency in Ottawa and with emphasis on rational priority-setting, a growing restiveness emerged among federal officials about "open-ended" arrangements in which federal expenditures are determined by provinces, local governments and institutions of post-secondary education. In the provinces, administrative rationalization made grants-in-aid less attractive than before because of their impact on program standards and expenditure-priorities. As we shall see in Chapter 6, the result was to eliminate most of the major shared-cost programs.

(3) The increasing concern of the provinces with fiscal policy as an instrument of economic stabilization may well sharpen federal-provincial conflict. As we shall see in Chapter 6 this has certainly been so in the case of Ontario, which has gone much farther than any other province in designing and implementing its own independent fiscal policy in terms of the generalized requirements of full employment, price stability and economic growth.

(4) The provinces have come increasingly to view taxation and expenditure by governments as instruments for deliberate policies of income redistribution and to challenge federal policies in terms of these redistributive goals. Not only Ottawa but most of the provinces have sponsored comprehensive fiscal investigations in the past decade, and the work of these groups has contributed greatly to provincial sophisication in fiscal matters. Thus Ontario waged a determined battle against federal proposals for reforming the individual income tax base in 1969, on the grounds that these proposals did not embody certain conditions regarded by the provinces as

equitable. Quebec's persistent and relatively successful pressures toward full provincial control over public welfare have been based on the alleged necessity of rationalizing all income-assistance programs under one jurisdiction. In respect to equity in taxation and public expenditures as in other matters the increasing sophistication of the provinces leads to more coherent policies and these policies to clashes with the federal government.

One of the most crucial elements of rationalization insofar as this impinges on federal-provincial relations has been the increasing influence of the intergovernmental managers, those officials not responsible for particular programs or other public activities but rather the interactions with other governments. At the federal level there appear to have been two impulses behind the development of such agencies as the FPRO and more recently a separate cabinet portfolio whose exclusive responsibilities are for relations with the provinces.[44] First, with the growth of interactions between the two orders of government it was deemed necessary for Ottawa to co-ordinate its various policies and to speak with a single and authoritative voice in relations with the provinces. Secondly, it was believed crucial that one agency and one cabinet member should be able to transmit the concerns of the provinces to the federal government. The first consideration appears to have been the dominant one in causing the provinces to create special agencies charged with carrying out federal-provincial relations.

Intergovernmental affairs agencies appear to contribute to federal-provincial conflict rather than accommodation. First, and in a negative sense, these central agencies restrict the capacity of program officials and departments to effect federal-provincial agreement based on professional and/or technical norms. It is reasonable to expect that, left to themselves, veterinarians will be able to agree most of the time on the standards and procedures related to the grading of meat, foresters, about forest management, and public health officials, about the control of communicable diseases. However, the thrust of federal-provincial relations agencies is to link narrower purposes with broader and more political ones, and in respect to these latter it is less likely that the federal and provincial governments will agree. The implicit and single-minded purpose of intergovernmental affairs managers at the provincial level is to safeguard and if possible to extend the range of jurisdictional autonomy, including of course the revenues that provinces have under their unshared control. Agencies of intergovernmental relations in the province do not of course have the responsibility for administering particular programs. Thus the objective is to guard and enhance provincial autonomy. The position of their federal counterparts is more complex and is partly devoted to sustaining single and authoritative channel for the provinces at the highest levels of the federal government. However, the FPRO and the Department of the Secretary of State for Federal-Provincial Relations are inevitably motivated in large part to sustain and enhance federal power, particularly of course when this power and the continuing existence of Confederation itself are under attack.

It seems impossible to escape the conclusion that for both orders of government jurisdictional autonomy has become an important independent value. This is perhaps most dramatically illustrated by the conduct of several of the provinces and of the federal government in the *Anti-Inflation Reference* decided by the Supreme Court of Canada in 1976.[45] The immediate issue was the constitutionality of the 1975 federal legislation controlling wages, prices and profits.[46] Only Alberta intervened to challenge the legal validity of this enactment. But the other issue at stake was whether the anti-inflation law would be upheld under the federal Parliament's emergency power or, alternatively, whether the legislation would be justified by resort to the national dimensions doctrine. This latter issue, the definition by the Court of the "Peace, Order and Good Government" power of Parliament in respect to economic matters as this would affect *future* exercises of federal jurisdiction, was regarded as being of crucial importance by the federal authorities and those of the provinces which intervened.

However, as Alan Cairns has recently argued, the federal and provincial governments have become progressively less disposed to press their respective interests with reference to constitutional and legal norms. The general denigration of the constitution was analyzed in Chapter 2. Cairns gives several examples of the federal government pursuing policies for which little or no constitutional justification could be found, and quotes what he accurately calls "a classic case of special pleading," the Report of Paul Hellyer's Task Force on Housing and Urban Development in 1969. "It is illogical, if not inconceivable, that the Government of Canada could have ministers dealing with fisheries, forestry, veteran affairs, and other matters which involve a minority of the population, but none to deal on a full-time basis with the urban problems which involve more than 70 per cent of the population, not to mention housing which involves virtually everyone." Cairns concludes,

> . . . the contemporary success in playing fast and loose with the [constitutional] division of powers has begun to produce diminishing returns. Flexibility now looks dangerously like intergovernmental anarchy. The federal-provincial game has gotten out of hand, and we are in danger of being left not with a flexible division of powers, but with a non-existent division.[46]

In general terms, the federal government has more opportunities than do the provinces for extending its range of action by non-constitutional means and can perhaps bring forward more plausible reasons for so doing. However, in recent years, as we have seen, the provinces have made an attempt to extend their influence to matters within federal jurisdiction on the double rationale that federal actions in respect to such matters impinge on provincial responsibilities and that the provincial governments have a generalized legitimacy to represent the interests of residents within their respective boundaries. The origins of this thrust would appear to be in the formulation of "co-operative federalism" made by Premier Jean Lesage of Quebec at the Federal-Provincial Conference of November 1963.[47] According to this view there were two imperatives. The first was a fastidious respect by Ottawa for matters within provincial jurisdiction; the second was that the provinces should have a "voice in determining tariff structures, transportation and even the monetary policies of Canada, fields which up to the present were considered as exclusively under federal government jurisdiction." This latter involvement should take place "through permanent Federal-Provincial organisms instituted for this purpose." The general rationale for the Quebec position was put in these terms: "If provincial and interprovincial policies may, according to the circumstances of the case, be made with or without federal government participation, those of the federal government should never be fixed without consulting the provinces for, inevitably, such policies affect the populations and the industries of the provinces which form Canada."[48]

Gordon Robertson has described the 1973 Western Economic Opportunities Conference as a "milestone" in the involvement of the provincial governments in matters wholly or exclusively within the jurisdiction of the federal government. The agenda of this meeting was almost wholly devoted to western grievances involving such matters as national transportation policies, tariffs and federal agricultural policies, and the provincial governments were confident and aggressive in assuming the role as spokesmen of their respective electorates. Robertson has made a useful distinction between negotiation and consultation in federal-provincial relations. Negotiation is "the familiar role of accommodating the direct impacts, financial or otherwise, which federal initiatives may have on the priorities, policies and programs of provincial governments" and consultation is the process of interaction between the two orders of government where matters within federal jurisdiction are involved. However, "the dynamics of [federal-provincial] conferences can leave the impression that the participants are in the midst of bargaining sessions when the federal government is, in reality, consulting the leaders of provincial governments on a decision that is its own to make." Robertson deplores the existing situation on several grounds. It confuses the public about the nature of federal and provincial jurisdiction. Robertson argues that the original intent of Confederation, and still a worthy objective, was to establish "a division and specialization of responsibilities and not to afford the voter two voices on any single issue." The existing arrangements do not permit the federal authorities an influence on the provinces analogous to the constraints the latter attempt to enforce on Ottawa. Robertson's basic explanation of the present role of the provinces in respect to matters within provincial jurisdiction is that "each of the central institutions of our federation is to some degree flawed as a forum for the fullest expression and reconciliation of regional interests."[49]

The most clearly formulated argument that the provinces are more legitimate than the federal government in articulating the aspirations and interests of Canadians is contained in the Report of the Task Force on Canadian Unity. The Task Force saw the present crisis in Canada in terms of the conflicts engendered by French-English dualism, and by regionalism. The provinces are the primary expressions of cultural duality and regional interests. Thus there should be a division of powers much more favourable to the provinces than is the existing constitution—the assignment of the residual power to the provinces, additional powers to the provinces in the field of culture and language including the removal of the restrictions imposed on Quebec under Section 133, constitutional limitations on the federal spending power, the elimination of reservation and disallowance, and so on. But from the point of view of my analysis, the more significant recommendations relate to the involvement of the provincial governments in matters which the Task Force assigns to federal jurisdiction. The major channel of such involvement would be through a new second chamber, the Council of the Federation, composed of delegates of the provincial governments. Although the Task Force recommends that "legislation and treaties within exclusive federal jurisdiction should not require the approval of the Council," this body would be deeply involved in a number of crucial matters which under the existing constitution are the responsibility of the federal Parliament and cabinet alone.

In summary, the institutions and processes of executive federalism are disposed towards conflict rather than harmony. Federal-provincial summitry along with the related phenomenon of administrative rationalization has weakened the capacity of the system to make piecemeal and incremental adjustments according to the norms of scientific and professional groupings. Even more crucially, the pursuit of jurisdictional autonomy increasingly takes place outside a shared acceptance of constitutional and legal norms about the respective powers and responsibilities of the two orders of government.

Notes

1. For one of the most lucid descriptions of classical federalism, see James Bryce's description of the U.S. system in his classic *The American Commonwealth*, published in 1893. "The characteristic feature and special in-

terest of the American Union is that it shows us two governments covering the same ground, yet distinct and separate in their action. It is like a great factory wherein two sets of machinery are at work, their revolving wheels apparently intermixed, their bands crossing one another, yet each doing its own work without touching or hampering one another. To keep the National government and the state governments each in the allotted sphere, preventing collision and friction between them, was the primary aim of those who formed the Constitution . . ." *Vol. I.* p. 325. However, Daniel Elazar's more recent research demonstrates that Bryce exaggerated federal-state isolation. See Daniel Elazar, *The American Partnership: Intergovernmental Cooperation in the Nineteenth Century United States,* Chicago: University of Chicago Press, 1962.

2. Thomas A. Hockin, *Government in Canada,* Toronto: McGraw-Hill Ryerson, 1976, p. 7.

3. Vernon C. Fowke, *Canadian Agricultural Policy,* Toronto: University of Toronto Press, 1946, reprinted in paperback 1978, p. 155. At a conference on the same matter in 1871, Fowke points out, British Columbia and Nova Scotia also attended.

4. J. A. Corry, *Difficulties of Divided Jurisdiction,* Ottawa: King's Printer, 1940.

5. William Kilbourn, *Pipe Line,* Toronto: Clark, Irwin and Company, 1970, pp. 29-30.

6. Gunnar Myrdal, *Beyond the Welfare State,* New Haven: Yale University Press, 1960, Chapter 10, "Economic Nationalism in the Western World."

7. Germain Julien and Marcel Proulx, *Les chevauchement des programmes fédéraux et québécois,* Québec: École nationale d'administration publique, 1978, (miméo), p. 33.

8. On *de facto* concurrency, see Barry Strayer, "The Flexibility of the BNA Act," in Trevor Lloyd and Jack McLeod, eds. *Agenda 1970: Proposals for a Creative Politics,* Toronto: University of Toronto Press, 1978, pp. 197-216.

9. Gérard Veilleux, "L'évolution des mécanismes de liaison intergouvernmentale," in Richard Simeon, ed., *Confrontation and Collaboration—Intergovernmental Relations in Canada Today,* Toronto: Institute of Public Administration of Canada, 1979, pp. 35-77.

10. A. R. Kear, "Cooperative Federalism: A Study of the Federal-Provincial Continuing Committee on Fiscal and Economic Matters" in J. Peter Meekison, Editor, *Canadian Federalism,* First Edition, Toronto: Methuen of Canada, 1968, *op. cit.,* pp. 305-317.

11. Quoted in Kear, *op. cit.,* pp. 309-310.

12. For the terms of reference as given to the Tax Structure Committee in October, 1964, see *Federal-Provincial Conference of Ministers of Finance and Provincial Treasurers,* Ottawa: Queen's Printer, Ottawa, 1969, Appendix G.

13. Donald V. Smiley, *Conditional Grants and Canadian Federalism,* Canadian Tax Paper No. 32, Toronto: Canadian Tax Foundation, 1963, pp. 37-42.

14. J. Stephan Dupré, *et al, Federalism and Policy Development: The Case of Adult Occupational Training in Ontario,* Toronto: University of Toronto Press, 1973.

15. Colin Campbell and George J. Szablowski, *The Super-Bureaucrats: Structure and Behaviour in Central Agencies*, Toronto: Macmillan of Canada, 1979, pp. 49-50. Italics in original text.

16. See two responses about secrecy-publicity. (1) That of Lester B. Pearson, "Three Canadian Prime Ministers Discuss the Office," in Thomas A. Hockin, ed., *Apex of Power: The Prime Minister and Political Leadership in Canada*, Second Edition, Scarborough: Prentice-Hall, 1977, pp. 255-256; and (2) Gordon Robertson, "The Role of Interministerial Conferences in the Decision-Making Process" in Simeon, *op. cit.*, pp. 85-86.

17. Pearson, *op. cit.*, p. 254.

18. *Report: A Future Together*, Ottawa: Supply and Services, 1979, p. 21.

19. Murray Beck, "The Maritimes: A Region or Three Provinces?" *Transactions of the Royal Society of Canada XV*, Fourth Series, 1977, p. 302.

20. J. E. Hodgetts, "Regional Interests and Policy in a Federal Structure," in J. Peter Meekison, ed., *Canadian Federalism: Myth or Reality?* Third Edition, Toronto: Methuen, 1977, p. 285.

21. Ibid., p. 290.

22. Beck, *op. cit.*,

23. Mildred Schwartz, *Politics and Territory: The Sociology of Regional Persistence in Canada*, Montreal: McGill-Queen's University Press, 1974, p. 5.

24. Richard Schultz, *Federalism and the Regulatory Process*, Federal-Provincial Relations Office, Ottawa, 1979, *mimeo*, Chapter 5.

25. Ibid., pp. 90-101.

26. Ibid., pp. 64-65.

27. *Report*, Dominion-Provincial Conference, Ottawa: Queen's Printer, 1960, pp. 126-127.

28. *Report*, Federal-Provincial Conference, Ottawa: Queen's Printer, 1963, pp. 44-46.

29. *Joint Provincial Statement*, delivered by the Honourable John Rhodes of Ontario to the Federal-Provincial Conference on Communications, May 13-14, 1975 (mimeo).

30. *Proposals on the Constitution, 1971-1978*, Collation by the Canadian Intergovernmental Conference Secretariat, Ottawa, 1978, pp. 94-95.

31. For an account of the Council of Maritime Premiers, see A. A. Lomas, "The Council of Maritime Premiers: Report and Evaluation after 5 years," Ibid. *Canadian Public Administration 20*, Spring 1977, pp. 188-199.

32. Ibid., p. 194.

33. On western interprovincial co-operation, see (1) Gerry T. Gartner, "A Review of Cooperation among the Western Provinces", *Canadian Public Administration 20*, Spring 1977, pp. 174-187; (2) M. Westmacott and P. Dore, "Interprovincial Cooperation in Western Canada: The Western Economic Opportunities Conference," in Meekison, *op. cit.*, 3rd ed., pp. 340-352; and (3) Premier Allan Blakeney "Western Provincial Cooperation," Ibid., pp. 238-245.

34. Gartner, *op. cit.*, pp. 178-179.

35. Western Premiers Task Force on Constitutional Trends, *Second Report*, 1978, p. 7.

36. The "intrusions" are classified in eight fields: (1) Consumer and Corporate

Affairs, (2) Resources, (3) Housing and Urban Development, (4) Economic Development, (5) Communications, (6) Immigration, Manpower and Labour, (7) Administration of Justice, (8) Interventions by the Government of Canada before the Supreme Court of Canada.

37. For Ontario-Quebec relations, see Kenneth McRoberts, "An Overview of Ontario-Québec Interprovincial Relations," in *Québec-Ontario Economic Relations*, Proceedings of York-ENAP Colloque held in Toronto, January 12-13, 1978, *mimeo*, pp. 215-270.

38. Ibid., p. 246.

39. David M. Cameron, "Urban Policy," in G. Bruce Doern and V. Seymour Wilson, eds., *Issues in Canadian Public Policy*, Toronto: Macmillan of Canada, 1974, p. 245. The full essay, printed on pp. 228-252 of Doern and Wilson, is a valuable account of the events leading up to the establishment of MSUA and its subsequent history to that date.

40. *Toronto Star*, November 22, 1973.

41. A. D. Careless, *Initiative and Response, The Adaptation of Canadian Federalism to Regional Economic Development*, McGill-Queen's University Press, Montreal and London, 1977, p. 206.

42. See two valuable articles by Bruce Doern, "Recent Changes in the Philosophy of Policy-Making in Canada", *Canadian Journal of Political Science IV*, June, 1971, pp. 243-264, "The Budgetary and Policy Role of the Federal Bureaucracy," in G. Bruce Doern and Peter Aucoin, eds., *The Structures of Policy-Making in Canada*, Toronto: Macmillan of Canada, 1971, pp. 79-112.

43. Ibid., pp. 104-105.

44. Veilleux, *op. cit.*, p. 43.

45. Peter Russell, "*The Anti-Inflation Case:* The Anatomy of a Constitutional Decision," *Canadian Public Administration 20*, Winter 1977, pp. 632-665.

46. "The Other Crisis of Canadian Federalism", Inaugural Address in the University of Edinburgh, 1978, University of Edinburgh, Centre of Canadian Studies, 1978. This paper was published in *Canadian Public Administration 22*, Summer 1979, pp. 175-195.

47. Ibid., pp. 36-47.

48. Ibid., p. 46.

49. Gordon Robertson, "The Role of Interministerial Conferences in the Decision-Making Process", in Richard Simeon, ed., *op. cit.*, p. 82. This is a particularly valuable article, found in full on pp. 78-88. For the view of Ontario's Deputy Minister of Intergovernmental Affairs, see Donald Stevenson, "The Role of Intergovernmental Conferences in the Decision-Making Process," *op. cit.*, pp. 89-98.

CHAPTER 5

THE POLITICS OF CANADIAN FEDERALISM

It is only within the past two decades that students of federalism have turned their attention to the study of political parties. Successive editions of K. C. Wheare's influential *Federal Government* exclude parties.[1] Neither does W. S. Livingston's perceptive analysis of the sociology of federalism deal with political parties as such.[2] There is a growing literature on political integration which focuses on the economic, cultural and attitudinal aspects of the building and maintenance of political communities but gives parties little or no attention in its analyses of these processes.[3]

Several recent books on comparative federalism by R. L. Watts,[4] Carl Friedrich[5] and Ivo D. Duchacek[6] give some place to party systems, but it is only William H. Riker's *Federalism: Origin, Operation, Significance*, published in 1964,[7] which makes political parties the crucial determinant of what form federations take. Riker's political explanation of federalism is in marked contrast both to those students who proceed exclusively or almost exclusively in terms of formal-legal and institutional forms and those who emphasize popular attitudes, degrees of integration and other circumstances outside the political system. There are, he claims, two explanatory foci through which federalism may best be investigated and understood. The first is the original political bargain concluded by the leaders of political jurisdictions who come together to form a federation. Certain of these leaders, if not all, will desire union to increase the diplomatic, military and economic power of themselves and their respective communities. Under modern conditions it is often more expedient to pursue such aggrandizement through negotiation rather than force and imperial expansion.[8] However, other leaders and other political communities are less urgent about the formation of a union and a bargain between centralization and decentralization is struck through the establishment of a federation. But once the original bargain is concluded, will it subsequently be sustained in a centralized or "peripheralized" form? Riker's second explanatory factor comes into operation—the degree of centralization in the party system. Thus,

> Whatever the general social conditions, if any, that sustain the federal bargain, there is one institutional condition that controls the nature of the bargain in all the instances here examined and in all others with which I am familiar. This is the structure of the party system, which may be regarded as the main variable intervening between the background social conditions and the specific nature of the federal bargain.[9]

Riker's political explanation of federalism can be summarized briefly: federations are centralized to the extent that national political parties can and do impose their wills on their respective provincial/state parties. This argument is suggestive in calling attention to the neglected role of the party system in federations. But Riker nowhere presents conclusive evidence for his assertion that parties do in fact "control" the nature of the federal bargain in the eight countries, including Canada, which he examines. In the absence of such evidence it seems plausible to argue that in some if not all of Riker's eight federations important decisions determining, in the short run at least, the degree of centralization or peripheralization are made by other institutions and processes than intraparty relations—by judicial review of the constitution, by what I called in the previous chapter "executive federalism" or by legislative committees at the national level drawing members from more than one party. Riker's attribution of primacy to intraparty relations in determining the shape of federal systems remains assertion and is devoid of any analysis of the widely divergent roles that parties do play in different political systems.

Relation between Federal and Provincial Parties

It may be useful in examining relations between federal and provincial parties to proceed from alternative models of federal party systems, which will be called "integrated" and "confederal" respectively.

INTEGRATED	CONFEDERAL
1. *Electoral dependence.* National and provincial parties of the same designation draw very largely on common voter allegiances to both.	1. *Electoral dependence.* National and provincial parties have significantly different bodies of voter allegiance. Changes in electoral support

When there are shifts in voter support at one level these are characteristically accompanied by shifts in the same direction at the other level in subsequent elections.

2. *Party organization.* The same party machinery is used to select and elect candidates of both national and provincial parties. There are authoritative processes within the parties to commit both levels to party policy.

3. *Party careers.* Those who pursue party careers characteristically move between national and provincial office. The most important careers are those involving popular election.

4. *Party finance.* Donors to political parties characteristically contribute to the party as such. Intraparty procedures distribute those funds between the two levels.

5. *Ideology.* Federal and provincial parties share a common ideology. This ideology distinguishes them from other parties in the political systems of both levels.

6. *Party symmetry.* The same political parties contest elections at both levels. The major federal parties are major parties at the provincial level.

for parties characteristically arise from circumstances prevailing at one level only and are not accompanied by changes in the same direction at the other level.

2. *Party organization.* The national and provincial parties are autonomous. This autonomy prevails in respect to nomination of party candidates, electoral competition and policy direction.

3. *Party careers.* Party careerists characteristically fulfil their ambitions through serving at only one level. The most crucial of these careers involve office by popular election.

4. *Party finance.* Donors to parties characteristically contribute to one level or the other separately. The federal and provincial parties are financially independent of one another.

5. *Ideology.* Federal and provincial parties characteristically do not share distinctive ideologies. Parties at both levels adjust themselves to the ideological currents prevailing among their respective activists and electorates.

6. *Party symmetry.* Federal and provincial elections often see different parties as the major contestants. Important parties are often wholly or largely oriented to political competition at one level rather than both.

These models can be applied to the Canadian party system, with particular but not exclusive emphasis on the two major parties.

Federal-Provincial Electoral Dependence

The electoral dependence of federal and provincial parties is an extraordinarily complex phenomenon which has only recently begun to be investigated. Sophisticated and inevitably costly survey research is needed to determine, for example, the extent to which Canadian voters perceive they live in one integrated political system or in two or more relatively discrete ones.[10] It is probable from the fragmentary evidence now available that the degree of dependence varies greatly among parties, regions and smaller areas within particular provinces, and much detailed work needs to be done even in the preliminary step of isolating the relevant variables.

The institutional forms under which Canadian elections take place clearly work toward the mutual independence of federal and provincial parties. With only a very few constitutional limitations, Parliament and the provincial legislatures have unfettered discretion to determine constituency boundaries, who may vote in their respective elections, and other circumstances shaping the electoral process. Elections at the two levels take place at different times and under different administrative auspices. It does indeed seem remarkable to a Canadian student of federalism that scholars of American politics give so little attention to the contrary circumstance in which a complex of intraparty dependencies must surely arise when voters make their choices at the same time and on the same ballot for candidates for elective offices at two or more levels. Although the Republic of India has retained most of the British parliamentary forms, R. L. Watts has pointed out that "with only a few exceptions, state elections have generally been called at the same time as Union elections, and . . . in these elections the candidates for state legislatures were finally selected by the All-India Board of the [Congress] Party."[11]

Some students of Canadian politics have propounded what has come to be called the "balance theory" of federal-provincial voting behaviour. Frank Underhill stated in 1955: "By some instinctive subconscious mental process the Canadian people have apparently decided that, since freedom depends upon a balance of power, they will balance the monopolistic power of the Liberal government in Ottawa by setting up the effective countervailing power not in Ottawa but the provincial capitals."[12] The late Robert MacGregor Dawson put it this way:

> The records suggest . . . that provincial electorates show a decided tendency to fall away from the party which gains control of the Dominion Parliament. The provinces would appear to feel happier when they are able to assert their independence of the party in control of the Dominion Parliament: and this tendency steadily grows and spreads and is virtually never reversed until a party change in Ottawa gives impetus in the opposite direction.[13]

Recent research appears to have invalidated the balance theory as formulated by Underhill and Dawson. The contrary hypothesis postulates a bandwagon effect, i.e. that a party's success at one level of the federal system contributes to its chances at the other level. The bandwagon hypothesis was tested by William Reeves and Roger Gibbins of the University of Calgary in a paper, unfortunately not yet published, to the Canadian Political Science Association in 1976 with reference to federal and provincial general elections in British Columbia (1928-1975), Alberta (1905-1975), Ontario (1867-1975), Quebec (1921-1975), Nova Scotia (1867-1975), and Newfoundland (1947-1975).[14] The findings presented by Reeves and Gibbins are very complex but may be summarized as follows.

First, in examining the correlation between the results of national elections and voter behaviour in subsequent provincial elections there was a bandwagon effect in Ontario, Quebec and Newfoundland, no discernible national impact in Alberta and Nova Scotia, and weak evidence of a balance effect in British Columbia. However, when these results are controlled by reference to the prior *provincial* election, *this* rather than the previous federal election, is the most reliable indicator.

Secondly, there were significant bandwagon effects running from provincial elections to subsequent federal elections.

Reeves' and Gibbins' general conclusions were these:

> . . . when cross-level effects exist within Canada's federated electoral system, they emanate from provincial rather than national elections. Independent national effects were not to be found . . . while persistent provincial effects were readily apparent. The provincial effects, furthermore, were transmitted by both sectionally-restricted and nationally-dominant political parties . . . . The interaction suggests a confederate style of federal politics, one in which the interprovincial integration by national electoral politics is minimal, and in which the provincial molding of national electoral politics is considerable.[15]

Other evidence also gives reason for rejecting the balance hypothesis:

(1) Howard Scarrow investigated patterns of "alternating party choice" in federal and provincial elections between 1930 and 1957,[16] with such choice being defined as "an election victory for a party at one level of government surrounded by election victories for another party at the other level of government." He found that of a total of 104 elections there had been alternating choices in only 16 and concluded "when a provincial electorate has registered a preference for one party over a number of years and then changes that preference, the change is reflected in both provincial and federal election results. . . . In Canada . . . as in other federations, the normal presumption is that a voter will exhibit relatively consistent voting behaviour in both federal and provincial elections."[17]

(2) In an article published in 1970 John Wilson and David Hoffman turned their attention to explaining the continuing weakness of the Liberal party in the provincial politics of Ontario while the Liberals dominated the province in federal elections. In investigating the

prevalence of a belief in the balance theory among a sample of Ontario voters they found that 52 per cent of their respondents disagreed with the theory and only a third agreed. However,

> . . . those who voted for the Liberal party in both (1965 federal and 1967 provincial) elections were actually more inclined to agree that the same party should not control both levels of government at the same time than were the federal Liberals. Nearly two-fifths of those who supported the Liberal party in 1965 and again in 1967 claimed to be adherents of the balance theory, while only 27 per cent and 17 per cent respectively of those federal Liberals who switched to the provincial Conservatives and to the provincial NDP gave such a response to the question.[18]

Furthermore "federal supporters of the Conservatives and the New Democrats who counted as consistent supporters of the balance theory—and who might have been expected to vote again for their party at the provincial level because of their opposition to the Liberals winning in Ontario as well—were actually more inclined than the sample as a whole to switch to the Liberal party in 1967."[19] Wilson and Hoffman conclude "the theory of balance has played little part in shaping the voting behaviour of Ontario citizens in recent years."[20]

(3) Jean Havel examined the voting behaviour of a sample of Sudbury voters in the federal general election of April, 1963, and the Ontario general election of September, 1963. He concluded, "There does not appear to be in Sudbury . . . any desire to balance power in Ottawa with power in Ontario. The interviewers discovered no indication of feeling in that direction."[21]

There has been a significant amount of recent survey research on federal-provincial voting behaviour and attempts to isolate the characteristics of "switchers" and to explain why some voters vote consistently for one party at successive federal and provincial elections and others do not. In reviewing this evidence from other findings and in presenting their own results from the three federal ridings centred around Waterloo, Toivo Miljan and Bruce Macnaughton conclude: "the phenomenon of voters switching from one party at one level of jurisdiction to another party at another level of jurisdiction is to be expected, and is not an 'aberration', but is an integral part of the Canadian federal system. . . . The electorate appears to make voting decisions at the two levels without reference to the other level."[22] The results of some of this research may be summarized briefly:

(1) John C. Courtney and David E. Smith investigated the voting behaviour in Saskatoon at a provincial general election in 1964 and a federal by-election two months later.[23] This constituency was an interesting one because it had a previous record of electing provincial

CCF-NDP and federal Conservative candidates and this record held in the 1964 elections. Of the 1075 voters in the sample 875 (81.4 per cent) voted for the same party both provincially and federally while 200 (18.6 per cent) supported different parties. The allocation of support of these 200 voters was as follows:

Party supported in federal by-election

Party supported in provincial election	CCF-NDP	Lib.	PC	Total
CCF-NDP	—	26	94	120
Lib.	—	—	58	58
PC	2	20	—	22
Total	2	46	152	200[24]

Courtney and Smith examined some of the characteristics of those who split their vote. Women split their vote to a greater extent than men. Voting articulation increased with age, except that splitting was highest in the 65-and-over age group. The occupational groups which split most frequently were the professional, sales and clerical groups and least frequently the service, transportation and managerial groups. Vote splitting increased with length of residence in the constituency.

(2) George Perlin and Patti Peppin undertook pilot surveys just before the Ontario provincial election of 1967 in the federal constituencies of Eglinton and Wellington South.[25] The first constituency had elected a Liberal in the federal general election of 1965 and a Conservative in the provincial election of 1963, while Wellington South had chosen a Conservative in 1965 and a Liberal in 1963. The results of the survey were as follows:

PERCENTAGES OF PARTY VOTE IN THE FIRST ELECTION OF EACH SET REMAINING CONSTANT AND CHANGING TO ANOTHER PARTY IN THE SECOND ELECTION

	Provincial-federal 1963-1965		Federal-provincial 1965-1967*		Provincial-Provincial 1963-1967*	
	%	N	%	N	%	N
Percentage remaining constant						
PC	54.1	46	66.3	55	77.6	66
Liberal	60.2	56	44.9	48	66.7	62
NDP	75.0	12	50.0	14	81.3	13
Percentage changing to another party						
PC	42.3	36	25.3	21	13.0	11

| Liberal | 34.4 | 32 | 41.1 | 44 | 22.6 | 21 |
| NDP | 25.0 | 4 | 39.3 | 11 | 18.8 | 3 |

* The calculation of 1967 preferences is based upon vote intentions rather than actual votes.[26]

Interestingly, Perlin and Peppin found that the usual demographic classifications (sex, age, income, education, occupation and religion) had no statistically significant relation to vote-switching. There were also suggestive results about the differing perceptions of federal and provincial politics:

> Among the more interesting findings . . . is the significantly greater influence attached by changers to leadership affect in federal politics. Personality generally seems to have been rather more important than we might have assumed since the (local) candidate is maintained at the federal level by more than 60 per cent of the changers and at the provincial level by as many as 47 per cent. Another comparison of interest is the greater frequency with which general past record is mentioned at the provincial level. It might be inferred from this that provincial politics is perceived more frequently in terms of generalized images, while in federal politics leader, candidate, policy and party are more frequently treated as independent objects.[27]

(3) Jean Laponce in his 1965 survey of the federal constituency of Vancouver-Burrard caught the provincial election of October 1963 between a series of federal elections in 1962, 1963 and 1965.[28] Between the federal and provincial elections of 1963, 49 per cent of the respondents "migrated" between one party and another, while between the two federal elections of 1962 and 1963 only 29 per cent changed parties. Of these migrants in the provincial election 93 per cent transferred to Social Credit; the NDP lost 8 per cent of its 1963 federal supporters to Social Credit and the Liberals and Conservatives 55 per cent and 62 per cent respectively. In the ensuing 1965 federal election the NDP recovered all its migrants; the Liberal and Conservative recovery rates were 60 and 71 per cent respectively. The federal-provincial switchers did not have significantly different demographic characteristics than the rest of the voting population. Laponce gives ideology a significant effect and he asserts: "The more ideological an electorate, the greater is the degree of perception of the boundaries around it and the less likely is the electorate to change in behaviour when moved from one political system to the other."[29] Thus the NDP neither gains nor loses significantly from federal-provincial migrations, while the Liberals, and to an even greater extent the Conservatives, are vulnerable to defections of their federal supporters to Social Credit in provincial elections in British Columbia.

(4) In the Wilson-Hoffman article to which reference has been made, the authors set out to explain the relative weakness of the Liberal party in recent Ontario politics, a weakness particularly striking because of the Liberal dominance of the province in federal elections. As we have seen, the balance theory was rejected. Aggregate results for the province indicate a close correlation between Liberal weakness and strength in provincial and federal elections respectively and voter-abstention at the provincial level. However, there are important regional variations. Liberal declines from federal to provincial elections accompanied by a corresponding increase in abstentions is most marked in the larger cities and the urbanized areas of the province from the Toronto-Hamilton areas to the Niagara Peninsula. In a number of rural constituencies of traditional Liberal strength the party's vote holds relatively consistent in both federal and provincial elections. All Ontario parties lose some of their federal supporters because of abstentions in provincial elections, but the Liberals lose more than others; in 1967 the provincial Liberals retained only 49 per cent of their 1965 federal supporters in Toronto and Hamilton. Throughout the province high-status federal Liberals were more prone than other voters to switch to the Conservatives in provincial elections, lower-status Liberals to abstain. Again there were regional variations, with this tendency most marked in the southern area of the province and particularly in Metropolitan Toronto.

(5) In their survey of the federal riding of Waterloo-Cambridge, Miljan and Macnaughton tested the demographic characteristics of switchers between the 1971 Ontario and 1972 federal elections in terms of sex, age, occupation, religion, length of residency, education, income, home ownership, union membership, ethnicity and subjective class.[30] "It was found that only the length of residency and the religion variables showed any statistically significant relationships at all between the non-switchers and the switchers." The religion variable was most consistent and showed that Presbyterian, United Church and "Other Protestant" had the greatest propensity to switch, while Roman Catholics, Anglicans and Lutherans tended toward party consistency. In terms of residence, those who had lived in the constituency between 11 and 15 years had the greatest tendency to switch, those with less than 3 years residency to vote for the same party.

(6) Although the investigation involved consistency of voting in the 1965 and 1968 federal elections, Lynn Macdonald's results are suggestive for federal-provincial voting behaviour. It was found that "switchers tend to move to a party more consistent with their social class, religion and ethnic group membership than their old party was."[31]

We still know very little about federal-provincial voting behaviour. The balance theory seems not to apply to recent circumstances. Laponce's finding in Vancouver-Burrard that ideological cleavages between parties discourages voter migration is probably true of other areas, although the very weak support for the New Democratic Party in provinces with NDP governments in the federal general election of 1974 might cause some qualifications of this. It is significant that on the basis of the Laponce, Perlin-Peppin and Miljan-Macnaughton studies, switchers appear not to differ from non-switchers on the basis of the usual demographic categories of age, sex, income, education and occupation. Much more evidence would be needed to demonstrate this conclusively, but it is plausible that voters make their decisions without reference to the other level of government although one might suppose, in the absence of empirical evidence, that this is less true of the Atlantic provinces where the parties are more highly integrated on federal-provincial lines than elsewhere in Canada. The Wilson-Hoffman analysis of federal-provincial voting in Ontario shows significant differences in behaviour among voters in particular regions and areas of the province. Such research as this should discourage easy generalizations about this kind of behaviour on a Canada-wide basis.

Despite our ignorance of the complexities of federal-provincial voting behaviour, we do at least know the outer limits of electoral dependence by the circumstance that parties at one level have been able to dominate particular provinces for long periods of time while remaining relatively weak at the other level or even absent from that level altogether. The provincial Conservatives have dominated Ontario for more than a generation while, in most federal elections, the Liberals won a majority of Ontario seats. In the Duplessis period the Quebec electorate sustained the Union Nationale *and* the federal Liberals. From 1958 onward the federal Conservatives were dominant in Saskatchewan but it was not until the mid-1970s that their provincial counterparts became a significant electoral force. The provincial strength of the CCF/NDP and of Social Credit in the western provinces has on many occasions not been carried over into national politics. Thus, apart perhaps from the Atlantic provinces where the classic two-party system has been sustained, any federal or provincial party with serious hopes of electoral success must gain the support of voters who either support other parties or abstain from voting in elections at the other level.

Party Organization

Apart from the investigation of party finance and national leadership conventions, there has been little published research on the extra-parliamentary organization of Canadian political parties. Walter D.

Young's study of the CCF between 1932 and 1961 is valuable[32] in this connection, as is David Smith's book-length analysis of the Saskatchewan Liberals between 1905 and 1975.[33] However it was not until Reginald Whitaker's monumental *The Government Party: Organizing and Financing the Liberal Party of Canada 1930-1958* appeared in 1974[34] that we had a major study of the extra-parliamentary organization of a major national party and one which emphasized the federal-provincial dimension of this organization. There is a crying need for studies of federal and provincial extra-parliamentary parties and the relations between the federal and provincial wings of the same parties in the past 20 years or so.

At the local level, many questions remain to be answered. Do the same party activists participate in both federal and provincial party activity? Or, alternatively, are large numbers oriented exclusively or almost exclusively toward one level or the other? Despite the increasing tendency towards separation of federal and provincial party organizations, the three major parties continue to promote the idea that federal and provincial wings are elements of the same team. To what extent is this mythology? One might suppose, in the absence of much evidence, that where parties are strong federally and weak provincially, or vice versa, there are tendencies encouraging activists to participate at only one level rather than both. But is this the case?

In a study presented in 1970, Henry Jacek, John McDonough, Ronald Shimuzu and Patrick Smith examined the federal-provincial activity of 180 party officials in three Hamilton constituencies.[35]

High Activity	Liberal	PC	NDP	Total
Provincial only	0	8	2	10
Provincially and federally	36	30	38	104
Federally only	30	16	2	48
At neither level	11	4	3	18
Total	77	58	45	180

This study indicated a very great variation among the parties in respect to integration on federal-provincial lines. The Liberal party was least integrated because the inducements to membership and activity are based largely on federal patronage, and the NDP most integrated because of common ideological and policy commitments. The Conservatives were between the two in degree of integration, with rather highly personalized patterns of allegiances among upper-status persons.

At the national level there has been an ongoing confederalization of the political parties, a tendency in the direction of the organizational separation of parties oriented to federal electoral success from provincial parties of the same nomenclature. Several factors appear to have been at work:

(1) Party Finance. Perhaps most crucially for party organization perhaps, federal and provincial wings of the same party have developed independent sources of party funds and there has been increasing public control over the raising and expenditure of such funds. These factors will be discussed later in the chapter.

(2) Increasing Conflict between Federal and Provincial Governments. The increasing conflict about matters of fundamental policy between the federal and provincial governments, and even between federal and provincial parties not in government, frustrates organizational integration between parties at the two levels. To take the extreme case, the organizational separation of the federal and Quebec wings of the Liberal party was effected in 1964 when the Lesage government was waging a vigorous fight for provincial autonomy against the Pearson administration in Ottawa. At a less fundamental level, there were conflicts in the mid-1970s between the national and Saskatchewan wings of the NDP about resource development policy. In some circumstances, certainly, the purely partisan interests of a party at one level, particularly if it is in power, adheres more closely to policy imperatives than to the electoral fortunes of its partisan counterpart at the other level.

(3) Different circumstances of electoral competition. Federal and provincial parties compete in different electoral arenas and these differing circumstances can and do frustrate their integration and cooperation. David Smith describes one set of such circumstances in his account of the conflicts between the federal and Saskatchewan Liberals in the early 1960s.[36] The provincial party under its new and vigorous leader Ross Thatcher had a single-minded devotion towards displacing the CCF government and in this effort adopted an explicitly right-wing ideology and attempted to win the support of voters who were disposed towards the Conservatives. On the other hand, to the federal Liberals the PCs rather than the NDP was the enemy. The Pearson Liberals regarded themselves as a left-of-centre party and in their minority position in the House of Commons as a result of the 1963 and 1965 elections needed the support of NDP legislators. What I shall later describe as the asymmetry of the Canadian party system, the circumstance that the party competitors and their relative strengths in the two political arenas differs markedly within particular provinces, frustrates the integration of federal and provincial party organizations. A rather dramatic example of this occurred in 1979 when the leader of the provincial Progressive Conservatives in British Columbia openly accused the national party of failing to support him and his colleagues because of an alleged agreement with the provincial Social Credit party. One of the most crucial variables in federal-provincial party relations relates to whether one or both parties is in power, or is out of power but a serious competitor, or is not even a serious competitor. Sometimes provincial

parties which are weak attract ideologues, and sometimes those primarily interested in the fruits of federal patronage. In such cases, relations with the national party oriented towards serious electoral competition are usually difficult.

(4) Party conventions. All federal and provincial party leaders are chosen by representative party conventions and the constitutions of most
parties provide for representative conventions to consider policy and
party organization on a regular basis.[37] Evidence would indicate that
such gatherings do not provide for the control or even crucial influence
of one wing of the party by the other. In general terms, provincial leaders attain their positions without the decisive intervention of influential leaders from the federal party organization. At both federal and
provincial leadership conventions the usual way of proceeding by successive secret ballots until one candidate has a clear majority frustrates
the exercise of power by persons who might otherwise control blocs of
votes. Thus in becoming party leaders, politicians have seldom incurred debts to organizations or leaders from the other level. Conventions devoted to organizational and policy matters have not been intensively studied, but the same kind of insulation of federal and provincial
parties would seem to prevail.

The circumstances under which the premiers of provinces commit
their own prestige and organizational resources in federal elections are
highly variable. Duplessis of Quebec and Frost of Ontario made such
commitments to the Diefenbaker Conservatives in 1957 and 1958, although neither had given such support to the federal party in 1953.
Robert Stanfield of Nova Scotia supported the Conservatives in 1965
while little help was given to the national party by Duff Roblin of Manitoba or John Robarts of Ontario. The late Ross Thatcher of Saskatchewan committed little of his support or that of his party organization
to the federal Liberals when he was in power between 1964 and 1971.
Quebec Liberals from 1960 onward appear to have given little assistance to their federal counterparts, particularly since the almost complete separation of the federal and Quebec wings of the party effected
in 1964. From 1935 onward the national Social Credit movement was
to a large extent the extension of the Alberta party. On the other hand,
Premier W. A. C. Bennett of British Columbia showed only a marginal
and intermittent interest in federal Social Credit politics. Only in the
CCF-NDP has there been a close integration of federal and provincial
party organizations.

The support of provincial party organizations is undoubtedly of assistance to federal politicians but, as the results of the 1968 general
elections demonstrate, it is by no means decisive. More perhaps than in
elections of the two decades before, the provincial Conservative and
Liberal parties throughout Canada were mobilized behind their federal

counterparts. The Conservatives had healed some of the internecine quarrels of the Diefenbaker years and the Liberals were riding on the wave of Trudeaumania. However, each of the two major national parties did well in those provinces where it was out of office provincially, with the exception of Nova Scotia. The Union Nationale and Ontario Conservatives supported the federal Conservatives, but the latter party received 21.3 per cent and 32.0 per cent of the popular vote respectively in these two provinces. On the other hand, with Liberal governments in power in Newfoundland, New Brunswick and Prince Edward Island, the federal Conservatives won 52.8 per cent, 49.7 per cent and 51.8 per cent of the popular vote compared with 31.4 per cent nationally. As for the Liberals, their proportion of the popular vote in provinces with Liberal administrations was 42.8 per cent in Newfoundland, 44.4 per cent in New Brunswick, 44.9 per cent in Prince Edward Island, and 27.1 per cent in Saskatchewan, compared with 45.5 per cent nationally. Only in Nova Scotia, where the Conservative proportion of the vote was the highest in the country (55.2 per cent) was a provincial party able to "deliver," and this result was no doubt due largely to the continuing personal popularity of the Conservative leader and former Nova Scotia Premier, Robert Stanfield. In fact, the relatively poor showing of the Liberals in Saskatchewan and Newfoundland—and perhaps that of the Conservatives in Manitoba—may be attributed to the decreasing popularity of provincial governments of those parties.

The confederalization of federal and provincial party organizations has been much more profound in respect to the Liberals than to the other two national parties, and the circumstances as they have arisen from the results of the 1979 federal election may result in changes in this dimension of Canadian federalism. The circumstance that the Liberals are not in power in any jurisdiction might result in some retreat from organizational autonomy in some provinces and the closer integration of federal and provincial Liberals. Both the attack of Prime Minister Trudeau on the provincial governments in the 1979 election campaign and the circumstance that the Conservative party which replaced his government is in power in seven of the provinces might also lead to increasing integration among the Progressive Conservatives in federal-provincial lines.

Something needs to be said about the partisan-political role of the cabinet. National extra-parliamentary associations of the two major parties were slow to develop in Canada and in each case the impetus towards the development of such organizations came when the party was in opposition. In office, cabinet ministers assumed the main responsibilities for party organization, including liaison with the provincial parties, and Whitaker has said this of the Liberal government which came to power in 1935:

The leading cabinet ministers not only held ministerial prerogatives over wide areas of appointments and issuing of contracts, but they represented the various regions of the country to the national government with the direct legitimacy of electoral support. Consequently there was never any real question that the locus of organizational responsibility would inevitably be located in the inner sanctum of the cabinet.[38]

In the Trudeau governments, the role of cabinet ministers in party organization appears to have been downgraded, particularly in the 1968-1972 period.[39] During his first term, Prime Minister Trudeau took steps to extend his range of political advice and political support well beyond that available to him from his cabinet—the establishment of regional desks in the PMO and the very great extension of the powers and resources of that office, the very influential role assumed by the Prime Minister's policy secretary Marc Lalonde, the attempts to democratize the national party and give it a more influential role in party policy, etc. There was also in the Prime Minister's Office a senior official whose sole responsibilities were giving advice on Governor-in-Council appointments and although there appear to be no published studies on how the role was performed, it is reasonable to suppose that the powers over personal patronage traditionally exercised by members of Canadian cabinets were thus curtailed. However, after the near-defeat of the Liberals in the 1972 general election there was a partial return to the earlier forms. A "political cabinet" was established consisting of parliamentarians and other party officials. Also, according to George Radwanski, the Prime Minister instituted in 1973 "a carefully structured system of regional political responsibility for his ministers, putting each minister in charge of a specified number of ridings."[40] Under this plan ministers were to visit each riding every six months, a senior member of the minister's staff was to visit non-Liberal ridings every two months, and every minister was to meet with the Liberal MP's in his area every two months. On the basis of such activities ministers were to give the Prime Minister bi-monthly reports on party organization within their respective areas, and Radwanski suggests that these requirements were strictly enforced.

The Clark government was in office too short a time for any changes in federal-provincial party relations to become evident. However, if this administration had had a longer incumbency, a higher degree of partisan integration than under the Liberals would likely have emerged because the PCs were in power in 7 provinces and because of the long experience of the Prime Minister in the extra-parliamentary activities of the party.

Aside from party organization as narrowly defined, the operations of the Ottawa cabinet are crucial to Canadian federalism. The early cabinets after Confederation were composed of persons most of whom were provincial or regional political bosses with bases of power independent of the Prime Minister. The circumstance persisted until the present generation but has now passed, and the last of the old breed of cabinet minister appears to have been James G. Gardiner who, as Minister of Agriculture, dominated Liberal politics in the prairie provinces between 1935 and 1957. The situation now is quite otherwise, although recent Prime Ministers have adhered to the older traditions of choosing their cabinets so as to "represent" the different provinces and regions of Canada. There are no published studies of the specifically political role of cabinet ministers in aggregating and articulating the interests specific to their provinces and regions, but it appears that this role has been vastly diminished.[41] Several obvious factors may be mentioned— election campaigns are increasingly contests among party leaders; the political resources of the Prime Minister's Office and the increasing politicization of the senior levels of the appointed bureaucracy have partially weakened the political influence of cabinet ministers; there appears to be some weakening of the patronage powers of members of the cabinet;[42] ministers are increasingly occupied with departmental and cabinet-committee responsibilities to the neglect of their political roles; cabinet ministers often come to office with little prior experience in politics and in some cases no doubt with a distaste for the political process. In general, the decreasing capacity of the cabinet to represent interests and aspirations which are explicitly provincial has contributed to the growing strength of the provincial governments and it is somewhat disheartening that current proposals to make the institutions of the central government more regionally representative have concentrated almost exclusively on the Supreme Court and the second chamber to the neglect of the more crucial and powerful institutions of the federal cabinet and appointed bureaucracy.

To the extent that in both federal and provincial politics the popularity of party leaders is more crucial than organization in determining levels of electoral support, the interdependence of federal and provincial politicians of the same party is weakened. Peter Regenstrief has said of national politics: "The personality orientation of Canadian parties is a functional ingredient of a political system in which social referents are weak mediators of political loyalties."[43] Certainly this appears to have been so in the Diefenbaker and Trudeau victories of 1958 and 1968, if not more generally true of the Canadian political system. Yet what leaders have at one level to assist their partisan colleagues at the other is for the most part organizational resources.

Another factor which may weaken federal-provincial electoral dependence is sometimes expressed in terms of the ripe-apple theory of governing parties, the theory that parties in power defeat themselves. According to this view every government party has a life cycle of indeterminate length. As it goes through this cycle it becomes increasingly complacent, arrogant, incapable both of sustaining its earlier basis of support and encompassing new groups in the electorate and so on. If this is in general true, a government party cannot stave off defeat by the support of its counterparts at the other level, nor is an opposition party crucially assisted in its efforts by such support.

Party Careers

According to the 1974 *Parliamentary Guide*, 35 Members of the House of Commons had contested one or more provincial elections and 12 had held seats in provincial legislatures. The party breakdown was this:

	Held provincial seats	Unsuccessfully contested provincial elections
Liberal	2	4
Progressive Conservative	5	9
New Democratic Party	5	7
Créditiste	0	3

Thus only 4.9 per cent of the 264 seats in the House of Commons were filled by former members of provincial legislatures, while 13.3 per cent were held by those who had contested provincial elections successfully or unsuccessfully. The party breakdown is interesting—38.7 per cent of the NDP Members had contested provincial elections while the corresponding percentages for the Progressive Conservatives and Liberals were 13.6 per cent and 5.9 per cent respectively.

Of the 565 members of provincial legislatures about whom the *Parliamentary Guide* gives information, only 30 or 5.3 per cent had contested federal elections, successfully or otherwise, and of these 12 or 2.1 per cent had been MPs.

In terms of recent federal-provincial relations it is significant to examine the membership of cabinets to determine the extent of the experience of their members at the other level.[44] The four cabinets noted below were those constituted in 1957, 1963, 1968 and 1979 by incoming prime ministers.

The Diefenbaker cabinet of 1957. Of the 21 ministers, 3 (Nowlan, Brooks and Churchill) had held provincial seats.

The Pearson cabinet of 1963. Of 24 ministers, 1 (Laing) had held a provincial seat.

The Trudeau cabinet of 1968. Of 28 ministers, 2 (Laing, Kierans) had held provincial seats.

The Clark cabinet of 1979. Of 30 ministers, 2 (Crosbie, Lawrence) had held provincial seats and had been senior provincial ministers. Interestingly and significantly, the new Minister of Finance, John Crosbie, had held that portfolio in the government of Newfoundland in 1972-1974.

Of the 186 provincial cabinet ministers about whom information is given in the 1974 *Parliamentary Guide*, only 5 had ever sat in the House of Commons while another 5 had unsuccessfully contested one or more federal elections. Only one of the provincial premiers—Schreyer of Manitoba—had contested a federal election.

In general, then, careers in elective office are to a large extent separated. So far as federal-provincial relations are concerned, ministers deal with one another in the absence of either personal experience or personal ambition related to the other order of government. In contrast with the recent situation, the Laurier cabinet of 13 members formed in 1896 contained no fewer than 3 former provincial premiers and was joined soon after by the most powerful figure in prairie politics, Clifford Sifton, who had formerly been Attorney-General of Manitoba. While it is very improbable that such a situation will be repeated, the present circumstance of the Progressive Conservatives being in power in Ottawa and 7 of the provinces may lead to an increasing number of elected officials having experience in both federal and provincial legislatures.

Party Finance

Long-run trends in party finance in Canada work in the direction of the mutual independence of the federal and provincial wings of the Liberal and Conservative parties. The most astute student of this subject, K. Z. Paltiel, has argued that this development has had a crucial disintegrative effect on Canadian federalism. He wrote of the older system:

> The traditional methods of financing the two old Canadian parties, the Liberals and the Conservatives, helped overcome the splintering effect of the provinces and provincial party organizations. This was accomplished through a highly centralized system of party finance. This system rested on a common basis: the centralized corporate industrial and financial structures located in Montreal and Toronto. It is common knowledge that the two old parties were largely financed from the same sources. These corporate contributors numbered in the hundreds rather than in the thousands. Under this system, provincial and even municipal elections, as well as federal elections, could be and were financed from the central party funds and sources. The traditional system of party finance had important integrative effects which helped overcome the centrifugal forces in Canadian political life. This beneficial result was made possible by the highly concentrated nature of Canadian industry and finance.[45]

In the period since the end of the Second World War the older system has been weakened. The rise of third parties has contributed to this trend. The increasing importance of natural resource development, primarily under provincial jurisdiction, has given corporate donors incentives to contribute directly to provincial parties. Paltiel described the more recent situation:

> . . . the British Columbia and Alberta wings of the federal Liberal and Conservative Parties have become largely self-supporting and contribute on occasion to the support of the Saskatchewan wing. Manitoba in the heyday of the Winnipeg Grain Exchange was self-supporting but now is a net importer of election funds. The rest of Canada, as far as the two major parties are concerned, are beneficiaries of transfer payments; they are in part political colonies except when some grass-roots movement has swept a minor party into power or a traditional party can exploit the advantages of incumbency by using office to gain funds by means fair or foul.[46]

The direct or indirect subsidy from the public purse of parties or of individual candidates for election works against the integration of federal and provincial parties by putting into the hands of parties and candidates resources quite independent of party decisions at the other level. Quebec in 1963 and Nova Scotia in 1969 enacted legislation providing for limits to the expenditure of parties and for subsidies to candidates of recognized parties. It is significant that the Quebec law was enacted at the same time that the Quebec Liberal Federation was in process of effecting an almost complete organizational separation from the federal Liberal party. A further amendment of 1974 to the Quebec legislation provides for public subsidies to the permanent organizations of recognized parties to enable each to "cover [its] current administration costs, ensure the propagation of its political program and coordinate the political action of its members."

The increasing public control of party expenditures and the subsidization of parties and candidates from public funds works against federal-provincial party integration. Such control has led to an elaborate system of record-keeping and reporting procedures whose concomitants are both formalization and the organizational disengagement in this dimension at least of federal and provincial party organizations. The direct or indirect subsidy of parties and/or candidates as prevails under federal law and, at the end of 1976, in Quebec, Ontario, Nova Scotia, and Saskatchewan gives parties at one level financial resources independent of party decisions at the other. Regulation of the source or amount of contributions to parties also frustrates federal-provincial transfers or prohibits them entirely, and the Ontario law so enacts:

> No political party, constituency association or candidate registered under the Act shall accept funds from a federal political party regis-

tered under the Election Expenses Act (Canada) except during a campaign period during which a registered party may accept from such a
federal political party an amount, not exceeding in the aggregate, $100
for each registered candidate endorsed by that registered party.

A somewhat different kind of issue related to cross-level transfers has
arisen under 1974 amendments to the federal Income Tax Act which
provide for deductions from individual income taxes of contributions
to registered parties and candidates. The position of the two major parties in the House of Commons is that funds so collected should be used
to support federal activities only, but spokesmen of the New Democratic Party, which has a stronger tradition of financial integration between the two levels, have argued that these monies should be expended on federal and provincial party activity as the parties
themselves choose.

Recent enactments providing for the recognition and regulation of
political parties thus frustrate intraparty integration on federal-provincial lines. Under federal law and the legislation of several of the provinces, the respective Chief Electoral Officers are responsible for enforcement of regulations relating to campaign finance. In Ontario there
has been established a Commission on Election Contributions and Expenses composed of a chairman appointed by the Lieutenant-Governor
in Council, the Chief Electoral Officer, a bencher of the Law Society of
Upper Canada appointed by the Lieutenant-Governor in Council, and
two representatives of each political party with at least four members in
the Legislative Assembly, if that party nominated candidates in at least
50 per cent of the electoral districts in the most recent general election.
Under Quebec legislation there is a Director-General of Party Finances
appointed for a seven-year term by the provincial prime minister under
the proviso that this choice be ratified by a two-thirds majority in the
National Assembly. To repeat, this kind of regulation of party finances—and in the case of federal parties of broadcasting—works
against the integration of federal and provincial parties.

Ideology

Party ideology would provide a basis for federal-provincial integration
of the parties if through Canada each of the parties was clearly distinguishable from the others on the basis of its ideological commitments.
However, both the national Liberal and Progressive Conservative parties are ideologically inclusive in the sense that each comprehends persons of divergent viewpoints and attempts to appeal to voters of widely
varying ideological persuasions. But even such differing ideological
dispositions as may exist between the two national parties do not

always or even usually distinguish Liberals and Conservatives in the provinces. We have seen how ideological differences complicated the relations between the federal and Saskatchewan Liberals in the 1960s. During this same period in which the Saskatchewan Liberals were almost monopolizing the right of the political spectrum in that province, the Lesage and Robichaud Liberal governments in Quebec and New Brunswick respectively were putting into operation very comprehensive programs of social and economic reform. In his study of Francophone federal and provincial Liberal activists, carried out in 1973, David Rayside found significant differences about such important matters as language rights in Quebec, a special status for Quebec, and whether or not the federal system was too highly centralized.[47] The ideological differences within the Progressive Conservative party appear not to fall along a federal-provincial axis, and with the exception of the right-wing dispositions of the Lyon Conservatives in Manitoba, most PC provincial administrations are middle-of-the-road in social and economic matters. One might thus hypothesize that the ideological divisions among Liberals are most clearly manifested in the federal and provincial wings of the party, and among the Conservatives within the national party. In general, a common and unifying ideology is not an influence towards federal-provincial integration within the major parties, and the national and provincial elements of each conform to the ideological dispositions of their respective leaders and the perceived imperatives of electoral success among their respective electorates.

The ideology shared by most members of the NDP does provide for a higher degree of integration on federal-provincial lines and this cohesion is manifested in party organization, party finance and party careers. Ideological conflict within the NDP does not characteristically occur between the federal and provincial elements of the party, despite recurring differences between the national party and its small and unstable Quebec wing and a recent situation in which the small New Brunswick party was taken over by persons on the far left of the political spectrum. However, the most dramatic ideological struggle within the NDP in recent years involved the left-wing Waffle which had a measure of support throughout Canada, although the Waffle was in effect ejected from the party by the Ontario rather than the national executive of the NDP.[48]

The constitutional division of powers between Parliament and the provinces appears to have an important impact on the influence of political ideology on federal-provincial party integration. Many, but of course by no means all, of the matters giving rise to left-right divisions are mainly or exclusively within provincial rather than federal jurisdiction—health, social security and education; collective bargaining and industrial standards for most of the labour force; and the exploitation of natural resources. In some of the provinces too, the NDP is a serious competitor for the powers of government. Thus within particular provinces there are occasional, or even permanent, ideological cleavages between the major political contenders that are more clear-cut than those in national politics.

Party Symmetry

Party symmetry is in a sense a residual category. In general, if the party system were symmetrical, with the same parties as the major competitors in all provinces, and in both federal and provincial elections, there would be important influences for integration. Conversely, asymmetry contains predispositions toward the confederal form.

At the end of 1979 the Canadian party system had many elements of asymmetry. Quebec and British Columbia were governed by administrations having no formal ties with national parties. The NDP was in power in Saskatchewan, and the official opposition in British Columbia and Manitoba. The Liberals were in power in no jurisdiction, but were the official opposition in the federal Parliament, Ontario and the four Atlantic provinces, and had no seats in the legislatures of the four western provinces. The Conservatives were in power in Ottawa, all the other provinces except Quebec, Saskatchewan and British Columbia, and the official opposition in Saskatchewan. Thus only in the four Atlantic provinces was the classic two-party system of Liberals and Conservatives sustained.

(Although it does not relate directly to this analysis, Maurice Pinard's suggestive theory of the rise of third parties in Canada may be mentioned parenthetically here for the light it sheds on party asymmetry.[49] He presents an impressive array of evidence from federal and provincial political history leading to the conclusion that where one party dominates a political system, effective opposition to that party is likely to find an oulet in a new party rather than a resurgence of strength in the weak opposition party. Thus "the indications are that whenever the opposition party (or the strongest of many opposition parties) fails to return at least a third of the votes while in opposition, it tends to be replaced by 'third parties'.")[50]

Asymmetry has direct consequences for intraparty relations, most of these consequences working in the direction of what I have called the confederal form. The existence in particular provinces of parties which are oriented exclusively or mainly to competition at one level or the other, rather than both, means either that large groups of voters switch allegiances between federal and provincial elections or that they abstain from voting, and probably encourages citizens to believe that they live in two relatively discrete political systems rather than an integrated system. Those seeking party careers will be predisposed by asymmetry toward service at one level rather than both in succession; at the extreme, an ambitious British Columbia Liberal is unlikely to be attracted to provincial politics and a Saskatchewan socialist with the goal of being a cabinet minister will perforce look toward Regina rather than Ottawa. If we assume, as is reasonable, that an important determinant of the success of a party in soliciting campaign funds is its prospects of electoral success, donors will be predisposed toward giving to one wing rather than both under conditions of asymmetry. Parties which are weak at one level sometimes evolve toward ideological sectarianism and sometimes become little more than groups of those interested more in patronage than electoral activity, to the embarrassment in both cases of the more serious politicians at the other level.

There are thus pervasive influences at work in the direction of autonomous federal and provincial party systems in Canada, i.e., toward the confederal form. However, several qualifications to this generalization should be made.

First, in the Atlantic provinces where the two-party system is sustained there is a higher degree of federal-provincial party integration than elsewhere in Canada.

Secondly, the parties differ in their degrees of integration. The Liberal party is least integrated and the circumstance of its being in power in Ottawa between 1963 and 1979 has given the Canadian party system as such an influential impulse toward confederalism. With the incumbent Clark government there may develop new forms of co-operation and integration among the national and provincial elements of the Progressive Conservative party. As we have seen, the traditions and circumstances of the NDP dispose that party in the direction of the integration of its federal and provincial wings.

Thirdly, partisan-political activity involves complexes of interpersonal relations which can and no doubt do exert important influences on interactions between federal and provincial wings and on government-to-government dealings. Of all important Canadian institutions, the two major parties are perhaps least subject to authoritative procedures regulating their internal workings. Despite the influences toward the confederal form, party leaders have important channels of access to their partisan counterparts at the other level. Again, despite the growing independence of federal and provincial party organizations, most active Liberals and Conservatives believe that they are in some general sense members of respective teams, and in most parts of the country and under most circumstances the notion is propagated that there is one party rather than semi-autonomous federal and provincial wings. Partisan activity involves hates and fears, personal allegiances and policy commitments, and in many circumstances these personal factors are important in the working of the federal system.

Despite these qualifications, the two major parties have increasingly manifested confederal forms. In doing so, these parties have almost ceased to be instruments of federal-provincial integration where the authoritative resolution of federal-provincial conflicts has become increasingly crucial for the stability if not the survival of Canadian federalism.

Elections and Federal-Provincial Conflict

If intraparty relations have a diminishing integrative capacity in the Canadian political system, it is conceivable that popular elections could be effective instruments to resolve disputes between the national government and dominant influences in particular provinces or regions. Perhaps the best available way to investigate this matter is to examine briefly four sets of elections in recent Canadian political history where federal-provincial relations have been of great salience.

(1) *Alberta, 1935.* In the Alberta provincial election of August 1935, the Social Credit party under William Aberhart came to power with 54.2 per cent of the popular vote. The party was elected on a platform of monetary reform which challenged some of the most crucial elements of national economic policies. Six weeks later in the federal general election the Alberta voters gave Social Credit 46.2 per cent of the vote and all but two of the province's 17 seats in the House of Commons, while on a country-wide basis the Liberals came to power with 44.8 per cent of the popular vote and 173 of 245 seats in the Commons. In the subsequent period the federal government was willing and able to obstruct Alberta's policies for monetary reform on a provincial basis.

(2) *Quebec 1939, 1940.* Premier Maurice Duplessis of Quebec unexpectedly called an election for October, 1939, with the alleged justification that Ottawa was illegitimately using the wartime emergency to encroach on provincial powers. Prime Minister King and Liberal cabinet ministers from Quebec took this challenge with the utmost seriousness. Two such ministers—Charles G. Power and Lucien Cardin—assumed direction of the provincial campaign, including raising funds from outside and inside the province and participating in the selection of local candidates. The four Liberal ministers from Quebec campaigned actively in the province and threatened to resign if the Union Nationale was sustained. The result was a decisive Liberal victory, with 53.5 per cent of the popular vote and 69 of the 86 seats in the Legislative Assembly. In the federal election of March 1940 the Liberals received 63.3 per cent of the Quebec popular vote and all but four of the province's 65 seats in the House of Commons.

(3) *Ontario 1940, 1943.* On January 18, 1940, Liberal Premier Hepburn of Ontario and George Drew, the leader of the Conservative Opposition in the province, jointly sponsored a resolution in the Provincial Parliament condemning the federal King government for not prosecuting the war effectively. The Prime Minister of Canada responded by requesting a dissolution of Parliament on January 25 and an election was held on March 29. Hepburn had in the recent past collaborated with both the Quebec Union Nationale and the federal and provincial Conservatives in attempting to displace Mackenzie King. In the 1940 election the federal Liberals increased their share of the popular vote in Ontario to 50.8 per cent from 42.4 per cent in 1935 and of seats from 56 to 57. Hepburn resigned as Premier in October 1942 and in August of the next year the Ontario Liberals sustained a disastrous defeat in the Ontario election, emerging with only 14 seats as against 38 for the Conservatives and 34 for the CCF.

(4) *Quebec 1968, 1970.* In the federal general election of June, 1968, Prime Minister Trudeau and the Liberal party campaigned in Quebec and throughout Canada on Trudeau's view of Canadian federalism. The party was sustained in Quebec with 53.6 per cent of the popular vote and 56 of 74 seats in the House of Commons. In the provincial general election of April, 1970 the Liberal party was returned to power in Quebec with 45 per cent of the popular vote and 72 of 108 seats in the National Assembly. The party had campaigned on a federalist platform.

There is an inevitable arbitrariness in interpreting the situations outlined above. In the Alberta and Ontario cases the results were relatively unequivocal. After the federal election of 1935 Ottawa was willing and able to frustrate Alberta's plans for monetary reform and so a national majority imposed its will on a provincial majority. The 1940 national election sustained the wartime policies of Prime Minister Mackenzie King against the challenge posed by Ontario—as well as Quebec—and the subsequent provincial election resulted in the defeat of the Ontario Liberals. The Quebec results of 1939 and 1940 installed in office in the province a government under heavy political obligations to the federal Liberal leadership, and rallied a provincial majority around that leadership and its policies. However, the Union Nationale was returned to power on a nationalist platform in 1944 and for at least 15 years afterward the provincial Liberals were seriously embarrassed by accusations that they were subservient to Ottawa.

If general elections were to be a method of resolving federal-provincial conflicts two conditions would have to be met:

First, some crucial aspect of federal-provincial contention would be so central to electoral competition that the voting results could reasonably be interpreted as a mandate for one side or the other in such contention.

Secondly, in particular provinces the electorate would be consistent in giving its majority support in successive federal and provincial elections to parties whose policies in federal-provincial relations were not inconsistent.

These two conditions are not often fulfilled.

Most general elections at both levels of government centre on personalities and policies not directly connected with federal-provincial relations. The four circumstances described above were atypical.

However, even when federal-provincial relations are highly salient in federal or provincial elections voters often give their support to parties with quite inconsistent policies and objectives. Quebec voters returned the Duplessis nationalists in the provincial elections of 1944, 1948, 1952 and 1956 but gave overwhelming support to the federal Liberals, who were more centralist than any party in peacetime Canadian history, in the elections of 1945, 1949, 1953 and 1957. During this period the Quebec electorate gave little effective support to the federal Conservatives, who were significantly more solicitous of provincial rights. Similarly, in every British Columbia election between 1952 and 1972, W. A. C. Bennett campaigned against federal power and other allegedly alien influences but the same electorate who responded to him gave majority support to other federal parties. Provincial autonomy is to a greater or lesser degree the electoral stock-in-trade of most provincial politicians seeking office. However, the electoral success of the most autonomist of these leaders has often little or nothing to do with resolving federal-provincial disputes in their favour.

The Canadian general election of May 22, 1979 was very interesting in terms of federal-provincial conflict because more than in any previous election the two parties espoused different views of federalism. The dominant theme of Prime Minister Trudeau's campaign was that of a strong central government along with the charge that the Progressive Conservative leader was a "puppet" of the provincial premiers. The Opposition leader had supported a somewhat more decentralized version of federalism and in 1977 he and the premiers of the provinces with Conservative governments had issued a statement giving in general terms a common view of the federal system along these lines. Because these conflicting views were joined in the campaign, it is reasonable to interpret the Conservative victory as a mandate for changes in Canadian federalism according to the broad imperatives espoused by that party. However, there is still a glaring inconsistency in the behaviour of provincial electorates, specifically that of Quebec, which demonstrates the weakness of general elections in resolving federal-provincial conflict. The same Quebec electorate which in 1976 had returned a Parti Québécois administration to power had in 1979 given overwhelming support to a party committed to strong central government.

The Party System and Executive Federalism

As we saw earlier in the chapter, Riker's attribution of the decisive role to political parties in federalism makes no analysis of the roles that parties actually perform in these political systems. In Canada as in other western democracies, parties appear to be of diminishing importance in the aggregation and articulation of citizen interests and the conversion of these into public policy.[51] This function of aggregation and articulation is increasingly performed by other institutions—by the departmental civil service, by pressure groups, by appointed advisory bodies, by quasi-independent boards, task forces, and royal commissions, etc. General elections have become increasingly personality contests among contending political leaders and the parties the instruments for the waging of such leadership-dominated campaigns. Thus the policy role of the parties is a relatively restricted one. Executive federalism itself has contributed to the decline as many of the more important decisions are arrived at through processes of federal-provincial interaction.

Political parties are thus of decreasing importance in the Canadian federal system. Partisan politics have relatively limited capacities for effecting the resolution of federal-provincial conflicts either through intraparty relations or general elections. We have also seen in Chapter 2 the restricted role of constitutional amendment and evolving patterns of judicial review in bringing about successive re-delineations of the powers of Ottawa and provinces as circumstances change. Thus very heavy burdens are thrown on intergovernmental relations in managing the federal system, i.e., on executive federalism.

The most obvious linkage between the partisan-political system and executive federalism is that the power of those who make the final and authoritative decisions in federal-provincial relations is legitimated by prior electoral success. Conversely, politicians in opposition at both levels are to an overwhelming degree "locked out," in Meisel's words, of effective influence in these matters. Federal-provincial relations absorb a relatively small amount of time in the debates of Parliament and the provincial legislatures, and under many circumstances these bodies have no real alternatives to ratifying decisions reached in intergovernmental negotiations. How then are electoral standings influenced by executive federalism?

Somewhat like sovereign states, Canadian provinces have fairly durable and persisting interests. Whatever administrations are in power,

Ontario is a large and wealthy province and Prince Edward Island a small and poor one. New Brunswick is inevitably more preoccupied with bilingualism than is Alberta. Every Quebec administration since 1944 has put a higher priority on autonomy than have other provinces. It is safe to predict that despite their egalitarian commitments, no NDP government of British Columbia or Ontario would press for higher equalization payments to less-favoured provinces. However, as is the case with sovereign states, these persisting interests do not prevent provincial leaders adopting different strategies in dealing with Ottawa, and ideology in some circumstances is of considerable importance in federal-provincial relations. Ideology appears, for example, to have determined the opposition of the CCF-NDP government of Saskatchewan in the early 1960s toward an inflexible formula for constitutional amendment and such opposition was ended by the displacement of that party by the Liberals in the provincial election of 1964. The personalized and erratic style of W. A. C. Bennett was of some consequence for federal-provincial relations. Premier Robarts of Ontario assumed a crucial role in attempting to reconcile conflicts between Quebec and the rest of Canada, but his successor William Davis has up to now given this activity less importance.

Provinces have thus persisting interests and provincial politicians in power have of course a persisting concern to press these interests in such a way as to be re-elected. Future electoral success at the provincial level has come to depend in large part on appropriate federal policies, particularly in respect to fiscal and energy matters. This, rather than the partisan complexion of the government in power in Ottawa, appears to be the crucial determinant of the stances of provincial leaders toward federal politics.

Provincial political parties, and most importantly those in power, have discretion in determining how much, if any, of their prestige and resources they will commit to their federal colleagues in federal elections. The outside limits of this discretion under the normal political rules are that provincial politicians will not do anything which aids the opposing parties. However, even these limits are sometimes exceeded. As we have seen, in the early part of the Second World War, Liberal Premier Hepburn of Ontario openly co-operated with the Conservatives in an attempt to oust the Liberal government of Prime Minister Mackenzie King. Just a few days before the federal general election of April, 1963, Premier Lesage delivered publicly what was widely interpreted as an ultimatum to both federal parties on future fiscal relations with the provinces; because the Liberals were expected to win the election, this statement was a considerable embarrassment to Mr. Pearson and his colleagues. In most circumstances, however, provincial parties will be more solicitous of the interests of their federal counterparts.

Within the context of federal-provincial relations as such, the partisan complexion of the governments involved is not crucial and it would indeed be unusual to see a Conference of Prime Ministers and Premiers divide on party lines. Both the permanent and occasional cleavages in this context are on axes other than partisan ones: between "have" and "have-not" provinces; between governments which put an urgent priority on bilingual and bicultural matters and those which do not; between Quebec and the other jurisdictions; between the heartland of Ontario and Quebec and the peripheral provinces. In recent years Ottawa's policies toward the provinces—most crucially in respect to fiscal matters and to regional economic development—have come to be based on rationalized criteria which do not take into account the partisan complexion of provincial governments. For example, in 1969 the Conservatives were displaced by the Liberals in Nova Scotia and in 1970 the Liberals by the Conservatives in New Brunswick, but it is improbable that in its dealings with Ottawa the position of either province was changed significantly. In broad terms, neither provincial electorates nor provincial parties can expect to enhance their influence to any marked degree by having governments of the same partisan complexion in power in the provincial capital as in Ottawa. From the federal point of view, whatever parties are in power provincially will press provincial interests. So far as policy matters are concerned, provincial administrators are not notably more or less compliant because of their partisan complexion, and federal politicians have no urgent interest in ensuring that their colleagues are in power provincially. This latter generalization must, however, be qualified in the case of Quebec, where there is a polarization of the provincial party system on federalist-separatist lines. The polarization of Quebec politics on the continuance of Confederation means almost inevitably that federal leaders will be oriented differently towards this political arena than toward others where the choices facing provincial electorates are less crucial. Cultural duality is the subject of Chapter 7.

Interest Groups and Canadian Federalism

Interest groups are of crucial importance in the political processes of Canada and other western nations. To the extent that such groups are successful in influencing public policy they must accommodate themselves to the structures by which power is organized within the political system. Yet it is almost inevitable that these influences will be to a greater or lesser degree reciprocal, and that governmental institutions will be shaped by, as well as shape, the structures and activities of interest groups. The essays in a recent collection *Pressure Group Behaviour in Canadian Politics*,[52] enhance our understanding of these relations:

—Helen Jones Dawson has discussed the profound impact of Canadian federalism among those interest groups concerned with matters where jurisdiction is divided among the federal and provincial governments (agriculture, labour, fisheries) or where jurisdictional lines are not clear (consumer protection, control of the environment).[53] Most of these organizations have federal structures in which the provincial federations dominate national headquarters; in fact many of these as described by Dawson appear to be in the strict sense of the terms confederal rather than federal, with individual members being able to participate nationally only through the provincial associations, national executives consisting of *ex officio* and other members of the provincial groups and the national associations being totally dependent for funds on the provincial bodies. In many cases the provincial groups tailor their policies to the provincial administrations and thus handicap themselves and their national headquarters in articulating national policies. Provincial associations are characteristically jealous of their national headquarters and resist locating these headquarters in Ottawa where they could be most effective or providing them with enough resources to develop professional expertise. Dawson concludes: "few national pressure groups have broken out of the vicious circle involving financing, membership and effectiveness, and as a result they are unable to offer services to their clientele which would demonstrate their effectiveness. It seems as if the centrifugal forces of federalism may have been more important to Canadian [pressure] groups than to similar American ones. . . ."

—in his essay "The Mining Industry and the Great Tax Reform Debate" M. W. Bucovetsky presents an intriguing case study of federalism and government—industry relations.[54] Historically, federal income tax legislation has been extraordinarily generous to the extractive industries. In its Report published in 1967 the Royal Commission on Taxation recommended that some of the most important of these privileges be eliminated within the framework of the Commission's proposals for a more rationalized and coherent system of federal taxation. Yet by the time tax reform was embodied in law in 1971 the mining industry had been able to retain most of the elements of its preferred position. The provincial governments were the most effective opponents of the Carter Commission's proposals as later modified in the federal White Paper on Taxation of August 1970. Bucovetsky explains the "potency" of the extractive industries in defending their tax privileges in terms of their "geographic localization." Thus:

> The mining and petroleum industries can bring intense political pressure to bear because mining shapes so many regionally distinct communities. Where mining exists, it tends to dominate. At the same time, the federal character of the constitution, the national diffusion of the

industry, and its common viewpoint on federal tax policy increase the number of political pressure points on which local influences can be brought to bear"[55]

It is argued that the major consequence of tax reform was to confirm the extractive industries more strongly than before as "the clients of the provinces." Subsequent to Bucovetsky's essay the vulnerability of these industries to the provincial governments has been manifested by radically higher provincial levies on these industries.

—David Kwavnick formulates and tests two significant hypotheses about the relationship between Canadian federalism and interest groups.[56] "First, it is hypothesized that the distribution of power between the central and regional governments influences the structure, cohesion and even the existence of interest groups; that is, that the strength and cohesion of interest groups will tend to mirror the strength, in their particular area of concern, of the government to which they enjoy access".[57] The validity of this proposition is confirmed by the history of the movements of university students in Canada during the 1950s and 1960s. The establishment of direct federal grants to universities in 1951 and the Canada Student Loan Plan of 1964 created the basis for a strong national movement of university students. However, Ottawa's 1966 action in withdrawing from direct support of the universities was crucial in the subsequent disintegration of the Canadian Union of Students. Prior to this event, the major French-language universities had withdrawn from the CUS and the strength and aggressiveness of the Union Générale des Étudiants du Québec resulted largely from the purposeful policies of the Quebec government in respect to higher education and the determination of the province to oust Ottawa from direct influence in these matters. Second,

> It may be hypothesized that if the federal distribution of powers does have consequences for the strength and cohesion of the interest groups enjoying access to the different levels of government, these groups may attempt to influence the distribution of powers between those governments. That is, the struggle for status, recognition and power between a national organization and a provincial organization may cause the leaders of these organizations to attempt to influence the distribution of powers between the federal and provincial governments.[58]

Kwavnick shows the workings of these influences in the relations between the Canadian Labour Congress and the Quebec-based Confederation of National Trade Unions. The main thrust of CLC policy has been to strengthen the power of the central government, that of the CNTU to strengthen the powers of the Quebec authorities, and these conflicting policies have reflected the access of the two labour groups to the two levels of government.[59]

The importance of interest groups in sustaining the federal system should not be underestimated. John Meisel has pointed out that in Canada and other western nations interest groups and other private organizations have come to perform many of the functions in interest-articulation and interest-aggregation formerly performed by political parties.[60] Peter Aucoin argues that recent changes in the policy process described in Chapter 4 as administrative rationalization have the effect of bringing about "a more public role for pressure groups" in which, more than in the past, these groups must extend their activities from private contacts with departments to central agencies like the Prime Minister's Office and Treasury Board, formulate their demands in the context of competing demands and government priorities, and engage in public discussion.[61] As the scope of public activity expands, more and more matters formerly of private concern are brought within the sphere of public decision and new groups are formed to promote and defend such interests, some of these financed largely or wholly by government itself. Yet because most of these interest groups have a greater or lesser amount of business to do with both levels of government, their structures and processes will inevitably be federal if action in influencing public policies is to be effective. Thus the boundaries of province and nation are crucial in delineating the territorial areas of action not only of governmental institutions but of private groups as well.

The relation between the activities of interest groups and the processes of executive federalism is a complex one. In his study *Federal-Provincial Diplomacy*, Richard Simeon argued that these processes tended to weaken the power of interest groups.[62] Several reasons were given for this conclusion. When a matter becomes a focus for federal-provincial negotiation, governments are motivated to regard other jurisdictions rather than interest groups as the most important actors. Governments have broader objectives than those of interest groups and under certain circumstances are willing to sacrifice the concerns of the latter to these objectives. Less than in some of the other western democracies are there formalized procedures in Canada for involving the representatives of interest groups in the making of public policy.

Simeon's general conclusions about the relation between interest group activity and executive federalism were reinforced by a study by Glyn R. Berry of the events leading up to the adoption of a national petroleum policy by the Trudeau government in late 1973.[63] Berry's analysis was that prior to the energy crisis governments in Canada had been "benevolently responsive" to the oil industry. However, once governments began to deal with energy as a matter of urgency and in terms of fundamental policy considerations "the industry seemed helpless to prevent measures that, only a year before, the government itself would have rejected as radical and unnecessary." Thus the petroleum corporations were so to speak frozen out of the policy process as governments began to respond to one another almost exclusively.

Richard Schultz's study of federal-provincial relations in respect to that part of the *National Transportation Act* of 1967 which provided for federal regulation over interprovincial trucking challenged Simeon's general conclusion about the impact of executive federalism on the activities of interest groups.[64] Schultz's criticism was that Simeon assumed a one-dimensional relation between interest groups and government in which demands flowed from group to government. This was not so in the circumstances of Schultz's case study where there developed a complex pattern of competition between the federal and provincial governments for the support of the major interest group involved, the Canadian Trucking Association, and the consequent influence of governments in the C.T.A. Schultz was also critical of Simeon's "governments-as-single-actors" model and described a very intricate pattern of unresolved relations *within* the federal government in which the political actors sought the support of forces outside government and in the provincial administrations.

In the state of our present knowledge we should be extremely cautious about making general statements about the relation between interest group activity and the processes of executive federalism. Some patterns of federal-provincial interaction, such as those related to the equalization of provincial revenues, appear to involve governments almost exclusively. In other circumstances, for example those analyzed by Schultz, interest groups are much more influential. And in yet other situations, such as those described by Berry, the relative influence of interest groups and intergovernmental negotiations in determining outcomes may change quickly and dramatically.[65] There are some impulses within governments to associate representatives of the major elements of the private sector in the making of economic policy in a more formal and institutionalized way, impulses towards what John Meisel has called "incipient corporatism."[66]

We also know all too little about how the attitudes and behaviour of individual Canadians influence the operations of the political institutions which govern them.[67] So far as the challenge to the federal system posed by Quebec nationalism is concerned, the recent findings of Michael Ornstein, Michael Stevenson and Paul Williams are that "To the extent that the contours of public opinion towards Quebec in English Canada can be said to be coherent, those contours do not correspond to the party divisions around which Canadian electoral politics are organized."[68] Thus it is suggested "The divisions among the supporters of each party are likely to be mirrored in divisions among the political elites within each party. This conflict makes it difficult to see how the political parties can serve to organize debate about Quebec in English Canada."[69] Also "The lack of coherent organization of these opinions [about Quebec in English Canada] will make it more difficult for political leaders to relate their opinion positions to public opinion.

It might also be seen as giving them considerable latitude for bargaining." This general conclusion is reached about the importance of elites and intra-elite relations. "In the absence of any consensus among their constituents, these debates within and among elites are likely to play the most important role in influencing political decisions."[71]

Notes

1. K. C. Wheare, *Federal Government*, London: Oxford University Press, Editions of 1946, 1951, 1953, 1963.
2. W. S. Livingston, *Federalism and Constitutional Change*, Toronto: Oxford University Press, 1956, Chapter 1, "The Character of Federalism"; and W. S. Livingston, "A Note on the Nature of Federalism," *Political Science Quarterly* LXVII, No. 1, March, 1952, pp. 81-95.
3. The most influential of the integration theorists is Karl Deutsch. See Karl Deutsch, *Nationalism and Social Communications*, New York: John Wiley & Sons, 1953; Karl Deutsch and William J. Foltz, eds., *Nation Building*, New York: Atherton Press, 1966; and Karl Deutsch, *The Nerves of Government*, New York: The Free Press, 1963.
4. R. L. Watts, *New Federations: Experiments in the Commonwealth*, Toronto: Oxford University Press, 1966.
5. Carl Friedrich, *Trends of Federalism in Theory and Practice*, New York: Praeger, 1968, particularly Chapter 5, "Federalism and Party System."
6. Ivo D. Duchacek, *Comparative Federalism: The Territorial Dimension of Politics*, New York: Holt, Rinehart and Winston, 1969, pp. 329-341. As well as the book-length treatments of federalism by Watts, Duchacek and Friedrich, the book of readings, Aaron Wildavsky, ed., *American Federalism in Perspective*, Boston: Little, Brown, 1967, has a long excerpt from Riker's book and, of the other twelve articles, four are devoted to federalism and the party systems of the United States, Canada and Australia.
7. William M. Riker, *Federalism: Origin, Operation, Significance*, Boston: Little, Brown, 1964, particularly Part I, "A Theory of Federalism," and pp. 135-136.
8. Riker, like C. J. Friedrich, seems to me to make an unduly clear-cut distinction between federalism and imperialism. See the latter's treatment in C. J. Friedrich, *Man and His Government*, New York: McGraw-Hill, 1963, Chapter 31, "Empire: Coercive World Order," and Chapter 32, "Federalism: Consensual World Order." However, in the Canadian case a major impetus to the original federal bargain was the prospect of a vast hinterland to be peopled, developed and exploited from the Canadian heartland of Ontario and Quebec. On the Canadian prairies during the 1930s we were sometimes told that the region was in the most humiliating of all possible circumstances as "a colony of a colony."
9. Riker, *op. cit.*, p. 136.
10. In a study of political perceptions, attitudes and behaviour in Vancouver, Burrard Jean Laponce asserted that the electors operate within three political systems—federal, provincial and American. He found "the greater

one's involvement with Canadian politics, the greater is the intellectual involvement with American affairs." Jean Laponce, *People vs. Politics,* Toronto: University of Toronto Press, 1969, p. 165.

11. R. L. Watts, *New Federations: Experiments in the Commonwealth,* Toronto: Oxford University Press, 1966, p. 338.

12. Frank Underhill, "Canadian Liberal Democracy in 1955," *Press and Party in Canada,* G. V. Ferguson and Frank Underhill, Toronto: Ryerson Press, 1955, pp. 39-40.

13. Robert MacGregor Dawson, *The Government of Canada,* Toronto: University of Toronto Press, 1946, p. 575.

14. William Reeves and Roger Gibbins, "The Balance Theory: An Empirical Look at the Interdependency of Federal-Provincial Electoral Behaviour," *mimeo.*

15. Ibid., p. 23.

16. Howard Scarrow, "Federal-provincial Voting Patterns in Canada," in John C. Courtney, ed., *Voting in Canada,* Toronto: Prentice-Hall of Canada, 1967, pp. 82-89.

17. Ibid., p. 84.

18. John Wilson and David Hoffman, "The Liberal Party in Contemporary Ontario Politics," *Canadian Journal of Political Science* III, No. 2., June 1970, p. 198. By permission of the authors and the Canadian Political Science Association. Emphasis in text.

19. Ibid., p. 199.

20. Ibid., p. 199.

21. Jean Havel, *Politics in Sudbury,* Sudbury: Laurentian University Press, 1966, p. 85.

22. Toivo Miljan and Bruce Macnaughton, "Federal-Provincial Party Support: The Case of the Waterloo Ridings," Paper prepared for the Annual Meeting of the Canadian Political Science Association, Edmonton, 1975 (*mimeo.*).

23. John C. Courtney and David E. Smith, "Voting in a Provincial General Election and a Federal By-Election: A Constituency Study of Saskatoon City," *Canadian Journal of Economics and Political Science* XXXII, No. 3., August, 1966, pp. 339-353. By permission of the authors and the Canadian Political Science Association.

24. Ibid., p. 344.

25. George Perlin and Patti Peppin, "Variations in Party Support in Federal and Provincial Elections: Some Hypotheses" *Canadian Journal of Political Science* IV, No. 2, June 1971, pp. 280-286. By permission of the authors and the Canadian Political Science Association.

26. Ibid., p. 281.

27. Ibid., p. 286. However, the authors suggest that the importance of federal "affect" in Ontario politics is atypical and that provincial affect is relatively more important in the Atlantic provinces.

28. Laponce, *op. cit.* On federal-provincial switching see pp. 168-176.

29. Ibid. p. 17.

30. Miljan and Macnaughton, *op. cit.* pp. 14-26.

31. Lynn Macdonald, "Party Identification, Stability and Change in Voting Behaviour: A Study of the 1968 Canadian Federal Election in Ontario," in Orest M. Kruhlak, Richard Schultz and Sidney I. Pobihuschy, Editors, *The*

Canadian Political Process: A Reader, Toronto: Holt, Rinehart and Winston of Canada, 1970, p. 273.

32. Walter D. Young, *The Anatomy of a Party: The National CCF 1932-1961,* Toronto: University of Toronto Press, 1969.

33. David Smith, *Prairie Liberalism: The Liberal Party in Saskatchewan 1905-1971,* Toronto: University of Toronto Press, 1975.

34. Reginald Whitaker, *The Government Party: Organizing and Financing the Liberal Party of Canada, 1930-1958,* Toronto: University of Toronto Press, 1974.

35. Henry Jacek, John McDonough, Ronald Shimuzu and Patrick Smith, "Federal-Provincial Integration in Ontario Party Organization—The Influence of Recruitment Patterns," Paper presented to the 1970 annual conference of the Canadian Political Science Association, *(mimeo),* p. 102.

36. Smith, *op. cit.,* pp. 290-296.

37. On party leadership conventions see (1) Donald V. Smiley "The National Party Leadership Convention: A Preliminary Analysis," *Canadian Journal of Political Science* I, December 1968, pp. 373-397; (2) John C. Courtney, *The Selection of National Party Leaders in Canada,* Toronto: Macmillan of Canada, 1973; (3) Lawrence Le Duc, "Party Decision-Making: Some Empirical Observations on the Leadership Selection Process" *Canadian Journal of Political Science* IV, March 1971, pp. 97-118; and (4) Robert Krause and Lawrence Le Duc, "Voting Behaviour and Electoral Strategies in the Progressive Conservative Leadership Convention of 1976," *Canadian Journal of Political Science* XII, March 1979, pp. 97-135.

38. Whitaker, *op. cit.,* p. 86.

39. See generally George Radwanski, *Trudeau,* Toronto: Macmillan of Canada, 1978, Chapters 8 and 9. In his reflections on his experience as a member of the Trudeau cabinet, Mitchell Sharp referred to the amount of time that ministers spent on policy matters in cabinet and in cabinet committees and suggested that if there had been more delegation to civil servants, ministers would have had more time to devote to reflection and to politics: Mitchell Sharp, "The Cabinet and the Public Service," in Thomas A. Hockin, Editor, *Apex of Power: The Prime Minister and Political Leadership in Canada,* Second Edition, Scarborough: Prentice-Hall of Canada, 1977, p. 182.

40. Radwanski, *op. cit.,* p. 272.

41. In his interview with Radwanski, Pierre Trudeau has attested to this: "I don't think I could operate in the kind of government system they have in Japan, for instance, or even Israel for that matter, where each minister brings his own power base," ibid., p. 188.

42. Whether this will continue under the Clark cabinet is of course conjectural.

43. *The Diefenbaker Interlude: Parties and Voting in Canada,* Toronto: Longmans, 1965, p. 24.

44. For career patterns of federal cabinet ministers in provincial politics since Confederation see Roman R. March, *The Myth of Parliament,* Prentice-Hall of Canada, Scarborough, 1974, pp. 72-73.

45. "Federalism and Party Finance: A Preliminary Sounding" in *Studies in Canadian Party Finance,* Committee on Election Expenses, Queen's

Printer, Ottawa, 1969. Reproduced by permission of Supply and Services, Ottawa. See also K. Z. Paltiel *Political Party Financing in Canada*, McGraw-Hill of Canada, Toronto, 1970 and Pattiel "Election Expenses" in David J. Bellamy, Ian H. Pammett and Donald C. Rowat, Editors, *The Provincial Political Systems*, Methuen of Canada, Toronto, 1976, pp. 161-176.

46. *Federalism and Party Finance*, p. 13. Reproduced by permission of Supply and Services, Ottawa.

47. "Federalism and the Party System: Provincial and Federal Liberals in the Province of Quebec" *Canadian Journal of Political Science XI*, September 1978, pp. 513-521.

48. Robert A. Hackett "The Waffle Conflict in the NDP" in Hugh G. Thorburn, Editor, *Party Politics in Canada*, Fourth Edition, Prentice-Hall of Canada, Scarborough, 1979, pp. 188-205.

49. Maurice Pinard, *The Rise of a Third Party: A Study in Crisis Politics*, Prentice-Hall, Englewood Cliffs, N.J., 1971.

50. P. 37.

51. See John Meisel's perceptive essay "The Decline of Party in Canada", in *Thorburn, op. cit.*, pp. 119-136.

52. Edited by A. Paul Pross, McGraw-Hill Ryerson, Toronto, 1975.

53. National Pressure Groups and the Federal Government", pp. 27-58. See particularly pp. 30-35.

54. Pp. 87-114.

55. P. 105.

56. "Interest Group Demands and the Federal Political System: Two Canadian Case Studies", pp. 69-86.

57. *Ibid.*, p. 72.

58. *Ibid.*

59. *Ibid.*, pp. 77-82.

60. John Meisel, "Recent Changes in Canadian Politics", in Hugh G. Thorburn, Editor, *Party Politics in Canada*, Second Edition, Prentice-Hall of Canada, Scarborough, 1967, pp. 35-36.

61. Peter Aucoin, "Pressure Group and Recent Changes in the Policy Process" in *Pross, op. cit.*, pp. 182-187.

62. Richard Simeon, *Federal-Provincial Diplomacy*, University of Toronto Press, 1972, pp. 280-283.

63. Glyn R. Berry, "The Oil Lobby and the Energy Crisis", *Canadian Public Administration 17*, Winter 1974, pp. 600-635.

64. Richard Schultz, "Interest Groups and Intergovernmental Negotiations: Caught in the Vise of Federalism" in J. Peter Meekison, Editor, *Canadian Federalism: Myth or Reality*, Third Edition, 1977, Methuen of Canada, Toronto, pp. 375-396.

65. For an imaginative analysis of changes in the strength and influence of government and private corporations related to the Saskatchewan potash industry see Jeanne Kirk Lau and Maureen Appel Molot "Multinational Corporations and Economic Nationalism: Control over Natural Resources in Canada," *World Development 6*, 1978, pp. 837-849. More generally on western resources see John Richards and Larry Pratt, *Prairie Capitalism*, McClelland and Stewart, Toronto, 1979.

66. "The Decline of Party", *op. cit.*, pp. 123-124. For a more extended discussion of the corporatist phenomenon in contemporary Canada see Section 4 of K. J. Rea and J. T. McLeod, *Business and Government in Canada: Selected Readings*, Second Edition, Methuen of Canada, Toronto, 1976, particularly essays by McLeod and Rea, Tuohy and Smiley.

67. See the thoughtful and provocative essay by John Shiry, "Mass Values and System Outputs: A Critique of Socialization Theory" in Jon H. Pammett and Michael S. Whittington, Editors, *Foundations of Political Culture: Political Socialization in Canada*, Macmillan of Canada, Toronto, 1976, pp. 36-58. Shiry challenges the "citizen input assumption" that mass wants, needs, attitudes, ideology and values are the primary determinants of the allocative outputs of the political system. The alternative view is that ". . . only institutions or institutional changes are viable sources of political demands". (p. 44).

68. Michael Ornstein, Michael Stevenson and Paul Williams, "The State of Mind: Public Perceptions of the Future of Canada," in R. B. Byers and Robert W. Reford, Editors, *Canada Challenged: The Viability of Confederation*, Canadian Institute of International Affairs, Toronto, 1979, p. 106.

69. Pp. 106-107.

70. P. 90.

71. P. 107.

CHAPTER 6
THE ECONOMIC DIMENSIONS OF CANADIAN FEDERALISM

The governmental and economic dimensions of Canadian nationhood and of the Canadian federal system are inextricably intertwined. So it has been from the first. A plausible argument can be made that in its purely constitutional dimensions the Confederation settlement was relatively conservative, but that in their vision of uniting the remaining British territories of North America into an integrated national economy the Fathers were bold, even foolhardy. We discussed in Chapter 2 some of the conservative aspects of the original constitutional settlement—the carry-over of the institutions of responsible parliamentary government under the Crown to the Dominion and the provinces, the continuance of the civil law tradition in Quebec and the common law in the provinces other than Quebec, the attenuation of the federal principle by quasi-unitary devices modelled along the lines of British Imperial rule. The impulses towards establishing a new economic nation were more imaginative and these impulses were manifested in a reasonably explicit form in the text of the British North America Act itself.[1]

—Section 146 made provision for the subsequent inclusion of Newfoundland, Prince Edward Island, British Columbia, Rupert's Land and the North-western Territory into the Dominion.

—Section 145 committed the Dominion to begin the construction of a railway linking Halifax and the St. Lawrence basin within six months of union.

—the division of jurisdiction under Sections 91, 92 and 95 gave the Dominion the powers believed to be necessary and appropriate to establishing an integrated transcontinental economy.

—Section 121 provided for a Canada-wide common market under these terms: "All Articles of the Growth, Produce, or Manufacture of any one of the Provinces, shall, from and after the Union, be admitted free into each of the other Provinces."

What Is a Contemporary Economic Nation?

It may be helpful in analyzing the economic dimensions of Canadian federalism to proceed by way of a schema of what in the contemporary world constitutes a nation in the economic sense. Explicitly or by implication each of these classifications points to imperatives for the public authorities in their relation to economic institutions and processes.

(1) *A nation is an economic union in which public policies safeguard the free movement of goods, people and capital within the nation's territorial boundaries.* A corollary is that there is a uniform set of restrictions applied to goods, people and capital entering or leaving the nation.

(2) *A nation is an economic community whose public authorities are committed to the nation-wide equalization of material resources on interpersonal and inter-territorial lines.* Such equalization can take many forms, but the most crucial ones to be discussed in this Chapter relate to the efforts of the government of Canada to ensure national minimum standards of personal incomes and of the range and quality of public services, and to enhance economic development in materially disadvantaged areas of the country.

(3) *A nation is an economic union in which governments undertake the responsibility for attempting to ensure relatively full employment and relative price stability.* Since the Keynesian revolution of the 1930s it has been recognized that the unhampered workings of capitalist market economies will not bring about the two objectives of the relatively full employment of resources and relative stability of prices, and the public authorities of such nations have accepted the responsibility of controlling the levels of aggregate demand to meet these imperatives.

(4) *A nation is an economic community which speaks with a single voice in dealing with other nations.* Whatever the domestic distribution of governmental powers in respect to economic policies, the nation has one set of public authorities which can speak for it and commit it in international interactions.

(5) *A nation is an economic community whose public authorities are charged with the reliability of energy supplies available to individuals and businesses.* This new dimension of economic nationhood has of course assumed a crucial importance in the 1970s.

(6) *An economic nation is a community in which the public author-*

ities assume a greater or lesser responsibility for the structure of the economy. Economic structure used in this sense is a residual category whose limits are somewhat indeterminate, but no government of a modern nation adopts a non-interventionist stance in respect to such matters as the balance between labour, industry and agriculture; urban concentration; foreign ownership; the national infrastructure of transportation and communications; labour mobility and the training of the labour force, and so on.

In this chapter each of these economic dimensions of economic nationhood will be discussed within the framework of federal-provincial relations.

The Common Market Dimension[2]

A common market is an economic unit within which there are no internal barriers to the movement of commodities, people and capital. As any reader who has had even a brief encounter with economics will know, the absence of such restrictions permits the market system to allocate the factors of production among alternative uses in such a way as to maximize the aggregate income of the community. Conversely, of course, and within the limiting assumptions of the economist, restrictions on the mobility of goods, people and capital decrease the income of the community. There are several economic advantages of larger common markets over smaller ones. Various areas can specialize in the production of commodities they can produce more efficiently than can other areas in the common market. Certain economies of scale allow goods to be produced at lower unit cost. It is reasonable to believe that larger markets call forth entrepreneurial performance of a higher quality. Superior occupational opportunities encourage the more ambitious and talented persons to undertake prolonged and specialized training and discourage the emigration of such persons after they are trained. Because of its wider range of economic activities the larger unit is less vulnerable to actions taken outside its borders and beyond its control.

The establishment of an integrated national economy and a common market extending over the northern half of the continent was one of the chief objectives of the Confederation settlement. There is reference after reference in the Confederation Debates to the complementarity of the Canadian and Maritime economies, the urgency of acquiring and developing a western hinterland, and the kind of general economic advantages of larger over smaller nations which I have mentioned in the paragraph above. Several of the powers vested in the Dominion were fairly explicitly directed to these ends—powers over trade and commerce; various aspects of interprovincial transportation and communication; banking, currency, interest and legal tender; patents; bankruptcy; naturalization and aliens and paramountcy in respect to agriculture and immigration—the latter two classes of subjects closely related to economic integration and development. In a negative sense, two clauses of the BNA Act enjoined provincial restrictions on the Dominion-wide common market:

—as we have seen, Section 121 enacted that "All Articles of the Growth, Produce, or Manufacture of any of the Provinces shall, from and after the Union, be admitted into each of the other Provinces." This clause prohibits the provinces from erecting tariff barriers against the products of one another.

—under Section 92(2) the taxation powers of the provinces were restricted to "Direct Taxation within the Province in order to the Raising of a Revenue for Provincial Purposes." This buttressed Section 121 and prohibits the levying of excise taxes at the producer level the effect of which is to encourage the sale of the commodities within the boundaries of jurisdictions which levy such taxes and discourage the movement of goods across provincial boundaries.

With the relatively restricted role of the provinces in economic matters contemplated by the Confederation settlement and which prevailed for several decades after 1867, the prescriptions on the provinces contained in Section 92(1) and 91(2) were adequate to the establishment and maintenance of a Canadian common market. It is no longer so. The following are some of the more important provincial restrictions on the free movement of labour, goods and capital within Canadian boundaries:[3]

—the purchasing policies of some of the provinces give preferences to provincially-based suppliers of goods and services. The Quebec government has defined such a policy for its own departments and public corporations more explicitly than have the other provinces. The magnitude of the purchases made by the provincial governments and their crown corporations is very great and preferential purchasing policies are considerable impediments to interprovincial trade.

—provincial boards responsible for the marketing of natural products impose barriers to the movement of these products across provincial boundaries. The constitutional position here is intricate, but the impulse of such provincial marketing boards is to protect provincial markets for provincial producers.

—the provinces control the licencing of the trades and professions and the exercise of such powers restricts labour mobility. A current dispute between Quebec and Ontario relates to the restriction imposed by the former province on Ontario residents working in the Quebec construction industry. More generally, there is a lack of reciprocity in tradesmen's qualifications enforced by the provinces, and members of the professions are licenced by provincial associations working under the authority of provincial legislation.

—the regulation of the trucking industry by the provinces works against mobility. Such regulation favours firms incorporated in one province against competition from outside.

—provinces can and do restrict the nation-wide mobility of capital by actions regulating the amalgamation or takeover of corporations. A spectacular instance of this occurred in early 1979 when the British Columbia government was successful in preventing Canadian Pacific Investments from acquiring control over Macmillan-Bloedel, the largest resource corporation in that province.

—the provincial regulation of the issuing of securities imposes barriers to the raising of capital on a Canada-wide basis. The most important of these barriers appear to be the different prospectus requirements imposed on companies wishing to raise capital.

—the provinces have recently imposed restrictions on the ownership of land by non-residents. Prince Edward Island has enacted legislation restricting the ownership of real property by non-residents and Saskatchewan the ownership of farm land.

—the provincial liquor control boards of the provinces confer advantages in provincially-produced beverages. The wine industries of Ontario and British Columbia have been major beneficiaries of such discrimination.

The examples given above relate for the most part to the mobility of the factors of production within Canada. Other provincial policies favour Canadians in one way or another against foreigners. For example, Ontario purchasing policies give preference to Canadian firms, some provinces charge foreign university students higher tuition fees than those paid by Canadians, and under the Ontario *Land Transfer Tax Act* of 1974 persons selling land to a non-resident of Canada are required to pay a tax not levied when land is conveyanced to a non-resident.

In his monograph Safarian has recommended two constitutional amendments which would extend Parliament's power to realize more completely the economic benefits of a Canadian common market.[4]

—Section 121 should be reworded this way: "All articles, services and persons in any one of the provinces shall be admitted to each of the other provinces free of duties, quantitative restrictions or charges or measures with similar effects."

—Section 91(2)—the federal trade and commerce power—should be extended by this wording: "The Regulation of Trade and Commerce, including such trade, commerce and ancilliary activity as, although carried out wholly within the province, shall be declared by the Parliament of Canada to be for the general advantage of Canada."

In a more general sense than Safarian, the Report of the Task Force on Canadian Unity recommended that Section 121 "be clarified to guarantee more effectively free trade between the provinces for all produce and manufactured goods, and be extended to include services."[5]

Within the context of the strong currents of provincialism which now prevail, it is unlikely that there will be significant relaxation of provincial challenges to the Canadian common market by way of either constitutional amendment or agreements among the provinces to forego such practices. There are perhaps possibilities in the more comprehensive interpretation that the Supreme Court has recently given to the trade and commerce power.

Canadians pay a heavy material price because of their failure to sustain a domestic common market. No one to my knowledge has attempted to measure the magnitude of this burden, and even with the most costly and sophisticated research such a measurement could only be based on arbitrary assumptions. It is often pointed out that Canada—along with Australia and Sweden—is the only western industrialized nation without access to a market of more than 100,000,000 people. This national disability is compounded by provincial barriers to the free movement of the factors of production within Canada itself.

The Equalization Dimension I: The Distribution of Revenues and Revenue Sources between Federal and Provincial Jurisdictions

The distribution of revenues and revenue sources between the central and the state/provincial governments is crucial to any federal system. In Canada as in other federations this is a matter of extraordinary complexity.

To clarify the general problem somewhat, we might hypothesize a situation in which a new federation is being established. Let us further hypothesize that the states/provinces are equal in their fiscal capacities, i.e., that equal rates of taxation will yield equal per capita revenues in each of the constituent jurisdictions. We might also assume that the needs for and the per unit costs of public services are equal throughout the projected federation. Under such circumstances the founders would no doubt allocate the tax sources between the central and state/provincial governments so that each order could carry out the responsibilities assigned to it without any need of financial transfers from the other.

The real world of federalism is infinitely more complicated than this hypothetical one. There are always significant variations among the fiscal capacities of the states or provinces, so that the poorer of these jurisdictions can support the services the constitution assigns to them at national average levels only by subjecting their residents to taxation rates above the national average—if they can support them at all. Beyond this, the relative importance of different kinds of public expenditure changes—at one time the more costly bundle of functions is that allocated to the cental government, while in another period the priorities are in the state/provincial domain. And the reliance of federal and provincial governments on different kinds of revenue sources shifts from time to time. There may be other kinds of what may roughly be called fiscal imbalance, such as those occasioned by the higher than average per capita costs of providing services in some provinces or the differential needs of some of these jurisdictions for particular services.

Attempts to alleviate what are perceived at any one time to be fiscal imbalances in a federal system can be effective by one or more of these kinds of transfers:

—a redistribution of functional responsibilities. For example, the constitutional amendment of 1940 vested exclusive jurisdiction for unemployment insurance in the Dominion.

—a redistribution of sources of taxation. For example, in 1971 the federal government abolished its tax on estates, thus allowing the provinces exclusive access to the taxation of inheritances and in the period prior to 1966 Ottawa on several occasions reduced its rates of personal income tax so that the provinces might increase theirs without extra net burdens on taxpayers.

—a redistribution of public revenues, almost always in practice in the form of grants from the central government to the provinces. For our examples here we have the various programs of conditional and unconditional subventions from Ottawa to the provinces which will be discussed later in this chapter.

Thomas J. Courchene has accurately pointed out that: "modifications in the nature and form of financial transfers from Ottawa to the provinces are equivalent to the *de facto* [re] distribution of power under the BNA Act."[6] To take the extreme case, whatever the legal distribution of powers, provincial autonomy was almost meaningless to the nearly bankrupt prairie provinces in the 1930s. Further, and this is Courchene's basic argument, the *form* that transfers take directly influences the actual scope of provincial power. If federal grants are made subject to detailed and stringent conditions, the provinces become little more than administrative agents of Ottawa in respect to these matters within provincial constitutional jurisdiction. On the other hand, unconditional federal subventions in fact enhance the powers of the provinces to do what they could not otherwise do. Apart from the 1940 amendment related to unemployment insurance and amendments of 1951 and 1964 concerning old age pensions, there have been no explicit constitutional changes in the allocation of responsibilities between the federal and provincial governments. Thus ongoing efforts to alleviate fiscal imbalances has been effected almost entirely through changes in the distribution of tax sources and public revenues.

The Confederation settlement of 1864-1867 gave what were then the most costly functions of government to the Dominion along with the power to raise revenues "by any Mode or System of Taxation." The provinces were limited to direct taxation and at the time of Confederation direct taxation was thought of largely in terms of taxes on real property normally levied by the municipal authorities. Thus provincial revenue-raising capacity was restricted to levies resulting from the development of natural resources and from incidental licence fees. Even though the functions assigned to these jurisdictions were not thought of as being very costly, the allocation of functions and revenue-raising capacities still left the provinces fiscally deficient. This original fiscal imbalance was to be alleviated by a scheme of annual grants by the Dominion to the provinces paid according to a schedule enacted as part of the BNA Act itself. Although the British North America Act of 1867 explicitly enacted that its terms of financial transfers to the provinces were to be "in full Settlement of all future Demands on Canada," this settlement was overturned within two years by a new schedule of payments devised by John A. Macdonald and his colleagues to counter Nova Scotia separation.[7] From that time until the Second World War what came to be called the "subsidy question" was a permanent source of contention between Ottawa and the provinces, despite a new settlement bargained out between the two levels in 1907 and enacted as an amendment to the BNA Act.[8] Writing in 1947 the late Robert MacGregor Dawson said this:

> This world of Dominion-Provincial finance has, indeed, an air of grotesque unreality, untrammeled by logic and the ordinary restrictions and meaning of words . . . The history of the subsidies demonstrates not only that final and unalterable agreements can be and are subject to frequent revision, but that population figures can be invented when the actual ones prove unsuitable; that debt allowances can be made for debts which have never existed; that natural resources can be returned and enjoyed and at the same time compensated for on the basis of their original alienation; and that when a subsidy is increased in order to equalize the treatment among the provinces, further adjustments become immediately necessary in order to overcome the injustices which have become occasioned by the very act of equalization.[9]

Behind all this manoeuvring Dawson saw the genuine need of the provinces for revenues to meet their needs.

The modern fiscal regime in Canada can somewhat arbitrarily be dated from the *Report of the Royal Commission on Dominion-Provincial Relations* published in 1940. The Rowell-Sirois Commission recommended a very new distribution of tax sources, revenues and responsibilities between the Dominion and the provinces. The federal government was to be given exclusive responsibility for unemployment insurance and a proposed system of contributory old age pensions, and exclusive access to the taxation of personal and corporate incomes and of estates. The existing system of statutory subsidies as provided for under the British North America Act was to be eliminated and the Dominion would assume the responsibility for provincial indebtedness. In place of the tangled web of subsidies there was to be a system of National Adjustment Grants paid by the Dominion so as "to enable each province (including its municipalities) without resort to heavier taxation than the Canadian average to provide adequate social, educational and developmental services." The thrust of the Commission's recommendation was in the direction of the administrative independence of the two levels and against federal schemes for making up the financial deficiencies of the provinces by conditional grants in aid of particular services.

Although a Dominion-Provincial Conference was convened in 1941 to discuss the Rowell-Sirois recommendations, the preoccupations of the federal authorities with the war along with the opposition of Quebec, Ontario and Alberta to the Commission and its work prevented a new sharing of revenues and responsibilities from being effected. Ottawa pre-empted exclusive access to taxation on estates, and individual and corporate incomes in 1942 and from this period until 1957 the urgency of the federal authorities' desire to assure their exclusive occupancy of these two fields caused them to design their schedule of payments to the provinces around the consideration of what would be necessary to induce Quebec and Ontario not to levy such taxes rather than, as Rowell-Sirois had suggested, the fiscal needs of the provinces in terms of equalization.

In retrospect, the most significant and lasting contribution of the Rowell-Sirois Commission was its approach to interprovincial fiscal equalization based on a rational evaluation of fiscal need. The Commission investigated, and it must have taken great forbearance to do so, the claims of the individual provinces for upward revision of their respective subsidies. The claims were in most cases based on the most questionable accounts of the purportedly contractual commitments incurred by Ottawa when the various provinces entered Confederation and the allegedly adverse effects of national tariff and transportation policies on the western and maritime provinces. The reasons the Commission gave for rejecting federal compensation based on the workings of the national policy were both principled and pragmatic. On the side of principle, it was asserted that, so far as national economic policies were concerned, the government of the Dominion was responsible to the House of Commons and the people of Canada rather than to the provinces. In practical terms, the burdens and benefits of national policies were so complex and so interrelated that it was impossible to evaluate with any precision their incidence on the various provinces and regions. Thus the Commission in rejecting these claims proposed a subsidy system based on provincial fiscal need. Such need was a great deal less subject to precise measurement than the Commission believed, and in particular the Commission ignored the circumstance that the costs of and needs for provincial and local services could not be evaluated without a great deal of subjectivity. Further, in the light of past and subsequent experience, it was patently unrealistic to suggest that the government of Canada would be willing to allow an independent fiscal commission in effect to determine the scale of subsidies to the provinces. On the other hand, the fundamental idea that Ottawa, through unconditional subsidies, should guarantee the revenues of the provinces to a national average has been an influential standard in federal-provincial fiscal relations from the publication of the Rowell-Sirois Report onward.

The Federal-Provincial Tax Sharing Arrangements Act of 1957 was of crucial importance in establishing a scheme whereby Ottawa would pay equalization grants to the provinces whether or not they levied their own taxes on individual and corporate incomes and on the proceeds of estates. The tax-rental system which had prevailed since 1942 had been breached in 1954 by Quebec's decision to levy its own taxes on individual incomes and Ontario was regarded as likely to move in the same direction. The 1957 arrangements provided that each province would receive an unconditional equalization payment from Ottawa equal to the amount necessary to bring its yields from taxes on individual and corporate incomes and succession duties up to the average per capita yield for the two provinces in which this yield was highest. These payments were to be made whether or not the provinces did in fact occupy such fields of taxation, under arrangements under which the provinces received a defined share of the three standard taxes or an abatement of federal taxes of the same amount.

Under the 1962-1967 taxation arrangements the system was again modified by divorcing the payments to the provinces from the yields to Ottawa of the three standard taxes. Thus the provinces were, so to speak, turned loose to make their own levies in respect to these forms of taxation. The federal government, however, offered to collect these taxes for the provinces if they adhered to the federal tax base at rates set by the provinces.

The equalization formula which came into effect in 1967 was based on a much broader set of revenue sources than the one which it replaced. Under the 1962-1967 arrangements such equalization took into account only the yields from income taxes, inheritance duties and natural resource revenues. The new formula included 16 provincial revenue sources. The number of revenue sources so used has been successively broadened and under the arrangements which came into effect in 1977 includes 29 items. This base comprises virtually all of the revenue sources which support the provinces, and from 1972 onward has included levies made by local governments for school purposes.[10] Under the 1977 arrangements only half of provincial revenues from the development of depleting natural resources is equalized.

The actual computation of provincial equalization payments is complex. The initial computation is a population-weighted average of provincial tax rates which is applied to each of the 29 tax sources. Then these average rates are applied to each province's own revenue base, which yields a calculation of the potential per capita revenue to the province. If a province's estimated per capita yields from all the tax sources is below national average per capita yields, the federal government makes up the deficiency. In the 1978-1979 fiscal year these estimated per capita equalization payments were made:

Newfoundland	$532
P.E.I.	633
Nova Scotia	462
New Brunswick	444
Quebec	214
Manitoba	233
Saskatchewan	30[11]

It must be emphasized that the equalization formula is geared to provincial revenue-raising capacity alone. In fact even with these subventions and other federal transfers which work in the direction of interprovincial equalization, the "have-not" provinces levy taxes at rates higher than those prevailing in the more prosperous jurisdictions. To take an example, Alberta does not impose a retail sales tax while such a levy in Newfoundland is 10 per cent. The other provincial levies fall between these extremes. The rates of personal income tax are higher in the have-not provinces. Although I have not found such comparative statistics available, it is reasonable to suppose that the "have" provinces are more generous with their local authorities and thus relieve the burdens which would otherwise fall on the municipal taxpayer, most importantly of course as these relate to levies on real property. Further, the equalization formula does not take into account differential provincial needs for public services or differences in per capita costs in providing them. Thus from time to time some provinces, usually the more prosperous ones, have complained that they are not given any consideration for very heavy expenses attendant on economic growth—for example, heavy capital expenditures necessary when new urban areas are being developed. There has been a long-standing grievance in British Columbia that the federal fiscal regime does not provide any relief for the high per capita costs of providing services in that province.

As in other federations, there is an ongoing competition among the central and regional governments for tax sources. The provinces are constitutionally prohibited from levying tariffs on interprovincial and international trade and from sales taxes at other than the retail level. Apart from these limitations, however, the two orders can in general raise revenues by any methods they wish. Competition for tax sources has been particularly intense in respect to income taxes and has often assumed the character of provincial pressures for "tax room" and, of course, federal resistance to such pressures. "Tax room" is a decrease in the rates of federal taxation so that the provinces can increase their rates without imposing heavier total burdens on the taxpayer. The story is a very complex one, but the general trend has been since 1966 for Ottawa to resist such provincial pressures, although in somewhat indeterminate ways the rates of federal tax do take into account the fiscal needs of the provinces. The situation is further complicated by the circumstance that Ottawa collects individual income taxes for all provinces except Quebec and corporate income taxes for all provinces except Quebec and Ontario. These collections are made according to the *rates* set by the respective provinces, e.g. for 1978 each resident of Ontario paid provincial income tax at 44 per cent of his federal liabilities. The price that the provinces pay for the administrative and political convenience of having Ottawa collect such taxes means that the federal authorities determine not only the tax base, i.e. the income on which taxes are levied, but also, in the case of levies on individuals, the progressiveness of the tax system. In recent years the federal government has shown some flexibility here in permitting individual provinces to make their own tax base more progressive by property tax and child credits but in terms of practical administration there are undoubtedly relatively strict limits imposed on provincial freedom of action.

The world petroleum crisis from 1973 onward brought complications in the distribution of revenues and revenue sources between the federal and provincial governments.[12] The fiscal arrangements which came into effect in 1972 provided for interprovincial equalization based on a formula which took into account all the major sources of provincial revenues, and in the next year the formula was extended to include taxes levied by the local governments for school purposes. Such revenue equalization had been decisive in bringing about a situation in which the per capita expenditures of the "have not" provinces in 1973-1974 was only 2 per cent below the national average, $1,234 as against $1,256.[13] However, the quadrupling of world petroleum prices by the Organization of Petroleum Exporting Countries in 1974 brought challenges to the revenue equalization system. It was calculated that if Alberta oil was sold at world prices energy royalties accruing to that province would increase about $2 billions annually.[14] The result under the existing equalization formula would be to make Ontario a have-not province and to subject Canadians to something like a 25 per cent increase in personal income taxes to finance the equalization payments.

The federal authorities undertook three measures to counter the imbalances in the fiscal system resulting from the new circumstances of
the world petroleum market:
—by means of an oil export tax the domestic price of Canadian petroleum was set well below the world level.
—the equalization formula was amended so that only one-third of any
   additional energy royalties beyond 1973-1974 levels would be included.
—it was provided by Ottawa that corporations in the resource development industries could no longer deduct royalties paid to the provinces from income as defined for federal tax purposes.

The fiscal arrangements which came into effect in 1977 include only
50 per cent of provincial revenues accruing from the development of
non-renewable resources in the equalization formula. In the wake of
the federal government's program of restraining expenditures announced in August 1978 there are likely to be other such changes. The
federal Minister of Finance in November of that year announced that
Ottawa intended to phase out of the equalization base provincial revenues accruing from the sale of crown leases for oil and gas exploration.
Because of the volatile nature of revenues derived from the development of depletable resources, it seems at least possible that within the
next few years this source will be eliminated entirely from the equalization formula.

The Equalization Dimension II: Equalizing the Range and Quality of Public Services

Unconditional fiscal transfers from the federal government to the provinces strengthen the capacities of the latter to provide services. However, the recipient jurisdictions can use these transfers at their discretion. Ottawa's attempts to equalize the range and quality of services
under provincial jurisdiction on a Canada-wide basis are effected
through various kinds of shared-cost arrangements.

Shared-cost programs involve financial concessions made available
by one level of government to compensate another level for part of the
costs incurred in providing particular services or facilities. One form of
this device is the conditional grant in which the recipient government
receives funds for performing functions according to standards which
are determined either unilaterally by the donor government or by the
two levels in collaboration.[15] The other variant provides the recipient
jurisdiction either with grants or tax abatements, sometimes a combination of the two, but does not involve any explicit controls of the standards imposed by the government making the fiscal transfer available.

The general effect of shared-cost arrangements is a higher expenditure on the aided service or facility than would be made by the jurisdictions responsible for these without such transfers. There are four kinds of justification made for such arrangements.

First, fiscal transfers to the provinces compensate the latter for the spillovers or external benefits arising from the provision of particular kinds of services. To take an obvious and important example, the emigration of graduates of Nova Scotia and Saskatchewan universities to Ontario and Alberta confers benefits on the latter provinces at the expense of the former. Economists will argue that jurisdictions which provide such external benefits will be disposed to spend on these services at lower than optimal levels in the absence of financial inducements from the other level of government.

Secondly, shared-cost programs enable the federal authorities to influence provincial policies which are deemed important in the attainment of specific federal objectives. To give two examples, the federal interest in an integrated system of national transportation impelled Ottawa to co-operate with the provinces in the building of the Trans-Canada Highway, and the perceived national interest in encouraging citizens to learn both of the official languages has led to a system of grants to the provinces for that purpose.

Thirdly, shared-cost arrangements contribute to the mobility of citizens within Canada.[16] Disparities in the range and quality of public services available in different provinces restrict such mobility by discouraging people from moving to jurisdictions where certain services are not provided at all or are of low quality. Further, provincial and local governments have incentives to provide certain services only to persons who have met certain residence requirements.

Fourthly, federal efforts to equalize the range and quality of services available on a Canada-wide basis is the manifestation of a sense of national community. The document *Federal-Provincial Grants and the Spending Power of Parliament*, introduced into the Federal-Provincial Constitutional Conference by Prime Minister Trudeau in June 1969, said this:

> Canadians everywhere now feel a sufficient sense of responsibility for their compatriots in other parts of the country that they are prepared to contribute to their well-being. . . . [One] of the most important ways of giving expression to this concern is by the provision to every citizen, wherever he lives, of adequate levels of public services—in particular of health, welfare and education services.[17]

Where such services that are regarded from time to time as being within the social minimum are under the legislative jurisdiction of the provinces, the shared-cost arrangement facilitates the imperatives of national community being met.

Beyond these justifications, various kinds of shared-cost programs allow the federal system to meet the circumstances that the constitution as judicially interpreted provides a relatively inflexible distribution of responsibilities between the federal and provincial governments and that, in general terms, the federal authorities have more ample revenue-raising capacities than do the provinces, certainly than the less prosperous provinces.

It seems that the first shared-cost program in the federal system was a parliamentary grant of $70,000 in 1872 for the establishment of provincial immigration officers in the United Kingdom and continental Europe.[18] The longest-standing continuous joint program still in existence is the Railway Grade Crossing Fund established in 1907. In 1912 a system of federal grants was established to stimulate provincial activity in agricultural education, and in 1919 other grants were provided to aid the provinces in the control of venereal disease, the establishment of provincial employment offices, and the building of highways. The first major federal-provincial effort in the field of welfare came in 1927 with the creation of a program of old age pensions available to those who met provincially-administered means tests.

The Rowell-Sirois Commission in its 1940 Report was in general hostile to conditional grants and, as we have seen, its solution was the transfer of some of the more costly welfare functions from provincial to Dominion jurisdiction, along with a program of equalization grants to be paid to the provinces without conditions attached. In a study *Difficulties of Divided Jurisdiction* prepared for the Commission, J. A. Corry argued that friction between the Dominion and the provinces in the operation of conditional grant programs was almost inevitable. Corry's basic argument was this:

> Hope for harmonious and efficient cooperation depends largely on the discovery of clear-cut objective criteria for measuring the activity-criteria which command agreement by their clarity. Such criteria are almost impossible to find.[19]

He was particularly critical of the grant-in-aid programs for old age pensions and for unemployment relief.

Despite the Rowell-Sirois recommendations there was a burgeoning of conditional grant programs in the 15 years after the end of the Second World War. Between 1946 and 1960 such programs increased from $4.11 to $22.11 per capita and in the latter year ranged from 33.0 per cent of provincial net general revenue in Prince Edward Island to 8.3 per cent in Quebec, with a national average of 15.7 per cent. The major programs were for building the Trans-Canada Highway, provincial hospital insurance, vocational education, income assistance to various categories of persons, assistance in the economic development of depressed rural areas and aid for several different kinds of health programs. The following generalizations can be made about the conditional grant system.

First, contrary to the analysis of the Rowell-Sirois Commission, these programs did not lead to any considerable amount of friction between the two levels of government. Apart from Quebec, which had participated in some of the arrangements and for principled reasons had refused to join others, the provincial governments offered little resistance to federal involvement in matters within their legislative jurisdiction and were glad to accept " 50-cent dollars", i.e., to spend their own revenues in ways which would qualify for federal assistance. At the operational level there was relative harmony among officials of such groupings as civil engineers, social workers, public health specialists and so on based on the professional norms of these groups. Such officials, characteristically functional specialists at the middle-levels of their respective federal and provincial departments, had self-interested incentives for collaborative behaviour because conditional grant programs had the general effect of increasing public expenditures on the aided facility or service beyond what those would have been in the absence of such grants.[20]

Secondly, federal assistance was given for fairly narrowly defined purposes. The corollary of this was a pattern of detailed and precise federal controls over the aided activities.

Thirdly, the various conditional grant programs were established in isolation from considerations of interprovincial revenue equalization. The operative justification was that grants-in-aid were for inducing the provinces to provide particular services or facilities at national minimum standards. Characteristically, these programs did not take into account the fiscal circumstances of the less prosperous provinces.

At the Federal-Provincial Conference of late July 1960 there was for the first time a concerted provincial attack on the rationale of conditional grants. This attack was led by Jean Lesage, who in the previous month had become Premier of Quebec. The new Quebec policy was to accept all the conditional grants the province was not then receiving— specifically those related to hospital insurance and the Trans-Canada Highway—but to press for federal withdrawal from fields within provincial jurisdiction under circumstances where provinces would be compensated by Ottawa for the increased financial responsibilities they were assuming. Such compensation in the Quebec view should take the form of "additional taxation rights specifically reserved for the provincial governments" and increases in equalization grants. The heads of government of the less prosperous provinces complained of the financial burdens placed on their jurisdictions by having to spend their own revenues to provide services in joint programs at federal standards. There were also criticisms of the administrative inflexibilities of conditional grant arrangements occasioned by the narrow definition by Ottawa of the purposes for which grants would be paid, the distortion of provincial expenditure-priorities inherent in such arrangements and, more generally, of federal encroachment on provincial jurisdiction.

From 1960 onward there were two broad patterns of change in the regime of conditional grants in the direction of making this regime more palatable to the provinces.

First, in 1965 Parliament enacted the Established Programs (Interim Arrangements) Act as a positive response by the Pearson government to Quebec's demands for fiscal and administrative autonomy.[21] Under the Act the provinces were given the alternative of contracting out of five established programs—hospital insurance; assistance for disabled, blind and old age pensions; unemployment assistance; vocational training; and grants for several specific purposes in public health. Provinces which chose this alternative were to be compensated by the lowering of federal income tax rates in these provinces, with the differences between the yields from such transfers and the amount these provinces would have received in conditional grants being made up by cash payments from Ottawa. During varying transitional periods as provided under the Act, non-participating provinces were to furnish the specified services under the same conditions as had prevailed under the previous arrangements. Only Quebec accepted the option made available under the 1965 legislation.

Secondly, there was a general movement towards giving grants for broader purposes which weakened or even eliminated entirely the detailed federal controls over provincial activities:

—in 1966 the federal government ended several programs in aid of technical and vocational education, and combined this with its program of per capita aid to universities in a general plan of assistance for post-secondary education. Under this new regime Ottawa would pay half the operating costs of post-secondary institutions or $15 per capita annually in the form of the transfer of tax points and cash payments.

—in 1966 came into effect the Canada Assistance Plan as an amalgamation of four schemes of federal grants for categorical public assistance programs—old age assistance, blind persons' allowances, disabled persons' allowances, and unemployment assistance.[22] There was here in effect a block grant for an important and costly area of provincial activity.

—in 1968 the federal government announced the phasing-out of the health grants for very specific provincial activities over a three-year period. Two years before a Health Resources Fund of $500 millions had been established to assist the provinces up to 1980 in the "planning, acquisition, construction, renovation and equipping of health training and research facilities."

By the mid-1970s about 90 per cent of the total conditional grant transfers to the provinces were made on behalf of four programs for broadly-defined purposes—post-secondary education, hospital insurance, medical insurance and welfare assistance. There had come to be a very considerable dissatisfaction in the federal government with these arrangements, with the exception of the Canada Assistance Plan. In each case these arrangements were "open-ended" in the sense that federal contributions depended on provincial expenditures and such expenditures were increasing proportionately more rapidly than G.N.P. Despite Ottawa's efforts to co-operate with the provinces in restraining the costs of post-secondary education and health services, the results were not very successful. Thus in the mid-1970's the federal authorities by unilateral decision announced restrictions on the increases in its contributions—15 per cent increase per year in those to post-secondary education and a sliding scale for medical insurance which would result in a maximum increase of 8½ per cent for 1978-1979 and subsequent years. At about the same time the federal government gave to the provinces the 5-year notice required by the Hospital Insurance and Diagnostic Services Act that the arrangements relating to hospital insurance be terminated and new arrangements undertaken. Federal restiveness with these increasingly costly and open-ended programs was also caused in part by the circumstance that large amounts of federal monies were being expended without effective control by Ottawa of the ways in which the provinces acted in respect to the aided services.

To widely varying degrees, the provinces themselves had become very critical of the conditional grant regime and in his Supplementary Budget of July 7, 1975 the Provincial Treasurer of Ontario brought this indictment against such programs:

> —Provincial priorities are distorted by the availability of federal dollars. The classic example of this, discussed below, was Medicare. Massive financial leverage by the federal government forced Ontario to join this program even though the Province already had a perfectly satisfactory system of medical insurance.
> —Capricious changes in policy by the federal government leave the provinces stranded to carry the burden of programs that were often imposed upon them in the first place. An example of this was the abrupt withdrawal of assistance to technical and vocational education in 1967.
> —Unilateral imposition of arbitrary ceilings on the rate of growth of federal contributions to established programs is unreasonable. It leaves provinces with an undue financial burden, and also creates great inequities because of the differential levels of service provided in different jurisdictions. Classic examples are the existing ceiling on post-secondary education and the ceilings on Medicare introduced in the recent federal budget.
> —Provincial administrative structures are interfered with. One famous

case concerned the offer of federal funds for the care of juvenile de-
linquents. In order to take advantage of this proposal, the Province
would have had to switch a whole administrative unit from one department to another. Recent discussions have led to a mutually satisfactory arrangement, but potential sharing was lost for many
years.
—Rigidly defined criteria for eligibility result in inequities, feuds and
distortions.
—Administrative costs are unnecessarily high.[23]

Under the Federal-Provincial Fiscal Arrangements and Established
Programs Financing Act which came into effect on April 1, 1977, federal financial assistance for medical insurance, hospital insurance and
post-secondary education came to be made in the form of unconditional transfers whose amount, unlike the previous arrangements, was
not determined by provincial expenditures on these functions.[24] The
formula by which such transfers is determined comprises both the
transfer of tax points of individual and corporate income tax *and* per
capita cash grants.[25] The Act also contained a new block grant program
for "extended health care services" available to persons not in inten-
sive-care hospitals.

The 1977 legislation meant the virtual liquidation of the conditional
grants regime in respect to medical and hospital services. (So far as
post-secondary education was concerned there was in fact no direct
control over standards under the previous arrangements).[26] Much of
the debate surrounding the 1977 measure focused on the question of
national standards and whether or not the federal government had
given up the ability to control these. Ottawa's official position at that
time and subsequently was that such standards had been safeguarded;
in respect to medical and hospital insurance these standards were designated as "comprehensiveness of coverage with regard to services,
universality of coverage with regard to people, accessibility to services
uninhibited by excessive user charges and non-profit administration by
a public agency." On the other hand, there would seem to be almost no
practical means by which the federal authorities could enforce their
will on a recalcitrant province. Section 28(2) of the Act in fact provides
that any enactment of Parliament between April 1, 1977 and March 31,
1982 which diminishes federal payments on behalf of these three programs is effective only with the consent of the province(s) so affected.
While in the strictest of legal terms no parliamentary enactment can
control the future legislation of Parliament, the understandings on
which the 1977 changes were based appear to be that the federal authorities were in fact giving up their power to control the provinces in
respect to medical and hospital insurance and post-secondary education. The issue is by no means an academic one. In early 1979 there has
been a great deal of debate about the circumstances in some provinces,

particularly Ontario and Alberta, where an increasing number of physicians have chosen not to participate in medical insurance plans and have thus challenged the principle of universality of access to medical services. It is also not improbable that the provincial governments themselves in a period of financial stringency will increasingly resort to co-insurance and deterrent fees in respect to hospital services both to recoup a portion of health costs and to restrict what may be regarded as the over-utilization of such services. To repeat, the federal authorities appear to have surrendered any real influence in determining—at least by direct means—the supply and nature of hospital and medical services available to Canadians.

After the 1977 legislation was enacted the most important conditional grant program was that for social assistance and social services under the Canada Assistance Plan which in the 1977-1978 fiscal year accounted for 62.0 per cent of all federal conditional payments to the provinces. After several years of discussion on the matter the Minister of National Health and Welfare introduced the Social Services Financing Act into Parliament on May 12, 1978 to provide in effect a block grant to the provinces for a wide variety of social services.[27] However the government later in 1978 decided not to re-introduce the legislation because of the significantly increased federal responsibilities it provided for in the light of Ottawa's decision in August of that year to embark on a policy of drastic fiscal restraint.

Apart from the Canada Assistance Plan there are several remaining conditional grant and shared-cost programs, most of them not involving large sums of money. The largest of these is in the field of bilingualism development for which an estimated $149.4 millions was expended in 1977-1978. In respect to this program certainly Ottawa is reluctant to impose its wishes on the provinces. In this fiscal year, Quebec received an estimated 51.4 per cent of total federal contributions when the province was restricting the rights of English, and, although the other provinces were in general terms expanding the development of French, there was little if any effective federal control of their activities.

The cost-sharing and conditional grant regime, including the system of fiscal transfers for health and post-secondary education under the 1977 legislation, is now very much influenced by the decision of the federal government in August 1978 to embark on a program of drastic expenditure restraint. On September 8, 1978 a joint statement by the Minsiter of Finance and the President of the Treasury Board spelled out the implications of this decision for expenditures.[28] After an intensive review of spending policies it was decided to hold federal expenditures for 1979-1980 to an increase of 8.9 per cent over the previous fiscal year although the growth in the GNP was estimated to be 11 per cent. This necessitated a $2.5 billion reduction in planned expenditures. Some

$370 millions of this was to be in reduced payments to the provinces, which the federal statement pointed out was only about 3.5 per cent of total fiscal transfers to the provincial government and a much less drastic reduction than the federal government was imposing on its own programs. About $150 millions were to be found in reductions to special purpose programs including the Health Resources Fund, the Public Utilities Income Tax Transfer, and the Bilingualism Development Program. The other $220 millions was to come from unconditional transfers under the 1977 legislation and from the Canada Assistance Plan. These latter are for the most part expressed in a contractual form and are under renegotiation with the provinces.

Unlike other federations Canada is now in the process of liquidating its regime of conditional grants. The major elements of this process have been traced in terms of the development from grants for relatively specific purposes to block grants for broadly defined functions to unconditional transfers. Certainly under the current circumstances of fiscal restraint and provincial assertiveness no important new grant-in-aid arrangements are under serious consideration and such restraint is resulting in the elimination of several of the smaller joint programs. As we saw in Chapter 3, the issue of constitutional restrictions on the federal spending power is on the agenda of federal-provincial constitutional discussions. However, in the immediate context of Canadian federalism the more critical issue is the ability of the provinces to finance programs established at their existing levels through federal conditional grants which were subsequently replaced by unconditional fiscal transfers or eliminated entirely. It is as yet too early to make any firm judgment about whether Ottawa's withdrawal from grants-in-aid will work towards widening the disparities among the provinces in the range and quality of public services but, particularly in a period of fiscal restraint, this is probable.

The Equalization Dimension III: Attempts to Narrow Interprovincial Economic Disparities

We have considered the attempts of the federal government to equalize provincial revenues and the range and standard of services provided by the provinces and their respective local governments. Along with the programs administered by the federal authorities themselves these have a redistributive effect on an interprovincial axis. In a study published in 1977 Geoffrey Young examined this redistributive effect in terms not only of revenue equalization but of shared-cost programs (post-secondary education, medicare, hospital insurance), family allowances, and old age security and unemployment insurance.[29] Using statistics from 1974 to 1976 Young found that the have-not provinces and their residents (i.e. all provinces but Ontario, Alberta and British Columbia) were beneficiaries except in the case of unemployment insurance in respect to which British Columbia was a beneficiary and Manitoba and Saskatchewan net losers.

Federal programs to equalize the range and standard of public services available throughout Canada do not *directly* contribute to the reduction of interprovincial and inter-regional economic disparities. These latter disparities are both deep and persistent and in the past two decades there have been more comprehensive efforts than ever before to deal with them. A 1977 study *Lving Together* published by the Economic Council of Canada has documented these disparities extensively. Some of the most significant differences are these:

Index of wages and salaries per worker in the labour force, 1975
(Canada = 100)

Atlantic region	Quebec	Ontario	Prairie Region	B.C.
83	93	109	95	105

Seasonally adjusted unemployment rate, percentages, June 1976

Atlantic region	Quebec	Ontario	Prairie Region	B.C.
11.3	7.8	6.3	4.2	8.8

Mean family income in dollars, 1970

Newf.	PEI.	N.S.	N.B.	Que.	Ont.	Man.	Sask.	Alta.	B.C.
6,680	6,989	7,858	7,479	9,260	10,661	8,646	7,328	9,475	10,019 [30]

There are many other measures of disparity and a certain arbitrariness about interpreting such measures as particular observers believe to be relevant. Regional and provincial aggregates conceal important intra-regional and intra-provincial differences. There are volatilities in the sub-national economies and measures taken at any particular time are thus somewhat misleading—at the most extreme, Saskatchewan is very much influenced by rapidly changing circumstances related to wheat. A plausible case can be made that we should look at disparities in terms broader than purely economic ones with attention to such social indicators as, for example, the quality of housing, the proportion of young people in institutions of post-secondary education, the incidence of crime and juvenile delinquency, the number of books read per capita, and the satisfactions or otherwise that persons in particular provinces and regions feel about their lives. With all these qualifications, the most chronically depressed parts of Canada in the Atlantic region and Quebec have several common characteristics—higher than average rates of unemployment, lower than average productivity per worker, relatively low per person and per family incomes, and the lack of opportunities for diversified and profitable employment.

Several contradictory explanations for the persistence of interprovincial and inter-regional economic disparities in Canada have been given. The general lines of these explanations can be noted briefly:

(1) The economic circumstances of the maritime and western regions result from the workings of national economic policies in favour of the commercial-industrial heartland of Ontario and Quebec. In his spirited account of Maritime grievances Paul MacEwan says this:

> . . . Confederation has so far failed Nova Scotia. It has failed the Maritimes. The national policy is clear and visible, and with inexorable tread the future is approaching, a future as bleak as the past, locked into a position of second class status, barred from the central market, cut off from investment capital, sitting on undeveloped resources, blocked from using the sea and forestalled from the advantages of free trade with natural markets.[31]

From the other end of the country this assertion was made by the submission of the western premiers to the Western Economic Opportunities Conference in 1973:

> . . . the pattern of [western] settlement and development has been influenced by the economic, financial and tax policies of the federal government, which early assisted the concentration of the nation's business and industrial activity in central Canada. These policies which have led to the concentration of financial and industrial resources and population have worked against the allocation of financial and productive resources to bring balance to the economies of all regions of Canada.

(2) Inter-provincial and inter-regional economic disparities arise from the differing natural and human endowments of the various areas of Canada as resources are allocated through the operations of the market system. Kenneth H. Norrie has examined the traditional arguments of westerners that the industrial structure of that region with its lack of secondary manufacturing is primarily the result of discriminatory national economic policies and asserts this counter-argument: ". . . the industrial structure of the West derives from its geographical isolation, relative lateness of settlement and small and diffused population base."[32] Norrie's general argument is that, apart from the taxation of natural resources, the real sources of western economic discontent are in the workings of the market economy rather than discriminatory federal policies.

(3) Regional economic disparities are primarily the result of foreign ownership of Canadian industry and the domination of the Canadian economy by the multinational corporation. This is the conclusion of Paul Phillips in his recent book on *Regional Disparities*. Phillips asserts: "Dominance by the continental American economy and the multinational corporation has effectively made the re-

gions of Canada into regions of the American economy. The very thing that the national policy and Confederation were designed to prevent has come about. . . ."[33] Because of these circumstances the federal government has lost the power to take effective action in reducing regional disparities through fiscal and monetary policies, policies to influence the location of industry, and measures to stimulate domestic activity in Research and Development.

Policies directed toward narrowing territorially-based economic disparities in Canada raise many complex issues, some empirical and some normative. Among the most important of these issues are the following:

(1) To what extent are regional disparities the result of inappropriate levels of aggregate demand in the economy? To the extent that such disparities can be narrowed by regulating aggregate demand, is it practical to have regionally-sensitive fiscal and/or monetary policies? This issue will be discussed in a later section of the Chapter.

(2) Where disparities are judged to be partly at least the result of inadequate structural circumstances prevailing in the provincial and regional economies, what is the appropriate "mix" of remedial policies? There are various possibilities here—measures to upgrade the skills of the labour force, to attract employment-producing enterprises to the region through taxation or other incentives, to provide a more effective infrastructure of transportation and other facilities encouraging to economic growth, etc.

(3) How effective are policies encouraging the out-migration of workers from disadvantaged areas in narrowing disparities? To the extent that such measures are effective on purely economic grounds, what counter-weight should be given to social factors, such as the value of preserving established communities and the kind of social cohesion that prevails in some of the more economically disadvantaged parts of Canada?

A. D. Careless in his book-length study of this matter has pointed out that the latter half of the 1950s was a "watershed," in that conditions at the time propelled the federal government into a new commitment to the reduction of regional differences in economic growth.[34] As we shall see in the next section, Ottawa officialdom in the immediate post-war years perceived the federal role in economic affairs as being centred on measures to ensure appropriate levels of aggregate demand. Such policies were understandably somewhat insensitive to inter-regional disparities in economic welfare and economic growth. However, from 1957 onward the Canadian economy was performing at a less adequate level than that of almost any other western country in terms of its balance of payments, economic growth, inflation, and unemployment. Expert opinion later suggested that these deficiencies in economic performance were in significant measure attributable to Ottawa's failure to regulate the levels of aggregate demand effectively by Keynesian-type policies.

The Diefenbaker years saw Ottawa turn its attention in a more explicit way than in the preceding period to an alleviation of the problems of slow-growth areas. Emphasis came to be given, and has remained, on structural solutions related to such things as industrial location, upgrading the skills of the labour force, specific solutions to the problems of declining industries and so on in contrast to an almost exclusive reliance on regulating the national levels of aggregate demand. The Report of the Royal Commission on Canada's Economic Prospects, published in 1957, had given much attention both to interregional differences in economic welfare and growth, and to the structural problems of the Canadian economy. Much more crucially, a sensitivity to the disadvantaged regions of Canada was in harmony with the dispositions of the Diefenbaker government and the appeal of the revived Progressive Conservative party to those areas and regions in less advantageous circumstances.

From the late 1950s onward there have been several initiatives in federal policies to alleviate the circumstances of less-favoured provinces and regions. As we have seen, the tax arrangements which came into effect in 1957 ended the rental system and provided for unconditional equalization payments to provinces whether or not they levied their own taxes on individual and corporate incomes. With the coming to power of the Diefenbaker government there came a program of Atlantic Province Adjustment Grants above the regular equalization payments and, at about the same time, a program of federal assistance for hydroelectric development was established in these provinces. In 1961 Parliament enacted the Agricultural Rehabilitation and Rural Development Act, the forerunner of later federal schemes for regional economic development. The aim of this program was to raise farm income by finding more profitable uses for marginal agricultural lands, by increasing employment opportunities in agricultural areas, and by enhancing the productivity of farm lands through soil conservation and the development of water supplies. The Minister of Agriculture was empowered to enter into agreements with the provinces to accomplish these objectives. In 1966 a Fund for Rural Economic Development of $50 millions was established. As the ARDA and FRED programs progressed, the emphasis shifted from land improvement toward the building of more effective social and economic infrastructures in depressed areas and toward training for employment in non-primary industry. The early 1960s also saw the creation of the Atlantic Development Board and a preliminary attempt to evolve a regional economic strategy in co-operation with the Atlantic provinces.

In 1963 the recently-elected federal Liberal government sponsored legislation providing for the encouragement of "industrial development in areas of chronic unemployment on a planned basis." This program as it developed provided for both tax relief incentives and cash grants to industry in such areas as were designated by the federal Area Development Authority. According to T. N. Brewis, such designations were made on the basis of the most inadequate statistics, and incentives were given to industry without any effective attempt to specify what objectives were being pursued.[35]

The Department of Regional Economic Expansion was established in 1969 under one of the most powerful ministers in the cabinet, Jean Marchand, with the responsibility of co-ordinating the various federal programs in regional economic development. Careless has analyzed some of the circumstances involved in Ottawa's shift away from the *ad hoc* and incrementalist approach to development to more co-ordinated policies. This general thrust was a reflection of the increasing disposition towards rationality in public policy which was a feature of the Trudeau approach to government described in Chapter 4. At the time of its establishment and subsequently DREE had the backing of the federal Finance Department and the Treasury Board, which favoured more precise and comprehensive formulations of federal objectives and more effective controls to ensure that federal monies expended for regional development met these objectives. In a more political sense the new directions reflected Ottawa's response to the increasing autonomism of Quebec and the other provinces by creating new dependencies on the federal government independent of the provincial administrations, and Careless said this

> The establishment of a virtually new constituency by Ottawa through increased direct spending, refusing the expansion of traditional transfer (to the provinces), and through elaborate provisions in DREE activities for the visible designation of all projects as clearly joint, constituted a new strategy in the assertion of federal power. The result of this process has been not only a shift of some provinces from a role of designing the component parts of a federally financed scheme to that of administrative agents within federal policy, but also the establishment of greater federal visibility in Canada for future tests of strength, particularly in fields of resource policy and urban affairs.[36]

There are two major DREE programs for economic development:

(1) There is the industrial incentives program of capital assistance to industry. These aids are available in all Canada except British Columbia, Alberta and that part of Ontario south of the Ottawa River.

(2) There are ten-year General Development Agreements concluded with all the provinces except Prince Edward Island. These are comprehensive agreements towards stimulating economic growth in depressed areas, and involve not only DREE and the provinces but other federal departments.

There are very great difficulties in measuring the impact of federal policies toward economic development in Canada and these are explored at length in the Economic Council of Canada study *Living Together*. Almost all that can be said with complete assurance is that the Atlantic provinces have, by any appropriate criteria, gained from DREE activities and these activities appear to have been important in reducing the net out-migration of people from Atlantic Canada to negligible proportions.

In direct efforts to stimulate economic development, i.e., in efforts other than those related to the management of aggregate demand, governments in Canada have embarked on an almost unchartered sea. Some of these issues and unresolved problems may be mentioned briefly:

(1) *The choice of policy instruments.* There continues to be a debate among specialists in economic development about the relative effectiveness of different policy instruments. For example, experts disagree about the emphasis which should be given to increasing investment expenditures on machinery and equipment as against enhancing the occupational skills of the labour force.

(2) *The appropriateness of direct measures to stimulate growth in depressed regions as against those to enhance the overall productivity of the national economy.* According to the Act establishing the Department, DREE's main responsibility is "to ensure that economic growth is dispersed widely enough across Canada to bring employment and earnings opportunities in the slow-growth regions as close as possible to those in the other parts of the country, without interfering with a high overall rate of national growth." In a root-and-branch attack on Canadian developmental policies from the early 1960s onward, Alan C. Green has argued that these goals might more effectively be pursued through the operations of the free market.[37] Specifically, Green criticizes federal policies toward regional development for their emphasis on "moving capital into low-income regions" and their weak commitment to "promoting labour emigration." In this view, the goals of national and regional development can and should be made compatible by decisive federal policies towards concentrating economic activity on the basis of the comparative advantages of provinces and regions. Another economist, R. Ian McAllister, is dismayed by the overlapping jurisdictions and intergovernmental friction characteristic of recent developmental policies in Canada and concludes: ". . . the question is whether the Canadian federal system of government has reached already a point where substantial dismantling might be in order— and that far greater emphasis might be placed on closer and more systematic planning with, and delegation to, the private sector."[38]

(3) *The extent to which regional development policies can be and should be harmonized with other national objectives and policies.* DREE does not operate programs of its own but rather is responsible

for co-ordinating the developmental activities of the provinces and of other federal departments and agencies. So far as the latter are concerned, economic development is so comprehensive a concept that it might reasonably be applied to all those parts of the central government concerned with social and economic matters. But is it either feasible or desirable that DREE should get its way with, say, the domestic programs of Industry, Trade and Commerce, with the Departments of Transportation and of Communications, and National Health and Welfare?[39] Is it legitimate that the activities of such federal crown corporations as Air Canada and the Industrial Development Bank be pressed into the service of regional development objectives? There are almost inherent conflicts in developmental policies between those public agencies like DREE which are specifically oriented to regions, and those oriented to particular sectors of the economy like communications, transportation, agriculture and resource development; it is by no means obvious that in cases of such conflict, regional objectives should always prevail.

Despite the vast amount of talk about the need for intergovernmental co-ordination in economic development, it is almost inevitable that the goals of various jurisdictions will remain to a large extent irreconcilable. As McAllister has pointed out, a municipality will see development almost exclusively in terms of employment and the generation of tax revenues within its boundaries.[40] The poorer provinces have a single-minded concern for the creation of jobs. A larger and more prosperous province like British Columbia or Ontario will have more complex goals related, for example, to the protection of the environment, foreign ownership and the intraprovincial dispersion of economic activity. Federal objectives will almost inevitably be more comprehensive still, and more characterized by aims which are not easily reconcilable with each other. These intergovernmental differences in objectives are compounded by the circumstance that in this policy area perhaps more than in any other there is a very vague constitutional delimitation of the powers and responsibilities of the two levels of government.

The positions of the more-favoured and less-favoured provinces in respect to federal efforts to narrow regional disparities are of course quite different.

From the point of view of the smaller and poorer jurisdictions of the Atlantic region, the extent of their reliance on federal developmental programs and the specificity of federal controls embedded in these programs gives these provinces little autonomy to formulate and implement their own economic and social objectives. Careless makes a vigorous and compelling argument that the commitment of the Trudeau government to rationalized and hierarchical procedures in decision-making has resulted in the sacrifice of the political diversity which he regards as an essential of federalism.[41]

The situation of the "have" provinces is of course different. The relatively limited involvement of DREE in these jurisdictions constitutes little threat to their autonomy—at the extremes, the average annual DREE expenditures in the 1969-1974 period were $13 per capita in Ontario and $15 per capita in British Columbia, compared with $807 per capita in Prince Edward Island and $386 per capita in New Brunswick. But so far as all the provinces are concerned, most crucially in the richer provinces, Ottawa's attempt to narrow regional disparities is a zero-sum game in the sense that if one province betters its relative position by whatever criteria are used, some other province must of necessity be in a worse position. With unsatisfactory economic conditions throughout Canada, it is almost inevitable that the richer provinces will to an increasing degree perceive Ottawa's attempts to alleviate inter-regional differences as contrary to their interests.

The Stabilization Dimension and Federal-Provincial Relations

In April 1945 the federal government committed itself to a full employment policy through the publication of the White Paper on Employment and Income.[42] The formulation contained in the White Paper was an application of the analysis of J. M. Keynes in his *General Theory of Employment, Interest and Money* published in 1936. In the broadest of terms, it can be said that the Keynesian theory demonstrated that the free movement of prices and interest rates could not be relied upon to bring about conditions of price stability with full employment. It was thus the responsibility of national governments to devise policies ensuring the appropriate levels of aggregate demand, demand categorized in this analysis as that (1) for consumers' goods, (2) for private capital goods, (3) for exports, and (4) for governmental facilities and services.

Canadian policy-makers, both elected and appointed, found very compelling at the end of the Second World War an analysis which purported to show how under peacetime conditions the federal government might effectively stabilize the economy without the extension of public ownership, the precise planning of objectives for particular sectors of the economy, or specific controls over wages, prices and profits. With the deprivations of the Great Depression very much in mind, full employment was almost a holy cause. Also, the Keynesians predicted that once the transition to peacetime conditions was made, capitalist economies would suffer chronic deficiencies of aggregate demand. These deficiencies could in part be made up by raising the levels of continuing expenditure on public services and, on this basis, the Canadian leadership combined their humanitarian dispositions with the perceived imperatives of full employment policy by proposing levels of spending on health and income-assistance higher than ever before believed to be practicable. Keynes had also argued that no country could carry out effective full employment policies in isolation, and this aspect of his analysis justified Canada and other nations in collaborating to establish a new international economic order on liberal lines. And finally, as T. N. Brewis has pointed out, "One of the chief attractions of the Keynesian theory was its association with an analytical formula which lent itself to ready administration."[43]

Keynes had of course developed his analysis within the environment of a unitary state, and this analysis as received in Canada at the end of the Second World War did not take into account the constraints of federalism in which two levels of government were involved in the formulation and execution of public policy. To Ottawa officialdom, these constraints were not conceived as being of very great importance. In 1945 the central government made 83 per cent of all public expenditures in Canada and while it was presumably expected that this proportion would decline with the return to peacetime conditions, the policy-makers of the central government no doubt assumed both that federal spending would remain dominant and that Ottawa would have a significant influence over the expenditure policies of the provincial and local authorities. On the taxation side it was an essential element of the federal government's design that it would continue to have exclusive access to levies on individual and corporate incomes. In general, the 1945 plans contained a very limited recognition of the need for intergovernmental collaboration in sustaining full employment and price stability. It was, however, suggested that the federal government co-operate with the provinces and municipalities in planning a "shelf" of public works to be undertaken when, in Ottawa's view, general economic conditions made this appropriate. In addition, it was urged that there should be federal-provincial co-operation in the development of natural resources.

In the decade after the Second World War, what I have elsewhere called the "New National Policy" provided a relatively coherent framework for federal action in economic matters. Writing in 1952 the late Vernon Fowke said:

> Lord Keynes' General Theory may well have done more to restore vitality and a sense of purpose to the dominion government than any single incident since the gold strikes in the Yukon in the late 1890's. At times within the past two years it has been a question whether all peacetime national policy might not be sustained under the head of full-employment policy. When baby bonuses and agricultural price support legislation are in danger of being regarded as mere instruments for the maintenance of full employment it is possible to suggest at least a temporary distortion of the national perspective . . .[44]

A more positive view of the Keynesian welfare-state in its Canadian variant was taken by Maurice Lamontagne, then Chairman of the Department of Economics at Laval University, in a paper presented in 1953, entitled "The Role of Government."[45] Lamontagne drew a sharp contrast between the place of government in the "First Industrial Revolution" based on coal, steam and steel, and the "Second Industrial Revolution" based on "oil, water and power, electricity and substitutes for steel." So far as Canada was concerned, the first of these revolutions could be dated from Confederation, the second from the First World War. Because of our particular circumstances, government in Canada had assumed a more important role in economic development during the earlier of these periods than was the case in most of the other western nations. But in the "Second Industrial Revolution" Canada was situated so that ". . . private initiative will continue to play the dynamic and dominant role in the field of long-term industrial development in Canada during the next decades. The role of government will be auxiliary and conditioning." However, government action was still needed to sustain short-term economic stability and its major roles would be in relation to "monetary policy, international trade policy, fiscal policy and public debt management." In terms of Canadian federalism, this would require a relatively high degree of centralization and in the 1954 book *Le Fédéralisme Canadien*[46] Lamontagne was harshly critical of the autonomist policies of Quebec, particularly as these were manifested in fiscal and social welfare matters.

By the late 1950s the Canadian economy was performing inadequately in comparison with those of the other industrialized nations of the western world in terms of the standards of full employment, price stability and economic growth. These inadequacies have continued to the present. It remains a matter of debate among specialists as to whether such deficiencies are in the main attributable to failures of the central government to manage the levels of aggregate demand effectively, or can be traced to structural problems in the national and regional economies. Wherever the truth lies, the federal government from the latter half of the 1950s onward ceased to rely as exclusively as before on Keynesian-type solutions and embarked on a wide variety of structural policies—efforts to narrow regional economic disparities, to enhance the skills of the labour force, to rationalize particular industries, to control the levels of foreign investment, to encourage energy self-sufficiency, to improve Canada's capacity in indigenous technological innovation, and so on. The deficiencies in economic performance also projected the provinces into a more active role in economic development than they had hitherto assumed, and they adopted measures such as seeking markets for their goods, soliciting foreign and domestic investment, directing more specifically the development of energy and natural resources, and engaging in different variants of indicative economic planning. Further, the centralized fiscal order which had been an inheritance of the Second World War was beginning to disintegrate with the decision of Quebec in 1954 to levy its own taxes on individual incomes, and the tax arrangements of 1957-1962 which paid equalization to the provinces, whether or not they "rented" exclusive occupancy of the income tax and succession duty fields to the federal government.

According to the Keynesian imperatives the major instrument of economic stabilization is fiscal policy, i.e. discretionary changes in the rates of taxation and of public expenditures. What then is the appropriate role of the provinces in fiscal policies oriented towards price stability, full employment and economic growth? A viewpoint which was at one time widely accepted was that in the absence of such provincial policies or of federal-provincial collaboration, provincial and local taxation and expenditures will be "perverse" in the sense that these jurisdictions in times of adversity will raise taxes and/or cut back on expenditures, and lower taxes and/or increase expenditures in prosperous periods. In its examination of provincial and municipal expenditures between 1945 and 1961, the federal Royal Commission on Taxation found that this had not been so and that these expenditures "did not exercise a destabilizing influence on the economy. ... The changes in provincial and municipal expenditures are as cyclically stable or more stable than the combined private and federal expenditures they replaced."[47] In the Commission's judgment this "built-in" stability was in large part the result of provinces and municipalities relying very heavily on indirect taxes when yields were "relatively insensitive to short-run fluctuations in the level of economic activity." The increasing reliance of the provinces on direct taxes, however, gave the Commission concern that this stability was being attenuated and it was recommended that the federal government resist pressures to withdraw further from the income tax field.

The Royal Commission on Taxation opposed independent stabilization policies by the provinces. It was argued that because of the effects of such policies outside the borders of the respective provinces, "unless each province took into account what all the other provinces and the federal government were doing, and were going to do, the individual provincial efforts could be offsetting, too extreme, or ill timed."[48] The alternative was federal-provincial co-operation in designing and implementing stabilization policies.

In his study prepared for the Ontario Committee on Taxation in 1967, Clarence L. Barber argued for independent provincial fiscal policies directed toward price stability, full employment and economic growth.[49] Barber pointed out that the larger provinces had both populations and incomes comparable to those of several industrialized nations. He examined the constraints on provincial policies which did not exist in the case of sovereign states—provinces cannot control their own monetary policies, exchange rates, or immigration policies. This did not, however, make it impractical or undesirable for provinces to have independent fiscal policies. There are of course leakages in provincial expenditures where the effects of changes in spending are partly experienced outside provincial borders and this "does seriously limit the effectiveness of provincial fiscal policy unless all or a number of provinces act in parallel fashion." However, since several of the smaller industrial nations have such leakages as great as the larger Canadian provinces, this limitation on the provinces is "a difference in degree rather than kind." In Barber's view, the key question was whether provinces had adequate borrowing capacity to sustain counter-cyclical policies. He was relatively optimistic that the provinces had such capacity in meeting cycles of "moderate amplitude." Thus the provinces, and in particular the larger ones, had the ability to carry out independent fiscal policies and Barber was convinced that it was appropriate they should do so. The control of expenditures in many important matters is within provincial rather than federal jurisdiction. There is regional variation in the need for policy measures and the federal government has a limited ability to meet these varying needs through its own policies. The most effective stabilization policies will of course be those carried out by all levels of government in co-operation. However, Barber felt that provincial pressure through fiscal policy was appropriate in order to change federal policies deemed inadequate to the needs of particular provinces or regions.

The Economic Council of Canada in its 1977 Report *Living Together: A Study of Regional Disparities* made a vigorous case for a "regionally differentiated stabilization policy."[50] A great deal of evidence was presented to show the differential impact of federal fiscal policy on the income and employment of different provinces and regions:

> . . . the 1965-73 experience suggests that Ontario benefits the most by a period of fiscal ease, but is also most affected by a tightening of fiscal policy. The Atlantic region, however, neither benefits greatly during periods of fiscal ease nor suffers much during periods of fiscal tightness. As for the remaining regions, the results for Quebec and the Prairies fall somewhere between those for Ontario and the Atlantic region; British Columbia exhibits the most erratic behaviour.

Thus because of these different impacts, fiscal policy should be applied regionally,

> at times when it is necessary to reduce aggregate demand because of inflationary periods or, for other reasons, attempts could be made to reduce it less in the high-unemployment regions, notably the Atlantic region and Quebec. When demand is being deliberately stimulated because national unemployment is high, one could try to stimulate it more in the high-unemployment regions.[51]

The Report was not very precise about the respective roles of Ottawa and the provinces in stabilization policies or the possibilities of intergovernmental collaboration. However, evidence which was presented showed the relatively large proportion of the impact of an economic stimulus on the province in which the stimulus was applied and this would appear to indicate the potential effectiveness of independent provincial fiscal policies:

Effect of an Increase in Construction Expenditure on the Income of the Province in which this was made relative to National Income (Per Cent)

Newfoundland	60
P.E.I.	53
Nova Scotia	64
New Brunswick	65
Quebec	81
Ontario	88
Manitoba	64
Saskatchewan	59
Alberta	68
British Columbia	75[52]

The relative autonomy of the provincial economies is attributed largely to the circumstance that ". . . more than half of the output produced in Canada is in the service sector, and the vast majority of services, must by their nature, be provided locally."

There appear to be no published studies on the extent to which the various provinces have designed fiscal policies toward economic stability and growth. The Ontario government has recently directed its fiscal policies in terms of the "full employment budget," defined as "a measure of the government surplus or deficit that would occur if the target of full employment were attained."[53] According to a 1971 Ontario Budget Paper,

> The most significant feature of the total public sector's fiscal impact on Ontario is a permanent full-employment surplus, implying a built-in tax drag on the provincial economy. This permanent tax-drag is due wholly to the financial operations of the federal government in Ontario.[54]

It was estimated that this permanent federal surplus, more influenced by discretionary changes in tax rates than in expenditure policies, was rapidly increasing—from 2.6 per cent of potential Gross Provincial Product in 1962 to 4.5 per cent of potential GPP in 1969.[55] Thus, according to the Ontario analysis, the net effect of federal policies was permanently "contractionary" in Ontario, and Ottawa's attempts to mitigate interprovincial disparities had frustrated full employment and economic growth in that province. From the Ontario perspective, provincial and municipal fiscal policies were necessary to counter the effect of federal action.

Federal fiscal policies directed towards stabilization have been almost entirely on the taxation rather than expenditure side. The levers most often used have been changes in capital consumption allowances, the rate of personal income taxes and the levels of exemptions, the manufacturers' sales tax and the corporation income tax. In a paper delivered in 1978, Y. Rabeau and R. Lacroix argued that "96 per cent of all federal government expenditures are not suitable for stabilization purposes."[56] This was so because most of such expenditures are made for purposes which are "recurrent" and thus not adjustable as stabilization imperatives dictate—expenditures on goods and services, transfer payments to individuals, interest on the public debt, and transfers to other governments which are for the most part in aid of recurrent expenditures made by these latter jurisdictions and for which, in many instances, Ottawa is bound by contractual or quasi-contractual agreements with these jurisdictions. Federal expenditures which are suitable for stabilization purposes are limited to those for gross fixed capital formation (GFCF), which have comprised about 3 per cent of recent federal budgets. The estimate is made that over 10 per cent of provincial budgets could be varied in terms of stabilization purposes. Rabeau and Lacroix go on to suggest a Stabilization Fund wholly provided by the federal government, which would be used by the provinces for stabilization purposes according to general conditions arrived at through federal-provincial agreement. The basic rationales for this proposal are that the provinces and local governments control the bulk of GFCF expenditures which are suitable for stabilization, but that these jurisdictions are too limited in their taxation and borrowing capacities to fund such spending themselves.

The second major instrument of stabilization is monetary policy, i.e. the control of the supply of money. As is the case with the regulation of taxation and public expenditures, the incidence of monetary policy on particular regions and provinces varies widely. However, although any layman's view is suspect here, there would appear to be few possibilities for either federal-provincial co-ordination in respect to such policies, or for a regionally sensitive monetary policy. This is so because national and international credit markets are national and international, and thus attempts to differentiate among provinces and regions would be subject to massive "leakages." Despite this, the Report of the Standing Senate Committee on National Finance, published in 1971, found some possibilities for regionally sensitive monetary policies by way of the Bank of Canada applying moral suasion on the chartered banks to give special attention to slow-growth areas in their lending.[57]

In the spring and summer of 1978 what seemed a hopeful event in the co-ordination of federal and provincial fiscal policies gave way to rancorous conflict between the two orders of government.[58] The federal Minister of Finance in his budget of April 10 proposed that the provinces reduce their sales taxes by three per cent for a six-month period in order to stimulate the economy. Ottawa would compensate the provinces for the loss of two-thirds of the revenue from such a reduction or, alternatively, compensation would be paid if a province wished to make a two per cent reduction and extend it for a further six months. In his Budget Speech the Minister indicated that the agreement of the provinces for such a scheme had been secured. Although what actually happened is not on the public record, the apparent "agreement" soon became unstuck. The response of the Quebec government was that the federal measure was an unwarranted intrusion on provincial jurisdiction and would do little to help that province. Quebec countered by eliminating entirely the sales tax on all clothing, textiles, shoes and furniture—products in which Quebec producers were dominant. After an acrimonious dispute between the two governments, Ottawa finally made cash compensation directly to Quebec taxpayers rather than to the government of the province. In the federal-provincial dispute, the premiers of the four western provinces had also criticized the "unilateral and intrusive" way in which the federal plan had been announced.

In the past decade both economists and the governments who design their policies in part at least in the light of economists' professional advice have become less confident than before about the possibilities of controlling national economies by Keynesian-type regulation of aggregate demand. Paul Samuelson, one of the world's most respected macro-economists whose textbook had instructed a generation of beginning students of economics in Keynesian theories, wrote this in 1974. "No mixed economy—not the U.S. or the U.K., Sweden or Switzerland, Germany or Japan, France or Italy—knows how to have sustained full employment."[59] The operative words here are "knows how," and economists have almost ceased to talk as they formerly did about "fine-tuning" the economy according to straightforward and easily determined trade-offs between inflation and unemployment. Whatever the possibilities of aggregate-demand policies in improving national economic performance, these are significantly limited by the lack of federal-provincial co-operation, particularly in respect to fiscal policies. It has become an established practice for the federal and provincial ministers of finance to meet early in each calendar year when the budgets of most of the provinces are in process of final preparation, and there is an almost continuous exchange of information among governments about fiscal matters. Yet as the federal measure of 1978 to induce the provinces to reduce their sales taxes showed in a dramatic way, effective collaboration about these matters is yet to be achieved.

The Energy Dimension and Canadian Federalism

The dramatic increases in oil prices imposed by the Organization of Petroleum Exporting Countries in 1973 has conferred upon national governments the imperative of attempting to ensure energy supplies within their respective jurisdictions. Just as this crisis has resulted in fundamental shifts of geopolitical power between oil-importing and oil-exporting nations and opened up new cleavages and conflicts among nations, so in Canada new advantages have been realized by provinces with natural endowments of fossil-fuels and new vulnerabilities experienced by provinces and regions deficient in such resources. In general terms, the energy crisis has directly or indirectly joined a group of crucial issues in public policy, federal-provincial relations, and the most fundamental aspects of national life—foreign ownership; the rights of native peoples; the protection of the natural environment; the respective roles of public and private enterprise in economic development; interprovincial fiscal equalization and other attempts to reduce interprovincial disparities; and persistent patterns of production and consumption developed on the basis of cheap and seemingly inexhaustible sources of energy.

The basic constitutional aspects of the distribution of powers in respect to fuel and energy matters can be outlined briefly.[60]

(1) Section 109 of the British North America Act of 1867 states:

> All Lands, Mines, Minerals, and Royalties belonging to the several Provinces of Canada, Nova Scotia, and New Brunswick at the Union, and all Sums then due or payable for such Lands, Mines, Minerals, or Royalties, shall belong to the several Provinces of Ontario, Quebec, Nova Scotia, and New Brunswick in which the same are situate or arise, subject to any Trusts existing in respect thereof, and to any Interest other than that of the Province in the Same.

These provisions were applied to the provinces of British Columbia, Prince Edward Island and Newfoundland when they entered Confederation. When Manitoba in 1870 and Alberta and Saskatchewan in 1905 attained provincial status the federal government retained control over the natural resources within their boundaries, and it was only in 1930 that these provinces attained an equal status with the others.

Apart from those resources alienated to private individuals and groups, the provinces own the resources within their respective boundaries. In general terms, most of the sub-surface rights in the three most westerly provinces have not been so alienated.[61] These powers of ownership give the provincial governments the authority to determine the rate at which resources are developed, the ways such development shall take place and the price of such resources within the province.

(2) Under its exclusive jurisdiction over trade and commerce and over "Lines of Steam or other Ships, Railways, Canals, Telegraphs, and other Works and Undertakings connecting the Province with any other or others of the Province, or extending beyond the Limits of the Province," the federal government is empowered to regulate the conditions under which resources pass into interprovincial and international trade, including the volume and price of these commodities and the facilities by which they are transported.

(3) The federal authorities have exclusive control over natural resources in the Yukon and Northwest Teritories. A 1967 advisory
opinion of the Supreme Court of Canada gave seabed resources off
the west coast to the federal government but there is an unresolved
and continuing dispute between Ottawa and the five easternmost
provinces about ownership of seabed resources.

(4) The powers of Parliament to raise monies by "any Mode or System
of Taxation" are limited only by the prohibition of Section 125
against the taxation of "Lands or Property" belonging to a province.

The summary account given above indicates only the "parameters of
jurisdiction"[62] about resource matters. There are inherent complexities
in the circumstance that so far as resources within provincial boundaries are concerned, the rights of ownership are exclusively provincial
but legislative jurisdiction over many aspects of resource development
is divided between Parliament and the provinces. Two areas of jurisdictional conflict may be mentioned briefly:

(1) The provinces through their ownership of resources may exercise
what A. R. Thompson and Howard R. Eddy call "de facto jurisdiction over interprovincial trade in resources".[63] Thompson and
Eddy give an example of this in relation to the issuance of licences
to develop natural gas which might without violating the law provide that such privileges be terminated if the gas were exported.
Also there is little doubt that provinces with resources can validly
take measures to ensure that these are available to consumers
within the provinces at more favourable prices than to those outside.

(2) The federal government through its taxation powers may qualify
provincial ownership rights over resources. The current tax on oil
exports from Canada is a recent and dramatic use of this power,
which obviously makes these resources less valuable to the oil-
producing provinces than they would otherwise be. The only limitation to the federal taxing power is contained in Section 125 of the
British North America Act which provides that no "Lands or Property" belonging to a province are subject to taxation. However,
whether he was stating a constitutionally valid position or not, the
federal Minister of Justice warned the provinces in November, 1974
that they could not escape federal resources taxes by setting up
crown corporations to take over the activities of private companies.[64]

Attention in the Canadian energy crisis has been focused on petroleum and petroleum products, although the rapid escalation in oil
prices from 1973 onward has resulted both in increases in the price of
natural gas and fundamental changes in the economic circumstances
surrounding the development of other sources of energy than the fossil
fuels. In 1961 the federal government adopted the National Oil Policy,

which ensured western oil the Canadian market from the Ottawa River westward while the rest of Canada would be supplied from cheaper foreign sources, mainly Venezuela and the Middle East.[65] This policy was adopted in the face of a world over-supply of petroleum and an essential element in it was that with the active support of the federal government markets for western Canadian oil would be found in the United States. By 1970 Canada had become self-sufficient in oil, with a domestic production of 1,476,000 barrels per day and a domestic demand of 1,466,000 barrels a day; in this year there were exports of 670,000 barrels a day from the provinces of origin (97.3 per cent from Alberta and Saskatchewan) with imports into Canada of 762,000 barrels per day.[66]

In the past generation, Canada along with other industrialized nations has developed an economic structure and a way of life based upon cheap and abundant energy. Energy costs as a proportion of GNP declined between 1950 and 1970 from 11.5 per cent to 8.9 per cent.[67] In these same two decades oil and natural gas as the sources of primary energy consumption increased from 31.0 per cent to 63.4 per cent while coal decreased from 41.9 per cent to 11.0 per cent.[68] Although these cheap and seemingly inexhaustible supplies of energy made this circumstance of less than crucial concern, Canada during this period became divided into provinces and regions that were high in energy consumption but relatively poor in their endowment of fuels for energy-generation, and provinces with abundant fuels to export outside their boundaries. Most dramatically, the provinces of Ontario and Quebec in 1970 accounted for 61.7 per cent of primary energy consumption in Canada, of which 57.4 per cent was oil and natural gas, but together produced almost none of these fossil fuels. At the other end of the spectrum, Alberta in 1970 produced 76.6 per cent of the total Canadian petroleum and 81.4 per cent of the nation's natural gas, while having only 10.5 per cent of Canada's total energy consumption and using only 8 per cent and 30.8 per cent of the country's oil and natural gas respectively.[69]

Under the National Oil Policy a set of stable, and harmonious relations developed. That western oil had a secure market west of the Ottawa River with domestic surpluses being exported to the United States was in the interest of the multinational oil companies, who also enjoyed generous tax concessions from both federal and provincial governments. The oil industry had brought unprecedented prosperity to Alberta and a significant degree of economic diversification to Saskatchewan. At the same time, those parts of Canada east of the Ottawa Valley line enjoyed the advantages of offshore oil cheaper than what they could have been supplied with from western Canada. Only those parts of Ontario which could otherwise have been supplied from offshore sources bore the economic burdens of the National Oil Policy, although with the prices prevailing up until 1973 this burden was not a very heavy one.

The energy crisis descended on Canada as on other nations with bewildering rapidity. Some rather hesitant measures were taken to restrict oil exports to the Unites States in the early months of 1973. A growing awareness of the imminent energy shortage, combined with the rapid escalation of world oil prices by the OPEC nations and the Arab oil embargo, led to more definite responses from the federal government later in the year—the introduction in September of a "voluntary" price freeze to January 31, 1974, the announcement of the extension of a pipeline to Montreal so that eastern markets could be served from western Canadian sources, and the imposition of an export tax on western crude oil. On December 6, 1973, Prime Minister Trudeau announced in the House of Commons a new national oil policy whose major elements were the following:

—the abolition of the Ottawa Valley line to give the western provinces a guaranteed outlet for increased production in the eastern provinces and to ensure supplies to these provinces.

—the early completion of a pipeline to Montreal so that eastern markets could be served from western sources.

—the early establishment of a publicly-owned Canadian petroleum company "principally to expedite exploration and development," and aggressive measures to intensify research on oil sands technology.

—the continuance of the export tax on domestic oil equal to the difference between the domestic price and the export price as determined by the National Energy Board.

—a short-term proposal to share the proceeds of the export tax on a 50/50 basis with the producing provinces, subject to a discussion of this and other related matters at a federal-provincial conference to be held in early 1974.

A Federal-Provincial Conference on Energy was held in Ottawa on January 22-23, 1974. The outcome of this Conference was that there would be a single price for oil throughout Canada, modified by transportation costs and differing levels of provincial taxes on that commodity. To attain that end, western oil would be made available to the Canadian market at prices significantly below those prevailing in the world market, while Ottawa would subsidize the costs of foreign oil largely from the proceeds of the export tax.

At the 1974 Conference the polar positions were clearly stated by the heads of the governments of Canada and Alberta.

Prime Minister Trudeau's opening statement put the energy crisis and Canadian policies to deal with it within an ideological formulation of Canada as a national community. On the international scene the recent dramatic shifts in power and welfare had come about by "the accidents of geology." However, we in Canada "need not reproduce in miniature the fragmented, sometimes brutal world vision I have just described." Canadians have pursued common purposes in the past through defining the social and economic rights of individuals and through various measures of interprovincial equalization. This concept of "fraternal responsibility" must now be extended to energy matters. Canada must thus move rapidly towards national self-sufficiency in oil both by securing the Canadian market for existing domestic supplies and by moving rapidly towards the development of new supplies of petroleum and other energy sources. In this process it would be necessary for oil prices to increase, both to honour the ownership rights of the producing provinces and to encourage the oil companies, with much more public involvement than in the past, to find and develop new supplies. Despite these provincial rights of ownership, the Prime Minister asked ". . . would it be reasonable for a province to receive continuing revenues which would give it the capacity to spend, in proportion to its population, three or four times as much as other provinces?"[70]

The Alberta position was stated with great forcefulness by Premier Peter Lougheed. When the National Oil Policy was adopted in 1961, and subsequently, Albertans wished to secure the whole Canadian market for western oil but for purely economic reasons this request was refused. Alberta was thus forced to seek export markets in the United States. Why now, when the advantages were reversed, should the rules of the game be changed? The federal export tax on oil was discriminatory, it was not imposed on the export of other natural resources such as lumber or the export, with federal approval, of Ontario electricity to the United States. Provincial ownership of resources is a fundamental element of Confederation and the export tax is "contrary to both the spirit and the intent of Confederation." Further, and most crucially, oil and natural gas are depleting, non-renewable resources and should be sold "only at prices which reflect fair value." Unlike other provinces, the Alberta economy rests on a base of resources which are exhaustible and are being quickly exhausted. In the decade or so immediately ahead it was thus necessary for the province to diversify its economic structure toward becoming less dependent on the sale of unprocessed natural resources, and current federal policies limiting the prices of oil were frustrating this objective.[71]

After the January Conference intensive discussions between the governments continued and on March 27, 1974 the Prime Ministers and Premiers at their meeting agreed that until June 1975 the price of crude oil would be set at $6.50 a barrel. Again, eastern Canadian consumers would be protected against increases in petroleum prices for foreign oil to the extent that such increases were not matched by increases in domestic petroleum prices, and this compensation program would be financed largely through the proceeds of the export tax on oil sent to the

United States. Thus "through the combination of the export charge and the oil import compensation program, it was possible for consumers throughout Canada to purchase petroleum products at prices that would have prevailed if pipelines had existed to supply all regions of the country with domestic petroleum."[72]

From the federal budget of May 6, 1974 energy matters in Canada have become entangled with a bitter federal-provincial conflict about the deductibility of provincial royalties and other levies made on the resource industries from corporate income as defined for federal tax purposes. (Earlier in this chapter the impact of higher oil prices on the regime of interprovincial fiscal equalization has been discussed). The non-deductibility of such provincial charges was announced in the federal budget of May, 1974. The government was defeated on this budget in the House of Commons, but subsequent to the election held on July 8 of that year this policy has been maintained by the Trudeau administration. At issue is the distribution of the rapidly escalating revenues derived from the development of non-renewable natural resources among the federal government, the provinces and the private corporations active in such development. Up until the 1970s both Ottawa and the provinces were notoriously generous in extending tax concessions to these industries.[73] The more recent disposition of governments to perceive the returns from resource development in terms of economic rent has led these jurisdictions to impose higher burdens on these corporations and the vast increases in revenues occasioned by the world energy crisis has of course enhanced the possibilities for diverting such revenues to the public purse. All the provinces have in the past years increased their levies on resource development. Ottawa sees in this an "erosion" of the corporation income tax base and argues that this base must be maintained, so that the federal government can both sustain effective stabilization policies and meet its expenditure responsibilities. The provinces have argued aggressively that the deductibility of royalties is an established principle of taxation, and that federal policy constitutes a direct challenge to the ownership of these resources by the provinces and to provincial management of such resources. This conflict has been particularly bitter in the case of the two oil-producing provinces and the Premier of Alberta claimed that federal policies were in contravention of the agreement on oil prices reached in March 1974.[74] Another set of crucial issues relates to the distribution of revenues between governments and the private corporations in the resource industries and appropriate measures to be taken to ensure that a significant part of industry's share is directed toward the exploration and development of Canadian resources rather than enhanced profits or investment outside Canada.[75]

On April 9-10, 1975 the First Ministers met in Ottawa with the major purpose of discussing the circumstances which would follow the freeze on domestic petroleum prices, which was to expire within the next two months. By this time the federal government was convinced that a significant increase in petroleum prices was necessary. This position seems to have resulted from the pressures of the producing provinces, the decreasing activity in oil exploration by private companies, the increasingly pessimistic estimates of domestic reserves of oil and a recognition of the need for energy conservation. This meeting was one of the least satisfactory ones in the recent history of federal-provincial conferences and adjourned without agreement on domestic oil prices, largely but by no means exclusively because of the refusal of Ontario to accept any price increases. The Ontario position was that in the increase of domestic oil prices from $2.70 per barrel to $6.50 per barrel over the past 18 months, some 90 per cent of the increased revenues had gone to the federal and producing governments and had done very little to enhance the supply of oil and natural gas, and that price increases would contribute to already severe inflationary pressures and to higher levels of unemployment.[76] Because the Conference could not agree the federal government set the domestic price of petroleum at $8.00 a barrel after the former arrangement expired, and in its budget of June 23, 1975 increased the excise tax on gasoline 10¢ per gallon. The Ontario government in its turn imposed a 90-day freeze on the increase from $6.50 to $8.00 per barrel on petroleum sold within the province.

In May 1977 Ottawa and the provinces concluded agreements on petroleum prices to the effect that the per barrel price would increase by $1 on July 1, 1978 and again on January 1, 1979. As a result of negotiations with Alberta the second increase was delayed until July 1, 1979 with a further one to take place on January 1, 1980.

Several more general aspects of the working of Canadian institutions of government during the ongoing energy crisis deserve brief consideration.

First, the energy situation has impelled governments to evolve more comprehensive and coherent policies towards energy, and such policies have led directly to severe inter-governmental conflict. When energy was cheap and in seemingly inexhaustible supply the public authorities did not much concern themselves with alternative energy sources, the impact of energy policies on the economy, or energy conservation. These circumstances have changed. The new coherence has both a conceptual and a related organizational dimension. Most crucially perhaps, federal policies have been organized around the broad goal of national self-sufficiency in energy. On the organizational side, prior to 1973 responsibility for energy matters was divided in the federal and provincial governments among several departments and agencies which carried on their activities with little relation to one another. These thrusts have been reflected as clearly as anywhere in Ontario where there has been established a Ministry of Energy with responsibility for various energy policies and an Ontario Energy Corporation to develop energy sources. In general terms this new degree of coherence has given rise to intergovernmental conflict as the various jurisdictions define their interests in respect to energy in a more clear-cut, expert and comprehensive way.

Secondly, the energy crisis has rapidly extended public involvement in energy matters and has launched the country on experiments in joint public-private ownership. The older mix of public-private involvement in energy development was featured by the dominance of government in the hydroelectric and nuclear fields, private ownership with public subsidies in coal, and a peculiarly unrestrained pattern of private ownership in respect to petroleum and natural gas. This has now changed, particularly in relation to the fossil fuels. Among other developments we have joint public-private participation in Syncrude and the Pan-Arctic consortium; the formation of a national petroleum company for exploration and development; the Alberta Energy Company and the Ontario Energy Corporation to undertake energy development in those provinces; and the actual setting of domestic petroleum prices by the federal government. In the cases of the Syncrude project for the development of the Alberta tar sands and the Pan-Arctic consortium for development of fossil-fuel resources in Northern Canada, there is a pattern of public-private ownership and control quite new in the Canadian experience. It is possible to foresee complications in such arrangements, not only between their public and private components but also in circumstances as that of Syncrude (with holdings by the federal and Alberta governments) where one or more governments holds equity shares under the jurisdiction of another; this was presumably the kind of consideration which has led Ottawa to block the participation of the government of Quebec in the Pan-Arctic consortium.

Thirdly, in the intense bargaining between the federal and provincial governments during the energy crisis, important and formerly influential interest groups have been rendered relatively ineffectual. Glyn R. Berry, in analyzing the circumstances of 1973 leading up to Prime Minister Trudeau's assertion of a new national petroleum policy on December 6 of that year, states: "During these developments the oil industry seemed helpless to prevent measures that, only a year before, the government itself would have rejected as radical and unnecessary."[77] Richard Simeon has said of the more general phenomenon ". . . the operation of the process (of federal-provincial negotiations) itself tends to freeze out interest groups."[78] Berry's analysis states that when decision-making on energy matters was relatively non-controversial, the federal and provincial governments were "benevolently responsive" to the interests of the oil industry. This lobby responded very ineffectually to the new circumstances, and the oil companies lost both their former degree of autonomy and their influence over policy, as other interest groups became mobilized against them and as governments began to deal with energy matters at the level of fundamental policy considerations.[79] In general, these close and harmonious relationships between industry and the public authorities were weakened as governments began to respond to one another to the virtual exclusion of other political actors.

Fourthly, and perhaps most crucially, the energy crisis has led, in respect to these matters, to a resurgence of power and purpose by the central government. Despite the hostility to nationalism expressed in Pierre Elliott Trudeau's academic writings, the Prime Minister's defence of the new national oil policy on December 6, 1973 and his opening speech to the Federal-Provincial Conference on Energy on January 22, 1974 were enunciated in explicitly nationalistic terms. Canada was and must remain, he argued, a "national community" and the new demands of "fraternity" in such a community made necessary national self-sufficiency in energy and decisive action by the national government to protect individual Canadian consumers and the provinces and regions of Canada against dislocations in the price and supply of energy, as well as the sharing of revenues accruing from energy development throughout the nation. These new imperatives projected the national government into many new activities in which it had hitherto done little or nothing—energy conservation, the development of new energy sources, the building of pipe-lines for oil and natural gas, the control of the domestic price of petroleum, emergency legislation allowing Ottawa to control the domestic supply of oil and so on. In all these circumstances, and others, new patterns of relations with the provinces have evolved.

The International Economic Dimension and Federal-Provincial Relations

In the most general sense the imperatives of economic nationhood require that one set of governmental authorities have the capacity to speak for and to commit the nation in international affairs. However, the constitutional division of powers over economic matters in Canada along with the increasing vigor and aggressiveness of the provinces in economic policy makes it almost inevitable that these latter jurisdictions will have a significant involvement in international economic interactions. There are two major kinds of such involvement. In some cases the provincial governments themselves assume the position of independent actors in relations with foreign individuals and business firms, and with foreign governments. Under other circumstances the provinces assert some influence over federal policies in international economic matters which are unequivocally within the jurisdiction of the government of Canada.

One example of the extent of the involvement of one province in international economic affairs was given by Premier Peter Lougheed in his Address in the Reply to the Speech from the Throne in the Legislative Assembly of Alberta on October 12, 1977.[80] The Premier began his discussion of his government's international activities by quoting from the communiqué of the Premiers' Conference of 1977 to the general effect that the provinces should play a "more prominent role" in Canadian-American relations. Here were some of the more specific Alberta involvements:

—in June 1977 the Premier and his Minister of Intergovernmental Affairs had visited Geneva in connection with the GATT negotiations. While there they had met with "chief negotiators for the United States, the European Economic Community, Japan, and the head of the secretariat that was involved, as well as, of course, the Canadian delegation."

—in the fall of 1977 the Premier had been to the Soviet Union in connection with Alberta wheat sales. "The main purpose of my visit . . . was that I wanted to see if . . . the Canadian government was basically out-negotiated by the United States." He had also met Premier Kosygin and discussed the possible sale of Alberta barley to the Soviet Union. In addition, the Premier and his colleagues made a visit to western Siberia to make an independent assessment of whether the CIA report on oil production in that region made public by President Carter was valid and determined that the American judgment was "probably exaggerated."

—the Premier had also visited Saudi Arabia and Iran. In the latter country he met with the Minister of Energy and discussed "price forecasts, investment policy, petrochemicals and production forecasts." Mr. Lougheed also discussed the sale of grain to these two countries.

While the extent of Alberta's international involvement in 1977 was more extensive than is usual for a provincial jurisdiction, there was here a somewhat dramatic example of how provincial economic interests impel such governments into action in the international economic arena.

There are a very large number of transborder relations between Canadian provinces and the American states, most often between jurisdictions which are geographically contiguous.[81] These interactions often relate to matters which are in a broad sense economic. In his analysis of such relations involving British Columbia, P. R. Johannson described the general quality of these transactions which appear to apply to other provinces as well:

Most interactions result from direct initiatives at the local level, rather than through formalized structures established between Canada and the United States. In the main, there is little use of formal written documents, but a strong tendency towards making "understandings" with other local governments. In part, this is because of constitutional prohibitions on this form of activity, in part, it is due to the level of authority involved, as the bureaucratic actor is not involved in written documentation between governments. Because of the numerical weight of bureaucratic interactions, the image . . . is one of largely informal contacts with neighbouring authorities who are charged with comparable governmental responsibilities.[82]

While these kinds of transborder relations do not in most cases involve fundamental matters of economic policy, it is at least possible that their cumulative effects might influence Canadian-American relations in important ways.

The actions of the provinces in economic affairs can and do complicate the relations between the government of Canada and other nations. Three examples can be given:

(1) In order to stimulate the economy, Ontario in 1975 reduced the sales tax on automobiles manufactured in North America but did not make a similar reduction for cars imported from Europe. This discrimination was contrary to Canada's obligations under GATT and under federal pressure was soon eliminated.

(2) Canada and the United States signed a treaty for the development of hydro-electric facilities on the Columbia River in 1961. Because of the subsequent disagreement of British Columbia with this settlement there was a renegotiation involving the Canadian and American governments and the government of British Columbia and a revised treaty was signed in 1964.

(3) The government of the United States was very critical of the action of the Saskatchewan government in nationalizing several American-controlled potash companies in 1975. This action brought about a complication of some significance in Canadian-American economic relations.

The increasing aggressiveness of the provinces has led to demands that these governments be more closely associated with the federal authorities in respect to international economic policies, particularly in the renegotiation of the General Agreement on Tariffs and Trade which takes place every ten years. The Report of the Western Premiers' Task Force on Constitutional Trends of 1977 said this

Although the federal government's responsibility for negotiating international trade agreements is clear . . . the Task Force viewed provincial output into the final position on international trade negotiations to be of utmost importance, given the significance of foreign market penetration to the realization of western economic objectives.

The liberalization of trade with the reduction of trade barriers is vital to the development in the west of a secure economic base; to aid industries reliant on natural growth through secondary industry; and to develop a strong manufacturing sector. As a result, the Task Force called for a more active and substantial role for the formulation of national policies in such areas as GATT negotiations.[83]

The federal government has continued to safeguard its exclusive prerogative of defining Canada's position in international trade matters but has in the past two years become more willing to consult with the provinces in respect to these policies. The renegotiation of the GATT agreements was the subject of a federal-provincial conference of Ministers of Finance and Industry in October 1977. Significantly, there seems to have evolved a high degree of support among the provinces, including even Ontario and Quebec, for trade liberalization in exchange for conesssions from other countries for Canadian exports.[84] The provinces are watching the GATT negotiations closely and three—Ontario, Quebec and Alberta—have sent independent delegations to Geneva to judge these proceedings at first hand and to present their positions to the Canadian delegation. When the negotiations are concluded there will of course be the need for federal-provincial collaboration on measures to cushion the impact on industries adversely affected by trade liberalization.

The Structural Dimension and Canadian Federalism

The political and economic structures both shaped and envisioned by the Confederation settlement of 1864-1867 were pre-eminently the manifestations of an impulse to establish a transcontinental economy in the remaining British territories of North America. With only slight exaggeration, Alfred Dubuc has written of this settlement "Confederation would be the political institution necessary for the pursuit of an economic project."[85] This original project and what I have called "the MacDonald-Laurier national policy" which was a fulfillment of it provided the economic foundations of Canadian nationhood until about the end of the First World War. There were three inter-related structural imperatives:

—to establish and sustain a strong industrial sector in the central heartland through a policy of high tariffs.
—to acquire and subsequently settle and develop a western hinterland.
—to provide for the integration of Canada on east-west lines through a railway system wholly on Canadian territory.[86]

Within the framework of this integrated economic structure the workings of the price system relatively unhampered by public control were expected to and did control the operation of the national economy.

The Macdonald-Laurier national policy provided a relatively high degree of coherence both for the economic activities of the federal government and for the Canadian economy itself in the first half-century after Confederation. It provided also a relatively limited scope for the provinces in economic policy. In his 1966 article Dubuc made a useful summary of some of the long-term developments which resulted in the increasing importance of the provinces in economic matters during the second 50 years of Canada's history:

> First, the discovery of extensive mineral resources has led to a considerable expansion of the domains and territory subject to provincial jurisdiction. Second, population growth and urbanization have caused expenditures on urban development to rise rapidly. Third, in the sector of primary activities, agriculture has yielded pride of place to mining. Fourth, a technological revolution, utilizing two great sources of energy, electricity and the internal combustion engine, has ushered in vast projects of dam construction and road development. Fifth, within the tertiary sector, the sector which has undergone the greatest development in the 20th century, there has been a continuous evolution of services in the fields of education, public health and social security.[87]

The developments to which Dubuc referred had become evident by the 1920s. The same decade manifested also a profound and lasting change in the economic circumstances of Canadian nationhood with the relative decline in the country's dependence on British capital and British markets and the increasing Canadian integration into the North American continental economy.

During the inter-war period the government of Canada developed no coherent set of national economic policies to replace those which had been fulfilled by the time of the First World War or to meet the new domestic and international circumstances facing the Canadian community. At the end of the Second World War, however, the federal government committed the national to measures which might together be called "the new National Policy."[88] As was the case in the previous period, there were three inter-related imperatives:

—the federal government would assume leadership in full employment policy through Keynesian-type measures to assure appropriate levels of aggregate demand, mainly through fiscal policy.

—because economists predicted that the peacetime economy would be subject to chronic deficiencies in aggregate demand, the federal government would assume leadership directed towards high and continuing spending on health and welfare.

—in co-operation with other nations, Canada would assist in the economic rehabilitation of the countries devastated by war and in the establishment of an international economic order on liberal foundations.

It is significant that unlike the earlier National Policy, the new measures undertaken by Ottawa at the end of the Second World War were *not* directed towards altering the structure of the Canadian economy—the general thrust of the Keynesian imperative was that once the public authorities had secured appropriate levels of aggregate demand the workings of the price system could be allowed to control economic operations.[89] There were, however, a number of other measures of a broadly structural nature undertaken in the years directly after 1945. For the most part these measures were in the direction of completing the national system of transportation and communication—the St. Lawrence Seaway, a complex of civil airports, the Trans-Canada Highway, the Trans-Canada Pipeline, broadcasting networks and so on. It may be mentioned almost parenthetically that in a somewhat paradoxical way these physical structures worked in the direction of both Canadian *and* continental integration.

By the late 1950s the Keynesian-type policies had ceased to yield satisfactory results in terms of employment, price stability and economic growth. This failure resulted in two very fundamental developments which still condition the economic circumstances of Canadian federalism.

First, the federal government was projected into a large number of economic policies of a structural nature. Some of these have already been mentioned—policies related to regional disparities, to upgrading the skills of the labour force, to ensuring energy self-sufficiency, to monitoring foreign ownership. Others concerned attempts to stimulate Research and Development, to rationalize particular industries and industrial sectors, to give consumers more adequate protection and, perhaps most crucially, to control or influence incomes. Most of these structural policies involved Ottawa in relations with the provinces if such measures were to be effective.

Secondly, the provinces were projected into a much more active role in economic affairs than they had hitherto played. There were aggressive attempts to encourage foreign investment and to seek foreign markets for provincial products. During the 1960s most of the provinces undertook various programs of indicative economic planning. Provincial governments undertook their own plans of regional development. In some cases the provinces emerged as independent actors in international economic affairs. Generally speaking, these jurisdictions became much more aggressive than ever before in shaping the structures and defending the interests of their respective provincial economies.

The structural dimension of Canadian federalism has been fundamentally altered by the piecemeal and gradual disintegration of what Donald Creighton called the "commercial Empire of the St. Lawrence." These changes will be analyzed in more detail in the next chapter.

As the commercial empire of the St. Lawrence has been subjected to strains, so in the United States there has been a rapid shift of economic power to the West and the South. The consequences of this latter shift for the structure of the Canadian economy and for Canadian-American economic and political relations has not so far as I know been analyzed. In his book *Power Shift*, Kirkpatrick Sale designates as the "Southern Rim" those areas of the United States south of the 37th Parallel which include North and South Carolina, Georgia, Florida, Tennessee, Alabama, Mississippi, Louisiana, Arkansas, Oklahoma, Texas, New Mexico, Arizona and the southern parts of Nevada and California.[90] If we take Canadian exports to the various states as an important indicator of Canadian-American integration, according to figures published in the *Financial Post* of May 12, 1979, total exports to the Southern Rim— including *all* of Nevada and California—were $4,684 millions compared with $24,137 millions to what Sale defines as the "Northeast",[91] and such sales to the "Rim" exceeds only marginally those to New York alone. The implications for Canada's role in the continental economy are obviously considerable when, in respect to trade and other matters, our strongest linkages are with that region of the United States which is in relative decline. It may also be conjectured that in economic competition between Canada and the United States, the Americans have the advantage that the states appear to have neither the power nor the impulse to erect the kind of barriers to the free movement of people, commodities and capital that have been established by the Canadian provinces.

Notes

1. See Donald Creighton, *British North America at Confederation*, A Study Prepared for the Royal Commission on Dominion-Provincial Relations, Ottawa: King's Printer, 1939, particularly Chapter IX, "The Division of Economic Powers at Confederation."
2. This section owes much to A. E. Safarian, *Canadian Federalism and Economic Integration*, Constitutional Study Prepared for the Government of Canada, Ottawa: Information Canada, 1974.
3. On provincial restrictions on the Canadian common market, see the articles, Carl S. Shoup, "Interregional Economic Barriers: The Canadian Provinces," and Michael S. Trebilcock, Gordon Kaiser and Robert S. Pritchard, "Restrictions on the Interprovincial Mobility of Resources: Goods, Capital and Labour," in *Intergovernmental Relations*, Toronto: Ontario Economic Council, 1977, pp. 81-100, and pp. 101-123 respectively. See also John S. Pattison, "Dividing the Power to Regulate", in *Canadian Confederation at*

   the Crossroads, Vancouver: The Fraser Institute, 1978, pp. 122-136, and Albert Breton, *"Discriminatory Government Policies in Federal Countries,"* Montreal: Private Planning Association of Canada, 1967.

4. Safarian, *op. cit.* pp. 98-102.

5. *A Future Together,* Ottawa: Minister of Supply and Services, 1979, p. 123.

6. Thomas J. Courchene, "The New Fiscal Arrangements and the Economics of Federalism", *Options,* Proceedings of the Conference on the Future of Confederation, Toronto: University of Toronto, 1977, p. 312.

7. For an account of these events see Donald Creighton, *John A. Macdonald: The Old Chieftain,* Toronto: Macmillan of Canada, 1955, Chapter I, "The Pacification of Nova Scotia (1867-1869)."

8. For a history of the subsidy question, see J. A. Maxwell, *Federal Subsidies to the Provincial Governments in Canada,* Harvard University Press, 1937.

9. Robert MacGregor Dawson, *The Government of Canada,* Toronto: University of Toronto Press, 1947, pp. 120-121.

10. For an analysis of the 1977 arrangements see Courchene, in *op. cit.,* and for a more general account of recent fiscal relations, see Perrin Lewis, "The Tangled Tale of Taxes and Transfers" in *Confederation at the Crossroads, op. cit.,* pp. 39-105. For earlier periods see A. Milton Moore, J. Harvey Perry and Donald I. Beach, *The Financing of Canadian Federation: The First Hundred Years,* Toronto: Canadian Tax Foundation, 1966.

11. Lewis, *op. cit.* p. 61.

12. For an account of the relation between this crisis and the equalization regime see Thomas J. Courchene, "Equalization Payments and Energy Royalties," in A. D. Scott, ed., *Natural Resource Revenues: A Test of Federalism,* Vancouver: University of British Columbia Press, 1976, pp. 73-107.

13. Courchene, *op. cit.,* pp. 91-92. Quotation from a statement of John Turner, then federal Minister of Finance.

14. Courchene, *Options, op. cit.* p. 325.

15. For accounts of federal conditional grants to the provinces at different periods of time, see Luella Gettys, *The Administration of Canadian Conditional Grants,* Chicago: Public Administration Service, 1938; Donald V. Smiley, *Conditional Grants and Canadian Federalism,* Toronto: Canadian Tax Foundation, 1963; and George E. Carter, *Canadian Conditional Grants since World War II,* Toronto: Canadian Tax Foundation, 1971.

16. Such provisions are made under the Canada Assistance Plan and were embodied in the programs of federal support for provincial hospital and medical insurance plans which prevailed until 1977.

17. The Right Honourable Pierre Elliott Trudeau, *Federal-Provincial Grants and the Spending Power of Parliament,* Queen's Printer, Ottawa, pp. 28-30.

18. Vernon C. Fowke, *Canadian Agricultural Policy,* Toronto: University of Toronto Press, 1946, 1978 reprint, p. 154.

19. J. A. Corry, *Difficulties of Divided Jurisdiction,* Ottawa: King's Printer, 1940, p. 30.

20. However, in the case of the adult occupational training program launched in 1966 there was an intense conflict between the federal and Ontario governments based largely on the divergent values of economists in Ottawa

and educationalists who dominated the program at the provincial level. See J. Stefan Dupré, David M. Cameron, Graeme H. McKechnie and Theodore B. Rotenberg, *Federalism and Policy Development: The Case of Adult Occupational Training in Ontario*, Toronto: University of Toronto Press, 1973.

21. For accounts of the opting-out arrangements, see J. S. Dupré, "Contracting Out: A Funny Thing Happened on the Way to the Centennial," *Report of the Proceedings of the Eighteenth Tax Conference, Toronto, 1964* and Carter *op. cit.*, Chapter 5, "The Development of Contracting Out and Tax Abatements."
    See also Claude Morin, *Quebec versus Ottawa*, Toronto: University of Toronto Press, 1976, Chapter 3.

22. Rand Dyck, "The Canadian Assistance Plan: The Ultimate in Cooperative Federalism," *Canadian Public Administration* 19, Winter 1976, pp. 587-602.

23. *Supplementary Actions to the 1975 Ontario Budget*, Toronto: Queen's Printer, 1975, "Ontario's Experience under Cost-Sharing," pp. 2-3. Emphasis in text.

24. Courchene, *op. cit.*, pp. 322-344.

25. It may be that Ottawa's decision to have about half the transfers in the form of cash payments was intended to make it easier for the federal authorities to move against provinces who did not maintain national standards. However, it seems to me unlikely that the federal government has any effective sanctions left in such circumstances.

26. It may, however, be claimed that, because compensation covered only operating but not capital expenditures, there was some influence on provincial expenditure priorities in post-secondary education.

27. For an account of the developments in this aspect of welfare, see Douglas Brown, *The Federal Year in Review 1977-1978*, Kingston: Queen's University Institute of Intergovernmental Relations, 1978, pp. 32-34.

28. Mimeo, Ottawa, 1978.

29. Geoffrey Young, "Federal-Provincial Grants and Equalization," in *Intergovernmental Relations*, pp. 39-54.

30. *Living Together, A Study of Regional Disparities*, Economic Council of Canada, Ottawa: Supply and Services, pp. 30-44.

31. Paul MacEwen, *Confederation and the Maritimes*, Windsor, Nova Scotia: Lancelot Press, 1976, p. 21.

32. "Some Comments on Prairie Economic Alienation," in J. Peter Meekison, ed., *Canadian Federalism: Myth or Reality?* Third Edition, Toronto: Methuen of Canada, 1977, pp. 325-339.

33. Paul Phillips, *Regional Disparities: Why Ontario Has So Much and the Others Can't Catch Up*, Toronto: James Lorimer, 1978.

34. A. D. Careless, *Initiative and Response: The Adaptation of Canadian Federalism to Regional Economic Development*, Montreal: McGill-Queen's University Press, 1977, Chapter 3.

35. T. N. Brewis, *Regional Economic Policies in Canada*, Toronto: Macmillan of Canada, 1969, pp. 162-163.

36. Careless, *op. cit.*, p. 207.

37. Alan C. Green, "Regional Economic Disparities," in Lawrence H. Officer

and Lawrence B. Smith, ed., *Issues in Canadian Public Policy*, Toronto: McGraw-Hill Ryerson, 1974, pp. 354-370. For another analysis of regional disparities by a free-market economist, see Thomas J. Courchene, "Avenues of Adjustment: The Transfer System and Regional Disparities," in *Confederation at the Crossroads, op. cit.* pp. 145-186.

38. R. Ian McAllister, "Some Economic Problems of a Federal System," Officer and Smith, *op. cit.*, p. 406.
39. For difficulties in this co-ordinating role, see R. W. Phidd, "Regional Development Policy," in G. Bruce Doern and V. Seymour Wilson, eds., *Issues in Canadian Public Policy*, Toronto: Macmillan of Canada, 1974.
40. McAllister, in Officer and Smith, *op. cit.*, p. 401.
41. Careless, *op. cit.*, pp. 213-218.
42. *Employment and Income with Special Reference to the Initial Period of Reconstruction*, Ottawa: King's Printer, 1945. For a series of papers published to commemorate the twentieth anniversary of the White Paper, see S. F. Kaliski, ed., *Canadian Economic Policy since the War*, Ottawa: Canadian Trade Committee, 1966. The account in this volume of the origins of the White Paper, by its author, W. A. Mackintosh, is particularly fascinating (pp. 9-21).
43. T. N. Brewis, "Economic Policy," in T. N. Brewis, H. E. English, A. D. Scott and Pauline Jewett, eds., *Canadian Economic Policy*, Toronto: Macmillan of Canada, 1961, pp. 150-151.
44. Vernon Fowke, "The National Policy—Old and New," *Canadian Journal of Economics and Political Science* 18, 1952, p. 285.
45. Maurice Lamontagne, "The Role of Government," in G. P. Gilmour, ed., *Canada's Tomorrow*, Toronto: Macmillan of Canada, pp. 117-152.
46. Maurice Lamontagne, *Le Fédéralisme Canadien*, Quebec: Les presses université Laval, 1954. See particularly "Epilogue: Le dilemme de la province du Québec," pp. 284-298.
47. *Report of the Royal Commission on Taxation, Volume II*, p. 93.
48. Ibid., pp. 102-103.
49. Clarence L. Barber, *Theory of Fiscal Policy as Applied to a Province*, A Study Prepared for the Ontario Committee on Taxation, Toronto: Queen's Printer, 1966.
50. *Living Together*, Chapter 6.
51. Ibid., and Chapter 10 for specific recommendations.
52. Ibid., p. 106.
53. The Honourable W. Darcy McKeough, *1971 Budget Ontario*, Toronto: Queen's Printer, 1971, Budget Paper A, "New Directions in Economic Policy Management in Canada," p. 45.
54. Ibid., p. 47.
55. Ibid., p. 49.
56. Y. Rabeau and R. Lacroix, "Economic Stabilization and the Regions," Paper delivered to a workshop on "The Political Economy of Confederation" held at Queen's University, November 8-10, 1978, mimeo, p. 3.
57. *The Report of the Standing Senate Committee on National Finance*, Ottawa: Queen's Printer, 1971, p. 70.
58. Brown, *op. cit.*, pp. 10-13.
59. *Newsweek*, August 19, 1974.

60. See Gerald V. La Forest, *Natural Resources and Public Property under the Canadian Constitution*, Toronto: University of Toronto Press, 1969; and A. R. Thompson and H. R. Eddy, "Jurisdictional Problems in Natural Resource Management in Canada," in W. D. Bennett et al., *Essays on Aspects of Resource Policy*, Science Council of Canada, Ottawa: Information Canada, 1973, pp. 67-96.
61. Thompson and Eddy state that in Alberta "approximately 86 per cent of mines and minerals remain in provincial ownership," ibid., pp. 75-76.
62. The term is used by Thompson and Eddy, ibid., p. 74.
63. Ibid., p. 74.
64. *Globe and Mail*, Toronto, November 27, 1974. On the federal taxation of provincial organs, see Gerald V. La Forest, *The Allocation of Taxing Powers under the Canadian Constitution*, Toronto: Canadian Tax Foundation, 1967, pp. 42-44.
65. For an account of the background of the National Oil Policy, see J. G. Debanné, "Oil and Canadian Policy," in Edward W. Erickson and Leonard Waverman, eds., *The Energy Question: An International Failure of Policy, Volume 2, North America*, Toronto: University of Toronto Press, 1974, pp. 125-136.
66. Computed from *An Energy Policy for Canada, Volume I.—Analysis*, Department of Energy, Mines and Resources, Ottawa: Information Canada, 1973, p. 39.
67. Advisory Committee on Energy, *Energy in Ontario: The Outlook and Policy Implications, Volume Two*, Toronto: Queen's Printer, 1973, p. 86.
68. *An Energy Policy For Canada*, p. 32.
69. Ibid., p. 33.
70. Opening Statement, Jan. 22, 1974, *mimeo*.
71. Statement, *mimeo*.
72. *Background Paper on the Canadian Energy Situation*, Prepared by the Government of Canada for the Conference of First Ministers, April 9-10, 1975, *mimeo*, p. 2.
73. See M. W. Bucovetsky, "The Mining Industry and the Great Tax Reform Debate," in A. Paul Pross, ed., *Pressure Group Behaviour in Canadian Politics*, Toronto: McGraw-Hill Ryerson, 1975, pp. 89-114.
74. See the correspondence on these matters between the Prime Minister and Premiers Lougheed and Blakeney between March 22, 1974 and November 22, 1974 as tabled in the House of Commons in late 1974. Available from the Prime Minister's Office.
75. This was a major issue of the April 1975 conference of First Ministers. The Saskatchewan government here presented a plan, unacceptable to Alberta, according to which all proceeds resulting from increases of the price of domestic oil above $6.50 a barrel be transferred to an Energy Security Fund to make Canada self-sufficient in energy.
76. Opening Statement of Premier William G. Davis (*mimeo.*).
77. Glyn R. Berry, "The Oil Lobby and the Energy Crisis", *Canadian Public Administration* 17, Winter 1974, p. 603.
78. Richard Simeon, *Federal-Provincial Diplomacy: The Making of Recent Policy in Canada*, Toronto: University of Toronto Press, 1972, p. 282.

79. Berry's article, *op. cit.*, pp. 630-635 is excellent on this. He states that as the crisis proceeded on the basis of federal-provincial negotiations of a constitutional nature and involving fundamental policy, the industry was left "clinging to redundant technical arguments," p. 634.

80. *Alberta Hansard*, pp. 1440-1443.

81. On state-provincial relations, see Roger F. Swanson *State-Provincial Interaction*, Washington, D.C.: Department of State, 1974; Richard H. Leach, Donald E. Walker and Thomas A. Levy, "Province-State Trans-Border Relations: A Preliminary Assessment," *Canadian Public Administration* 16 Fall 1973, pp. 468-482; and P. R. Johannson, "British Columbia Relations with the United States," *Canadian Public Administration* 21, Summer 1978, pp. 212-233.

82. Johannson, *op. cit.*, p. 226.

83. *The Report of the Western Premiers' Task Force on Constitutional Trends*, 1977, p. 13.

84. Brown, *op. cit.*, p. 22.

85. Alfred Dubuc, "The Decline of Confederation and the New Nationalism," in Peter Russell, ed., *Nationalism in Canada*, Toronto: McGraw-Hill of Canada, 1966, p. 116.

86. There is a substantial literature on the national policy. See Fowke's work cited in Notes 18 and 44 as well as his *The National Policy and the Wheat Economy*, Toronto: University of Toronto Press, 1957. See also W. A. Mackintosh, *The Economic Background of Dominion-Provincial Relations*, Carleton Library, Toronto: McClelland and Stewart, 1964, Chapters 2-4; John H. Dales, *The Protective Tariff in Canada's Development*, Toronto: University of Toronto Press, 1966; and R. Craig Brown, *Canada's National Policy 1883-1900*, Princeton, N.J., Princeton University Press, 1964.

87. Dubuc, *op. cit.*, p. 121.

88. Donald V. Smiley, *Constitutional Adaptation and Canadian Federalism since 1945*, Documents of the Royal Commission on Bilingualism and Biculturalism, Ottawa: Queen's Printer, 1970, Chapter II.

89. In his review of the Rowell-Sirois Report, Harold Innis had made a vigorous criticism to the effect that the Report had avoided a solution to the regional "disequilibrium" in the Canadian economy resulting from the national policy: Harold Innis, *Canadian Journal of Economics and Political Science*, 6, 1940, pp. 562-571.

90. Kirkpatrick Sale, *Power Shift*, New York: Random House, 1975.

91. The Northeast includes Maine, Vermont, New Hampshire, Massachusetts, Rhode Island, Connecticut, Pennsylvania, New York, Ohio, Indiana, Michigan, Wisconsin and Illinois.

CHAPTER 7

CULTURAL DUALITY AND CANADIAN FEDERALISM

The Report of the Task Force on Canadian Unity published in January 1979 said,

> We believe that the heart of the present crisis is to be discovered in the intersecting conflicts created by two kinds of cleavage in Canadian society and by the political agencies which express and mediate them. The first and most pressing cleavage is that old Canadian division between 'the French' and 'the English'. . . . The second cleavage is that which divides the various regions of Canada and their populations from one another.[1]

The Dominion of Canada was established as a federation, albeit a federation of a somewhat centralized kind, primarily because of French-English duality. Most of the Fathers of Confederation from the Province of Canada and some of those from the Maritime colonies as well very much preferred a "legislative union," a unitary constitutional regime in which the powers of whatever sub-national jurisdictions there were would be held at the discretion of the central government. Yet the French-Canadian leaders would not have it that way, as George Brown stated in the Confederation Debates, "We had either to take a Federal union or drop the negotiations."[2]

To understand anything of how cultural duality impinged on Confederation it is necessary to examine briefly the development of French-English relations in the United Province of Canada under the regime provided for by the Act of Union.[3] The Act of Union enacted by the Parliament of the United Kingdom in 1840 was the response of the Imperial authorities to the rebellions of 1837 in each of the Canadas and to the famous Report of Lord Durham, who was sent to British North America to examine and to deal with the circumstances which had climaxed in those rebellions. The Report made two major recommendations. First, it was proposed that Canada be granted responsible government, that the Governor appointed by the Imperial authorities carry out his executive functions—so far as these related to colonial rather than Imperial matters—through ministers who had the continuing support of majorities in the colonial legislature. Second, there should be a legislative union of the two Canadas with the avowed intention of assimilating the French into the English language and culture.

The Imperial government rejected Durham's proposal for responsible government, although this was granted in 1848, but accepted his recommendation for legislative union. The Act of Union provided for a single legislature for Canada, with equal membership from each of the two sections, which from the Constitutional Act of 1791 had had their own legislative assemblies, legislative councils and executive councils. This equality in the 1840 Act was explicitly designed to swamp the French. In 1841 Lower Canada (Quebec) had a population of about 670,000, Upper Canada (Ontario) of about 480,000. It was anticipated that the English Canadians from Upper Canada would join with their counterparts from the other section to render the French a permanent minority. Further, the Act provided that the proceedings of the Legislative Assembly and the Legislative Council be in the English language only.

Both Lord Durham and the Imperial government of the day held highly unrealistic notions about the disappearance of the French language and culture in Canada. It was naïvely and confidently expected that once the government of the United Kingdom took decisive action in rendering the French a permanent political minority, this group, through its leaders, would choose early and easy assimilation into the dominant culture. This was not to be. The French-Canadian community again demonstrated its tenacity for survival and no Imperial authority, much less the English-Canadian politicians, ever seriously considered the draconian measures that might have led to such assimilation. Throughout the period from 1841 to 1867 the French group in the Canadian legislature manifested a higher degree of cohesion than that of the English Canadians, and were thus in many circumstances able to exercise a decisive influence.

Under the Act of Union régime there developed several quasi-federal devices in response to cultural and linguistic duality:
—from the action of the Governor, Lord Bagot, in bringing the French leader Lafontaine into the executive council in 1842, Canada was governed by ministries with a leader from each of the two sections. There were sixteen such ministries between this date and 1867.

—there was some recognition of the double-majority rule. Under this procedure measures peculiarly applicable to one or the other section were enacted only with the consent of a majority of the legislators from that section.

—apart from the heads of government, there was a considerable bifurcation in the executive council and the departments of government. Such prevailed in education, the departments of the provincial secretaries and attorneys-general, public works, Indian affairs and fisheries.

—prior to Queen Victoria's decision in 1857 to make Ottawa the permanent seat of government, the capital perambulated between the two sections. There was a move from Kingston to Montreal in 1844, and in 1849 it was decided to rotate the seat of government between Quebec City and Toronto every four years.

—in 1848 the United Kingdom Parliament repealed those sections of the Act of Union providing that all records of the legislative assembly and legislative council be in English only. The next year the Governor, Lord Elgin, gave symbolic recognition to bilingualism by reading the Speech from the Throne in both languages.

In broad terms, the Canadian politicians after 1840 very quickly and decisively rejected the assimilationist premises of the Durham Report and the Act of Union and moved toward a very high degree of what contemporary students of government call "consociationalism."[4] These consociational devices have already been mentioned—legislative groupings confined to English or French members, the double-majority procedure, English-French bifurcation in the political executive and appointed bureaucracy, the official recognition of the two languages. Yet these devices both reflected English-French duality and contributed to English-French conflict. J. M. S. Careless has said of the period between 1841 and 1857

> . . . for all the quasi-federal structure in Canada, there was no effective separation of sectional from common concerns within the single legislature. The cumbersome expedient had frequently confused the two, and so made for angry friction. Certainly Upper or Lower Canadians tended to adopt the view that the province was one or two just as the occasion suited them . . . If quasi-federalism was a response to duality, it aggravated rather than resolved inherent Canadian differences.[5]

Most crucially, the province from the mid-1850s onward was brought to political deadlock by insistent demands from important elements in Upper Canada for representation by population. That section grew much more rapidly than the other and was now under-represented in the Legislative Assembly. These demands for "rep by pop" were very easily transmuted, particularly by the Clear Grits, into anti-French and anti-Catholic sentiments. Understandably, the French were steadfastly unwilling to yield to these pressures against a settlement that was originally designed to assimilate them but was now working in their favour. Further, despite the growing cohesion of legislative parties in this period, there was continuing political instability as a succession of dual ministries failed to maintain the continuing support of legislative majorities over extended periods.

Cultural Duality and the Confederation Settlement

The political settlement worked out by the British North American leaders from the late summer of 1864 onward, and in its main outlines enacted by the United Kingdom Parliament as the British North America Act of 1867, was in large part a response to political deadlock in the province of Canada, a deadlock in large degree brought about by cultural polarization. It is, however, a mistake to regard Confederation as exclusively or perhaps even primarily a French-English bargain.[6] The broad outlines of this settlement were worked out in the coalition cabinet of the province of Canada in 1864[7] and then in a sense "sold" to the leaders of New Brunswick and Nova Scotia, and in this second step cultural and linguistic matters were of little importance. Furthermore, over all these negotiations hung the apprehension of American political, economic and military aggression, with the British North American response of establishing a second transcontinental nation under British parliamentary institutions and within the British Empire.

In a negative sense, the Confederation settlement was a decisive rejection of the consociational and dualistic devices that had developed in Canada under the Act of Union. There was to be a single Prime Minister for the Dominion. By implication, the double-majority principle was rejected. There was to be no bifurcation of cabinet posts or administrative departments. In broad terms, a federal division of legislative powers was to be the major constitutional recognition of cultural duality in the new Dominion, with those matters in which the two groups differed most markedly being assigned to the jurisdiction of the provinces. The powerful Liberal leader George Brown spoke of the projected union in these terms:

> The questions that used to excite the most hostile feelings among us have been taken away from the General Legislature, and placed under the control of the local bodies. No man need hereafter be debarred from success in public life because his views however popular in his own section are unpopular in the other;—for he will not have to deal with sectional questions.[8]

On the French-Canadian side, George Étienne Cartier asserted that what was being created was a "new political nationality" and in regard to this nationality the cultural backgrounds and allegiances of citizens were irrelevant.[9] The implication was that those powers necessary to the welfare and survival of the French-Canadian community of Quebec were vested in the provinces and that the exercise by the Dominion of its jurisdiction over military and economic affairs was of no direct consequence to the integrity of that community.

It is, however, a mistake to believe that the French-Canadian leadership posited any kind of absolute distinction between those matters deemed essential to the interests of this group and those which were not. As we shall see in Chapter 8, it was not anticipated that the institutions of the central government would work in an entirely majoritarian way and on this basis French Canadians could realistically expect to exercise a continuing influence in Ottawa. Quebec was to be represented in the cabinet of the Dominion. Legislative parties were less cohesively organized than they subsequently became and this looseness gave cultural and sectional groupings effective power. Quebec was to have equal representation with Ontario and the Maritime provinces, the latter considered as a unit, in the Senate.

Apart from the federal division of legislative powers, the British North America Act contained several other provisions directly related to cultural and linguistic duality:
—Section 133 specified that:

> Either the English or the French language may be used by any Person in the Debates of the Houses of the Parliament of Canada and of the Houses of the Legislature of Quebec; and both those Languages shall be used in the respective Records and Journals of those Houses; and either of those Languages may be used by any Person or in any Pleading or Process in or issuing from any Court of Canada established under this Act, and in or from all or any of the Courts of Quebec.
>
> The Acts of the Parliament of Canada and of the Legislature of Quebec shall be printed and published in both those languages.

There was here a precise and limited recognition of linguistic duality in the operations of the Dominion and Quebec governments but no constitutional definition of language rights in the other provinces.
—Section 93 conferred on the provinces exclusive jurisdiction over education with the limitation that they could not override the educational rights of Protestant and Roman Catholic minorities existing "by Law" at the time of Union or later so established. If these rights were encroached upon by a province, there could be an appeal to the federal cabinet and if the cabinet's decision was not executed by the offending province Parliament might enact "remedial Laws" to give effect to this decision. It may be noted that in the pre-Confederation period and for some decades after, the differentiation between French and English was perceived much more in terms of religion than of language.
—Section 94 contemplated the early assimilation of laws related to property and civil rights in the provinces other than Quebec into a uniform code under the Dominion. This section, which was never

implemented, did not include Quebec, whose private law was based on the civil code rather than, as in other parts of the Dominion, on the English common law.

—Several provisions of the Act attempted to preserve the rights of the English-speaking community of Quebec rendered by Confederation a minority in the affairs of that province. These provisions guaranteed representation in Parliament and in the Quebec Legislature to areas of the province with English majorities.

French-English Relations: Confederation to 1960

Confederation did not eliminate conflict between the English and French communities. In the period between 1867 and the end of the Second World War the most bitter of these conflicts involved two sets of matters: the position of French and Catholic minorities outside Quebec and Canadian orientations in external affairs as a member of the British Empire/Commonwealth. When they were mobilized as such, English Canadians in these conflicts got their way. Issues like these— the rights of the French outside Quebec and foreign policy orientations—rather than the protection of the French-Canadian community of Quebec by safeguarding and extending provincial powers, constituted the major sources of French-English tension up to the past generation. Quebec from the late 1880s onward emerged as a defender of provincial rights. Yet this was not the major axis of cultural conflict, and in fact Ontario was the more consistent defender of provincial autonomy, perhaps because the latter never had interests in defending the federal power against actions of the other provinces as had Quebec in respect to French and Catholic minorities.

Despite the conflicts mentioned above, there were certain patterns of French-English relations which developed to make Canada prior to the 1960s one of the most stable of the western nations:

(1) *The federal division of legislative powers.* As we have seen, the basic rationale of the division of legislative powers established at Confederation was to vest in the provinces control over those matters where the cultures differed most markedly, while Dominion powers had no such cultural incidence. Up until at least the First World War the major activities of the federal government related to national economic development and in respect to these policies the interests of French and English were not perceived to be in opposition. On the other side, Ottawa for the most part did not involve itself in those matters within provincial jurisdiction believed to be most crucial to the French language and culture. In general then, the division of legislative powers and governmental responsibilities contributed to harmony between the two groups.

(2) *Institutional self-segregation.* From 1759 there was sustained in Quebec what one might call a counter-culture, with its own justify-

ing system of political, economic and religious thought. Pierre
Elliott Trudeau wrote in 1954,

> . . . against the English, Protestant, democratic, materialistic, commer-
> cial and later industrial world, our nationalism worked out a defensive
> system in which all the opposition forces were stressed: the French
> language, authoritarianism, idealism, rural life and later the return to
> the soil.[10]

The historian Michel Brunet says the dominant currents of French-
Canadian thought were "l'agriculturisme, l'anti-étatisme et le messianisme".[11] These institutions and their justifying values did not
in any direct way challenge Anglo-Saxon political and economic
power either in Quebec or in Canada as such, and at the individual
level most Anglophones and Francophones could pursue their occupational and other objectives without obstruction from members
of the other group.

(3) *Mediation "at the summit"*. Traditionally, the most important of
Anglophone-Francophone political relations have been mediated
by leaders of the élites of the two communities. In federal politics
Anglophone party leaders have either had their Quebec lieutenants
or—as has been the case with the Conservatives for most of the time
since the death of Georges-Étienne Cartier in 1873—have been trying with some urgency to find someone to play this role effectively.
Although the Quebec lieutenant was by no means a co-prime minister when the party was in power, he had characteristically a wider
scope of discretion in Quebec affairs than did ministers from the
other provinces in respect to the areas they represented.[12] In the
Quebec cabinet there was usually a cabinet minister from the English-speaking community—often the Minister of Revenue—representing Anglophone business interests.

(4) *The traditional French-Canadian distrust of the state*. French
Canadians have traditionally distrusted government, even governments in which they themselves have had a numerical dominance.
According to Trudeau's analysis, because French Canadians received democratic institutions not through their own efforts but by
the will of the English-speaking community, they came to value democracy not for itself but as an instrument of ethnic survival.[13] The
Church remained jealous of its privileges and erected a system of
social and religious thought which was both authoritarian and anti-
statist. Although successive Quebec governments mounted a stub-
born defence of provincial autonomy against real or alleged federal
encroachments, there was little disposition to use these provincial
powers imaginatively. A doctrinaire adherence to anti-statist values became a justification for French-Canadian political and religious leaders to co-operate in the economic domination of Quebec
by Anglo-Saxon capital.

(5) *The defence of historic, prescriptive rights.* Prior to the 1960s, French-Canadian leaders saw the welfare and integrity of their community primarily in terms of an unyielding defence of historic and prescriptive rights, particularly as these rights were embodied in the Confederation settlement. From the 1880s onward such interests were often defined in terms of the theory of Confederation as a compact either among the provinces or between the English and French communities.[14] The corollary of course was that the terms of Confederation could not legitimately be altered without the consent of the original partners.

These circumstances, taken together, gave a degree of stability to Anglophone-Francophone relations and to Canadian federalism. Institutional differentiation based on contrary value-systems made the individual and group objectives of members of the two communities relatively compatible. The mediation of community relations through the élites provided a regularized procedure for managing the demands of each group on the other. Anti-statism in Quebec facilitated both the domination of the province by English-speaking business interests and, particularly in the period between 1945 and 1960, the extension of federal powers in harmony with the preferences both of Canadians outside Quebec for national leadership and inside Quebec for public action to meet emergent social needs. Adherence by French Canadians to one version or other of the compact theory was an affirmation of the continuing legitimacy within Quebec of the federal system.

Quebec in the 1960s and the Quiet Revolution

Each of the stabilizing elements which has been discussed in the preceding section was abruptly challenged by the so-called Quiet Revolution of Quebec in the 1960s. Despite the speed and the comprehensiveness of change, these developments had their roots in the past. Many years before the death of Maurice Duplessis in 1959, the traditional institutions of Quebec and their justifying ideologies had become progressively less relevant to the circumstances of an industrialized community exposed to a modern and modernizing world. The formulations of the Duplessis era and later Quebec nationalism differed in many important respects but were similar in that they tended to equate Quebec with French Canada, and were for the most part indifferent to the recognition of cultural and linguistic duality in federal institutions or in provinces and areas of Canada outside Quebec where there were significant concentrations of French-speaking people. On the other hand, the older nationalism was primarily defensive and the new currents of thought and policy much less so.[15] In turning from "*survivance*" to "*épanouissement*" the Quebec leadership decisively altered the older patterns of relations between Anglophones and Francophones.

(1) *Conflicts over the federal division of legislative powers.* By the 1960s the original division of legislative powers by which the provinces were given control over those matters directly impinging on culture had broken down. Mainly through the exercise of the spending power, Ottawa was now directly involved in health, welfare, higher education, vocational training and other such matters wholly or largely within provincial jurisdiction. Further, as we shall see, the Lesage government and its successors defined the survival and integrity of the Francophone community in Quebec largely in terms of the control by the province of its own economic development, and this brought about a challenge to federal powers.

(2) *A breakdown in institutional self-segregation.* What the sociologist Hubert Guindon has called "a new middle class" had developed in Quebec in response to urbanization and industrialization.[16] During the Duplessis period this emergent class had been rendered impotent both by the traditional political and religious leadership and by the Anglophone centres of corporate power. The new groups were committed both by ideology and class interest to the rationalization and modernization of Quebec society. Their frame of reference was secular, materialistic and democratic. Because corporate business was for the most part an Anglo-Saxon preserve, the new middle class turned to public institutions and in the main to the government of Quebec. This kind of development inevitably brought about new conflicts between the French-Canadian elites and centres of business and governmental power dominated by English-speaking Canadians.

(3) *An end to anti-statism.* After the election of the Lesage administration in 1960, dominant currents of thought and policy in Quebec turned away from the older suspicion of the state and came to see the provincial government as the major instrument by which Quebec society might be reformed. The interests of the new middle class lay in the expansion of the public sector and in the bureaucratization of public and private institutions. This led inevitably to the displacement of the Church from its dominance in health, education and welfare—as well as to the bureaucratization of the Church itself and the declining political influence of its leaders—and to more intervention than before in the private sector by the provincial authorities.

(4) *Complications in elite accommodation.* From 1960 onward there was overt conflict among the Quebec élites which inhibited the older kinds of élite accommodation between Francophones and Anglophones both within Quebec and outside. During the early

1960s a frequent question asked by English-speaking Canadians was, "What does Quebec want? The meaning was undoubtedly, "Who speaks for Quebec?" and confusion was made worse because, as one French-Canadian scholar pointed out in 1968, "Actually too many individuals among the élite are speaking in the name of the whole French-Canadian population."[17] The overt and vigorous conflicts within Francophone Quebec undoubtedly became more salient for relations between the two communities as an increasing number of Anglophone Canadians came to interest themselves in Quebec affairs. In the federal political parties, the new currents in Quebec were weakly manifested through the Progressive Conservatives[18] and the NDP, and between the retirement of the Right Honourable Louis St. Laurent in 1958 and the period immediately after the general election of 1965, no authoritative spokesman for Quebec emerged from the federal Liberal caucus. The results of the federal election of 1962 further confused the situation, as the Créditistes displaced the Progressive Conservatives as the major opposition to the Liberals in Quebec federal politics on a program which was at the same time federalist, anti-élitist and based on traditional French-Canadian values.[19] In the redefinition of Quebec's relations with the rest of Canada a number of alternatives from revolutionary separatism to co-operative federalism were proposed and vigorously expounded. By the mid-1960s the older patterns of élite accommodation between the Francophone and Anglophone communities appeared in retrospect to have been relatively tidy and straightforward.

(5) *The turning away from historic, prescriptive rights.* There was little disposition in the 1960s to defend Quebec's rights in terms of the compact theory of Confederation. Pierre Carignan said of prevailing constitutional attitudes in 1966,

> . . . il semble que la majorité des Québécois d'expression française sont prêts à rejeter la constitution dans sa forme actuelle. N'ayant pu convaincre leurs compatriotes que la constitution constitue un pacte, ils ont eux-mêmes cessé de la croire: en conséquence, ils ne se sentent plus liés par elle et remettent tout en question.[20]

As we saw in Chapter 3 in their acceptance and later rejection of the Fulton-Favreau formula for constitutional amendment, the Lesage Liberals were caught in the crossfire between changing attitudes. Interestingly, the direct challenge to the Fulton-Favreau formula, whose rigidities were a manifestation of constitutional conservatism, was made by the Union Nationale. Writing in 1965 when he was Leader of the Opposition, Daniel Johnson pointed out that Canadians had lived under five constitutions—those of 1763, 1774, 1791, 1841 and 1867—and said,

Les constitutions sont faites pour les hommes et non les hommes pour les constitutions. *Quant les conditions changent, c'est aux structures juridiques de s'adapter aux circonstances nouvelles* . . . Et les conditions ont changé depuis 1867.[21]

In harmony with the new circumstances Johnson defined Quebec's position not in terms of historically acquired rights but on the basis of the inherent right of nations to self-determination.

The changes effected by the Lesage government were in the direction of reform of both the private and the public institutions of Quebec. Progress was made in creating a merit civil service, and some of the most able persons in the province were hired either as full-time officials or part-time advisers. Some of the grosser forms of patronage endemic to Quebec politics were eliminated, and in 1963 came legislation which both limited campaign expenditures and provided generous subsidies to candidates of recognized political parties. Through the Société Générale de Financement private and public funds were channelled into Quebec industry and some attempts were made to rationalize such industry. A provincial Department of Education was established and a comprehensive program of educational reform undertaken from the kindergarten to university levels. Health and welfare systems were rationalized and bureaucratized. Hydro-electric resources were brought under public ownership, significantly increasing the opportunities for French-speaking Quebeckers, particularly in the professional and management categories. There was a new emphasis by the provincial authorities on linguistic and cultural matters, including contacts with the French-speaking world in Europe and Africa. Comprehensive programs of provincial and regional economic planning were devised and some progress was made in their implementation.

Despite the speed and comprehensiveness of reform, the changes being effected by the Lesage government were very much the same as those which had been undertaken in other parts of Canada but over a longer period of time. There were of course some differences. Understandably, these developments in Quebec had repercussions upon the relations between the Francophone and Anglophone communities which were absent from modernizing trends elsewhere in the country. In the eastern part of Quebec the province sponsored the first large-scale program of development through *"animation sociale"* which had ever been undertaken in Canada. The bureaucratization and rationalization of public services involved new relations between the religious and public authorities in Quebec much more than in the other provinces. On the whole, however, the reforms undertaken in Quebec were in the direction of bringing its institutions in harmony with those of other western democracies. This circumstance created an essential sympathy for the province and its new leadership within the federal government and among Canadians throughout the country. For the first time in the history of Canada the source of change was coming from Quebec.

The Lesage government postulated the interests of Quebec largely in terms of an extension of the autonomy of the province as the precondition of cultural integrity. The Premier said this at the Federal-Provincial Conference of November 1963:

> ... we must exercise constant vigilance. Nobody in Quebec believes that a given measure,—aid to municipalities, the contributory pension programme, or federal assistance to technical education, for example—can, in itself, lead French Canada to assimilation by the English-speaking majority. Nor does anyone believe that any one of these measures, taken simply, is of a nature to threaten our entire cultural heritage. However, we must be systematically opposed to any federal move, whatever it may be, that reduces, in fact, or attacks the field of provincial jurisdiction. We absolutely cannot, even if it concerns a question which appears to be only a secondary one, remain passive in the face of federal initiative which are judged to be detrimental to the exercise of powers entrusted to the provinces. In fact, it is the whole of these measures that must be considered, and it is against each of the items comprising the whole that we must be opposed, because each of them is a threat to the autonomy of the provinces, a threat which constitutes a precedent which is later invoked to justify threats of increasingly detrimental effect.
>
> In short, we are not defending the autonomy of the provinces because it is a question of principle, but rather because autonomy is to us the basic condition, not of our survival which is assured from now on, but of our assertion as a people . . .[22]

In terms of the general formulation quoted above, the Lesage administration made very specific demands on Ottawa, and pressed these demands in an effective way through the elected leadership and their extraordinarily sophisticated senior advisers. I have said elsewhere of these developments.

> Such pressures [toward enhanced provincial discretion] arose as much from the requirements of particular Quebec policies as from a generalized disposition toward autonomy on ideological grounds. . . .
> The provincial administration was motivated to increase its range of effective discretion because it had very ambitious plans for reform and, to a greater or lesser degree, specific activities of the federal government stood in its path.[23]

There were three classes of demands on the federal government:
(1) *For financial autonomy and financial resources.* The reforms undertaken by the Lesage administration were expensive and the Quebec authorities, with of course support from other provinces, pressed for both higher unconditional subsidies from Ottawa and decreases in federal income tax rates so that the province could in-

crease its revenues without at the same time increasing the burdens on its taxpayers.

(2) *For a withdrawal of federal involvement from matters within provincial legislative jurisdiction.* Particularly in the period between 1945 and 1960 the federal government had involved itself in a very large number of matters within provincial jurisdiction, largely through the exercise of the spending power. The Lesage government demanded such encroachments cease, on the double grounds that they threatened the integrity of the French-Canadian community and interfered with provincial objectives and priorities. In particular, Quebec demanded that in respect to existing and future shared-cost programs the province be allowed to contract out without either itself or Quebec residents being thereby subjected to financial penalties. Also, the province demanded that the Canada Pension Plan be not applied within Quebec, which would have instead its own scheme of contributory retirement pensions.

(3) *For more institutionalized procedures of intergovernmental collaboration.* In its quest for autonomy the Lesage administration showed a basic distrust of the informal and segmented pattern of relations between the provinces and the federal government. As we saw in Chapter 4, the Quebec government centralized the control of its relations with outside jurisdiction in a Department created for that purpose and under the direct supervision of the Premier. One of the basic elements of Quebec's formulation of co-operative federalism was a fastidious respect by Ottawa for matters within provincial jurisdiction. However, because most federal economic policies had direct and immediate implications for the provinces, Quebec demanded that there be established regularized patterns of federal-provincial consultation in respect to these policies.[24] There was also the desire to institutionalize procedures of interprovincial co-operation.

Throughout its six years in office the Lesage government failed to evolve a coherent constitutional policy, and in particular failed to formulate an unequivocal answer to the question of whether Quebec required explicit constitutional changes to give it a wider jurisdiction than that wanted or needed by the other provinces. In his last year in power Premier Lesage and his chief constitutional advisor, Paul Gérin-Lajoie, the Minister of Education, came to speak in a specific way about a *statut particulier* for Quebec.[25] However, these statements could be read either as a rationalization of the existing contracting-out arrangements, and their future application to other federal-provincial activities, or a rather generalized demand for explicit constitutional change. The specific demands of Quebec for autonomy had been spectacularly successful and because of this—and perhaps because of conflicting pressures operating within and on the government—the Premier and his colleagues chose to proceed in a piecemeal way rather than directing their activities toward comprehensive constitutional reform.

As a result of the general election of June 1966 the Union Nationale under the leadership of Daniel Johnson succeeded to power in Quebec. The anomalies of the electoral system allowed the UN to win a narrow majority in the Legislative Assembly, with 40.8 per cent of the popular vote as against 47.4 per cent for the Liberals. The Liberals had failed when in office to effect a comprehensive electoral redistribution because, so Mr. Lesage claimed after the 1966 election, Section 80 of the BNA Act precluded the legislature from altering the boundaries of twelve electoral districts which in 1867 had English-speaking majorities, without the consent of a majority of the sitting members of the Assembly from those districts.[26]

With the coming to power of the Union Nationale, the focus of Quebec pressures shifted somewhat from the specific demands for provincial autonomy which had characterized the Lesage period to broader and more symbolic matters of constitutional reform and of the role of the province in international affairs. By reason of ideology and the basis of its electoral support the Union Nationale was less interventionist than its predecessor and thus felt less urgency about effecting specific changes which would have brought it into conflict with federal policies. Further, a continuation of reform at the pace set by the Lesage government was impossible without imposing intolerable burdens on the Quebec taxpayer.

While in opposition, the United Nationale had been persistently critical of what it claimed to be the pragmatism and opportunism of the Lesage government in constitutional affairs. The party was instrumental in having the Legislative Assembly establish a committee on the constitution in 1963 to hear interested and expert opinion and to stimulate debate on these matters. The UN led the struggle against the Fulton-Favreau formula for constitutional amendment and challenged the Lesage government to fight the forthcoming general election on its acceptance of this proposal. Daniel Johnson in 1965 had published his *Egalité ou Indépendance*,[27] which called for a radical reform of the Canadian constitution on binational lines. After coming to power the Union Nationale continued to place a high priority on comprehensive constitutional change. In retrospect, this may be explained as an attempt to reconcile conflicts within the cabinet and the party—as well as the wider Quebec society—on the place of Quebec in Confederation. There were undoubtedly many traditional UN politicians whose basic commitment was to the continuation of federalism in a revised form. Other and younger members of the party espoused even the more thoroughgoing variants of Quebec nationalism. All could be brought to at least transient agreement on the desirability of constitutional change on binational lines, but the successive premiers, Johnson and Bertrand, resorted to exquisite equivocation on the urgency of change. On some occasions, such changes were pressed stridently in terms that suggested their almost immediate acceptance was necessary if separation was to be avoided. At other times, the tone if not the substance of Quebec's position was moderate.

The major policy issue on which the federal and Quebec governments came into conflict in the 1966-1970 period involved the province's role in international affairs.[28] Under the Lesage administration Quebec had extended its economic and cultural contacts abroad with the opening of several quasi-diplomatic offices in Europe and the United States. The government had asserted its right to participate independently in international relations in respect to matters within provincial legislative jurisdiction, but a major conflict with Ottawa over this issue had been avoided. After the Union Nationale came to power there was a series of incidents involving Quebec's participation in international affairs and both federal and provincial governments were disposed to carry on this struggle in doctrinaire and symbolic terms. Ottawa came to believe that France, with the connivance of its African allies, was engaged in a deliberate policy of encouraging Quebec's international pretensions in an attempt to destroy the Canadian federation, or at the very least to challenge its stability by involving themselves in domestic Canadian affairs. In waging this conflict Ottawa put great emphasis on the abstract principle that foreign policy was indivisible and that in both law and practice there was a vast gulf between sovereign states and other governments.[29] The Quebec authorities on their part were disposed to assert in a symbolic way their right to independent participation in external affairs within the broad but indeterminate limits set by France and the French-speaking nations of Africa.

The Responses to the New Quebec

During the 1960s there developed among supporters of the federal system, both English-speaking and French-speaking, the judgment that under the new circumstances of Quebec the survival of Confederation dictated a much enhanced and more explicit recognition of French-English duality in the Canadian community as such. Among the English-speaking elites certainly there was more of a disposition than at any previous time in the country's history to assert a dualistic view of Canada which has been defined as " . . . the view which holds that the most significant cleavage in Canadian society is the line dividing English from French, and which identifies as the major challenge to domestic statecraft the establishment of harmonious and just relations between the English-speaking and French-speaking communities of Canada."[30] Ramsay Cook pithily expressed this perspective in the In-

troduction to his *Canada and the French-Canadian Question* published in 1966, "Canada and the French-Canadian question is really the
Canadian question."[31] The Terms of Reference of the Royal Commission on Bilingualism and Biculturalism defined the "Canadian Confederation" as "an equal partnership between the two founding races."[32]
And certainly Pierre Elliott Trudeau espoused a view of Canada which
is primarily dualistic both before and after his entry into elective politics.

Apart from ideological redefinitions, there have been other responses
to the modernized Quebec which developed from 1960 onward:

*(1) Accession to Quebec's demands for fiscal and administrative au-
tonomy.* Particularly after the coming to power of the Pearson administration in Ottawa in April 1963, the federal government was relatively
acquiescent in yielding to Quebec pressures for an enhanced range of
fiscal and administrative autonomy. On several occasions prior to 1966
the federal authorities extended the range of provincial "tax room" and
increased the scale of unconditional subsidies to the provinces. Parliament in 1965 enacted the Established Programs (Interim Arrangements) Act permitting the provinces to contract out of several established grant-in-aid programs with full fiscal compensation. After a
lengthy series of negotiations between the federal and Quebec governments it was agreed that the Canada Pension Plan should not apply
within Quebec.[33] Two other programs, student loans and youth allowances, which elsewhere in the country were funded and administered
by the federal authorities, were in Quebec undertaken by the province
with unconditional fiscal compensation from Ottawa.

(2) Constitutional Review and Reform. As we saw in Chapter 3, the
process of constitutional reform begun by the Confederation for Tomorrow Conference in 1967 and ended shortly after the Victoria Conference of 1971 was a direct response to the circumstances of Quebec.
While the more recent efforts at constitutional review which may be
dated from Ottawa's proposals of June 1978 were directed at a much
broader set of grievances than those emanating from Quebec, the federal authorities at least derived much of their urgency for reform from
the incumbency of the PQ and the perceived necessity of putting together a package of federal reforms before the Quebec referendum.

(3) Reforms in the federal civil service. In April 1966 Prime Minister
Pearson announced a new linguistic regime in the federal public service.[34] This was the first such federal policy related to this matter, although from a 1938 amendment to the Civil Service Act onward there
had been a requirement that in recruitment to local positions the Civil
Service Commission should ensure that a successful candidate had a
knowledge of either English or French if this was the language "of the
majority of the persons with whom he is required to do business."

The Prime Minister's statement so enunciated the new policy:

> The government hopes and expects that, within a reasonable period of years, a state of affairs will be reached in the public service whereby
> (a) it will be a normal practice for oral or written communications within the service to be made in either official language at the option of the person making them, in the knowledge that they will be understood by those directly concerned;
> (b) communications with the public will normally be in either official language having regard to the person being served;
> (c) the linguistic and cultural values of both English-speaking and French-speaking Canadians will be reflected through civil service recruitment and training.

A Report of the Royal Commission on Bilingualism and Biculturalism on "The Federal Administration" published in 1969 made a detailed analysis of the participation of Anglophones and Francophones in the public service as well as of linguistic usage in the operations of the bureaucracy.[35] The Commission attributed the "precipitous decline" in the French-speaking proportion of the public service between 1918 and 1946—from 22 per cent to 13 per cent—to the workings of the merit principle adopted in the former year. According to the Report "both Francophone and Anglophone federal politicians and public servants accepted the prevailing orthodoxies linking unilingualism with rationality and efficiency"[36] and "the Civil Service Commission and the departmental chiefs did not relate language use and participation to the goal of bureaucratic efficiency." In 1965 some 21.5 per cent of federal departmental civil servants had French as their mother tongue but it was reported that

> Only in two of the 22 larger departments and agencies did [persons with French mother-tongue] make up 22 per cent of the staff earning $10,000 or more—the departments of the Secretary of State and the Post Office (26 and 45 per cent respectively). At the level earning less than $10,000 a year, 10 of the 17 departments and agencies for which data were available had staffs that were more than 22 per cent of French mother tongue. They were obviously concentrated in the lower levels of the federal administration.[37]

Outside Quebec, and most crucially in Ottawa itself, English was the working language of the civil service and the Commission asserted "Ability and willingness to work in English appear to be conditions of advancement in the Public Service for those of French mother tongue."

In June 1973 Parliament confirmed the general principles of the 1966 policies by a Resolution which directed the government to identify the official-language requirements of all positions in the departmental civil service and to ensure a greater use of French at all levels in the service. On November 21, 1974 the President of the Treasury Board tabled a statement in the House of Commons to the effect that language requirements had been established for 281,664 positions in the departmental public service:

—60 per cent of positions were defined as those in which English was essential, 13 per cent French essential, 19 per cent bilingual, and in 8 per cent either language might qualify.

—in the National Capital Region 45 per cent of 79,939 positions required bilingual capacities.

—the bilingual positions were so described by occupational category:

Category	Number of Positions	% of Category Bilingual
Executive	963	93
Administrative and Foreign Service	16,805	37
Scientific and Professional	7,002	27
Technical	4,137	15
Administrative/Support	19,482	25
Operational	4,835	5

By 1975 the way in which the federal bilingualism program had been implemented was under attack both from the Commissioner of Official Languages and in a massive report prepared for the government under the direction of Dr. Gilles Bibeau of the University of Montreal. The major thrust of the Bibeau Report was that the 53,000 bilingual positions which existed in 1973-1974 had been so classified without any detailed evaluation of the needs for the second language on the job, and the recommendations were made that the number of bilingual positions be reduced by relating these more closely to functional needs, but that the standards of competence in the second language be raised. In his 1975 Report the Commissioner of Official Languages published a survey made by the Treasury Board Secretariat of some 3,762 graduates of courses in English and French which showed that, of 2,670 graduates of French-language courses, 83 per cent spent less than 20 per cent of their working time in that langauge and 61 per cent less than 10 per cent of such time.[39] The Commissioner questioned pointedly whether the estimated expenditure of $9,150 on the linguistic education of each of these persons was justified.[40]

Partly no doubt in response to the kinds of criticisms outlined above, the President of the Treasury Board issued in September 1977 a statement of revised government policies in respect to the official languages in the public service. Among the more important changes were these:

—the less discriminating approach to bilingual classification was to be replaced by a principle which would "base the language requirements of positions on the specific and actual work-related need for one or both languages to carry out the duties of each position."

—under broad guidelines set by the Public Service Commission the responsibilities for language classification and for second-language
training formerly assumed by the Commission were to be devolved
on the departments and agencies.

—most of the federal crown corporations were to be included in the linguistic regime prevailing in the departmental public service,

—by 1983 the government was to end its policies of "appointments of
unilingual persons to bilingual positions conditional on these persons acquiring the capacity in the second langauge, language instruction at public expense, and salary bonuses for bilingual employees."

The 1977 Report of the Public Service Commission gave a detailed
account of Anglophone and Francophone participation in the departmental public service. Among some of the most important findings
were these:

—there had been steady though modest increases in the proportion of
Francophones since 1973. Despite austerity, this proportion increased from 26.2 per cent to 27.2 per cent between 1976 and 1977
and in the same year from 31.8 per cent to 32.4 per cent in the National Capital Region.

—14.1 per cent of public servants said they used French most frequently at work.

—there were very wide variations in the proportions of Francophones
in the various departments and agencies. In 12 such departments
with more than 5,000 employees this proportion ranged from a high
of 33.0 per cent in Employment and Immigration to a low of 12.4 per
cent in Fisheries and Environment. In general terms, there was a high
concentration of Francophones in language-related activities.
(teachers, translators etc.), and a low concentration in scientific and
technical groupings.

—at all levels of the service the termination rate of Francophones was
higher than that of Anglophones. The Commission was dissatisfied
with its efforts to recruit Francophone graduates of colleges and universities and on this basis was anxious that the higher termination
rates "might wipe out the gains of the past decade."

—in 36.1 per cent of the public servants who were in the officer category, 22.7 per cent were Francophones. Of the 1,268 persons in the
"senior executive" category 21.0 per cent were Francophones.[41]

(4) *The Federal Official Languages Act.* In 1967 the Royal Commission
on Bilingualism and Biculturalism published its Report on The Official
Languages and in 1969 Parliament enacted The Official Languages Act.
Article 2 of the Act declared "The English and French languages are
the official languages of Canada for all purposes of the Parliament and
Government of Canada, and possess and enjoy equality of status and

equal rights and privileges as to their use in all the institutions of the Parliament and Government of Canada." The major thrust of this legislation was to ensure that citizens could communicate with the government of Canada in whichever of the official languages they chose, at least in places and situations where there was a sufficient demand for English or French to make this feasible. In order to police the operations of the Act a Commissioner of Official Languages was appointed during good behaviour and for a seven-year term. The Supreme Court of Canada in a 1974 decision upheld the constitutionality of the Official Languages Act as a valid exercise of Parliament's power to legislate for the "Peace, Order, and Good Government of Canada."

It is impossible to summarize the enhancement of the capacity of the federal government to communicate with French-speaking Canadians over the last decade, although successive Annual Reports of the Commissioner of Official Languages Act give invaluable and detailed accounts of such policies and the difficulties encountered in implementing them. The ability of federal institutions to communicate with citizens in the French language and the levels of Francophone participation in these institutions are related in a complex way. In a formal sense the bilingual requirement might be met by a public service made up wholly of Anglophones fluent in French. However, in practical terms Francophones will continue to be disproportionately represented in bilingual positions and of course will almost wholly monopolize positions where French is the only required language; for example, in 1971 some 81.7 per cent of appointments to bilingual positions were of persons whose "preferred language of work" was French, although this proportion dropped dramatically to 55.1 per cent in 1974.[42] As we have seen, the policies adopted in 1977 emphasize the functional capacity of federal institutions to serve citizens in both official languages. The decrease in the number of positions requiring bilingual capacities—along with Ottawa's intention of phasing out its own activities in teaching official languages to civil servants—will almost inevitably work in the direction of decreasing Francophone participation unless effective counter-measures in recruiting Francophones are taken.

Sections 10 to 18 of the Official Languages Act provided that the Governor in Council might by proclamation establish "bilingual districts" where 10 per cent or more of the population was of an official-language minority.[43] In such districts the services of federal departments and agencies would be available in both languages. The Act also gave the Governor in Council the authority to enter into agreements with provinces for the provision of federal, provincial, municipal and educational services in the minority language. The federal government has not proclaimed bilingual districts either in respect to federal services alone or to services provided by all levels of government. In its Report of 1975 the Bilingual Districts Advisory Board under the chairmanship of Paul Fox proposed 30 bilingual districts, including at least one in every province except British Columbia.[44] All of the province of New Brunswick was thus classified. Significantly, the majority of the Board recommended against Montreal being made a bilingual district on the major ground that English-speaking citizens in this metropolitan centre experienced no outstanding difficulties in being served in English and that the classification of Montreal as a bilingual district was thus inappropriate. It seems unlikely that the federal authorities will proclaim bilingual districts in the forseeable future.

(5) *"French power"* in the *Federal Cabinet.* Provincial representation in the first cabinet of the new Dominion was a crucial element of the Confederation settlement. As agreed upon by the British North American leaders in 1866, the first Executive Council was to have 5 ministers from Ontario—including the Prime Minister—4 from Quebec and 2 from each of the Maritime provinces.[45] This provincial balance was in aggregate terms perpetuated in succeeding decades and between 1867 and 1965 some 30.4 per cent of cabinet ministers were from Quebec, a proportion very close to that province's persistent proportion of the total Canadian population.[46] However, such aggregates give an inaccurate indication of French-Canadian influence, as Francophones tended to occupy such portfolios as Justice, Public Works and the Post Office with a heavy patronage orientation and to be denied the leadership of departments with responsibilities for economic policy. Thus Pierre Elliott Trudeau wrote in 1962 "with the sole exception of Laurier, I fail to see a single French Canadian in more than three-quarters of a century whose presence in the federal cabinet might be considered indispensable to the history of Canada as written—except at election time"[47] The later composition of Trudeau's own cabinets in a somewhat dramatic way reversed the historic pattern and between 1968 and 1973 French Canadians had been appointed to the following portfolios with important responsibilities for economic policy—Energy, Mines and Resources; Indian Affairs and Northern Development; Industry, Trade and Commerce; Manpower and Immigration; and Regional Economic Expansion. The appointment of the Honourable Jean Chretien as Canada's first French-Canadian Minister of Finance in 1977 was also a break with the historic pattern. In the general election of May 1979 only two Progressive Conservatives were elected from Quebec and of these one was an Anglophone. However, new Prime Minister Clark showed extraordinary urgency in strengthening the Francophone membership of his government and in the cabinet which took office in early June 1979 there were three Francophone Senators, including two with major portfolios.

(6) *The Francophone Minorities Outside Quebec.* According to the 1976 mid-term census by Statistics Canada there are 905,440 persons

outside Quebec of French mother tongue. 76.8 per cent of this official-language minority lives in Ontario and New Brunswick, with 462,075 and 233,8975 persons respectively. There have been several efforts on the part of the federal government and the governments of the provinces with English-speaking majorities to enhance the position of these minorities. A plausible case can be made that on an individual basis the Official Languages Act benefited Francophones outside Quebec more than French-speaking persons in that province. Although recent statistics appear not to be available to demonstrate this, it is widely believed that members of the Francophone minorities—particularly Franco-Ontarians—were the major beneficiaries of efforts of the federal government to increase the proportions of Francophones in the technical, professional and executive categories of the departmental public service.[48] There has been a vast expansion of the French-language networks of the Canadian Broadcasting Corporation outside Quebec. From 1971 onward the provinces have received federal grants for various kinds of programs in their respective minority official languages. Among the provinces with large Francophone minorities, New Brunswick enacted its own Official Languages Act in 1969 very much along the lines of the federal enactment of the same year, although much of the Act was not proclaimed in force until 1977. Ontario has significantly extended its services to Francophones, specifically in public education—including university education—and the court system.[49] In widely varying degrees the other provinces have extended opportunities for French-language education.[50]

(7) Foreign policy. To some extent, Canadian foreign policy has come since 1960 to give more attention to French-language nations than was so in the past. In response to Quebec pressure for participation in international affairs, Ottawa has given positive recognition to the provincial governments in international relations which involve matters within the constitutional jurisdiction of the provinces. The most dramatic change in the new emphasis given to the Francophone world has been in the attention given in Canadian policy to the French-speaking nations of Africa;[51] for example in 1961-1965 Canada gave 10.7 times as much aid to English-speaking Africa as to Francophone Africa, while in 1972-1973 these English-speaking nations received only 71 per cent of the assistance given to French-speaking African countries.[52]

The response of the government of Canada, and to a more limited extent of the provinces with English-speaking majorities, to the circumstances created by the new Quebec was thus a multifaceted one and not, as critics have claimed, based exclusively on linguistic reforms.[53] However, the centrepiece so to speak of the federal response *was* language policy as embodied in the Official Languages Act. The rationale of such policies was elaborated in a document *A National Understand-*

ing issued by the government of Canada in 1977.⁵⁴ Much of the argument was focused on the circumstances of the official-language minorities.

> The federal government rejects the concepts of a Canada divided into two mutually exclusive unilingual separate countries or two mutually exclusive unilingual regions within one country. While these two options have a superficial appearance of dissimilarity, they amount in practice to the same thing, a province or state of Quebec that is unilingual French-speaking and the rest of Canada or a truncated Canada, which is unilingual English-speaking.⁵⁵

Such unilingual policies would, in Ottawa's view, deny all Canadians "the heritage of one country, would compromise the roughly 8 per cent of citizens who belong to official-language minorities and would not allow the federal government to assume any responsibilities for the strengthening and preservation of the French language and culture." *A National Understanding* was written in part at least as a response to the policies of the Bourassa and Lévesque governments which required the children of immigrants to be educated in French. While the appropriateness of Quebec remaining a predominantly French-language community was recognized, it was believed to be preferable that " . . . immigrants should be attracted to the French language educational system for reasons that do not include coercion."

In general terms, the developments in Quebec during the 1960s brought about a hitherto unprecedented situation in English-French relations in Canada. From the Conquest of 1759 onward these relations had involved a stable and profoundly conservative society resisting changes to its integrity and survival coming from a more dynamic community. Now the forces for change in the Canadian Confederation were coming from Quebec itself.

Quebec and Canadian Federalism under the Bourassa Regime

In 1969 Robert Bourassa succeeded Jean Lesage as leader of the Quebec Liberal party. The Quebec general election of April 29, 1970 returned the Liberals to power with 45 per cent of the popular votes and 72 of the 108 seats in the National Assembly.⁵⁶ In the next election of October 30, 1973 the Bourassa government won a massive victory with 102 of 110 seats in the National Assembly and 54 per cent of the popular votes. This latter election returned Quebec to its two-party tradition with the virtual elimination of the Union Nationale and Créditiste parties as significant political forces in the province, and polarized the province on separatist-federalist lines, since the Parti Québécois increased its proportion of the popular vote from 1970 from 23 to 30 per cent and won 6 legislative seats.

The Bourassa government was less disposed than its predecessors of the 1960s to advance the province's interests by rhetorical and symbolic appeals to Quebec nationalism. In formulating the general rationale of its policies, it spoke of the cultural sovereignty of the province within the framework of Canadian federalism as a set of economic devices which were profitable to Quebec. On the side of what it defined as culture, the Bourassa government was very aggressive. Its linguistic legislation, enacted as Bill 22, will be discussed later. In collaboration with the other provinces it worked to restrict the jurisdiction of the federal government in the field of telecommunications and expanded the facilities of Radio-Quebec. It extended provincial activities in the field of immigration and in 1971 concluded an arrangement with Ottawa by which "orientation officers" of the Quebec Department of Immigration might work in federal immigration offices outside Canada. In the aftermath of the Victoria Conference, Quebec concluded arrangements with the federal authorities whereby the provinces might exercise a significant range of discretion over the allocation of federal family allowance payments. Also in 1971 an agreement was signed with Ottawa providing for Quebec participation with the French-language nations in the International Agency for Cultural and Scientific Cooperation. If it had remained in office it seems likely that the Bourassa government would have mounted a direct challenge to such federal cultural agencies as the Canada Council and the National Film Board.

As we have seen, the Bourassa administration in a piecemeal and pragmatic way had a relatively high degree of success in enlarging the province's scope of autonomy. However, in this quest for autonomy perhaps the most dramatic successes were in the field of interprovincial co-operation. Premier Lesage convened the first of the annual conferences of provincial premiers in 1960, and he frequently expressed the view that co-operation among the provinces should be developed as a substitute for federal action in some cases and as a prelude to federal-provincial co-operation in others. Yet relatively little was accomplished in this direction in the 1960s. However, in reviewing the events of 1973 Premier Bourassa could say:

> The most striking aspect of recent developments in Canadian federalism is the fact that the provincial governments have been adopting increasingly similar attitudes towards most problems. The provinces have in fact arrived at an identity of views on how to approach and solve most of Canada's economic and social problems. This identity of views finds expression in joint efforts to bring about a greater decentralization of the federal system, particularly in the following areas:
> 1. Federal finances: it is hoped to obtain a distribution of the resources that is more in keeping with the constitutional responsi-

bilities of the federal government and the provincial governments.
2. Economic development, particularly respecting the problems of regional disparities and unemployment.
3. Social development, with special emphasis on social security programs.
4. Cultural identity.[57]

The Bourassa government was thus committed to "fédéralisme rentable," profitable federalism, with the corollary that Quebec's separation from Canada as proposed by the Parti Québécois would be economically disastrous. With the formation of the PQ in 1968 the Liberals had lost most of those elements of Quebec society most urgent about modernization and social reform and because of this, along with the virtual elimination of the Union Nationale and Créditiste parties in the 1973 election, had come almost to monopolize the right of the Quebec political spectrum. The party attempted to wage its 1976 campaign almost exclusively on the issue of separatism rather than its own political record, but its reputation among the electorate for arrogance, insensitivity and corruption led to its defeat.[58]

Linguistic Conflict

As we have seen, a major element of the response to the new Quebec by the federal authorities and in widely varying degrees the governments of the other provinces was in the direction of enhancing the position of the French language in the Canadian community as such. Within Quebec these efforts have not been widely applauded, even by those committed to the federalist cause. In some cases bilingualism has been seen as an irrelevant diversion, in others an attempt by Ottawa to frustrate Quebec efforts to secure the dominance of the French language within that province.

It is interesting to inquire why linguistic conflicts have come to be so central to English-French relations in Canada:

—with the modernization of Quebec, most crucially perhaps with the decline of Roman Catholicism in that province, language has come to be the most significant differentiation between the two communities. From Lord Durham's Report of 1840, to André Siegfried's *The Race Question in Canada* in 1907, to A. R. M. Lower's "Two Ways of Life: the Primary Antithesis of Canadian History" in 1943, to the Report of the Quebec Royal Commission of Inquiry into Constitutional Problems in 1956 there is a remarkable similarity in the ways these communities and the relations between them have been depicted. Pierre Elliott Trudeau pithily summed up the French-English dialectic in his *La grève de l'amiante* published in 1956: ". . . pitted against an English, Protestant, democratic, materialistic, business-minded, and later industrial environment, our nationalism's system of self-preservation glorified every contrary tendency; and made a cult of the French language, Catholicism, authoritarianism, idealism, the rural way of life, including later, the myth of a 'return to the land'."[59] While there has been relatively little systematic examination of the differences between Anglophones and Francophones since 1960[60] it is reasonable to believe that these differences are less profound than in earlier periods of Canadian history. The statements of leaders of mainstream Quebec nationalism do not refer to the distinctive values of the two societies as the justification for Quebec independence and René Lévesque wrote in 1968, "Being ourselves is essentially a matter of developing and keeping a personality that has survived for three and a half centuries. At the core of this personality is the fact that we speak French."[61] On the other hand, the socialist scholar Marcel Rioux has asserted that ". . . a culture and a nation whose only distinctive trait was language would soon cease to be a culture and a nation."[62] Rioux's general argument is against a Quebec strategy of "catching up," i.e. establishing a society conforming to North American norms and in favour of a socialist Quebec. In broad terms, however, the passing of the traditional Quebec appears to have narrowed the differences between the two Canadian communities apart from linguistic differences and raised the salience of language.

—almost by their nature, relations involving language are a zero-sum game in which payoffs beneficial to all participants are very difficult or even impossible to achieve. If persons with two different "first" languages interact, it is almost inevitable that one will have to give way wholly or partly in respect to linguistic usage, except under relatively rare conditions in which both parties are fluently bilingual—or at least have fluent "receptive" capacities so that each person can express himself in the language with which he is more familiar and yet be understood by the other. The same general situation prevails in respect to collectivities. On the basis of deductive economic analysis Albert Breton argues that in the North American context the material costs of communication between English and French will be borne almost exclusively by the French.[63] Federal and Quebec language legislation attempts to shift part of the burden. In terms of language, there are three labour markets in Canada—one for bilinguals, one for those who speak French only, and one for those who speak English only. The federal Official Languages Act extends this market for bilinguals, the majority of whom are Francophones. Quebec legislation securing French as the language of work extends the market for French unilinguals, restricts that for English unilinguals, and has less determinate effects on the opportunities for bilingual persons. In these as in other cases of linguistic interactions, winners and losers are clearly and decisively defined.

—the modernization of Quebec and its openness to the external world are perceived by many Francophones to make the French language and culture more vulnerable than it was in the past. This is combined with what many believe is the demographic vulnerability of Francophone Quebec. Although demographers have differed about certain aspects of the matter, the rapid decline in the birth-rate of Quebec Francophones combined with the continuing disposition of persons in the province of non-English, non-French backgrounds to assimilate into the English-speaking community have been used to justify legislative measures to secure and enhance the position of the French language.

—the sociologist Hubert Guindon attributes the pressure of language legislation in contemporary Quebec to the circumstance that the occupational opportunities of the "new middle class" are now blocked.[64] In the early days of the Quiet Revolution adequate opportunities for such persons were available in the expanding public and para-public institutions of the province. More recently these institutions became fully staffed and the local and provincial governments of Quebec like those elsewhere have worked under financial constraints. This then set up a pressure for these modernized elites to extend their individual and collective opportunities in the private sector from which they have remained blocked, opportunities of course to be available in a French-language environment.

Bill 22 enacted by the National Assembly of Quebec in 1974 was the first major attempt of a government in that province to establish the dominance of the French language.[65] The opening clause of the legislation declared that French was to be the "official language" of Quebec. Apart from certain school boards servicing Anglophones, French was to be the internal language of communications in the provincial and local governments. With certain exceptions, persons who wished to attain qualification to practice in the professions were required to demonstrate a working knowledge of French. Under the guidance of a board, Régie de la langue française, private businesses were to be directed to establish French as the language of work and after completing their "francization" requirements would be given certificates necessary, with again some exceptions, to enable them to do business with the Quebec government. So far as public education was concerned, the future entry of children into schools where English was the language of instruction was to be limited to those who had already acquired a sufficient knowledge of English and school boards were charged with assigning children to English- or French-language schools according to these principles.

Bill 22 challenged for the first time the coequal status that the English and French languages had developed in the public affairs and private businesses of Quebec. Understandably this legislation was strenuously opposed by non-Francophone elements in the province, more strenuously perhaps by relatively recent immigrants against whom the educational provisions of Bill 22 were directed than by longer-term residents of the province who were mainly of British origin and by the leaders of private business. The enactment gave sweeping discretionary powers to the provincial government and to school boards in applying its provisions and such discretion was displeasing both to non-Francophones and to Québécois nationalists, the latter fearing that the dominance of French could thus be weakened.

Bill 101, at first symbolically called Bill 1, as enacted by the National Assembly in 1977 was an extension of the principles of Bill 22 with some significant modifications. In general terms, the new legislation is more specific than the former and confers less discretionary authority on provincial and local officials. Important provisions related to place names and to the names of businesses, language used in advertising etc., attempted to ensure that Quebec would be visually French. It was in its educational provisions that Bill 101 differed most markedly from its predecessor. Children were eligible to receive instruction in English-language schools only under the following conditions: (a) either parent had received his or her elementary education in English in Quebec; (b) either parent had received elementary education in English outside Quebec but was domiciled in Quebec at the time the Act came into effect; (c) they were already receiving instruction in English-language schools at the time the Act went into effect, in which case their younger brothers and sisters were also eligible; (d) they were children of members of the Canadian Armed Forces temporarily assigned to Quebec, or of persons who were members of international agencies or representatives of foreign governments; (e) they were children or persons studying or working in Quebec for a period of not more than three years, providing one or other of the parents had been educated in English or that one of their children had already begun or had completed his or her education in English. There was also a provision whereby English-speaking children from provinces which had completed a reciprocity agreement with Quebec might be enrolled in English-language schools. However, Premier Lévesque was unsuccessful in gaining the willingness of any of the other provinces to enter into such arrangements when the matter was discussed at the annual Premiers' Conference held in St. Andrew's, New Brunswick in August, 1977.

Bill 101 also went beyond its predecessor by challenging directly what most constitutional scholars have believed to be the protections of Section 133 of the British North America Act for linguistic duality in the legislature and courts of Quebec. Article 7 declared French to be "the language of the legislature and the courts in Quebec." It was further stipulated in Article 8 that legislative bills be drafted in French and be tabled in the National Assembly, passed and assented to in that language. Article 9 enacted that "only the French text of the statutes and regulations is official," and Article 13 that all the judgments of Quebec courts must be "drawn up in French or be accompanied by a duly authenticated French version." In Quebec legal circles there has been some support for the view that the provisions of Section 133 providing for the rights of the two languages in the legislature and courts of the province are a part of the provincial constitution and thus may be altered or eliminated by the Quebec legislature by Section 92(1) of the BNA Act which allows each province to amend its own constitution "except as regards the Office of Lieutenant-Governor." However, Judge Deschênes of the Superior Court of Montreal rejected this view and declared unconstitutional Articles 7-13 of Bill 101 as contrary to Section 133 in a judgment delivered in early 1978.[66]*

Even more directly than Bill 22, Bill 101 challenged the duality of Quebec society that had prevailed since the Conquest. Edward McWhinney has recently written of these two enactments that "language reform became the means of effecting the progressive transfer of economic decision-making in Quebec from an older Anglo-Saxon élite to the emerging new French-Canadian commercial élite."[67] As we have seen, this kind of change is explicitly contrary to the policies of the federal government in its support for linguistic and cultural duality. However, the Trudeau cabinet resisted pressures either to disallow Bill 101 or to refer it to the Supreme Court of Canada for an opinion about the constitutionality of certain of its provisions. Further, Quebec received in 1977-1978 some $76.9 millions from Ottawa for bilingual programs, 51.2 per cent of all federal grants to the provinces for such purposes.

The Parti Québécois[68]

The Parti Québécois was formed in 1968 as a union of two independence movements, Le Rassemblement pour l'Indépendance nationale and Le Ralliement National. In October 1967 René Lévesque and several of his more nationalistic colleagues and supporters had resigned from the Quebec Liberal party because of the failure of that party to accept a program based on the political sovereignty of Quebec and a continuing economic association with Canada. Apart from its commitment to Quebec nationalism, the PQ's program of domestic reform is in general terms similar to that of social democratic parties in western Europe and to the New Democratic Party. Like the NDP also, the PQ's internal structures provide for a high degree of intraparty democracy. In general

---

* In December 1979 the Supreme Court of Canada upheld this decision and declared Section 133 of the BNA Act took precedence over the sections of Bill 101 at issue.

terms, the Parti Québécois is the institutional outlet for those elements of Québécois society in the vanguard of modernization.

The Part Québécois contested the 1970 provincial election and won 7 seats in the National Assembly with 23 per cent of the popular vote. In the 1973 general election the PQ received 30 per cent of the popular vote but only 6 seats.

After the Quebec provincial election of 1973 in which the Bourassa Liberals won 102 of 110 seats in the National Assembly with 54.2 per cent of the popular vote, the PQ undertook a careful review of its strategy. The independence issue had dominated the election and largely because of this Quebec politics had reverted to their historic two-party form with the virtual elimination of the Union Nationale and the provincial Créditistes. According to the evidence presented by Maurice Pinard and Richard Hamilton, support for Quebec independence among the electorate was growing relatively slowly and thus the PQ was faced with the task, if it hoped to come to power in the forseeable future, of gaining the support of voters who did not favour independence.[69] The immediate solution, as it was adopted at the PQ's 1974 national convention, promised that if the party came to power there would be a referendum on independence during its first term of office and that steps towards independence would be taken only after a positive result in such a referendum.

The PQ's attempt at dissociating support for the party and support for Quebec independence was spectacularly successfully in the 1976 provincial election, by which it came to power with 41.4 per cent of the popular votes yielding 71 of 110 seats in the National Assembly. During the election campaign the party emphasized its own program of social and economic reform, the need for effective political leadership and the inadequacies of the Bourassa government rather than independence. This was apparently in harmony with the priorities of the Quebec electorate; in the survey of a representative sample of Quebec adults taken 10-15 days before the election, Hamilton and Pinard found that for only 15 per cent was independence the "most important" or "next most important" issue, while some 70 per cent accorded the "management of the economy" such significance and, of the French Canadians opposed to independence, only 8 per cent named this as the "most important" or "next most important issue."[70] The PQ's victory can thus be explained largely in terms of its effective dissociation of the election and the future referendum on independence and the party's consequent ability to win the support of voters not committed to the sovereignty of Quebec. The Parti Québécois was also aided by the extreme unpopularity of the Bourassa regime which had come to prevail in all elements of Quebec society and by the partial recrudescence of the Union Nationale gained with the support of large numbers of non-Francophones in the Montreal region who were alienated by Bill 22.

Although the PQ had fought the 1976 election campaign almost entirely on the need for effective political leadership and on its program of social and economic reform, it emphasized the national issue in its first months in power. At the first ministers' conference held in early December 1976 Premier Lévesque assumed a belligerent stance and early the next year his officials presented financial statistics purporting to show that Quebec was disadvantaged by the federal system. In his speech to the prestigious Economic Club of New York in January 1977—a speech broadcast by the major Canadian television networks—Lévesque again emphasized the independence issue. Much of the political debate in Quebec during 1977 revolved around the linguistic issue and Bill 101. Meanwhile, facing relative financial stringency, the government proceeded slowly with its program of economic and social reform.

Sovereignty-Association and the Referendum

From its origins the Parti Québécois has combined its program of the political sovereignty of Quebec with that of a continuing economic association with Canada. This combination appears to be in general harmony with the preferences of the Quebec electorate in the sense that there is ample evidence from survey research to demonstrate that sovereignty-association is much more acceptable than independence in its fullest sense. From time to time the PQ has given different emphasis to the sovereignty and the association elements of its program and in different circumstances party leaders have given somewhat divergent answers as to what economic association is to include. A statement *Égal à égal* issued by the executive council of the party, to be submitted to the national congress later in 1979, included these elements:

—there is to be the free circulation of commodities within the boundaries of Canada-Quebec, qualified by the right of each state to protect its agricultural producers, to engage in programs of temporary aid for economic development, and to maintain preferential programs of purchasing.

—there is to be a common Canada-Quebec tariff against goods coming into that community from outside.

—with certain exceptions, there is to be free circulation of capital within Canada-Quebec.

—there is to be a common currency.

—there is to be free movement of people within Canada-Quebec.[71]

The document also proposes that if an economic association with Canada is impossible to attain, the government should again consult with the citizens of Quebec, presumably by way of a second referendum or a general election, to ascertain whether Quebec is to become sovereign in the most complete legal sense.

In late 1978, a lengthy study, *L'Option*, was published by two PQ members of the Quebec National Assembly, Jean-Pierre Charbonneau and Gilbert Paquette.[72] The latter part of this book dealt at length with the content and structures of possible forms of association between a sovereign Quebec and Canada in the light of the experience of such contemporary international associations as Benelux, the Nordic Union and the European Economic Community. The Charbonneau-Paquette study is not of course an official statement of the PQ, but because of the personal influence of the authors within that movement and because they have studied the matter at hand in considerable depth it is reasonable to suppose that this book will have considerable influence within the party.

In terms of the content of economic association strictly defined, Charbonneau and Paquette do not diverge significantly from the proposals of *Égal à égal*, although there is a tentative and inconclusive discussion of the possibilities of an integration of the transportation systems of the two nations. However, there are recommendations for other aspects of association than the economic:

—it is suggested that the two nations could "harmonize" the establishment of diplomatic and consular services abroad to bring about a more complete coverage than either could sustain by itself.

—Canada and Quebec would be associated jointly in the protection of the native peoples and of French-Canadian and Anglo-Quebec minorities.

L'Option goes further than any previous study in detailing the possible institutional structures of association between Canada and a sovereign Quebec:

—the major decisional agency would be a council of four ministers delegated by each of the two governments. The council would direct the Secretariat of the Canada-Quebec authority and such bipartite committees as were established to facilitate the work of the authority. In the proceedings of the council each nation would cast a single vote and unanimity would be necessary for any decision.

—a court of justice would interpret the act of association of Canada and Quebec. This would be composed of four judges from each of the states and a chairman from Canada and Quebec in rotation. All these appointments would be subject to the approval of both governments.

—there would be an interparliamentary consultative council of 115 members. Fifty of these would be nominated from each of the Legislatures of Canada and Quebec according to the party representation in these bodies and 5 each from the councils of the minorities (native peoples, Anglo-Quebeckers, the French Canadians).[73]

The Parti Québécois is committed to holding a referendum on Quebec's constitutional future within its first term of office. According to pronouncements of party leaders the electorate would be asked to give the government "a mandate to negotiate" a new relation with Canada, presumably along the lines of the sovereignty-association alternative.

The general conditions for the Quebec referendum were specified in a White Paper *Consulting the People of Quebec* issued under the name of Robert Burns, Minister of State for Electoral and Parliamentary Reform in August 1977.[74] The White Paper purports to derive the referendum procedure from those which governed the British plebiscite of 1975 in which voters were asked whether they wished the United Kingdom to remain a member of the European Economic Community. More specifically:

—the question to be settled by the referendum would be submitted to the National Assembly by the government and there debated.

—those eligible to vote in the referendum were to be persons otherwise eligible to vote in provincial elections and the referendum was to be administered by the same authorities and the same procedures as prevail in such elections.

—those supporting each of the options would organize themselves into *ad hoc* committees and only these organizations would be entitled to receive financial assistance from the state or from private sources, or to incur campaign expenses.

—each of the *ad hoc* committees was to receive the same amount of public funds to conduct its campaign.

—each committee would be allowed to spend up to 50 cents for each voter on the electoral roll.

—the committees would be permitted to draw financial support from only three sources: from the state contribution, from members of the electorate according to the same provisions which govern the financing of political parties and from the parties themselves which would be permitted to donate no more than 25 cents per voter to the organizations.

Quebec nationalism as manifested by the PQ has polarized Quebec society along the axis of the national issue and undoubtedly this polarization will be intensified as the referendum campaign approaches. In the long run, however, the most decisive influence of the PQ has been perhaps to change the self-identification of citizens from French Canadians to Québécois, and Don and Věra Murray point out that even Pierre Elliott Trudeau has given up using the former expression when speaking in Quebec.[75] Although the results of such changes in perception are difficult to assess in any precise way, there is here a crucial and no doubt irreversible development in the circumstances of French-English relations in Canada.

Notes

1. *A Future Together: Observations and Recommendations*, Ottawa: Supply and Services, 1979, p. 21.
2. *Parliamentary Debates on Confederation at British North American Provinces, 1865*, King's Printer, Ottawa, 1951, p. 108.
3. The Act of Union period has been intensively studied by several contemporary scholars. See particularly in relation to this discussion J. M. S. Careless, *The Union of The Canadas: The Growth of Canadian Institutions*, Toronto: McClelland and Stewart, 1967, and J. E. Hodgetts, *Pioneer Public Service: An Administrative History of the United Canadas 1841-1867*, Toronto: University of Toronto Press, 1955. For the roots of federalism in this period, see W. G. Ormsby, *The Emergence of The Federal Concept in Canada, 1839-1845*, Toronto: University of Toronto Press, 1969.
4. See the collection of essays edited by Kenneth McRae, *Consociational Democracy, Political Accommodation in Segmented Societies*, Carleton Library Series, Toronto: McClelland and Stewart, 1974.
5. From *Union of the Canadas* by J. M. S. Careless (p. 210), reprinted by permission of the Canadian Publishers, McClelland and Stewart Limited, Toronto.
6. For a cogent criticism of recent attempts to see Confederation in these terms, see Donald Creighton's essay "The Use and Abuse of History," in Creighton, *Towards the Discovery of Canada*, Toronto: Macmillan of Canada, Toronto, 1972, pp. 65-83.
7. Because of the traditions of cabinet secrecy—and the casual way in which cabinets of that day carried on their internal business—we know very little about these negotiations except for references by participants in the Confederation Debates, particularly Macdonald and Brown.
8. *Confederation Debates*, p. 96.
9. Ibid., pp. 53-61.
10. (trans.) In Pierre Elliott Trudeau (editeur), *La grève de l'amiante*, Québec, Université Laval Presse, 1954, p. 12. See also Trudeau's essay, "Some Obstacles to Democracy in Quebec," in Pierre Elliott Trudeau, *Federalism and the French Canadians*, Toronto: Macmillan of Canada, 1968, pp. 103-123.
11. Michel Brunet, "Trois dominantes de la pensée canadienne-française; l'agriculturisme, l'anti-étatisme et la messianisme," in *La présence anglaise et les canadiens*, Montreal: Beauchemin, 1964, pp. 113-166.
12. See generally Frederick W. Gibson, ed., *Cabinet Formation and Bicultural Relations: Seven Case Studies*, Studies of the Royal Commission on Bilingualism and Biculturalism, Ottawa: Queen's Printer, 1970, and more particularly Gibson's conclusions "Co-Prime Minister, Chief Lieutenant or Provincial Spokesman," pp. 155-159 and ff.
13. Pierre Elliott Trudeau, *Federalism and the French Canadians*, Toronto: Macmillan at Canada, 1968. "Regardless of how liberal were the conqueror's political institutions, they had no intrinsic value in the minds of the people who had not desired them, never learned to use them and finally only accepted them as a means of loosening the conqueror's grip." p. 106.

14. For a history of the compact theories, see Ramsay Cook, *Provincial Auton-omy, Minority Rights and the Compact Theory, 1867-1921*, Studies of the Royal Commission on Bilingualism and Biculturalism, Ottawa: Queen's Printer, 1969. See also R. Arès, S.J., *Dossier sur le pacte fédératif de 1867*, Montreal: Les Éditions Bellarmin, 1967.

15. See Leon Dion, "The Origin and Character of the Nationalism of Growth", *Canadian Forum*, Vol. XIII, No. 516, January 1964, pp. 229-233; and H. Guindon, "Social Unrest, Social Class and Quebec's Bureaucratic Revo-lution", *Queen's Quarterly* LXXXI (Summer 1964), pp. 150-162.

16. Hubert Guindon, "Two Cultures: An Essay on Nationalism, Class and Eth-nic Tension," in *The Canadian Political Process*, Toronto: Orest Kruhlak, Richard Schultz and Sidney Pobihuschy, ed., Holt, Rinehart and Winston of Canada, 1970, pp. 75-93.

17. Fernand Ouellett in *Quebec: Year Eight*, Glendon College Forum, Toronto: C.B.C. Publications, 1968, p. 80.

18. For accounts of the failure of Prime Minister Diefenbaker in respect to Que-bec by two former Conservative MPs from that privince, see Pierre Sevigny, *This Game of Politics*, Toronto: McClelland and Stewart, 1965 and Vincent Brassard, *Les insolences d'un ex-deputé*, Montreal: Distributions Eclair, n.d. (1963?)

19. Maurice Pinard, *The Rise of a Third Party: A Study in Crisis Politics*, Eng-lewood Cliffs, NJ.: Prentice-Hall Inc., 1971.

20. *Le Devoir*, 29 Octobre, 1966.

21. Daniel Johnson, *Égalité ou Indépendance*, Éditions Renaissance, Montreal, p. 35. Emphasis in text.

22. *Federal-Provincial Conference, 1963*, Ottawa: Queen's Printer, 1964, p. 40.

23. Donald V. Smiley, *The Canadian Political Nationality*, Toronto: Methuen of Canada, 1967, pp. 66-67.

24. *Federal-Provincial Conference, 1963*, pp. 44-46.

25. For the Premier's statement see his Ste. Foy speech reprinted in *Le Devoir*, 23 et 24 décembre 1965. Paul Gérin-Lajoie spoke along similar lines to the 1965 Couchiching Conference. Toronto: Gordon Hawkins, ed., *Concepts of Federalism*, Canadian Institute on Public Affairs, 1965, pp. 62-68.

26. The provisions of Section 80 were nullified by the National Assembly after the 1970 election.

27. Johnson, *op. cit.*

28. For an account of those incidents see Edward McWhinney, "Canadian Fed-eralism: Foreign Affairs and Treaty Power," in *The Confederation Chal-lenge, Background Papers and Reports, Volume 2*, Ontario Advisory Com-mittee on Confederation, Toronto: Queen's Printer, 1970, pp. 115-152.

29. For the federal position, see the Honourable Paul Martin, *Federalism and International Relations*, Ottawa: Queen's Printer, 1968; and the Honour-able Mitchell Sharp, *Federalism and International Conferences on Educa-tion*, Ottawa: Queen's Printer, 1968. See also Jacques Brossard, André Patry, et Elisabeth Weiser, *Les pouvoirs extérieurs du Québec*, Montréal: Les Presses de l'Université de Montréal, 1967.

30. David R. Cameron "Dualism and the Concept of National Unity," in John H. Redekop, ed., *Approaches to Canadian Politics*, Scarborough: Prentice-Hall of Canada, 1978, p. 237.

31. Ramsay Cook, *Canada and the French-Canadian Question*, Toronto: Macmillan of Canada, 1966, p. 2.

32. *Report of the Royal Commission on Bilingualism and Biculturalism Book I, The Official Languages*, Ottawa: Queen's Printer, 1967, p. 173.

33. For accounts of the pension issue see Kenneth Bryden, *Old Age Pensions and Policy-Making in Canada*, Montreal: McGill-Queen's University Press, 1974, Chapter 8; Richard Simeon, *Federal-Provincial Diplomacy*, Toronto: University of Toronto Press, 1972, Chapter 3; and Peter C. Newman, *The Distemper of Our Times*, Toronto: McClelland and Stewart, 1968, Chapter 22.

34. For a general discussion, see V. Seymour Wilson, "Language Policy" in G. Bruce Doern and V. Seymour Wilson, eds., *Issues in Canadian Public Policy*, Toronto: Macmillan of Canada, 1974, pp. 253-285.

35. *Report of the Royal Commission on Bilingualism and Biculturalism, Book III, The Work World*, Ottawa: Queen's Printer, 1969.

36. Ibid., p. 111.

37. Ibid., pp. 211-213.

38. *Official Languages in the Public Service of Canada, A Report by the Honourable Jean Chretien President of the Treasury Board*, Nov. 21, 1974. (mimeo)

39. Ottawa: Information Canada, 1976, p. 8.

40. Ibid., p. 7.

41. See Chapter 4 and Appendices to the Report.

42. *Report, Commissioner of Official Languages, 1973-74*, Information Canada, Ottawa, 1974, p. 395.

43. This was in harmony with the 1967 Report on *Official Languages of the Royal Commission on Bilingualism and Biculturalism*.

44. *Report of the Bilingual Districts Advisory Board*, Ottawa: Information Canada, 1975.

45. W. L. Morton, "The Cabinet of 1867," in Frederick W. Gibson, ed., *Cabinet Formation and Bicultural Relations*, Studies of the Royal Commission on Bilingualism and Biculturalism, Ottawa: Queen's Printer, 1970, p. 5.

46. Richard J. Van Loon and Michael S. Whittington, *The Canadian Political System*, Toronto: McGraw-Hill of Canada, 1971, pp. 346-350.

47. Pierre Elliott Trudeau, "The New Treason of the Intellectuals," in Trudeau, *Federalism and the French Canadians*, p. 166.

48. In his 1965 study of a representative group of Francophone middle-level public servants in the federal government, the late Christopher Beattie found that 51 per cent came from Quebec and 40 per cent from Ontario. Christopher Beattie, *Minority Men in a Majority Setting*, Carleton Library Original, Toronto: McClelland and Stewart, 1975, p. 12.

49. For reforms in education, see T. H. B. Symons, "Ontario's Quiet Revolution," in R. M. Burns, ed., *One Country or Two?* Montreal: McGill-Queen's University Press, 1971, pp. 169-204.

50. For a comprehensive report, see *The State of Minority Language Education in the Ten Provinces of Canada*, Council of Ministers of Education, Toronto, 1978 (mimeo).

51. Louis Sabourin, "Canada and Francophone Africa," in Peyton V. Lyon and Tareq Y. Ismael, eds., *Canada and the Third World*, Toronto: Macmillan of Canada, 1976, pp. 133-161.

52. Conrad Winn, "Bicultural Policy", in Conrad Winn and John McMenemy, *Political Parties in Canada*, Toronto: McGraw-Hill Ryerson, 1976, p. 196.

54. For example, see Denis Smith's criticism of "Ottawa's narrowly legalistic and linguistic approach to Quebec nationalism", "Preparing For Independence", Editorial, *Canadian Forum*, January 1977, p. 4.

55. *A National Understanding*, Ottawa: Ministry of Supply and Services, 1977, p. 41.

56. For an analysis of this election, see Vincent Lemieux, Marcel Gilbert et André Blais, *Une élection de réalignment: l'élection du 29 avril 1970 au Québec*, Montréal: Cahiers de Cité Libre, 1970.

57. Communiqué of December 22, 1973, Government of Quebec, *mimeo*, pp. 10-11.

58. Maurice Pinard and Richard Hamilton, "The Parti Québécois Comes to Power: An Analysis of the 1976 Quebec Election," *Canadian Journal of Political Science*, 11, pp. 748-752.

59. Pierre Elliott Trudeau, "La grève de l'amiante," translated and quoted in Ramsay Cook, ed., *French-Canadian Nationalism*, Toronto: Macmillan of Canada, 1969, p. 33.

60. But see the empirical evidence presented by John Meisel in his "Values, Language and Politics in Canada," in John Meisel, *Working Papers on Canadian Politics*, Montreal: McGill-Queen's University Press, 1972, pp. 127-181.

61. René Lévesque, *An Option for Quebec*, Toronto: McClelland and Stewart, 1968, p. 14.

62. Marcel Rioux, *Quebec in Question*, Toronto: James Lewis and Samuel, 1971, p. 132.

63. Albert Breton, *Bilingualism: An Economic Approach*, Montreal: C. D. Howe Research Institute, 1978. For a similar analysis see Jean-Luc Migué, *Nationalistic Policies in Canada: An Economic Approach*, Montreal: C. D. Howe Research Institute, 1979, pp. 30-36.

64. Hubert Guindon, "The Modernization of Quebec and the Legitimacy of the Quebec State," in Daniel Glenday, Hubert Guindon and Allan Turowitz, eds., *Modernization and the Canadian State*, Toronto: Macmillan of Canada, 1978, pp. 230-234.

65. See on recent Quebec language legislation, Edward McWhinney, *Quebec and the Constitution 1960-1978*, Toronto: University of Toronto Press, 1979, Chapter 6 "Quebec Acts: Bills 22 and 101."

66. *Blaikie et al C. Procureur-général de la Province de Québec et Procureur-général du Canada*, 85 D.L.R. (3d), 252, (1978). The Gendron Commission on language in Quebec heard evidence that Section 133 in its Quebec aspects could be overridden by provincial action under Section 92(1). See the paper of Henri Brun and Jean K. Sampson in the Commission's Report, 2 *Les droits linguistiques*, Quebec, 1972, pp. 372-377.

67. McWhinney, *op. cit.*, p. viii.

68. The writings of Don and Věra Murray on the Parti Québécois are very useful. See Věra Murray, *Le Parti québécois: de la fondation à la prise du pouvoir*, Montréal: Cahiers du Québec/Hurtubise HMH, 1976; Don and Věra Murray, *De Bourassa à Lévesque*, Montréal: Éditions Quinze, 1978; and Don and Věra Murray, "The Parti Québécois: From Opposition to Power,"

in Hugh G. Thorburn, ed., *Party Politics in Canada*, 4th Edition, Scarborough: 1979, pp. 243-252.

69. Hamilton and Pinard, *op. cit.*, pp. 742-748.

70. Ibid., p. 746.

71. Maurice Pinard and Richard Hamilton, "The Independence Issue and the Polarization of the Electorate" *Canadian Journal of Political Science*, X, June 1977, pp. 215-259. In a poll conducted for the CBC in March 1977, Pinard and Hamilton found 16 per cent of the Quebec sample in favour of independence, and 32 per cent favouring sovereignty-association. Hamilton and Pinard, The Parti Québécois Comes to Power," p. 744 n.

72. Jean Pierre Charbonneau and Gilbert Paquette, *L'Option*, Montréal: Les Editions de L'homme, 1978.

73. Ibid., pp. 471-493.

74. *Consulting the People of Quebec*, Québec: Gouvernement du Québec, 1977.

75. Don and Věra Murray, *De Bourassa à Lévesque*, p. 257.

CHAPTER 8

THE COMPOUNDED CRISIS OF CANADIAN FEDERALISM

Up until now the analysis has been focused almost exclusively on the Canadian governmental system and in Chapter 1 I suggested that in contemporary Canada governments themselves have a considerable capacity to shape their respective national and provincial societies. Yet this is not the whole story and it would be perverse not to recognize the important and, in the long run decisive, impact of underlying economic and social structures in the political system. The basic argument of this Chapter is that the current Canadian crisis involves *both* these structures *and* the form that the governmental system has taken.

In the structural dimension, what might be designated as the "compounded crisis of Canadian federalism" is a result of simultaneous and in all likelihood irreversible changes in three sets of relations which have in the most elemental way determined Canadian nationhood. These relations are those between (1) The English-speaking and French-speaking elements of Canada, (2) The central heartland of Ontario/Quebec and the regions to the east and west of this heartland, and (3) Canadian and American structures of political and economic power. The Confederation settlement of 1864-1867—along with the subsequent national economic policies of the Macdonald Conservatives and Laurier Liberals which were an elaboration of this settlement—was a coherent response to these sets of interactions.[1] If Canadian nationhood is in any genuine sense to be re-established, new and equally coherent solutions to all three of these underlying relations must be found.

The most influential voices in Canadian political debate during the past two decades have been preoccupied almost exclusively with one or, more rarely two, dimensions of Canadian nationhood to the neglect of the other(s). Several such examples could be given. Those like Pierre Elliott Trudeau who have been primarily concerned with French-English relations have failed to think creatively about either continentalism or centre-periphery relations. English-speaking intellectuals in their support of Canadian cultural and economic nationalism have often sympathized with a Quebec nationalism whose explicit objective it is to destroy Confederation. Supporters of the claims of the peripheral regions of Canada have often viewed cultural duality as an irrelevant diversion." The French-English contradiction which appears to separate Ontario from Quebec serves only to force even more federal attention towards this region, almost always at the expense of the West and the Maritimes."[2] The Report of the Task Force on Canadian Unity published in early 1979 addresses itself to cultural duality and regionalism but ignores the continental dimension entirely. It would be tedious to give more such examples.

Manifestations of the Decline of Canadian Nationhood

There are several manifestations of the decline of Canadian nationhood.

Canada is only in a very imperfect sense an economic community. A fundamental prerequisite of nationhood in its economic dimension is the free movement of people, commodities and capital within the national boundaries. Yet as we saw in Chapter 6 the provinces have increasingly compromised what economists call factor mobility through preferential purchasing policies, barriers on the movement of natural products between provinces, occupational licensure, and so on. These kinds of restrictions are for the most part prohibited in the case of nations within the European Economic Community. The federal government has neither the will nor the constitutional powers to remove these barriers to movement between provinces, and Canadians are thus denied the full material benefits of nationhood. Furthermore, it is at least possible to contemplate a situation in which such internal obstructions to mobility would make it difficult or impossible for Canadians to attain membership in other free trade areas or international economic communities.[3]

The federal government has a declining capacity to commit Canada in international relations. An increasing number of matters of international action are wholly or exclusively within the legislative jurisdiction of the provinces. In respect to such matters, Canada can be an effective actor only if there is co-operation between the federal and provincial governments. Under the current circumstances of conflict between the two orders, such co-operation is often absent. The provinces to widely varying degrees have become independent actors in international economic and cultural relations and have become increasingly insistent that they be involved in the formulation of national economic policies even when these are unequivocally within Ottawa's jurisdiction.

The capacity of the federal government to effect interprovincial and interpersonal equalization appears to be in decline. As we saw in Chapter 6, Canada had by 1974 attained a regime of interprovincial revenue equalization in which the per capita provincial-municipal expenditures of the "have-not" provinces were very close to the national average. Largely because of developments in the international petroleum market, Ottawa has now moved away from full revenue equalization and it is reasonable to expect that increasing financial stringency will lead the federal authorities to compromise this principle even further. In the dimension of interpersonal equalization, Ottawa appears to have a declining capacity to sustain the national welfare state that was established largely under federal leadership. The crucial area here is access to medical and hospital services. In the past two decades there have been important national commitments that Canadians will pay for such services when they are well rather than when they are ill and that no citizen will be denied these amenities when he needs them because of his financial circumstances. The conversion of federal payments for hospital and medical insurance from conditional to unconditional transfers under the 1977 legislation makes it impossible for Ottawa to ensure universal accessibility except by drastic measures which would undoubtedly excaberate federal-provincial tensions to a very marked degree. Yet such accessibility is being challenged by the decision of physicians to opt out of provincial plans, and it is very likely that provincial governments themselves will come to support deterrent or "coinsurance" arrangements related to medical and/or hospital services for reasons of fiscal stringency.

There is a decline in the strength of a Canadian political nationality as Canadians increasingly emphasize culture/language/ethnicity as the foundation of political organization and political allegiance. In 1865 George Étienne Cartier spoke of the creation of a Canadian "political nationality with which neither the national origin nor the religion of any individual would interfere;"[4] in 1965 the Terms of Reference of the Royal Commission on Bilingualism and Biculturalism spoke of Confederation in terms of "an equal partnership between the two founding races."[5] The second definition appears to be overtaking the first, certainly among French Canadians and those in the other linguistic community who accept their claims. More than at any time in the past, however, English-speaking Canadians have come to accept what

Kenneth McNaught has called "a non-racial view of nationality"[6] as is demonstrated by an immigration policy explicitly setting aside racial and ethnic origin as criteria for eligibility, human rights legislation enjoining discrimination of racial and ethnic grounds, the relative toleration of old-stock Canadians of British origin for those of other groups attaining positions of power and status, the glorification of the multicultural mosaic and so on. The view is challenged by those who view Canada primarily or exclusively through the prism of cultural/linguistic duality whether this is formulated in terms of binationalism or the perspectives of Pierre Elliott Trudeau and the Royal Commission on Bilingualism and Biculturalism. I shall argue in Chapter 9 that this preoccupation with language and culture is destructive of Canada as a *political* community.

The decline of Canadian nationhood means then that the country is denied many of the material benefits of a domestic common market, that the central government is decreasingly effective as an international actor and as an agent of interpersonal and interprovincial equalization, and that culture rather than nationality is increasingly the principle of political organization and political allegiance.

The First Axis: French-English Relations

Canada is now comprised of two modernized and modernizing linguistic communities rather than one. *This* is the essential element in contemporary English-French relations. The sociologist Hubert Guindon has made a highly suggestive analysis of "the social contract underlying the Canadian Confederation of 1867" which "worked smoothly" until the 1960s and has since been challenged by the modernization of the French-speaking part of Quebec society.[7] The partners to this "tacit agreement" were the English merchant class of Montreal and the Catholic clergy in Quebec."[8] The crucial element of the bargain was an institutional division of the labour force with the surplus population of French Catholics becoming "the unskilled and semi-skilled labour force of industrial capitalism" while the technical and managerial personnel would be English-speaking. Beyond that, the provinces were granted jurisdiction over health, welfare and education—services provided through local units of administration under the control of the Church.[9]

Modernization changed the social contract by destroying the power of the Catholic Church, and the provincial government rather than the Church quickly became the major institutional expression of Québécois society. The public sector expanded very rapidly and in the first decade of the Quiet Revolution provided adequate employment opportunities for members of the "new middle class". More recently, however, this sector has become almost fully staffed and there are increasing pressures challenging the dominance of the private sector by English-speaking élites.

As we saw in Chapter 7, the major response of the federal government to Quebec nationalism has been a linguistic one following very closely the recommendations of the Royal Commission on Bilingualism and Biculturalism in its Report on the Official Languages. Up until the mid-1970s, this kind of response was supported by what one observer has called an "élite phalanx" in English-speaking Canada and among Francophone federalists in Quebec and one could oppose it in respectable circles only at his peril. Guindon's critique of the official-languages policies is devastating[10] and in my view essentially accurate. In his assessment, this policy did not either appreciably increase the Francophone share of the federal bureaucracy or arrest the accelerated assimilation of French Canadians outside Quebec. At the same time it awakened the antipathies of English-speaking Canadians against Francophones and created ambiguities for immigrants within Quebec. It is the essence of Guindon's argument that what is needed is "the full participation of Québécois in their political economy."[11] Thus "Quebec is the only province in Canada that has a double economy, in labour force terms, neatly segregated along language lines. The credibility of the Canadian federal state will ultimately stand or fall on this issue."[12] In general, the federal response to the imperatives of modernization in Quebec has been irrelevant or worse.

The modernization of Quebec society has led to the enhanced influence of what Henry Milner has designated as the "state middle class" directly or indirectly linked to the provincial government. This group includes such occupations as ". . . teachers, professors, psychologists, technicians, journalists, planners, economists, broadcasters, nurses, physiotherapists and other health semi-professionals, social workers, social animators, community organizers, trade union officials, professional athletes, artists, entertainers, scientists, as well as members of the 'older' professions (medicine, law, engineering etc.) employed directly or indirectly in the public sector."[13] Milner estimates that this stratum, including dependents, would comprise 300,000 to 350,000 persons which is roughly 7 per cent of the Francophone population of Quebec.

The political expression of the new middle class in Quebec, including of course the state middle class, is the Parti Québécois. Věra Murray's study of the social origins of Liberal and PQ candidates in the 1970 and 1973 elections showed that the former drew 22.9 per cent of its candidates from the "nouvelle class moyen" and the latter 53.2 per cent with this defined as "des employés des services publics et para-publics (professeurs, enseignants, journalistes, conseillers, criminologues, sociologues, politicologues, économistes, etc.) mais aussi les catégories telles que ingénieurs, contremaîtres, superviseurs, etc.)".[14] There is ample evidence that support both for the PQ and for independence among Québécois comes disproportionately from urban-dwellers, from the younger, from the more affluent and from the better-educated.[15] On the basis of both the social character of its leadership and the kind of support it receives from the wider electorate, it might be plausible to accept the prospect of the virtually inevitable victory of Quebec independence.

Yet countervailing forces might come to prevail. The PQ's coming to power in November 1976 was in large measure attributable to the success of René Lévesque and his colleagues in winning the support of large numbers of voters who did not favour Quebec independence.[16] However, with one or more plebiscites on the independence issue in the offing it appears unlikely that the PQ will be able to maintain the same high level of dissociation between its electoral support and that for the central element of its program. Thus the unpopularity of the party arising from sources unrelated to independence might well compromise the cause of independence or apprehensions about independence could lower popular support for the party. Further, through language legislation and other measures successive governments of Quebec have shown considerable capacity to pursue the interests and enhance the confidence of Québécois society within the federal system. Because of this it is at least possible that many French-speaking Quebeckers will come to find Confederation less than intolerable. The PQ has held out the prospect that sovereignty can be attained at little or no material cost or dislocation through the negotiation of a continuing economic association with Canada. When it becomes apparent to the Quebec electorate, as I think it must, that this is impossible a very new situation that the present will exist.

Since its establishment in 1969, the Parti Québécois has supported the solution of what has come to be called "sovereignty-association." So far as I am aware, neither the party as such or any of its influential leaders have diverged at any time from the announced goal of political sovereignty. There will no longer be a common constitution from which the political institutions of Canada and Quebec draw their legal authority. There will be no common Parliament enacting laws and levying taxes which bind Québécois and Canadians. Quebec will become a member of the United Nations and other associations of sovereign states. There has been considerably more ambiguity about the economic association side of the PQ formula but its essential elements appear to be a customs union with a common Canada-Quebec external tariff and no barriers to the free movement of goods within the boundaries of Canada-Quebec, the free movement of persons between the two nations, and a common currency and monetary policy.[17]

It appears that the Quebec electorate in the referendum will be asked whether or not it is willing to give the government "the mandate to negotiate" an economic association with Canada. According to the preference of Premier Lévesque and most of his colleagues, such an association would be negotiated simultaneously with Quebec attaining political sovereignty rather than afterward.

In the first Edition of *Canada in Question* published in 1972 I argued that a Canada-Quebec economic union along the lines suggested by the PQ was the "least available alternative" in the future relations between Quebec and the rest of the Canadian community. I still believe this position is sound. Since the Quebec election of November 1976 the most powerful Canadian politicians outside Quebec have declared economic association between Canada and a sovereign Quebec to be unacceptable—and these politicians include the leaders of all three of the major national political parties, the Conference of Premiers of the Western Provinces, and the Premier of Ontario. Several influential business leaders have taken the same view. The response of spokesmen of the Parti Québécois to this rejection of economic association was that these political and business leaders were merely trying to influence the Quebec voters in the referendum but that once a favourable mandate for the sovereignty-association is attained the Canadians for motives of economic self-interest will be willing to negotiate a new relation along these lines.

So far as economic association has a customs and monetary union as its essential elements, this is an attempt to sustain the National Policy of Ontario and Quebec domination over the regions to the east and west of the heartland.[18] This structure is already under pressure, specifically from the West. The 1976 census saw the combined population of the four western provinces exceed that of Quebec for the first time in Canadian history; obviously the western and Atlantic provinces with their dispositions toward lower tariffs would be relatively more influential in Canada-without-Quebec than under Confederation. Also the 1976 census showed that in the period since 1971 the growth in population of Montreal which had been built and sustained by the National Policy was 2.7 per cent compared with an average of all metropolitan areas of over 100,000 of 7.0 per cent and 7.7 per cent in Toronto, 7.8 per cent in Vancouver, 11.7 per cent in Edmonton and 16.5 per cent in Calgary.[19] So far as a monetary union is concerned, westerners have regarded Montreal-Toronto domination of the Canadian financial system as one of their historic grievances and are unlikely to wish to share a common central bank with a sovereign Quebec. In general, the sovereignty-association formula is an attempt to sustain the National Policy after its political underpinnings are removed and in circumstances where this structure of political and economic domination of the peripheral regions is already under sustained and effective attack.

In the political dimension, it appears unlikely that Canadians would be willing to confer on the government of a smaller and poorer nation a veto over the most crucial aspects of national economic policy. John Holmes, in another context, has asserted that Canada's dispositions are towards international rather than supranational associations and that we prefer membership in groupings like NATO and the Commonwealth where we retain our freedom to define and pursue the national interest.[20] If Quebec should become sovereign it is likely that these dispositions would prevail and the record of our relations with the British Empire/Commonwealth indicates the Canadian unwillingness to let a *prior* pattern of political and economic integration to be used as a rationale to inhibit subsequent freedom of action. So far as trade and monetary policies are concerned, it seems probable that Canadians would choose to associate with a sovereign Quebec through such multilateral organizations as GATT and IMF rather than the special relationship of sovereignty-association.

It is difficult to see how the devices of the PQ alternative would work. Canada would still be organized on federal lines and the complexities of a tripartite division of powers among Canada-Quebec, federal, and provincial authorities would be almost intolerable. Because of conflicts of interest involving Quebec, the government of Canada, and the provinces, the common Quebec-Canada authority could be expected to be an ineffectual and perhaps unreliable participant in international economic affairs. As those who are married will agree, dualistic unions of equals are the most difficult of institutions to operate; when decisions are made the stark alternatives are agreement or deadlock, and deadlock by definition benefits the partner who wants to preserve some existing situation rather than the one who wishes change. So far as a monetary union is concerned, how could the authorities of a central bank operate effectively either on a day-to-day or longer term basis with conflicting directives from two national governments? And, as in the case with tariffs, the differential impact of monetary policies on Canada and Quebec would make such conflicts between the two nations likely.

There would appear to be almost insurmountable difficulties in effecting sovereignty and economic association simultaneously. What authorities would negotiate for Canada in respect to the latter? It could hardly be the federal government because so long as Confederation exists this includes representatives of Quebec. And neither the provinces individually nor any grouping of them could play this role because the matters under negotiation are under federal jurisdiction. From a procedural point of view, it would be much easier to bring about economic association *after* Quebec had attained sovereignty in the fullest legal sense. Sovereignty could be effected by the United

Kingdom Parliament enacting an amendment to the British North America Act to the effect that the Constitution of Canada as therein defined did not after some specified date apply to Quebec. Under the existing conventions of the constitution such action would be taken in response to a Joint Address of the Senate and House of Commons of Canada after the assent of all the provinces had been secured.[21] After Quebec and Canada had attained sovereignty the two new nations might of course enter into any kind of joint arrangements on which they could agree.

There has been a good deal of loose thinking about the probable response of the government of Canada to a favourable popular verdict for the PQ alternative in the referendum. According to one line of argument, such a result would force the federal authorities to negotiate something along the lines of economic association. This is not, I believe, so. The economic association alternative has not been widely discussed outside Quebec, but when and if it is, it would seem likely to be rejected for the political and economic reasons I have already outlined. Neither would the PQ have increased leverage in negotiating provincial interests within the existing federal system. Because of the Quebec government's commitment to sovereignty, it has *now* little bargaining power in the normal course of federal-provincial relations. The probable stance of Ottawa in response to a favourable popular verdict for sovereignty-association would be to assert that, of all the provincial governments, Quebec alone had no mandate to press for a better deal within the federal system. In general, the PQ's bargaining power is very much dissipated when Canadians come to realize that sovereignty in the fullest legal sense is preferable to economic association.

So long as the Parti Québécois remains in power it is almost inevitable that the ancestral antipathies between English and French in Canada will be exacerbated. The PQ is the institutional expression of the national pride and the national grievances of Québécois, and as the plebiscite campaign intensifies Premier Lévésque and his supporters will increasingly play on this pride and those grievances. It appears likely that somewhat similar sentiments will be activated in English-speaking Canada. The PQ assumption is that the Anglo-Canadian is preeminently an economic man who will respond to Quebec's expressed desire for sovereignty-association on the basis of calculations of material advantage alone. This assumption has potentially catastrophic consequences. After all, those issues which in the past have most bitterly divided English and French have not been economic but rather religion and language in education, military conscription and the orientation of Canada's external policies, and more recently language use in air-traffic control. It can confidently be predicted that future relations between English and French—whether within a common federal system or outside—will be decisively influenced by non-economic factors. In the short run of the referendum and its aftermath the PQ has very much underestimated the emotional commitment of large numbers of Canadians to Confederation and the strength of the resistance to be overcome before Canada can be destroyed as a political community.

The referendum is unlikely to lead directly to any decisive resolution of the relations between Canada and Quebec. The Quebec electorate will be asked by its government to vote in favour of an alternative which as I have argued is in all likelihood unavailable. It is impossible for an outsider to make any informed assessment of the intentions of the PQ leaders about their course of action if economic association cannot be negotiated, apart from the reasonably explicit promise that there would be a subsequent plebiscite or general election before steps were taken in the direction of sovereignty in its fullest sense. Yet there is ample evidence that only a relatively small minority of the Quebec public favours what one might designate as "sovereignty neat."

The relations between Canada's two linguistic communities thus remain in a confused and inconclusive state with no immediate prospects of resolution. The Parti Québécois remains committed to an alternative that appears unavailable, yet without very radical changes in Quebec opinion there will not be more than minority support for sovereignty in its most complete sense. On the other hand, the linguistic solution as a response to Quebec nationalism which is accepted by the three major political parties of Canada appears both irrelevant to Quebec's needs and instrumental in exacerbating the antipathy of English-speaking Canadians towards their fellow citizens of the other linguistic community. It may be that when Canadians in both Quebec and outside that province come to look at the alternatives cool-headedly they will decide that the creation of two or more jurisdictions possessing sovereignty in the fullest legal sense would be less than calamitous. A more hopeful alternative would be that along the general lines of Claude Ryan's formulation based on an unequivocal commitment to Quebec as a distinctive society along with an equally unequivocal commitment that that society remain with some reformed version of the Canadian federal system.

The Second Axis: The Centre and the Peripheries

The domination of the Atlantic and western regions of Canada by the Ontario-Quebec heartland has been and remains a continuing circumstance of Confederation. This domination includes not only politics and the economy as these are narrowly defined, but also such matters as broadcasting and the development of the arts, along with the capacity of institutions in the heartland to determine what things are on the Canadian agenda for discussion and resolution.

The position of the Atlantic region is very different from that of the West. The easternmost provinces remain relatively poor, undeveloped and overwhelmingly dependent on Ottawa for maintaining standards of public services and employment opportunities even at levels below the national average. There are no immediate prospects for this situation to be changed in its essential elements,* and the decreasing capacity of the federal government to effect interprovincial equalization in revenues and in the range and quality of public services may even result in its worsening. The Atlantic region is of course challenged by the prospect of Quebec sovereignty in a more direct and critical way than are other parts of Canada. In a purely economic sense, Ontario along with the four western provinces and the North would be a viable nation—actually one without some of the handicaps of the existing Confederation. The Atlantic provinces are obviously more exposed.

It is the four western provinces rather than those bordering on the Atlantic which have come to impose significant strains on the Canadian Confederation. Beyond the specific grievances of the western provinces in economic matters, residents of that region came in the 1960s to feel themselves outside the mainstream of national life by the acceptance in Ottawa and among the elites of the central heartland of a formulation of Canada and the Canadian experience which had little relevance to western circumstances and traditions. Donald Creighton in an essay published in 1966 criticized this emergent orthodoxy which asserted the primacy of cultural values in these terms: "It grotesquely exaggerated the importance of language and culture: it absurdly minimized the importance of everything else."[22] This new way of looking at Canada was most fully embodied in the Reports of the Royal Commission on Bilingualism and Biculturalism, and the views of Pierre Elliott Trudeau. This formulation involved relatively few changes for the West as such.[23] However in its general perspectives—as well as those which came to prevail within the federal government and the universities and media of central Canada—there was the assertion that cultural duality was *the* central element of Canadian life and that all responsible Canadians must put aside other concerns to deal with English-French relations. Western Canada never accepted this dualist view of Confederation.

Western Canada was from the first, and to a considerable extent remains, an economic colony of the country's central heartland. Chester Martin asserted of the transfer of Rupert's Land and the "North-Western Territory" to Canada in 1870: "It transformed the original Domin-

---

* This was written before the discovery of what appear to be large-scale oil reserves off the coast of Newfoundland. Whether the economy and position of that province in Confederation is on the verge of radical change is still in doubt.

ion from a federation of equal provinces each by a fundamental section (109 of the British North America Act) vested with control of its own lands, into a veritable empire in its own right, with a domain of public lands five times the area of the original Dominion, under direct federal administration."[24] Despite the conferring of the jurisdiction over natural resources on the prairie provinces in 1930, the relations between the central heartland of Canada and its western hinterland have continued to be regulated by the classic devices and principles of mercantilism:

1. metropolitan policies have confined the hinterland to the production of staple products exported from the hinterland in a raw or semi-finished state;
2. metropolitan policies have required the hinterland to buy the manufactured goods of the heartland;
3. capital development in the hinterland has been carried out by institutions controlled in the heartland;
4. in external economic relations, the interests of the hinterland have been sacrificed to those of the heartland;
5. the hinterland and the heartland have been physically linked by transportation facilities controlled by and operated for the benefit of the heartland;
6. many of the crucial aspects of hinterland-heartland relations have been carried out through the instrumentalities of large business organizations protected by the heartland authorities from both foreign and hinterland competition.

The economic dominance of the prairie region by the commercial-industrial heartland was sustained by political institutions and processes patterned explicitly on those of British Imperial rule. Lewis H. Thomas has written this of Ottawa's attitudes and policies in the period immediately after the acquisition of the western territories by the Dominion:

> The imperial-colonial relationship and the process of gradual, unsystematic evolution in that relationship were so familiar, and in many of their aspects so acceptable, as to be one of the assumptions of Canadian political thought. It is not surprising therefore to find the federal government embracing, without any hesitation, the prerogatives of "imperial" authority in the North-West.[25]

The Governor of the Territory appointed by the Dominion played an important and often decisive role in the area until, after prolonged struggle, responsible government was granted in 1897. Prior to the prairie provinces being given control over their natural resources in 1930, the Dominion, acting through the Department of the Interior, set the essential patterns of regional settlement and development. When the provinces of Alberta and Saskatchewan were established in 1905, the boundaries were drawn according to the designs of Dominion politicians rather than the needs or desires of residents of the North-West and these provinces began their political lives with premiers chosen by the Laurier government. The federal cabinet used its powers of disallowance more frequently to restrain the western provinces than the others.[26] This pattern of internal colonialism—still prevailing in its essential elements in the Yukon and Northwest Territories—was in marked contrast to the American pattern. One of the last acts of the Continental Congress before its work ended in 1787 was the North-West Ordinance providing for the future government of areas outside the boundaries of the existing states. The North-West Ordinance specified in some detail the circumstances under which new states equal in constitutional status to the existing ones should be established and by 1870 some 18 states had been so established.[27]

From the challenge raised by Manitoba against the monopoly clause of the CPR charter in the 1880s onwards, there have been western Canadian revolts against that region's place in Confederation—revolts expressed through the various farmers' movements, Progressivism, the Social Credit and CCF parties, and some influential elements of Diefenbaker Conservatism. These pressures have from time to time had a considerable success as manifested in the cancellation of the C.P.R. monopoly clause in 1888, the Crow's Nest Pass differential, Liberal tariff reforms in the 1920s, the establishment of the Prairie Farm Rehabilitation Administration in the Great Depression, the National Oil Policy of 1961, and the recent commitment of the federal government to freight-rate structures based on the costs of service and the removing of some of the restrictions on the provincial governments owning equity stock in chartered banks.

After the relatively weak showing of the federal Liberals in the general election of 1972, Prime Minister Trudeau convened a Western Economic Opportunities Conference in Calgary in July 1973 among leaders of the four western provinces and the central government. The provincial premiers were able to eliminate from the agenda of the Calgary meeting such subjects as energy and resource development matters and fiscal equalization on which the interests of the individual western provinces diverged from one another, and thus to evolve a group of common recommendations on such matters as agriculture, transportation and economic development. In his opening statement to the Conference the Prime Minister showed a shrewd realization of the basic issues at stake by contrasting the "old national policy" based on a "central Canadian 'metropole' with an agricultural and resource hinterland" with current needs for a "new national policy" of "more balanced and diversified regional growth throughout the country."[28] However, as the Conference proceeded the western Premiers were able to demonstrate that certain elements of Ottawa's industrial strategy—specifically measures to strengthen research and development and the established secondary manufacturing sector—were working to perpetuate or even to exaggerate the economic dominance of Central Canada.

It is common to talk of "western alienation." The use of this term is unfortunate because, as David Elton and Roger Gibbins have pointed out, contemporary western protest manifests few of the characteristics of political alienation—it is not expressed as apathy toward or estrangement from the polity and it is not the response of groups who are poor, dispossessed, and socially and economically marginal.[29] Rather it is a broad influence in a region increasingly prosperous and increasingly confident and is in large part supported by the more privileged elements in that region. Further, in contrast with Quebec, there are no separatist movements of any consequence in the West and western movements of protest are overwhelmingly directed toward "a demand for greater inclusion in, rather than withdrawal from, the broader Canadian society."[30] Although there are strong pressures in the direction of securing provincial autonomy, many of the government powers crucial to the West are necessarily and unequivocally within federal jurisdiction—tariffs, interprovincial transportation, control of the monetary system and so on. The most fundamental of the western demands are that these national powers be exercised in ways more compatible with western interests.

In a broad sense, the economic strategies of the western provinces are centred on the development of natural resources and the processing of such resources in the region rather than sending them to Central Canada or abroad in a raw or semi-finished state. The resource-based economies of the West are of course becoming much more diversified with the discovery and development of new staples—potash, petroleum, uranium, and natural gas. Because of the relative sparsity of its population and its geographical isolation, staple development rather than the rapid expansion of secondary manufacturing provides the major foundation for western economic development.[31]

Within the general context of western regionalism, Alberta has emerged as a province "pas comme les autres," largely but by no means exclusively because of its ownership of most of the known Canadian supplies of fossil fuels. The Alberta situation is intriguing in the sense that one of its economic sectors is based on the older agricultural staples and the other in the new staples of petroleum and natural gas. Some of the other elements of Alberta's distinctive position within the Canadian federation can be mentioned briefly:

—Alberta is Canada's newest province in terms of development. It was the last part of North America to come under agricultural settlement. Even more importantly for current circumstances, the discovery of petroleum at Leduc in 1947 decisively altered the structure of the economy in a way not experienced by the other provinces. The energy crisis of the 1970s has of course enhanced Alberta's economic strength.

—Alberta is a politically aberrant province. From 1911 to 1979 it did not have a government of the same partisan complexion as that in power in Ottawa. It has also tended to send opposition rather than government members to the House of Commons; in 11 federal general elections from 1945 to 1974 inclusive, 26.4 per cent were won by the party returned to power and 73.6 per cent by opposition parties. However, if we except the elections of 1957, 1958 and 1962, in which the Progressive Conservatives were returned, only 12.0 per cent of the seats went to the governing Liberals. With the possible exception of Douglas Harkness as Minister of Agriculture, and later as Minister of National Defence in the Diefenbaker government, Alberta had not produced an important member of a federal cabinet between R. B. Bennett and the defeat of the Trudeau government in 1979. Liberal ministers from Alberta in the Liberal cabinets since the Second World War such as Mackinnon, Prudham, Hays, Olson, Mahoney and Horner, made little impact on national politics. In provincial politics, more than any other province, Alberta has been characterized by one-party dominance, and since it was established in 1905 it has had only three changes of government—in 1921, 1935, and 1971.

—in the Alberta Heritage Fund there is one of the largest pools of liquid capital in the western world.[32] The Fund was established in 1976 under legislation which provided that 30 per cent of Alberta's non-renewable resource revenue, mainly oil and natural gas royalties, be "set aside and invested for the benefit of the people of Alberta in future years." In late 1978 the Fund was worth $4 billions and was projected to be worth $10 billions by 1983. About three-quarters of the present Fund is invested in marketable securities and most of the rest in various forms of investment within the province—Syncrude, the Alberta Energy Company, the Alberta Housing Corporation and the Alberta Home Mortgage Corporation. Alberta has also bought bond issues of the provinces of Newfoundland, New Brunswick and Manitoba, leading to an interesting speculation for Canadian federalism that the Alberta government might in part displace the capital markets of the eastern United States as a major source of borrowing by the governments of the other provinces and their public corporations. Certainly the possession of the Heritage Fund confers on Alberta opportunities not available to any other province to strengthen and diversify the provincial economy and even to gain control of national business enterprises.

—the Alberta government in its policies of economic development has become the instrument of a relatively cohesive "class," and there are some interesting parallels between this and the relation between the Quebec state and the new middle class of that province.[33] Larry Pratt has summarized the Alberta situation in this way:

> . . . the powers and resources of an interventionist positive government are being employed to nurture the development, and to defend

the province-building interests of an ascendant class of indigenous business entrepreneurs, urban professionals and state administrators. The objectives of this nascent class are to strengthen its control over the Albertan economy, to reduce Alberta's dependence on outside economics and political forces, and to diversify the provincial economy before depleting oil and natural gas reserves are exhausted.[34]

—in its programs of economic development Alberta has developed patterns of relations between government and private enterprise which are somewhat outside the Canadian tradition.[35] As is well known, federal and provincial governments have relied heavily on public ownership in the form of the crown corporation for a wide variety of purposes. Successive Alberta governments, in part on ideological grounds, have avoided this pattern and have preferred to proceed through joint public-private ventures, particularly of course in the field of energy development.

On the basis of its circumstances, the Alberta government has developed a relatively coherent economic strategy. This strategy involves the preservation of provincial autonomy in resource development and the sale of petroleum and natural gas as near to those any buyer will pay as possible. Efforts are being made to establish a petrochemical industry in the province and in general to diversify the Alberta economy. There are also provincial policies by which Albertans are given preferential treatment in terms of employment and of investment opportunities in the development of the province's resources. Attempts are also being made to disperse economic development outside the Edmonton and Calgary metropolitan areas. With these measures directed rather specifically toward Alberta, the province co-operates with other jurisdictions of the region in attempts to influence federal policies in respect to agriculture, transportation and tariffs. These provincial interests are pressed against the federal authorities in an aggressive and sophisticated way through the Department of Federal and Intergovernmental Affairs, established soon after the Lougheed government came to power and modelled on the corresponding Department in Quebec. The government manifests extraordinary urgency about its policies of economic development in the anticipation that the reserves of conventional petroleum, on which the province's peculiarly favourable situation is in large part based, will soon be exhausted.

Although the diversification of the Saskatchewan economy has had less profound effects than that in Alberta, the same general pattern has occurred with the development of petroleum, uranium and potash. Petroleum supplies are relatively limited, of poor quality and, like the conventional reserves in Alberta, are expected to be exhausted in the forseeable future. Uranium is subject to the very great uncertainties of national and international markets. The situation in respect to potash is much more favourable.[36] Within Saskatchewan boundaries are estimated to be 40 per cent of the world's supply of this mineral, the reserves are of high quality, and are accessible through conventional mining methods, and are for all practical purposes in inexhaustible supply. Because of its overwhelming dependence on the volatilities of the wheat economy, the income of the Saskatchewan community has been more variable than that of any other province. The diversification of the Saskatchewan economy works towards a lesser degree of instability and with this diversification and the relative prosperity of the agricultural sector the province is on the verge of passing from "have not" to "have" status in terms of the federal scheme of revenue equalization.

The western provinces, more specifically Alberta and Saskatchewan, have ample reasons to believe that institutions of the federal government have been instruments to frustrate the region's new economic aspirations. The oil export tax instituted in 1974 which cushioned the consumers of oil-importing provinces against world petroleum prices was in effect a subsidy to these consumers and to the economies of these provinces by Alberta and Saskatchewan—a subsidy, as westerners point out, with no counterpart in respect to other resources such as Ontario's hydroelectricity and uranium and Quebec asbestos. The federal decision in 1974 not to allow private corporations in the resource industries to deduct provincial royalties from their taxable income is also regarded by westerners as a move by Ottawa to frustrate regional development. Recent decisions of the Supreme Court of Canada extending the scope of federal powers over "Trade and Commerce" and narrowing provincial taxation powers in effect restrict provincial ownership of natural resources. The western governments have been particularly exercised by the apparently growing federal practice of supporting private litigants who are attacking the constitutional validity of provincial legislation.[37]

The success of the governments of the western provinces in furthering regional interests will be dependent in considerable part on the effectiveness of interprovincial co-operation. The Western Economic Opportunities Conference of 1973 was a crucial event in stimulating such co-operation. In effect the provinces out-manoeuvered Ottawa by setting the agenda of the Conference to include those matters on which the westerners could agree and excluding matters on which their interests differed. Just as importantly, WEOC brought British Columbia into the framework of western interprovincial co-operation, although prior to 1973 this co-operation had been limited to a much looser kind of interaction among the governments of the prairie provinces alone. Through its Task Force on Constitutional Trends established in 1976, the western governments have undertaken a detailed monitoring of federal "intrusions" into provincial powers and more generally on federal policies which are seen as hostile to western interests.[38] Quebec's relative ineffectiveness in the ongoing processes of federal-provincial relations since November 1976 makes the westerners by far the strongest opponents of Ottawa's powers.

The Third Axis: Canadian-American Relations

As Canadians approach the 1980s, relations with the United States are much lower on the public agenda than was the case in the previous decade. It may be useful to speculate why this is so.

First, there is the Canadian preoccupation with domestic problems. In particular, the crisis of Canadian nationhood is now perceived almost exclusively in terms of the immediate challenge of post-November 1976 Quebec rather than the persistent circumstances of various aspects of American power.

Secondly, post-Watergate United States projects a much more benevolent image than did the Americans during the previous decade. Over the longer sweep of history, it seems possible to base a Canadian national feeling on anti-American foundations only when the Americans themselves are undergoing severe difficulties in their domestic and/or foreign policies, as was the case in the 1860s and 1960s.

Thirdly, President Nixon's administration seemed to decide that Canada would not obtain exemption from the application of United States' economic policies to other foreign nations. Until the imposition of exchange controls by the American government in August 1971, it was a topic of lively debate among Canadians as to whether it was appropriate from time to time to seek such exemptions, but now this broad alternative of such a "special relationship" has been precluded by the Americans themselves.

In the 1960s and early years of the last decade, the issue of direct foreign investment in the Canadian economy, most crucially of course investment by American multinational corporations, was one of the central focuses of Canadian public debate.[39] This debate has for the most part passed. So far as governments themselves are concerned, the perceived necessity to create more jobs has overridden any of the earlier concerns about foreign control of the Canadian economy. In a speech given to the Council on Foreign Relations in New York on February 15, 1979, the federal Minister of Finance, Jean Chretien, asserted "I can state categorically that the Government of Canada welcomes foreign investment." Chretien went on to point out that from the inception of the Foreign Investment Review Act in 1974 until the end of 1978, the government had dealt with 954 applications for takeovers, of which 786 were allowed, and 797 proposals for establishing new businesses, of which 685 were allowed. In addition, under the government's new proposals for banking legislation, foreign banks would be permitted to participate in the Canadian market with essentially the same banking powers as are available to Canadian banks. While, so far as I know, an evaluative study of the Foreign Investment Review Agency has not been published it appears that the major effect of this body's work is not to restrict foreign investment but rather to influence such investors, whether establishing new enterprises or taking over existing ones, to bring what the Agency and government define as "significant benefit to Canada."

Interestingly, the federal policy of screening foreign investment has not led to conflict with the provinces. Section 2(2) of the 1974 enactment provides that the criteria in defining whether an investment is of significant benefit to Canada should include the compatibility of such investment with "national industrial and economic policies, taking into consideration industrial and economic policy objectives enunciated by the legislature or government of any province likely to be significantly affected." Beyond this general statement, the Act does not provide for consultation with the provinces or what weight provincial wishes are to be given in the screening process. However, so far as I am aware, there has been no objection by a provincial government to any decision by Ottawa respecting foreign investment and even the sharp-eyed researchers working for the Western Premiers' Task Force on Constitutional Trends have not been able to fault the federal government here for policies allegedly contrary to provincial interests. In general, it may be surmised that the relatively permissive stance of FIRA and the government towards foreign investment is generally compatible with the perceived interests of the provinces in encouraging such investment. Further, the decline in economic nationalism in the English-speaking community of Canada has removed in part at least one of the differences between this community and Quebec, as such nationalism in its pan-Canadian variant was never a French-Canadian cause.

In an article published in 1974, Daniel Latouche asserted that the Parti Québécois had "not worked out or even thought in systematic fashion about its future relations—intergovernmental or transnational—with the United States."[40] Latouche attributed this to "a widespread belief among the PQ leadership that [after independence] it should be easier to work out mutually satisfactory relations with Americans than with Canadians."[41] So far as published information is available, it appears that the Parti Québécois has made little progress in this direction.[42] Since its election the government has increased its efforts to influence American elite opinion by reassurances that Quebec independence would not in any significant way create political or economic instability in the United States' northern borders. The PQ leadership at least seems to be veering away from the policies of pacifism and non-alignment which it adopted in its earlier years, although this change has not been subjected to prolonged debate within the party itself. In a *Time* interview on February 13, 1979 Premier Lévesque said "it would be completely nutty, not to keep the basic Western ties, including NATO" and a few weeks later the Minister of Intergovernmental Affairs, Claude Morin, suggested that it would be appropriate for Quebec to remain committed to the western defence system, including both NATO and NORAD.[43]

President Carter and his administration have given general support for the preservation of the Canadian federation but have repeatedly asserted a policy of non-interference in the relations between Quebec and the wider Canadian community. In an article published in 1977, Alfred Hero Jr., perhaps the most informed student of United States-Quebec relations, pointed out that for the most part even the relatively small number of Americans informed about Canadian affairs found their interlocutors among English-speaking Canadians and bilingual and federalist French Canadians.[44] Even with more aggressive and sophisticated efforts to cultivate American opinion on the part of the PQ, it is reasonable to expect that opinion to be characterized by a bias against Quebec independence.

One can only surmise how the relevant élites of the United States government and the business community now perceive American interests in Canada, and how these élites would react to an intensification of the Canada-Quebec conflict or to Quebec independence.[45] It is reasonable to believe that what these élites want from Canada is a continuance of military, economic and political stability on the United States' northern borders. This general disposition in itself creates hostility to the PQ and its destabilizing objective of Quebec independence. If Quebec were to become sovereign, a significant number of Canada-U.S. arrangements would have to be renegotiated on a trilateral basis, perhaps most crucially those providing for the military defence of the continent, the various activities of the International Joint Commission and the St. Lawrence Seaway, and the Auto Pact. Again one can only surmise how the Americans would define their national interests in such circumstances and what linkages they would make among different issues—for example, Byers and Leyton-Brown speculate that " . . . a prowestern (Quebec) policy stance would be a precondition for fruitful negotiations in the economic sphere, while an anti-western or non-aligned posture would seriously affect even the initiation of negotiations."[46]

The economic objectives of the PQ government have also given rise to considerable uneasiness in American business circles, although one can only guess how much of this arises from the social-democratic commitments of the government and how much from apprehension about the dislocations which would arise from Quebec independence. The party's program commits it to a somewhat restrictive and nationalistic policy in respect to foreign investment. However, apart from the government's moves to acquire controlling interests in the Asbestos Corporation of America, such policies have not been implemented by the PQ government. The Lévesque administration appears very sensitive to its ability, and that of Québec Hydro, to borrow funds at favourable rates in the capital markets of the eastern United States. In more general terms, both by its relatively conservative economic policies and by the explicit statements of its leaders, the PQ government has attempted to convey a message of reassurance to American business elites.

What is the relationship between the ongoing processes of continental economic integration and the workings of the Canadian federal system? There is a strain of argument that provincialism equals continentalism and that only a strong and purposeful national government can effectively resist these influences. Donald Creighton put this argument in its most uncompromising form. In an article "Watching the Sun Quietly Set on Canada," published in 1971, he described the two persistent dangers to Canadian survival as "internationalism" and "provincialism and localism."[47] Creighton saw internationalism in its Canadian variant as a cover for American imperialism, and provincialism—particularly as this was expressed in the demand for a special status for Quebec—as a formula for national disintegration. There was here a Confederation fundamentalism, an argument that Canada could survive only if the elements of the 1864-1867 settlement were preserved in all their essentials. A somewhat similar line of analysis relating provincialism to continental economic integration proceeds by way of emphasizing the breakdown of the "Macdonald-Laurier national policy" of national integration on east-west lines through the trilogy of encouraging economic development in the central heartland, settlement of the West, and the building of railways with various kinds of government assistance.[48] This policy made an independent nation possible because north-south pulls were counterbalanced by the integration of the Canadian economy with that of the United Kingdom. However, with the relative decline of the latter, the integration of the provinces and regions with contiguous areas of the United States proceeds without impediment. This integration is based largely on the export of Canadian staple products in raw or semi-finished form. The provinces which under the constitution own these resources have encouraged their development by multinational corporations, mainly American corporations. Again, provincialism leads to continentalism.

There is, however, another possibility. It is what one might call provincial economic nationalism in which particular provinces strive against the integration of their economies into either the continental or the Canadian frameworks. In his analysis of resource development policies in Ontario in the last decade of the nineteenth century and the early years of the twentieth, H. V. Nelles has given an account in terms of what he calls "the manufacturing condition" which demanded that "Ontario's resources be manufactured into finished products within the boundaries of the province."[49] Those provincial business interests supporting the "manufacturing condition" were successful in securing provincial legislation prohibiting the export of uncut logs and pulp-wood from provincial crown lands, and in spite of the opposition of the federal authorities to such measures these were decisive to the establishment of strong lumbering and pulp and paper industries in Ontario. To widely varying degrees, the provinces with natural resources are now disposed towards measures encouraging the processing of natural resources in the provinces of origin. As we have seen, Alberta has established its own variant of provincial economic nationalism. In a more general sense, the various measures of provinces to obstruct the free movement of persons, commodities and capital over provincial boundaries which have been discussed in Chapter 6 work against both Canadian *and* continental integration.

The most overt form of American control over the actions of the provinces relates to the capital borrowing of these governments and their crown corporations. The nature of this control has not so far as I know been the subject of systematic study but it appears that the major institutions of the capital market in the eastern United States subject the policies, actual and projected, of these governments and their public corporations to expert and detailed scrutiny. The financial consequences of their respective ratings in the American capital markets are very high for the provinces, and their incentives to tailor even the most fundamental of their policies to the institutional investors in these markets are very pressing. Certainly this scrutiny is more detailed, sophisticated, and influential than that of the provincial legislatures.

Provincial economic policies have in the past complicated the relations between the government of Canada and that of the United States and have very great potentialities for doing so in the future. Ottawa faced considerable complications of this kind as a result of Ontario's pursuit of the manufacturing condition described by Nelles. Early in 1961 a treaty for the development of the Columbia River was signed between the United States and Canada, but subsequent objections of the government of British Columbia to its terms resulted in a process of renegotiation, which was of a trilateral character involving Ottawa, Washington and Victoria, culminating in a modified treaty in 1964.[50] There were vigorous objections by the United States government to the action of Saskatchewan in nationalizing American firms in the potash industry in 1975. The Americans have obvious and direct interests in Alberta policies related to resource development.

Along with Quebec nationalism and the growing economic strength of the western provinces, the influence of multinational corporations and of the American government over the Canadian economy has weakened, and is weakening, the capacity of Ottawa to structure and control that economy. Incumbent federal governments are still held accountable for many circumstances over which their power is so constrained by other influences as to be somewhat marginal—prices, the rates of unemployment, the balance of payments, interest rates, and the strength or otherwise of the Canadian dollar. There has not yet been any coherent federal response to this dependence.

The Institutional Crisis

Successive federal governments in Canada have failed to evolve coherent and effective responses to the structural challenges to nationhood— to American power in its various dimensions, to the new modernized Quebec, to the stronger and more confident West. The ineffectualness of the apparatus of the central government is overwhelming and palpable to any person exposed to Ottawa even briefly. One of the most sensitive of Canadian scholars has said this of the federal bureaucracy.

> . . . it seems to be largely made up—not of the dedicated professionals of other years—but of career-oriented managerial men who would be no doubt (and sometimes are) just as happy in Bay Street as in Ottawa. In the hands of this rootless managerial class rather a lot of human and political sensitivity seems to have been lost, if ever it could have survived among the potted plants in those fenestrated towers which have replaced the Victorian blocks and shabby Bank Street offices of the past.[51]

In the absence of effective substantive policies, the gargantuan Ottawa apparatus manifests a single-minded dedication to political and administrative self-preservation. A large part of the incapacity of this apparatus to shape the Canadian economy and Canadian society arises from the circumstances that interests which are territorially delimited have ceased to find an effective outlet through the institutions and processes of the federal government. Canada is in the most elemental way a federal society, and the general thrust of its political institutions is to strengthen territorially based particularisms. If we take these particularisms as givens, there are two alternative ways that they may find outlets through a set of political institutions. The first is that these are channelled within the structures and processes of the central government itself. The second option is a federal division of powers in which responsibility for those matters were territorial differences are most profound is conferred on the states or provinces. Most federal systems are a mix of these two devices. It is my basic argument that since Confederation Canada has moved away from a situation in which territorially based interests and aspirations received an effective outlet through the central government. Thus in Mallory's terms, displacement in Ottawa of "political sensitivity" by managerialism is a reflection of the circumstance that the federal apparatus to alarming degrees has ceased to represent interests other than its own political and bureaucratic survival.

The Confederation settlement contemplated a centralized federal system. Most of what were then regarded as the major functions of government were vested in the Dominion. But although this settlement provided for the dominance of the central government, it seems to have been taken for granted that provincial and regional interests would find an effective outlet through these institutions centred in Ottawa. P. B. Waite has asserted that, "Cartier, like Sir Etienne Taché, was confident, perhaps too confident, that French-Canadian privileges could be defended better by French-Canadian ministers in a central government than by a local [provincial] legislature." Waite's general argument is that those who designed the Confederation settlement did not think of the "federal principle" as being embodied in the co-ordinate jurisdictions of the Dominion and provincial governments, but rather in the composition of the central legislature, and in particular "in the balance between the House of Commons on the one hand and the Senate on the other".[52]

To trace the decreasing sensitivity of the national government to influences which are specifically provincial or regional would be to write the history of Canadian political institutions over more than a century. Yet it may be useful to look in a summary fashion at this dimension of national institutions in terms of how these emerged at Confederation and where we arrived in the late 1970s.

The Senate

(a) At Confederation. The composition of the upper legislative chamber was by far the most contentious issue resolved by the Fathers of Confederation. It was from the first agreed that the House of Commons would be formed on the basis of representation in proportion to the population of the provinces and, as Waite has argued, the federal principle was in large measure embodied in the relations between the House and the Senate, with the latter body formed of equal numbers of members from Quebec, Ontario and the two Maritime provinces.

(b) Today. Whatever the usefulness of the Senate, it has never been an effective outlet for provincial attitudes and interests. In his authoritative study of that institution, Robert A. Mackay concluded: "The Senate . . . has rarely been appealed to as the champion of provincial or sectional rights and, even when appealed to, has not consistently supported claims to such rights."[53] For example, no sophisticated observer would look to the Senate as a primary channel for contemporary Quebec nationalism or western regionalism.

The Parties in the House of Commons

(a) *At Confederation.* It was not until the end of the nineteenth century that two cohesive parties in the House of Commons came into being.[54] As in the pre-Confederation period, legislative parties during the early years of the Dominion were coalitions, often of a relatively loose nature, around several political leaders and characteristically these leaders had a base of support that was exclusively provincial or regional.

(b) *Today.* It is unnecessary to emphasize the relative cohesiveness of political parties in the contemporary House of Commons, particularly in the case of the government party. Although there are countervailing influences at work to enhance the independence of private Members, the long-term trends have been in the other direction. So far as the government party is concerned, the dominance of the prime minister is strengthened by the circumstance that many MPs owe their election largely to his popularity, his powers of bringing about a dissolution, and his control over many preferments which Members desire. Prime ministerial government is incompatible with the effective representation of territorially bounded interests.

The Prime Minister and his Cabinet

(a) *At Confederation.* An historian has said of the first government of the Dominion:

> It would have been wrong to suppose that Macdonald was leading a centralized party. He was rather the chief of a coalition of groups in which each obeyed a regional leader, rather than Macdonald himself. To keep the confidence of the majority, Macdonald knew he must negotiate with these leaders. In this spirit the cabinet was to be, in a certain sense, a chamber of political compensation, where the provincial spokesmen traded their support in return for concessions to their regions.[55]

(b) *Today.* Canadian prime ministers have come increasingly to dominate their cabinets on the basis of their continuing personal popularity with the mass electorate. There are many reasons for this dominance. So far as the Liberals in particular are concerned, the extra-parliamentary party apparatus is devoted almost entirely to national political success and is very much centred on the person of the prime minister. Elections are increasingly contests among competing party leaders. Between elections the prime minister has easy and immediate access to the mass media when he wants it. The national party leadership convention provides for voting by secret ballot and aspirants are thus not required to come to terms with provincial and regional blocs. The staff services available to the head of government through the Prime Minister's Office and the Privy Council Office are enormous.

Less than in earlier periods are cabinet ministers persons with bases of political power in their regions independent of the Prime Minister. Recent Prime Ministers, including Mr. Trudeau and Mr. Clark, have continued to follow the traditional patterns of regional and provincial representation in constituting their cabinets but ministers are less effective than before in articulating interests which are explicitly regional. Further, as the late Donald Gow pointed out, ministers have virtually no staffs involved with the areas they purportedly represent and the departments under their control are "oriented to stress values associated with industrial and social structures and aggregates" rather than particular cultures or regions.[56]

The new procedures of decision-making in what Stefan Dupré has called the "institutionalized cabinet" also frustrate the articulation of provincial or regional interests by cabinet ministers. The major thrust here is to decrease the relative autonomy of ministers and the departments working under their direction. This autonomy is restricted by the increasing power of central agencies over departments—most crucially the Prime Minister's office, the Privy Council office, the Federal-Provincial Relations office, and the Treasury Board—along with the increasing importance of cabinet committees in the decision-making process.

The Federal Bureaucracy

(a) *At Confederation.* At the time of Confederation and for some time decades after, the departments of government had a very high degree of autonomy in the recruitment of federal civil servants and positions were characteristically filled by political patronage. Thus to the extent that the cabinet included members of the various provinces and regions—and the early bureaucracy was in a relative sense geographically dispersed—there were strong influences at work to keep the federal civil service broadly representative of regions and provinces.

(b) *Today.* The establishment of the merit system in the Canadian civil service, particularly with the reform measures of 1918, has had the effect of decreasing the representivity of the federal public service on provincial or cultural lines. This impact has been abundantly demonstrated in terms of the declining proportion of Francophones, particularly in the professional and executive categories, from the end of the First World War until recent efforts were undertaken by the Pearson and Trudeau governments to remedy this imbalance.

It is prudent, however, not to attribute undue importance to the provincial and cultural origins of civil servants in sensitizing them to the values and interests of these regions and cultures. Bureaucracies, including that of the government of Canada, are successful in socializing their members to common values and bureaucratic behaviour is determined more decisively by the requirements of bureaucratic roles rather than by the class or regional or cultural backgrounds of the incumbents of these positions. Much more important in decreasing the sensitivity of federal departments and agencies is the multifaceted phenomenon of managerialism. The managerial ethos is to treat questions which are essentially political as technical—in Karl Mannheim's view, to reduce the political to the administrative.[57] Further, the bureaucratic apparatus in Ottawa is characterized by an ever-increasing number of agencies which are not directly involved in either providing services or carrying out regulatory activities. The clienteles of such agencies are thus within the governmental system itself and on a week-to-week basis there is little or no incentive for them to be responsive to attitudes and interests outside government, including of course those specific to particular provinces and regions.

The relative incapacity of national political institutions to represent interests and attitudes which are territorially bounded is reinforced by the workings of the Canadian electoral system. In a classic article published in 1968, Alan Cairns demonstrated both that the federal electoral system contributed to regional cleavages in national politics and made the issues so raised extraordinarily difficult to resolve.[58] One of Cairns' basic points was that this system grossly distorts the size of party representation in the House of Commons in terms of the popular votes that particular parties have won in provinces or regions. To take a crucial example, in general elections from 1921 to 1965 inclusive there had been 5.6 times as many Liberal as Conservative MPs elected from Quebec, although in terms of the proportion of the popular vote the ratio was 1.9 to 1. As few opposition members are elected from Quebec, so the electoral system works against the presence of Alberta MPs in the government party in the House of Commons. More generally, this system reinforces the Liberals as an Ontario/Quebec party and the Progressive Conservatives as the party of what Peter Newman has called "Outer Canada." For example, in the 1974 general election the Liberals received 49 per cent of the popular vote and 71.0 per cent of the seats in the two provinces of the central heartland, and the Conservatives 44.2 per cent of the votes and 65.0 per cent of the seats from the rest of Canada.

To the extent that the workings of the electoral system deny particular provinces or regions effective and continuing representation on the government side of the House of Commons, these areas will understandably come to believe they are left out of crucial decisions in national affairs. There is reason to believe this alienation is cumulative, if only because the parties which are weak in particular parts of the country will have difficulties there in gaining the services as candidates or otherwise of able and ambitious people. The dominance over provinces and regions by particular parties encourages national politicians in some cases to neglect particular areas and in others to seek their support through unduly generous promises or policies. Most importantly from the viewpoint of Canadian federalism, the lack of adequate provincial representation on the government side of the House of Commons confers on the provincial administrations of such areas the almost exclusive privilege of speaking for these sentiments and interests.

The perceived lack of representivity in the institutions of the government of Canada has led to many of the current proposals for constitutional reform—the reconstitution of the second chamber as a House of the Federation or House of the Provinces, the participation of the provinces in the choice of judges of the Supreme Court of Canada, revisions in the federal electoral system, provincial participation in the selection of members of federal regulatory agencies, and so on. The *First Report of the Ontario Advisory Committee on Confederation*, published in April 1978, saw the "two broad options for the future" as "either a wholesale decentralization of power in favour of provincial or regional autonomy, or fundamental reform of federal institutions to make them more responsive to regional and provincial interests in the evolution of national policy."[59] In the Committee's view the provincial *governments* were the necessary and appropriate articulators of provincial and regional interests, and what was needed was "constitutionally involving the provincial governments in the formulation of, and responsibility for, national policy decisions, as well as the organization of vital national institutions such as the Supreme Court and the major regulatory agencies."[60]

Would the government of Canada be less ineffectual in meeting the basic structural challenges to nationhood if it were restructured in the direction of giving greater representivity to provincial and regional interests, specifically as these are articulated by the provincial governments themselves? Would these latter governments be less urgent than now about safeguarding and extending their range of fiscal and administrative autonomy if such reforms were implemented? My own expectations of such changes are very limited. None of them deals in any direct way with the crucial power centre of the federal government, i.e. the cabinet and the departmental civil service, but focus on what may be called without exaggeration the peripheral institutions of the second chamber of Parliament and the Supreme Court of Canada. I would also expect these proposals to have little effect in dampening the ardour of the provinces for their own autonomy. In general terms, the Canadian political system is a system of executive dominance, and constitutional reforms which do not in a direct way change the structures and operations of cabinets and appointed bureaucracies are of somewhat marginal significance. And such institutional reforms as have been proposed seem to have few prospects in themselves for bringing about coherent and effective responses to the structural challenges to Canadian nationhood.

Notes

1. There is a very extensive literature on the National Policy. For the Confederation settlement, see Donald Creighton, *British North America at Confederation*, A Study Prepared for the Royal Commission on Dominion-Provincial Relations, Ottawa: King's Printer, 1939. For later developments see R. Craig Brown, *Canada's National Policy 1883-1900*, Princeton N.J., Princeton University Press, 1964. A synoptic account of the literature and issues is my article, "Canada and the Quest for a National Policy," *Canadian Journal of Political Science* VIII, March 1975, pp. 40-62.
2. David Jay Bercuson "Canada's Burden of Unity: An Introduction," in David Jay Bercuson, ed., *Canada and the Burden of Unity*, Toronto: Macmillan of Canada, 1977, p. 2. This is a series of essays by maritime and prairie scholars on their respective regions.
3. Enthusiasts for Canadian-American free trade, particularly those writing under the auspices of the Economic Council of Canada, seem not to have taken the internal obstructions to the free flow of the factors of production within Canada into account. This is particularly striking in the account by political scientist Peyton Lyon in his *Canada-United States Free Trade and Canadian Independence*, Ottawa: Economic Council of Canada, Information Canada, 1975.
4. *Parliamentary Debates on Confederation of British North American Provinces*, February 7, 1865, King's Printer, Ottawa, 1951, p. 60.
5. *Report of the Royal Commission on Bilingualism and Biculturalism, Book I, The Official Languages*, Ottawa: Queen's Printer, 1967, p. 173.
6. Kenneth McNaught, "The National Outlook of English-speaking Canadians," in Peter Russell, ed., *Nationalism in Canada*, Toronto: McGraw-Hill of Canada, 1966, p. 63.
7. Hubert Guindon, "The Modernization of Quebec and the Legitimacy of the Canadian State", in Daniel Glenday, Hubert Guindon and Allan Turowitz, eds., *Modernization and the Canadian State*, Toronto: Macmillan of Canada, 1978, pp. 212-246.
8. Ibid., p. 235.
9. The English-speaking minority of Quebec also received constitutional protections in education under Section 93, and protection for the areas in which they predominated in the legislature of Quebec as well as the Senate of Canada.
10. Guindon, *op. cit.*, pp. 217-244.
11. Ibid., p. 245.
12. Ibid., p. 217.
13. Henry Milner, *Politics in the New Quebec*, Toronto: McClelland and Stewart, 1978, p. 94.

14. Věra Murray, *Le Parti québécois: de la fondation à la prise du pouvoir*, Montréal: Cahiers du Québec/Hurtubise HMH, 1976, pp. 33-34.

15. Maurice Pinard and Richard Hamilton, "The Parti Québécois Comes to Power: An Analysis of the 1976 Quebec Election," *Canadian Journal of Political Science* XI, December 1978, pp. 762-765.

16. Ibid., pp. 745-748.

17. *Égal à égal*, Québec:, Conseil exécutif du parti Québécois, 1978. For a very comprehensive account of what two PQ members of the Quebec National Assembly understand as sovereignty-association see, Jean-Pierre Charbonneau et Gilbert Paquette, *L'Option*, Volume 2, Montréal: Les Éditions de l'homme, 1978.

18. It may even be more accurate to speak of the domination of the commercial-industrial complex of Montreal-Toronto of its Canadian hinterland, including areas of Ontario and Quebec itself.

19. Warren E. Kalbach and Wayne E. McVey, *The Demographic Basis of Canadian Society*, Second Edition, Toronto: McGraw-Hill Ryerson, 1979, pp. 142-143. Canada's second National Policy city, Winnipeg, grew only 5.2 per cent in the 1971-76 period.

20. John Holmes, "Nationalism in Canadian Foreign Policy," in John Holmes, *The Better Part of Valour: Essays in Canadian Diplomacy*, Carleton Library, Toronto: McClelland and Stewart, 1970, pp. 28-43.

21. For a contrary argument that, according to the "rules and values entrenched in the [Canadian] constitutional document" an amendment ending Quebec's membership in Confederation might validly be effected without the consent of the other provinces, see John Claydon and John Whyte, "Legal Aspects of Quebec's Claim for Independence," in Richard Simeon, ed., *Must Canada Fail?* Montreal: McGill-Queen's University Press, 1977, pp. 275-280.

22. Donald Creighton, "The Myth of Biculturalism," in Donald Creighton, *Towards the Discovery of Canada*, Toronto: Macmillan of Canada, 1972, p. 257.

23. The Report of the Royal Commission on Bilingualism and Biculturalism on Official Languages, published in 1967, showed that according to the 1961 census of the 54 census divisions in Canada which had official-language minorities of 10 per cent or more, only 6 were in the western provinces, and of these 4 were in Manitoba, one each in Saskatchewan and Alberta, and none in British Columbia. While the Commission's recommendation was that public services be provided in both official languages not in these districts but in bilingual districts drawn up by another procedure where the minority was more than 10 per cent, it is apparent that little was to be changed in the three most westerly provinces.

24. Chester Martin, *Dominion Lands Policy*, edited and with an Introduction by Lewis H. Thomas, Carleton Library Series, Toronto: McClelland and Stewart, 1973, p. 9.

25. Lewis M. Thomas, *The Struggle for Responsible Government in the North-West Territories 1870-1897*, Second Edition, Toronto: University of Toronto Press, 1978, p. 4.

26. Although aggregate figures are perhaps not very meaningful, of the 112 times that provincial bills were disallowed, 85 involved the legislatures of

the western provinces—Manitoba (28), Saskatchewan (3), Alberta (11) and British Columbia (43). Tabulated from G. V. La Forest, *Disallowance and Reservation of Provincial Legislation*, Ottawa: Department of Justice, 1955, pp. 83-101.

27. Thomas, *op. cit.*, p. 5.

28. Pierre Elliott Trudeau, *Opening Speech*, July 24, 1973, *mimeo.*

29. David Elton and Roger Gibbins, "Western Alienation and Political Culture," in Richard Schultz, Orest M. Kruhlak and John C. Terry, eds., *The Canadian Political Process*, Third Edition, Toronto: Holt, Rinehart and Winston of Canada, 1979, p. 83.

30. Ibid., p. 83. For another excellent account of the political position of the West in Confederation, see David E. Smith, "Western Politics and National Unity," in Bercuson, *op. cit.* pp. 142-168.

31. For an economist's argument that most of the economic disabilities of the West arise from market factors rather than the allegedly discriminatory effects of national policies, see Kenneth H. Norrie, "Some Comments on Prairie Economic Alienation," in J. Peter Meekison, ed., *Canadian Federalism: Myth or Reality*. Third Edition, Toronto: Methuen of Canada, 1977, pp. 325-339.

32. For an account of the Heritage Fund, see Peter Foster, "Heritage of Wealth, Legacy of Envy," in *Financial Post*, November 25, 1978, Supplement on Western Canada, pp. 4-5.

33. See John Richards and Larry Pratt, "Oil and Social Class in Alberta: The Bourgeoisie Take Power," *The Canadian Forum*, October-November 1978, pp. 6-14; and Larry Pratt, "The State and Province-Building: Alberta's Development Strategy," in Leo Panitch, ed., *The Canadian State: Political Economy and Political Power*, Toronto: University of Toronto Press, 1977, pp. 133-162.

34. Ibid., p. 133.

35. Ibid.

36. On the Saskatchewan potash industry I am indebted to unpublished research of Maureen Appel Molot and Jeanne Kirk Laux.

37. The Second Annual *Report* of the Western Premiers' Task Force on Constitutional Trends, published in 1978 said this: "During the past four years (from January 1973 to January 1977) the Federal Government has attacked the validity of provincial legislation in nine of the approximately ten cases in which provincial legislation has been challenged . . . in the Supreme Court of Canada. . . . Furthermore, the provinces are concerned that the Federal Government has allied itself with the plaintiff in court cases challenging the constitutionality of provincial resource legislation. It is felt that the co-plaintiff strategy represents an unnecessarily aggressive approach by the Federal Government to this matter," p. 30.

38. *First Report*, mimeo, 1977, *Second Report*, *op. cit.*

39. There is a very extensive literature on foreign direct investment in Canada. See particularly *Foreign Direct Investment in Canada*, (The Gray Report), Ottawa: Information Canada, 1972; A. E. Safarian, *Foreign Ownership of Canadian Industry*, Toronto: McGraw-Hill of Canada, 1966; and Kari Levitt, *Silent Surrender*, Toronto: Macmillan of Canada, 1970.

40. Daniel Latouche, "Quebec and the North American Subsystem: One Possible Scenario," *International Organization* 28, Autumn 1974, p. 959.

41. Ibid., p. 960.
42. Even the very detailed plans for sovereignty-association worked out by Charbonneau and Paquette, *op. cit.*, pay almost no attention to the American dimension.
43. Toronto *Globe and Mail*, March 9, 1978.
44. Alfred Hero Jr., "Quelques réactions americaines au regime du parti québécois depuis le 15 novembre 1976," *Études internationales* 28, juin 1977, p. 356.
45. I am very much indebted here to a paper, as yet unpublished, by my colleagues R. B. Byers and David Leyton-Brown, "United States-Quebec Relations: Implications of an Autonomous Quebec," for an analysis of the military and other issues involved.
46. Ibid., pp. 12-13.
47. Republished as Donald Creighton, "Canadian Nationalism and Its Opponents," in Donald Creighton, *Towards the Discovery of Canada*, Toronto: Macmillan of Canada, 1972, pp. 271-285.
48. Hugh C. J. Aitken, *American Capital and Canadian Resources*, Cambridge, Mass.: Harvard University Press, 1961.
49. H. V. Nelles, "Empire Ontario: The Problems of Resource Development," in Donald Swainson, ed., *Oliver Mowat's Ontario*, Toronto: Macmillan of Canada, 1972, pp. 189-190. See also Nelle's more detailed analysis in his excellent *The Politics of Development: Forests, Mines and Hydro-Electric Power in Ontario 1849-1941*, Toronto: Macmillan of Canada, 1974.
50. For a very detailed account within the analytic framework of decision theory, see Neil A. Swainson, *Conflict over the Columbia*, Montreal: McGill-Queen's University Press, 1979.
51. J. R. Mallory, "Confederation: The Ambiguous Bargain," *Journal of Canadian Studies* 12, July 1977, p. 20.
52. P. B. Waite, *The Life and Times of Confederation 1864-1867*, Toronto: University of Toronto Press, 1962, p. 110.
53. Robert A. Mackay, *The Unreformed Senate of Canada*, Revised Edition, Carleton Library, Toronto: McClelland and Stewart, 1963, p. 113.
54. On the early parties, see Escott Reid's classic article "The Rise of National Parties in Canada," in Hugh G. Thorburn, ed., *Party Politics in Canada*, Fourth Edition, Scarborough: Prentice-Hall of Canada, 1979, pp. 12-20.
55. Jean Hamelin, *The First Years of Confederation*, Centennial Historical Booklet, No. 3, Ottawa: Centennial Commission, 1967, pp. 3-4.
56. Donald Gow, *Canadian Federal and Political Institutions: A Role Analysis*, Unpublished Ph.D. dissertation, Queen's University, 1967, p. 114.
57. Karl Mannheim, *Ideology and Utopia*, Harvest Book Edition, New York: Harcourt, Brace, (1957?), p. 119.
58. "The Electoral System and the Party System in Canada 1921-1965" *Canadian Journal of Political Science* 1, March, 1968, pp. 55-80.
59. *First Report of the Ontario Advisory Committee on Confederation*, Toronto: 1978, p. 2.
60. Ibid., p. 3.

CHAPTER 9

IS THERE BASIS FOR POLITICAL COMMUNITY IN CANADA?

This last chapter attempts in a tentative way to deal with the question of whether there is a basis for political community in contemporary Canada. It is not the normal disposition of Canadians, even of those who are scholars, to ask this kind of fundamental question. However, the current crisis of the Canadian Confederation appears to make this kind of inquiry more urgent than at any time in the past.

The Non-Philosophic Nature of Canadian Political Discourse

In explaining Mackenzie King's longevity as Prime Minister, Frank Underhill wrote in 1944 of ". . . our Canadian preference, in spite of the clearness of our physical climate, for living constantly in an atmosphere of mental haze. We never make issues clear to ourselves. We never define our differences so that they can be understood clearly or resolved."[1] Certainly in their political debates, even as these debates have engaged articulate and intellectually sophisticated people, Canadians have been loath to raise first order, broadly philosophic questions—questions of freedom and equality, of the basis of human rights, of political obligation and of the standards by which political regimes are to be judged. Our political tradition differs here very markedly from the American. In the fateful quarter-century from the imposition of the Stamp Act to the coming into effect of the Constitution residents of the Thirteen Colonies and later the United States of America debated and in some crucial instances resolved the most fundamental questions of political legitimacy and political order—all this within the context of a heady eighteenth-century faith that by studying the past and the present rational men might discover the permanent principles of government and that, when these principles were found, they could be applied to the design of new political institutions. This original tradition of principled political debate among Americans was perpetuated by the challenge to the Union in the middle years of the next century and, in our generation, largely through the controversies involving various kinds of issues about civil rights.

Unlike Americans and Frenchmen in the eighteenth century—and Englishmen in the seventeenth—Canadians have never experienced the kind of decisive break with their political past which would have impelled them to debate and resolve fundamental political questions. Our tradition of political discourse is pervasively conservative and legitimist. This constitutional conservatism has permeated even the thought and the action of those on the left-wing of the Canadian political spectrum, as is demonstrated by the consistency with which the CCF and NDP have defended the rights of Parliament and established human rights. So far as French-Canadian thought was dominated by Catholicism, this was implicitly and sometimes explicitly according to the teaching of St. Paul in *Romans*, Chapter 13:

> Let every soul be subject unto the higher powers. For there is no power but of God: the powers that be are ordained of God. Whoever therefore resisteth the power, resisteth the ordinances of God: and they that resist shall receive to themselves damnation.

Among English-speaking Canadians there has been the acceptance, even the glorification, of a political and constitutional tradition based on continuity and ordered change.

The pervasive legitimism of the Canadian tradition has decisively shaped the political inquiry and political discourse which has engaged scholars. Donald Creighton pointed out in his Presidential Address to the Canadian Historical Association in 1957:

> . . . the economists, political scientists, lawyers, literary critics and art critics of Canadian universities show a marked preference for the historical method. Canadian scholars, in any and every academic discipline, are far more likely to be historians than they are to be theorists or philosophers.[2]

The results of this disposition had been pithily summarized by Creighton's colleague Underhill a decade before: "In Canada we have no revolutionary tradition and our historians, political scientists and philosophers have assiduously tried to educate us to be proud of this fact."[3]

With the challenges to Confederation occasioned by the new circumstances of Quebec, and with the vast amount of debate about this situa-
tion, one might reasonably have expected a more philosophic dimen-
sion in Canadian political discourse. It has not been so. So far as
Canadian federalism is concerned, the only genuinely philosophic
analysis that has ever been made is the *Report of the Quebec Royal
Commission of Inquiry on Constitutional Problems,* published in 1956.
In its discussion of "Culture, Nation and Society," and of the place of
Quebec within Confederation, the Tremblay Commission posited the
Canadian situation as essentially that of two Christian cultures, one
French and Catholic and the other Anglo-Saxon and Protestant in in-
spiration, both menaced by the ongoing pressures of materialism and
technological change.[4] Paradoxically, this elegant formulation of Catholic conservatism came within less than a decade of the displacement
of the influence of such a variant of social thought within Quebec itself.
But the challenge of the Tremblay Commission to debate the political
order within the framework of first-order principles has not been taken
up. For example, when the Royal Commission on Bilingualism and Biculturalism came to write its Report on the Official Languages there
was a fragmentary and inconclusive attempt to define "biculturalism,"
followed by a retreat from any serious attempt to answer the fundamental questions raised by Tremblay about the relation between culture
and political organization.[5] More recently, the *Report of the Task Force
on National Unity* posits the primacy of Quebec and the other provinces as the essential elements of the political community without any
analysis of why in normative terms their claims are to be preferred to
those of the wider Canadian community. So far as Quebec nationalism
is concerned, the situation has not been much better. In the most influential variants of this nationalist thought, Quebec sovereignty is por-
trayed as a natural and inevitable culmination of the pressures of this
society for autonomy which have existed since the Conquest, along
with assertions rather than philosophic argument about the right of
Quebec as a nation to self-determination.

The ways of thinking and acting imbedded in the federal tradition itself may well have disposed Canadians not to deal with political matters by reference to first-order principles. This was the argument advanced by Thomas Hockin in a perceptive essay, "Federalist Style in
International Politics," published in 1968. Hockin's basic point was
that the ineffectuality of Canadian action in international affairs was
less a result of "our status as a middle power" than of our "*domestic
habits of mind, our Canadian political style.*" (Emphasis Hockin's.)
These habits, this style, result from the imperatives of federalism: ". . .
the diversity of the federal system's components may impel its political
leaders to avoid ultimate questions of purpose in order to maintain a
minimal common denominator of consensus."[6] This domestic con-

sensus, inappropriately in Hockin's view applied by Canadians to international politics, is based not on substantive purposes but rather on procedure. But this Canadian preoccupation with procedure and organizational machinery in international affairs renders the nation's actions ineffective because such an approach is irrelevant to situations where fundamental conflicts of a substantive nature are engaged.

The Question at Issue: Cultural Nationhood and Political Organization

What is involved in the current Confederation debate is the relation between nationhood in a cultural/ethnic/linguistic sense, and political organization. It is not within my competence nor is it my purpose to define culture in any exact way. From one point of view, those who share a culture share definitions covering every aspect of activity that is distinctively human—for example, definitions of what is edible food, what is play, what is the appropriate relation between the sexes, who is a friend and who an enemy. A nation in this sense involves not only a sharing of such definitions but also a feeling of group identification, a sense of a common history, and common hopes for the future. The relation between culture and language is an intricate one, but it is reasonable to assert that the most pervasive differentiation between cultures is linguistic, and it is almost impossible to conceive of a nation in the cultural sense unless its members share a common language.

Nations in the cultural/linguistic/ethnic sense have existed for many centuries but it is only since the French Revolution that such nations have demanded political institutions under their own control.[7] So far as the European world was concerned, the characteristic form of political organization prior to this time was the empire or dynasty including many nationalities. The French Revolution for the first time based the credentials of political organization on the popular sovereignty of a particular people and the resistance to the subsequent conquest by the French of other peoples was for the most part based on the demands that these latter should not be ruled by foreigners. Within the European context, the culmination of the movement towards national self-determination was the Peace Settlement at the end of the First World War and the creation of several new nations from the elements of the Russian, Turkish and Austro-Hungarian Empires. The second phase of the general movement occurred after 1945 with the successful demands of Asian and African people that they not be ruled by Europeans. We are now in a third phase with the challenges to multinational states in the developed world—the pressures of Scottish, Flemish, Basque and of course Quebec nationalism, for example. In a general sense the movement towards national self-determination is, as it has been for nearly two centuries, a profoundly destabilizing one which challenges and has challenged nearly every political community not the expression of a single culture and language.

Two very different views of the relations between nation and political organization were given by the nineteenth century English liberals John Stuart Mill and Lord Acton. Similar perspectives on nationhood and its political claims are at the foundations of the contemporary Canadian debate.

In his *Considerations on Representative Government*, published in 1861, Mill said this:

> Free institutions are next to impossible in a country made up of different nationalities. Among a people without fellow-feeling, especially if they read and speak different languages, the united public opinion, necessary to the working of representative government cannot exist. The influences which form opinions and decide political acts are different in different parts of the country. . . . The same incidents, the same acts, the same system of government, affect them in different ways, and each fears more injuries to itself from the other nationalities than from the common arbiter, the state.[8]

Under some circumstances, claimed Mill, stability in such divided communities might be achieved by an army composed of members of the various national groups but whose loyalties were to the state rather than the groups from which they were drawn. However, ". . . it is in general a necessary condition of free institutions that the boundaries of governments should coincide in the main with those of nationalities." When this coincidence was impossible representative institutions could develop only through the admixture and assimilation of national groups constrained to living within a single political community.

Mill's views on nationality were essentially the same as those expressed by another liberal, Lord Durham, in his famous Report on the Affairs on British North America in 1840.[9] Durham's general diagnosis of the situation in Lower Canada has often been quoted: "I expected to find a contest between a government and a people: I found two nations warring in the bosom of a single state: I found a struggle not of principles, but of races: and I perceived that it would be idle to attempt any amelioration of laws or institutions until we could first succeed in terminating the deadly animosity that now separates the inhabitants of Lower Canada into the hostile divisions of English and French."[10] He went on: "The national feud forces itself on the very senses, irresistibly and palpably, as the origin or the essence of every dispute which divides the community; we discover that dissensions, which appear to have another origin, are but forms of this constant and all-pervading quarrel; and that every contest is one of French and English at the outset, or becomes so ere it has run its course." As is well known, Durham's solution was the early assimilation of the French:

I entertain no doubts as to the national character which must be given to Lower Canada: it must be that of the British Empire. . . . Without effecting the change so rapidly or so roughly as to shock the feelings and trample on the welfare of the existing generation, it must henceforth be the first and steady purpose of the British Government to establish an English population, with English laws and language, in the Province, and to trust its government to none but a decidedly English legislature."[11]

In the year after Mill's *Considerations on Representative Government* was published, there appeared Lord Acton's essay on "Nationality," which gave a contradictory view of the proper relation between nationhood and political organization. Acton's argument was directed against the national-state as the embodiment of the will of a single nationality. Of such he said ". . . nationality is founded on the perpetuation and supremacy of the collective will, of which the unity of the nation is the necessary condition, to which every other influence must defer, and against whom no obligation enjoys authority, and all resistance is tyrannical." The alternative commensurate with liberty is the multinational state:

While the theory of unity makes the nation a source of despotism and revolution, the theory of liberty regards it as the bulwark of self-government, and the foremost limit to the excessive power of the state. Private rights, which are sacrificed to the unity, are preserved by the union of nations. No power can so efficiently resist the tendencies of centralisation, of corruption, and of abolutism, as that which is the vastest that can be included in a State. . . . The co-existence of several nations under the same State is a test, as well as the best security of its freedom.[12]

As Acton's disciple Pierre Trudeau has put it, "It is not the concept of *nation* that is retrograde; it is the idea that the nation must necessarily be sovereign."[13] (Emphasis Trudeau's.)

Both Mill and Acton were concerned with important and persistent ideals of liberalism. Mill's emphasis was on the "fellow feeling" necessary to representative government in the context of free and widespread public discussion. Acton's concern was with effective restrictions on the powers of the centralized and centralizing state. In the contemporary Canadian context does federalism offer the reconciliation between these two ideals through a regime in which cultural nations can sustain their integrity by benign possession of a range of governmental powers short of sovereignty in its fullest legal sense?[14]

Cultural Nationhood and Canadian Federalism

Before embarking on the federal experiment the politicians of the United Province of Canada evolved a set of political institutions and

habits which went a very long distance in refuting the assumptions of
Durham and Mill that the politics of nationally divided societies must
inevitably revolve around inter-racial tensions.

Durham was in the very short run at least proved in error about the
strength of the disposition of the French to survive, the kinds of measures necessary to assimilate them, and the possibilities of English-
French co-operation. The devices which evolved in the Province of
Canada in the two decades after the Act of Union of 1840 conform very
closely to what modern students of government call "consociationalism."[15] Consociationalism is a way of governing, through representative institutions, societies composed of groupings distinguished by
language, ethnicity or religion (or a combination of two or more of
these). Under such circumstances the most crucial of the processes of
politics are the accommodations between political elites representing
these subcultures, elites who are committed to the continuance of the
political community and who retain the support of the citizens of the
respective subcultures which they represent. I have discussed in
Chapter 2 some of these consociational devices developed by the Canadians—political groupings representing English or French, the double-
majority rule, double-headed ministries, the bifurcation of government
departments, and so on. The major influences leading to the breakdown of consociationalism were the persistent demands of the Upper
Canadians for representation by population in the Legislative Assembly, and by consequence the recrudescence of political conflict between the two sections.

The Confederation settlement, in so far as it was an attempt to resolve
the political deadlock between the English and French of Canada, provided a new answer to the relation between cultural/linguistic nationality and political organization. In this dimension, as we saw in
Chapter 2, the basic formula was to confer on the provinces exclusive
legislative jurisdiction over those matters in respect to which the two
cultural/linguistic communities differed most profoundly, along with
certain limited protection for the rights of the English and French languages and for the educational rights of the denominational minorities
in the provinces. So far as this element of the Confederation settlement
received a theoretical defence, it was given in George Étienne Cartier's
vision of a Canadian "political nationality, with which neither the national origin, nor the religion of any individual would interfere." Cartier was influenced in part by the United Kingdom political nationality
composed of members of the English, Scottish, Welsh and Irish nations. It can also be noted that the Act of Union of 1707 uniting England
and Scotland gave the latter protection for its distinct systems of law,
religion and education, and that these protections foreshadowed in a
broad way the safeguards conferred on the French Canadians of Quebec
under the BNA Act.

Not even the most fervent admirers of Cartier would accord him a high ranking as an original political thinker, and so one should avoid reading too much into his vision of a Canadian political nationality.[16] These, however, would appear to be his assumptions:

—being a Canadian was a political matter and neither religion nor national origin should influence a citizen's political rights or political obligations.

—those governmental powers necessary to the integrity and survival of the French-Canadian society of Quebec were within provincial rather than Dominion jurisdiction.

—whatever axes of cleavage would develop in respect to matters within Dominion jurisdiction would not divide people on ethnic/cultural/linguistic lines.

Cartier's vision of a Canadian political nationality was not realized in the subsequent development of the Dominion.

First, there was a profound and persistent impulse by Canadians of British extraction to deny other citizens an equal status. In one sense the Confederation settlement was flawed in that it did not deal in any explicit way with the constitutional and political relations between the new Dominion and the United Kingdom. As it happened, the "little Englandism" so influential in both Britain and British North America gave way within less than a generation to master-race imperialism which perhaps reached its zenith during the First World War. In a multitude of ways loyalty came to be associated with Britishness, and Canadians of French and other national origins were relegated to subordinate roles in Canadian affairs.

Secondly, the Dominion authorities failed to take action to secure the linguistic and educational rights of the French-speaking minorities in the provinces. From the refusal of the federal cabinet in the early 1870s to disallow New Brunswick legislation challenging the privileges of Catholic and French-speaking schools in that province, Ottawa was never willing to take effective action to safeguard cultural/linguistic/religious duality against English-speaking and Protestant provincial majorities. It can persuasively be argued that this failure contributed powerfully to French Canadians being thrown back on the Quebec government alone as the bulwark of their national rights.[17]

Thirdly, the federal authorities extended their powers to include matters of a direct cultural incidence. As we have seen in earlier chapters, this occurred most dramatically in the period after the Second World War through the exercise of the federal spending power in respect to matters within the legislative jurisdiction of the provinces.

Despite what I have said above, Cartier's vision of what Kenneth McNaught has called "a non-racial view of nationality" has never been extinguished in Canada.[18] In fact, this has become the dominant view among English-speaking Canadians during the past generation. There have been several circumstances at work here—the decline in British imperial power, the decreasing proportion of Canadians with familial and other links to the United Kingdom, the weakening disposition to believe that particular races or cultures are inherently superior to others, and so on. There are many evidences of the passing of cultural and ethnic nationalism. Canadian immigration policy enjoins racial and ethnic criteria for the selection of immigrants. Federal and provincial legislation prohibits discrimination on ethnic and racial lines in employment and other aspects of economic and social life. There is a glorification in official and semi-official ideology of Canada as a multicultural mosaic and in certain quarters a profound impulse towards the "unhyphenated Canadian." Canadians of British extraction show an increasing acceptance of persons of other backgrounds attaining positions of power and prestige in various aspects of Canadian life. And in a negative sense, the adverse public reaction to the two-nations view of Canada which caused the New Democratic Party and the Progressive Conservatives of a decade ago to terminate their flirtation with this doctrine is a manifestation of the rejection by English-speaking Canadians of culture as the essential element of political organization.

Can Cultural Nationalism Be Contained?

Let us return to the question of whether federalism provides a possible reconciliation between cultural nationalism and the establishment and sustaining of binational or multinational political communities. If the claims of political organization and political allegiance are regarded as adhering to culture, the answer would have to be "no." On this basis citizens of a "nation" have no reason for assenting to being governed under a system where they share a range of important state powers with those who are by definition foreigners, and in any clash between the authorities of one's own "nation" and those of the central government, support must be given to the former.

Stable and effective political institutions are seldom based on the kind of rigid logic I have outlined above. Federalism might thus provide some grounds for the reconciliation of cultural nationalism and the membership of nations in a wider political community under the general circumstance of a broad consensus about the range of powers short of sovereignty that "nations" require to ensure their integrity and survival. This was the essential consensus of the Confederation settlement or, more accurately, the condition under which the French-Canadian Fathers agreed to the formation of the new political community. Put more concretely, there was a distribution of governmental powers which assigned economic matters to the Dominion and matters regarded as having a direct cultural incidence to the provinces.

Most of the recent proposals for constitutional reform are based implicitly or explicitly on the dominance of the federal authorities over economic matters and of the provinces over those defined as cultural. In practice of course it is impossible to design federal and provincial compartments of a "watertight" nature along economic/cultural lines. The situation is further complicated by the circumstance that although Quebec has more urgency than other jurisdictions about extending its range of control over what are defined as cultural matters, it is in several dimensions the province most closely integrated into the Canada-wide economy. Conversely, of course, the three westernmost provinces with lesser concerns about culture are preoccupied with provincial autonomy in economic development, specifically in the exploitation and control of natural resources.

In more general terms, the range of activities undertaken by modern governments makes it increasingly likely that cultural nations will be disposed towards sovereignty in its most complete legal sense. Before the modern era nations existed and in many cases thrived within the framework of multinational dynasties or empires but, as Cobban has pointed out, the impulses towards national self-determination arose at the time of the French Revolution as a response to the centralized and centralizing national state established in France.[19] Under contemporary circumstances the scope of functions undertaken by modern government means that for those who exercise it or desire to do so the stakes of state power are higher than ever before and that national elites have more incentives to attempt to capture the state apparatus in the name of national self-determination.[20] Further, the extent and pervasiveness of the responsibilities assumed by modern governments give cultural nations—or those who claim to speak in their name—plausible if not conclusive reasons for asserting that national integrity is in jeopardy if the state is not under the unshared control of their respective nationals.

The disposition of contemporary cultural nationalism, in its Canadian variants at least, is to define culture broadly and to assert the necessity of a comprehensive and pervasive pattern of state activity in the defence of cultural survival and integrity. This statist thrust is shown very clearly in the Parti Québécois. In a frequently quoted interview given to *Le Devoir* in 1963 René Lévesque, then a member of the Lesage cabinet, spoke of the "denationalized" man as "disoriented, incomplete" and thus degraded, while as a member of a dynamic nation the person feels "magnified, prouder and stronger."[21] Lévesque's emphasis in this interview was on the Quebec state as the key instrument for the economic emancipation of the Quebec people. More recently, Quebec nationalists have emphasized state activity in relation to language and culture. Bill 101 provides for more detailed and comprehensive public regulation of linguistic usage than exists in any other western nation. The document *Le politique québécoise du développement culturel*, published by the Quebec government in 1978, calls for an aggressive and coherent policy for Quebec's cultural development and defines culture broadly to include housing, health, leisure, work, mass communications, arts and letters, scientific research, archives and other records of the past, architecture and so on.[22] Don and Vera Murray quote Dr. Camille Laurin in relation to what they call "la foi presque illimitée des péquistes dans les bienfaits de l'action étatique" in his speech to the National Assembly on July 19, 1977. "Il est vrai de dire que c'est la liberté qui opprime et la loi qui libère, car seul l'Etat possède la responsabilité, le droit et surtout le pouvoir d'atténuer, de corriger et d'éliminer ces inégalités qui constituent pour plusieurs une entrouve à l'exercice de leurs droits individuels".[23] As Pierre Elliott Trudeau pointed out in a 1963 critique of Quebec nationalism, "The state was nothing in Quebec: now it must be everything."[24]

Although there are nascent elements of liberalism in the commitment to a non-ethnic political nationality which persists among English-speaking Canadians, the core of *this* tradition is also statist and conservative. John Porter wrote in 1967:

> English and French Canadians are more alike in their conservatism, traditionalism, religiosity, authoritarianism and elitist values than the spokesmen of either group are prepared to admit. . . . In all the present concern for biculturalism we might raise the question of whether, after all, there is not a single culture in Canada in which the core values are conservative . . . .[25]

English-speaking nationalists in Canada are of course pre-occupied with various aspects of American power and influence. But in staking out the nationalist position, leaders of this broad current of opinion are not disposed to make the kind of distinction between culture and economics which even the PQ supports in its program of Quebec sovereignty *and* economic association with Canada. Abraham Rotstein wrote in 1969 "America is total environment: it envelops us as a mist, penetrating every sphere of our cultural, political, economic, and social environment."[26] And to resist this "total environment," it is of course necessary to develop a total and, inevitably statist, response.

My general argument is that once the state is defined primarily as the instrument of cultural survival and integrity there are almost inevitable dispositions for nations in the cultural sense to demand a range of governmental powers so extensive as to be incompatible with federalism. English-speaking nationalists have had a prevailingly benevolent disposition toward Quebec nationalism and one of the intellectual leaders of this former movement said in 1977: "It is not quite axiomatic that a victory for the independence movement in Quebec must be a defeat for Canada; it is just conceivable that the two nationalist movements could develop in a way which would reinforce the confidence and will to survive of both communities."[27] It is not completely clear from the context just what Smith *would* regard as a "defeat for Canada". It is difficult for me at least to think of Canada as anything more and anything other than a political community of an inevitably federal nature. But is a federal political community organized on a two-nations premise possible?

The Two-Nations Response

Cultural nationalism in Quebec as elsewhere gives culture the dominant place in political organization and political allegiance. The response of some English-speaking intellectuals is to urge the creation of an English-Canadian nation as a response to Quebec nationalism.[28]

In institutional terms, the two-nations Canada is incompatible with the working of the federal system. English-speaking Canada has no political instrument for furthering its collective purposes because control of the federal government is shared with Québécois, and because neither in law nor in practice are the governments of the provinces with English-speaking majorities so organized as to act in concert. Thus even if the national aspirations of Québécois could be contained within some federal distribution of powers, the stimulation of the national aspirations of English-speaking Canadians as such would almost inevitably lead this group in the direction of creating a political instrument for the embodiment of these aspirations which would destroy Confederation.

In another dimension the establishment of an English-Canadian nation would make necessary the desertion of the vision of a non-ethnic basis for political nationality which I have argued is now an influential even a dominant element of the way in which non-Québécois Canadians perceive themselves and their political community. To use an analogy which is not totally misleading, the cause of Christian ecumenicism might well be furthered if the denominations belonging to the World Council of Churches regrouped themselves under one hierarchy to associate with the Vatican. Yet if Baptists or Presbyterians assented to such a measure they would cease in any identifiable way to be Baptists or Presbyterians because these religious traditions are based in large measure on convictions about church organization. Similarly, if English-speaking Canadians should come to act as if the claims of political community and political allegiance were cultural/linguistic, they would be denying an essential element of their tradition.

Canada-without-Quebec may well be established through the withdrawal of Quebec from the common political community. Yet it is very unlikely that this new nation would find its credentials in culture and language.[29] It is also probable, almost certain, that this nation would be

federal and thus based on the divided loyalties which I would argue
cultural nationalism denies.

On What Conditions Can a Canadian Political Community Be Re-established?[30]

I would argue that there is an adequate foundation for a renewed political community in Canada only if two conditions are met.

First, there must be a recrudescence of Cartier's vision of a political
nationality not based on culture and ethnicity.

Secondly, there must be a discriminating limitation of the powers of
the state and a strengthening of the voluntarist institutions of society.

The non-ethnic view of nationality has been challenged not only by
cultural nationalism in its Québécois and English-Canadian variants,
but also by the formulations of the Royal Commission on Bilingualism
and Biculturalism and of the recently departed Trudeau government.
The Terms of Reference of the Royal Commission spoke of the "Canadian Confederation" as an "equal partnership between the two founding races" and, almost as an afterthought, made mention of the "contribution made by the other ethnic groups to the cultural enrichment of
Canada." There was here the assertion that Confederation and the political community which developed out of it were to be regarded almost
exclusively in ethnic and cultural terms. There was the perpetuation of
the archaic usage of race—which in contemporary language is taken to
refer to physical rather than cultural differentiation—with the false corollary that individuals are, so to speak, stuck with their cultural origins
as they are with their genetic inheritances. There was the relegation of
citizens whose origins were neither British nor French to the "cultural
enrichment of Canada." The support of multiculturalism by the Trudeau government from the early 1970s onward did nothing to correct
these errors. The assertion that while Canada had two official languages there was no official culture made a false dissociation between
language and culture. And although policies towards state support of
the activities of ethnic groups were on the surface liberal and pluralis-
tic, the penetration and control of such associations by government
which was inherent in such support weakened the voluntarist principle. Even more fundamentally, multi-culturalism was based on the
promise that Canada was essentially a community of cultures rather
than a political community.

The formulation of the Canadian Confederation primarily or even exclusively in cultural/ethnic terms is inherently divisive and in the long
run destructive of Canada. Because of their experiences and their interests, the non-ethnic view of nationality is almost inevitably the disposition of those Canadians whose antecedents are neither British nor

French. At least in those parts of Canada outside Quebec where there are small numbers of French Canadians, citizens whose origins are British are more likely to accept the same non-racial view of nationality than a formulation based on French-English duality. It is to emphasize the obvious to point out, first, that the ongoing concentration of the French-speaking community of Canada within the limits of the Soo-Moncton line (and the concentration of the English-speaking population of Quebec in the Montreal area), means that a decreasing proportion of Canadians experience French-English duality as a circumstance of daily life and, secondly, that the tilt westward of power and population is towards a region where such duality has few roots.[31]

The second precondition for the re-establishment of political community is some considerable limitation of the powers of government and a consequent strengthening of social institutions interposed between the citizen and the bureaucratized institutions of big government. In respect to the growth of government, our attention has been too much on the economic, too little on what one may describe broadly as social. Yet it is this latter area where recent extensions of state power are perhaps more consequential—the penetration of family life and of leisure-time activities; the harnessing of the arts, letters and sciences to nationalistic purposes as defined by the state authorities; the conversion of "amateur" athletics from the domains of voluntary association to that of government; the financing of other voluntary organizations, including interest groups and cultural association, by the state; the assumption by politicians of the role of enunciating the highest ideals of the community. In a culturally diverse society, it is reasonable to expect common political institutions to be sustained and respected only if there is some restriction on the range of activities undertaken by those institutions. Otherwise members of the different nations as culturally defined will have insistent impulses to accede to unshared power over the state apparatus.

Quebec and the Right to Self-Determination[32]

There has been a good deal of heated and inconclusive recent debate in Canada about Quebec's right to self-determination. In so far as this right is being asserted by non-revolutionary Quebec nationalists, the right is one that the Quebec nation is not *now* claiming but may do so under indeterminate circumstances in the future. Some persons disposed towards the maintenance of the federal system have even claimed that if other Canadians make what is regarded as a symbolic and generous gesture in recognizing Quebec's right to self-determination, Québécois will be less likely than otherwise to opt for independence.

A further complication arises when a nation as culturally defined wishes to change its status within an existing political community by reforms short of assuming sovereignty in the most complete legal sense. The claims of the Dene nation of Northwest Canada, as those were articulated in the hearings of the Berger inquiry, were for the settlement of the land claims of the indigenous peoples and for forms of local and regional autonomy according to the needs and traditions of these people.[33] And of course the preferred alternative of the Parti Québécois is not sovereignty in its most complete sense, but rather sovereignty-association. Abraham Rotstein as editor of the *Canadian Forum* in 1971 supported the claim that "Quebec has the absolute right to self-determination up to and including independence."[34] The difficulty here is with "up to". Read literally, it would give the Quebec nation the unilateral right to determine its place in and relationships with the wider Canadian community. Even if one were to assent to the general principle that a nation as culturally defined is entitled to some range of governmental powers under its unshared control, it is patently illogical to assert its unilateral claim to determine the nature and extent of these powers so long as this nation is comprehended within a particular union and ruled under the constitutional procedures of that union, because such a claim would deny the same powers to other members of that political association. Thus the right to national self-determination can only mean the right of a nation to sovereignty in its fullest sense.

The Canadian constitution contains a procedure by which Quebec might accede to sovereignty. According to the opinions of most specialists in these matters, such a change could be effected by the United Kingdom Parliament amending the British North America Act on request contained in a Joint Address of the Senate and House of Commons of Canada and, according to the prevailing conventions of the constitution, this request would be made only after the assent of all the provinces had been obtained. It must, however, be emphasized that neither Parliament nor the provinces with English-speaking majorities have any *constitutional* obligation to agree to Quebec's withdrawal from the Canadian federal system. As is the case with other powers conferred by the constitution on the federal and provincial authorities, such jurisdiction can be exercised at the discretion of the authorities to whom such powers are granted.

Quebec's right to self-determination is usually adduced from international law and from various conventions of the United Nations to which Canada is bound. In order to make such a case one would have to give his assent to the general principle as enunciated in the international sphere and then to the judgment that Quebec qualified as a nation eligible to assert this right. To a layman the principle itself appears somewhat dubious, at least if it is stated in an unqualified way.[35]

First, most of the sovereign nations which have given assent to it are demonstrably unwilling to apply it to their own domestic circumstances. Thus, for example, the Spanish government denies this right to the Basques, the Iranians to the Kurds, and the rulers of the Soviet Union to the Baltic peoples.

Secondly, the principle appears to deny existing political communities the right to take even peaceful and non-coercive means to frustrate their own destruction. If stated in an absolute way, the principle of national self-determination would make it illegitimate for, say, the Canadian Broadcasting Corporation to be used as an instrument to oppose Quebec separatism or for the Canadian government to give financial assistance to private groups and/or politial parties opposing separatism.

Thirdly, there is a contradictory principle embodied in international law and convention enjoining sovereign states from intervening in the domestic affairs of other states to contribute to the latters' disintegration. If this principle is held to override the right to national self-determination, nations already contained within broader political communities have a right for which there is no remedy beyond their own power to assert it without the assistance of other sovereign states.

Most of those who have supported Quebec's rights to national self-determination have proceeded, explicitly or implicitly, on the basis of what one might call an optimistic scenario.[36] This scenario postulates that the claim to Quebec sovereignty is made after the will of the Quebec electorate has opted for this result through processes which are unequivocally peaceful and democratic. It seems also to be taken for granted that "Quebec" is defined as what is now within the territorial limits of that province. There are of course other possibilities. Could this right validly be asserted on the basis of a unilateral declaration of independence without the consultation of the Quebec electorate through a plebiscite or referendum? Or, alternatively, what if the Quebec and Canadian authorities disagreed about the procedures by which the plebiscite was held and/or the validity of its results? In such circumstances, would such a judgment by other Canadians be an infringment of Quebec's right to national self-determination? What if the present boundaries of Quebec and Canada were subjected to challenge—say, by a renewal of Quebec's claims to Labrador, by the expressed wish of French-speaking communities contiguous to Quebec in New Brunswick and Ontario to join Quebec, by Canadians pressing to restrict the territorial boundaries of Quebec to their pre-1912 limits? In my view, it is unlikely that the Canadian nation could be destroyed without intense political conflict because very intense vested interests, both material and emotional, would be engaged. Thus it would seem to me to be imprudent for the governmental authorities of Canada to bind themselves to specific courses of action as to what they would do in the event that the public authorities of Quebec should, under the indeterminate circumstances of the future, claim self-determination.

If, however, the optimistic scenario should prevail it would in my view be inappropriate for the government of Canada and for Canadians to resist Quebec's claim to sovereignty in its fullest sense. The normative principle here is government by consent, the liberal principle that the good political community is based on a maximum of agreement and a minimum of coercion. "Government by consent" has philosophic difficulties which I have neither the desire nor the competence to explore here.[37] However, in the current context it can be seen in terms of the consent of individual citizens and groups of citizens to be governed by persons chosen and laws enacted through the procedures of a particular constitutional regime. Under some conditions, this "consent" will be granted in a very grudging way on the basis that the individuals or groups concerned perceive no other available alternative. The Declaration of the representatives of the Dene nation of the Northwest Territories contained these statements,

> The Dene find themselves as part of a country. That country is Canada. But the Government of Canada is not the Government of the Dene. The Government of the Northwest Territories is not the government of the Dene. These governments were not the choice of the Dene, they were imposed upon the Dene. ... And while there are realities we are forced to submit to, such as the existence of a country called Canada, we insist on the right to self-determination as a distinct people and the recognition of the Dene Nation.[38]

Prior to the 1960s there was a pervasive strain of conservative nationalism in Quebec which would have taken the same general position as that contained in the Dene Declaration, and Léon Dion has said that in spite of the many pro-separatist statements in Abbé Groulx's writings, "One gets the impression that, when he looked at matters dispassionately, he never thought the separatists' dream achievable."[39] It is obvious that this kind of pessimism does not prevail among contemporary Quebec nationalists, despite their commitment to a continuing economic association with Canada. The civilized values of Canadian liberal democracy would preclude the sustaining of a political community in which a large element was contained in that community against its expressed will.[40]

Notes

1. Frank Underhill, *In Search of Canadian Liberalism*, Toronto: Macmillan of Canada, 1960, p. 118.
2. Donald Creighton, "Doctrine and Interpretation of History," in Donald Creighton, *Towards the Discovery of Canada*, Toronto: Macmillan of Canada, 1972, p. 29.
3. Underhill, *op. cit.*, p. 12.

4. See *Report of the Quebec Royal Commission of Inquiry on Constitutional Problems*, Volume II, Third Part, "The Province of Quebec and the French-Canadian Case," particularly Chapters I and II.

5. *Report of the Royal Commission on Bilingualism and Biculturalism*, Ottawa: Queen's Printer, 1967, pp. xxx-xxxviii.

6. Thomas Hockin, "Federalist style in International Politics," in Stephen Clarkson, ed., *An Independent for Foreign Policy for Canada?* Toronto: McClelland and Stewart, pp. 119-130.

7. The best general historical and analytical treatment of this question that I know is Alfred Cobban, *The Nation State and National Self-Determination*, London: Collins, 1969.

8. John Stuart Mill, *Utilitarianism, Liberty and Representative Government*, London: J. M. Dent, Everyman Library, p. 361.

9. Durham *was* a liberal and one of a very advanced kind. It has been the orthodox view in Canada that in the two major recommendations of his Report that Durham was right and progressive in his advocacy of responsible government and wrong and reactionary in his advocacy of the early and complete assimilation of the French. Ms. Janet Ajzenstat is writing a doctoral dissertation in the Department of Political Economy of the University of Toronto which challenges this conventional wisdom in asserting the coherence of Durham's political thought and I thank her for letting me read her work.

10. *Lord Durham's Report*, edited by Gerald M. Craig, Carleton Library, Toronto: McClelland and Stewart, 1963, pp. 22-23.

11. Ibid., p. 146.

12. Lord Acton, *Essays on Freedom and Power*, New York: Meridian Books, 1957, Chapter V.

13. Pierre Elliott Trudeau, "New Treason of the Intellectuals," in Pierre Elliott Trudeau, *Federalism and the French Canadians*, Toronto: Macmillan of Canada, 1968, p. 151.

14. See Trudeau, *op. cit.*, particularly the last four essays. Although Cobban does not specify federalism in the juridical sense, his general solution to the reconciliation of nationalism with viable and stable nation status is "regional autonomy." Cobban, *op. cit.* Chapter XIV, "Self-Determination as a Regional Problem."

15. See the very useful collection of essays *Consociational Democracy: Political Accommodation in Segmented Societies*, edited by Kenneth McRae, Carleton Library, Toronto: McClelland and Stewart, 1974.

16. For an analysis which assigns Cartier a very modest capacity in this direction, see Jean-Charles Bonenfant, "Les idées politiques de George-Étienne Cartier," in Marcel Hamelin, ed., *Les idées politiques des premiers ministres du Canada*, Ottawa: Les Éditions de l'Université d'Ottawa, 1969, pp. 31-50.

17. This is the argument of W. L. Morton in his essay "Confederation, 1870-1896: The End of the Macdonaldian Constitution and the Return to Duality," *Journal of Canadian Studies* 1, No. 1, 1966, pp. 11-24.

18. See generally the seminal essay, Kenneth McNaught, "The National Outlook of English-speaking Canadians," in Peter Russell, ed., *Nationalism in Canada*, Toronto: McGraw-Hill of Canada, 1966, pp. 61-71.

19. Cobban, *op. cit.*, pp. 247-248.
20. Donald Smiley, "Federalism, Nationalism and the Scope of Public Activity in Canada," in Russell, *op. cit.*, pp. 85-111.
21. René Lévesque, "From *Le Devoir*, July 5, 1963" in Frank Scott and Michael Oliver, eds., *Quebec States her Case*, Toronto: Macmillan of Canada, 1964, p. 134.
22. *Le politique québécoise du développement culturel*, Québec, 1978.
23. Don and Věra Murray, *De Bourassa à Lévesque*, Montréal: Les Éditions Quinze, 1978, p. 255
24. Pierre Elliott Trudeau, "Quebec and the Constitutional Problem," in Trudeau, *op. cit.*, p. 18.
25. John Porter, "Conservatism: The Deep Bond in an Embattled Marriage," in William Kilbourn, ed., *Canada: A Guide to the Peaceable Kingdom*, Toronto: Macmillan of Canada, 1970, p. 267.
26. Abraham Rotstein, "Binding Prometheus," in A. Rotstein, *The Precarious Homestead*, Toronto: New Press, 1973, p. 183.
27. "Choosing our Distance," in Janice L. Murray, ed., *Canadian Cultural Nationalism*, New York: New York University Press, 1977, p. 118.
28. Many examples could be given here but one of the most straightforward is Hugh L. Thorburn, "Needed! A New Look at the Two-Nations Theory," *Queen's Quarterly* LXXX, Summer 1973, pp. 268-273.
29. Thus the patent unreality of the study by the two PQ members of the Quebec National Assembly, Jean-Pierre Charbonneau et Gilbert Paquette, *L'Option*, Québec: Les Editions de l'homme, 1978, pp. 445-459. Charbonneau and Paquette project not only an economic association between Canada and a sovereign Quebec but also the joint regulation of the rights of Franco-Canadians, Anglo-Quebeckers, and the indigenous peoples.
30. See the penetrating philosophical essay by William Mathie, "Political Community and the Canadian Experience: Reflections on Nationalism, Federalism and Unity," *Canadian Journal of Political Science* XII, March 1979, pp. 3-20.
31. For a sensitive expression of prairie views on Confederation, including cultural duality, see J. A. Archer, "The Prairie Perspective," in R. M. Burns, ed., *One Country or Two?* Montreal: McGill-Queen's University Press, 1971, pp. 231-252. Archer's later account of western views after the 1976 Quebec election are, "The Prairie Perspective in 1977," in Richard Simeon, ed., *Must Canada Fail?* Montreal: McGill-Queen's University Press, 1977, pp. 73-84.
32. My views in this section have been very much influenced by David R. Cameron's excellent book, *Nationalism, Self-Determination and the Quebec Question*, Toronto: Macmillan of Canada, 1974. For an exhaustive survey of the legal issues involved in Quebec's claims to self-determination, see Jacques Brossard, *L'accession à la souveraineté et le cas du Québec*, Montréal, Les Presses de l'Université de Montréal, 1976.
33. For these statements, see Mel Watkins, ed., *Dene Nation: The Colony Within*, Toronto: University of Toronto Press, 1977, pp. 3-17.
34. Abraham Rotstein, "Postscript," in Abraham Rotstein, ed., *Power Corrupted: The October Crisis and the Repression of Quebec*, Toronto: New Press, 1971, p. 1.

35. See David Cameron's lucid analysis in Chapter 6, "Self-Determination in International Relations and International Law," in Cameron, *op. cit.*

36. See contrasting scenarios by Richard Simeon, "Scenarios for Separation," in Burns, *op. cit.*, pp. 73-94.

37. For such a discussion, see P. H. Partridge, *Consent and Consensus*, New York: Praeger, 1971.

38. Watkins *op. cit.*, p. 4.

39. Léon Dion, "Politics and Nationalism in Quebec," in Léon Dion, *Quebec: The Unfinished Revolution*, Montreal: McGill-Queen's University Press, 1976, p. 118.

40. Cameron, *op. cit.*, Chapter 10 "Love of One's Own and Love of the Good."

APPENDIX A

TOWARDS FURTHER INVESTIGATION

There is an extensive literature related directly or indirectly to Canadian federalism. Without such a literature *this* book could not have been written. Yet there are still major gaps in our understanding of the federal system. What I suggest below may impel students to fill these gaps. I am aware that in respect to some of these things investigation is already going on and my comments here may be a prod towards the results of such analysis being put in published form.

First, and in my view most crucially, we need work on the linkages between political culture and the operations of our major political institutions. There is an increasing literature of the attitudes and perceptions of Canadians based on survey research. There is also a growing volume of studies on the working of political institutions and of the policy outputs of such institutions. But we know almost nothing about the relations between political culture and the operations of governments. This judgment can be made more concrete by reference to the basic question of national unity and the survival of the Canadian federation. In *Working Papers on Canadian Politics*, John Meisel presented the results of his investigation of the linguistic capacities and linguistic usages of his respondents in English and French and their political attitudes.[1] Meisel's sensitive and impressionistic concluding essay in the same book makes this judgment:

> It is my guess, admittedly based on only very general and unsubstantiated observations, that on the French side the general population is able and prepared to make the necessary adjustment in its aims and methods of achieving them, but that a substantial number of leaders is

incapable and unwilling to accept conditions necessary for a Canadian solution. The opposite situation seems to obtain in English Canada.[2]

In a recent paper Michael D. Ornstein, H. Michael Stevenson and A. Paul M. Williams presented evidence that among non-French respondents outside Quebec there was majority support in Ontario, the Prairies and British Columbia, for negotiating an economic association with an independent Quebec,[3] although the governments of all these provinces have taken forthright stands against this position. As was the case with Meisel, the relations between mass public attitudes on questions of French-English relations and the conduct of governments are explained by Ornstein and his colleagues in an unsatisfactorily impressionistic way.[4]

Secondly, we now have enough case studies of the operations of executive federalism for someone to put together a "propositional inventory" about federal-provincial and interprovincial relations in contemporary Canada,—perhaps somewhat along the lines that John Terry and Richard Schultz have done for Canadian electoral behaviour.[5] Such an inventory of generalizations would do a great deal to clarify what we now know, or think we know, about these processes and institutions and where further research is needed.

Thirdly, we *do* need further investigation of the institutions and processes of executive federalism. We lack even a preliminary study of the institution of the first ministers' conference. There is also work to be done on the central agencies of the federal and provincial governments explicitly charged with responsibilities for intergovernmental relations.

Fourthly, there is a need for studies of the workings of the courts— most crucially of course the Supreme Court of Canada—in judicial review of the constitution based on first-hand observation. Peter Russell's paper on the 1976 Anti-Inflation reference should be a model here.[6]

Fifthly, we very much need studies of province-building. The essays contained in the collection edited by Bellamy, Pammett and Rowat on *Provincial Political Systems*[7] and that by Robin on provincial parties[8] vary in quality and are only a start for the serious study of comparative provincial politics and government. My own notion of what needs to be done is modelled on the superb recent study of Alberta and Saskatchewan by John Richards and Larry Pratt.[9]

Sixthly, those of us whose interests are of the nuts-and-bolts variety very much require the illumination of the political philosophers. C. B. Macpherson has pointed out that there are a considerable number of such persons with distinguished international reputations teaching in Canadian universities.[10] Yet with relatively few exceptions these political philosophers have not turned their attention to an examination of the "inarticulate major premises" of Canadian political institutions and

Canadian political discourse. My model *here* is the recent penetrating essay by William Mathie on Canadian political community.[11]

Notes

1. John Meisel, "Values, Language and Politics in Canada," in John Meisel, *Working Papers on Canadian Politics*, Montreal: McGill-Queen's University Press, 1972, pp. 127-182.
2. John Meisel, " 'Cancel Out and Pass On': A View of Canada's Present Options," in Ibid., p. 214.
3. Michael D. Ornstein, H. Michael Stevenson, and Paul M. Williams, "The State of Mind: Public Perceptions of the Future of Canada," in R. B. Byers and Robert W. Reford, ed., *Canada Challenged: The Viability of Confederation*, Toronto: Canadian Institute of International Affairs, 1979, p. 68.
4. In their conclusions Ornstein, Stevenson and Williams come to some hypotheses which very much invite being followed up. For example, in respect to English-Canadian attitudes they say: "The divisions among the supporters of each party are likely to be mirrored in divisions among the political élites within each party. This conflict makes it difficult to see how the political parties can serve to organize debate about Quebec in English Canada." Ibid., pp. 106-107.
5. John Terry and Richard Schultz, "Canadian Electoral Behaviour: A Propositional Inventory," in Orest M. Kruhlak, Richard Schultz and Sidney B. Pobihushchy, eds., *The Canadian Political Process*, Revised Editions, Toronto: Holt, Rinehart and Winston of Canada, 1973, pp. 248-285.
6. Peter Russell, "The *Anti-Inflation* Case: The Anatomy of A Constitutional Decision," *Canadian Public Administration* 20, Winter 1977, pp. 632-665.
7. David J. Bellamy, Jon H. Pammett and Donald C. Rowat, eds., *The Provincial Political Systems: Comparative Essays*, Toronto: Methuen of Canada, 1976.
8. Martin Robin, ed., *Canadian Provincial Politics: The Party Systems of the Ten Provinces*, Second Edition, Toronto: Prentice-Hall of Canada, 1978.
9. John Richards and Larry Pratt, *Prairie Capitalism: Power and Influence in the New West*, Toronto: McClelland and Stewart, 1979.
10. C. B. Macpherson, "After Strange Gods: Canadian Political Science in 1973," in T. N. Greensburg and G. L. Reuber, eds., *Perspectives in the Social Sciences in Canada*, Toronto: University of Toronto Press, 1974, p. 60.
11. William Mathie, "Political Community and the Canadian Experience: Reflections on Federalism, Nationalism and Unity," *Canadian Journal of Political Science* XII, March 1979, pp. 3-20.

Selected Bibliography

Bibliographical Assistance

Students may find these bibliographical references helpful:

1. *Federalism and Intergovernmental Relations in Australia, Canada, the United States and Other Countries*, Institute of Intergovernmental Relations, Queen's University, 1967, (mimeo), with supplements made subsequent to 1967.
2. Grace F. Heggie, *Canadian Political Parties 1867-1968: A Historical Bibliography*, Toronto: Macmillan of Canada, 1977.
3. W. E. Grasham and Germain Julien, *Canadian Public Administration Bibliography*, Toronto, Institute of Public Administration of Canada, 1972, and 1974 Supplement.
4. Brian Land, "A Description and Guide to the Use of Canadian Government Publications," in Paul W. Fox, ed., *Politics: Canada*, Fourth Edition, Toronto: McGraw-Hill Ryerson, 1977, pp. 638-653.

These groups provide invaluable documentary assistance to students of Canadian federalism:

1. The Institute for Intergovernmental Relations, Queen's University, Kingston, Ontario is developing a publishing program. Its *Federal Year in Review* of which two editions—1976-1977 and 1977-1978—are available is an invaluable record of conferences, judicial decisions, policy changes etc. relating to Canadian federalism. The Institute is also developing a series of "Occasional Papers" and monographs.
2. The Canadian Tax Foundation, 100 University Avenue, Toronto, Ontario has invaluable resources for those concerned with the fiscal aspects of Canadian federalism. Its annual publication *The National Finances* chronicles taxation and expenditure measures of the federal government, and less regularly *Provincial and Municipal Finances* does this for the other jurisdictions. Its quarterly *Canadian Tax Journal* contains analysis and information related to fiscal affairs. The Foundation also publishes monographs, several of them related to fiscal federalism.
3. The C. D. Howe Research Institute, 2064 Sun Life Building, Montreal, Quebec, publishes materials on Canadian economic policy, much of which relates directly or indirectly to federalism. It has a series of monographs and occasional papers *Accent Quebec* on various economic aspects of the Quebec situation.
4. The Canadian Intergovernmental Conference Secretariat, Ottawa makes available documents related to intergovernmental conferences.

These institutions outside Canada provide a focus for comparative federalism:

1. The Centre for Research on Federal Financial Relations, The Australian National University, Canberra, Australia, publishes an extensive monograph series on fiscal federalism.
2. The Center for the Study of Federalism, Temple University, Philadelphia, Pa., is mainly concerned with American federalism, but has some dispositions towards comparative studies. Its quarterly *Publius: The Journal of Federalism* is invaluable for students of comparative federalism.

Among academic quarterlies, The *Canadian Journal of Political Science, Canadian Public Administration, Canadian Public Policy* and the *Journal of Canadian Studies* feature articles and reviews directly or indirectly related to Canadian federalism.

There are also useful bibliographies for students of Canadian government and politics in Paul Fox, ed., *Politics: Canada*, Fourth Edition, Toronto: McGraw-Hill Ryerson, 1977, and in Richard Van Loon and Michael Whittington, *The Canadian Political System*, Second Edition, Toronto: McGraw-Hill Ryerson, 1976. There is a very full bibliography on French Canada in Vol. I, No. 1 of the *Canadian Journal of Political Science*, April 1968.

General and Comparative References on Federalism

Birch, A.H., *Federalism, Finance and Social Legislation in Canada, Australia and the United States*, Oxford: Clarendon Press, 1955.

Bowie, R.R. and Friedrich, C.J., Editors, *Studies in Federalism*, Boston: Little, Brown, 1954.

Brady, Alexander, *Democracy in the Dominions*, Toronto: University of Toronto Press, 1948.

Breton, Albert and Scott, Anthony, *The Economic Constitution of Federal States*, Toronto: University of Toronto Press, 1978.

Dicey, A.V., *Introduction to the Study of the Law of the Constitution*, Macmillan, London: Seventh Edition, 1908. Particularly Chapter III "Parliamentary Sovereignty and Federalism."

Duchachek, Ivo D., *Comparative Federalism: The Territorial Dimension of Politics*, New York: Holt, Rinehart and Winston, 1970.

Earle, Valerie, Editor, *Federalism: Infinite Variety in Theory and Practice*, Ithaca, Illinois: F.E. Peacock, 1968.

Franck, Thomas M. et al., *Why Federations Fail*, New York: New York University Press, 1968.

Friedrich, Carl J. *Trends of Federalism in Theory and Practice*, New York: Praeger, 1968.

Livingston, W.S., *Federalism and Constitutional Change*, Oxford: Clarendon Press, 1956.

Macmahon, A.W., Editor, *Federalism, Mature and Emergent*, New York: Doubleday, 1955.

Mathews, Russell, Editor, *Making Federalism Work*, Canberra: The Centre for Research on Federal Financial Relations, Australian National University, 1976.

McWhinney, E., *Comparative Federalism*, Toronto: University of Toronto Press, 1962.

McWhinney, E., *Judicial Review in the English-Speaking World*, Fourth Edition, Toronto: University of Toronto Press, 1969.

May, R.J., *Federalism and Fiscal Adjustment*, Oxford: Clarendon Press, 1969.

Oates, Wallace E., *Fiscal Federalism*, New York: Harcourt Brace, Jovanovich, 1972.

Riker, William H., *Federalism: Origin, Operation, Significance*, Boston: Little, Brown, 1964.

Sawer, G.A., *Modern Federalism*, London: C.A. Watts, 1969.

Watts, R.L., *New Federations: Experiments in the Commonwealth*, Oxford: Clarendon Press, 1966.

Watts, R.L., *Multicultural Societies and Federalism*, Studies of the Royal Commission on Bilingualism and Biculturalism, Ottawa: Information Canada, 1970.

Wheare, K.C., *Federal Government*, Fourth Edition, New York: Oxford University Press, 1963.

Wildavsky, Aaron, Editor, *American Federalism in Perspective*, Boston: Little, Brown, 1967.

General References on Canadian Federalism

Since the Quebec election of November 1976, there have been several symposia and collections of essays on various aspects of the crisis in Canadian federalism:

Berkowitz, S.D., and Logan, Robert K., Editors, *Canada's Third Option*, Toronto: Macmillan of Canada, 1978.

Byers, R.B., and Reford, Robert W., Editors, *Canada Challenged: The Viability of Confederation*, Toronto: Canadian Institute of International Affairs, 1979.

Études Internationales VII, Juin 1977, *Le Canada et le Québec*, Centre des relations internationales, Université Laval.

Fraser Institute, *Canada at the Crossroads*, Vancouver: Fraser Institute, 1978.

Journal of Canadian Studies 12, July, 1977, *Thinking About Separation*.

French G. Stanley, Editor, *Confederation: Philosophers Look at Canadian Confederation*, Montreal, The Canadian Philosophical Association, 1979.

Options, Proceedings of the Conference on the Future of the Canadian Federation, University of Toronto, 1977.

Simeon, Richard, Editor, *Must Canada Fail?* Montreal: McGill-Queen's University Press, 1977.

These are other general references on Canadian federalism:

Beck, J.M., Editor, *The Shaping of Canadian Federalism*, Toronto: Copp, Clark, 1971.

Bercuson, David Jay, Editor, *Canada and the Burden of Unity*, Toronto: Macmillan of Canada, 1977.

Black, Edwin R. *Divided Loyalties: Canadian Concepts of Federalism*, Montreal: McGill-Queen's University Press, 1975.

Browne, G.P., Editor, *Documents on the Confederation of British North America*, Toronto: McClelland and Stewart, 1969.

Creighton, Donald, *Towards the Discovery of Canada*, Toronto: Macmillan of Canada, 1972.

Crepeau, P.-A. and Macpherson, C.B., Editors, *The Future of Canadian Federalism*, Toronto and Montréal: The University of Toronto Press and Les Presses de l'Université de Montréal, 1965.

Hawkins, Gordon, Editor, *Concepts of Federalism*, Toronto: Canadian Institute on Public Affairs, 1965.

Lalande, Gilles, *Pourquoi le fédéralisme*. Montréal: H.M.H. Hurtubise, 1972.

Lower, A.R.M., Scott, Frank et al., Editors, *Evolving Canadian Federalism*, Durham, N.C.: Duke University Press, 1958.

Ormsby, W.G. *The Emergence of the Federal Concept in Canada 1839-1845*, Toronto: University of Toronto Press, 1954.

Ryerson, Stanley, *Unequal Union*, Toronto: Progress Books, 1968.

Smiley, Donald, *The Canadian Political Nationality*, Toronto: Methuen of Canada, 1967.

Smiley, Donald, *Constitutional Adaptation and Canadian Federalism since 1945*, Documents of the Royal Commission on Bilingualism and Biculturalism, Ottawa: Queen's Printer, 1970.

Stevenson, Garth, "Federalism and the Political Economy of the Canadian State," in Panitch, Leo, Editor, *The Canadian State: Political Economy and Political Power*, Toronto: University of Toronto Press, 1977, pp. 71-100.

Stevenson, Garth, *Unfulfilled Union: Canadian Federalism and National Unity*, Toronto: Macmillan of Canada, 1979.

Trudeau, Pierre Elliott, *Federalism and the French Canadians*, Toronto: Macmillan of Canada, 1968.

Waite, Peter, *The Life and Times of Confederation, 1864-1867*, Toronto: University of Toronto Press, 1962.

The Canadian Constitution and Constitutional Change

There are four widely used recent texts in Canadian constitutional law.

Atkey, Ronald G., and Lyon, J. Noel, *Canadian Constitutional Law in a Modern Perspective*, Toronto: University of Toronto Press, 1970.

Laskin, Bora, *Canadian Constitutional Law*, Fourth Edition, Revised by Albert S. Abel, Toronto: Carswell, 1975.

Hogg, Peter, *Constitutional Law of Canada*, Toronto: Carswell, 1978.

Whyte, J.D., and Lederman, W.R., *Canadian Constitutional Law*, Second Edition, Toronto: Butterworths, 1977.

Alone of these texts, Hogg's book is topical rather than based on the case-method, and because of this non-lawyers may find it more useful than the others. Hogg has also a bibliography, pp. 477-485.

The Canadian Intergovernmental Affairs Secretariat, Ottawa has published two valuable documents on the process of constitutional change

—*The Constitutional Review*, 1968-1971, Secretary's Report.

—*Proposals on the Constitution, 1971-1978*, Collation.

The verbatim reports of the Constitutional Conferences of February 1968, February 1969 and December 1969 are available from Supply and Services, Ottawa.

The following are the more comprehensive and detailed proposals for constitutional reform which have been made in the past decade and a half:

1. Alberta, *Harmony in Diversity: A New Federalism for Canada*, Edmonton, 1978.
2. British Columbia, *Constitutional Proposals*, Victoria, September, 1978.
3. Canadian Bar Association, *Towards a New Canada*, Committee on the Constitution, Canadian Bar Association, 1978.
4. Elton, David, et. al., *Alternatives: Towards the Development of an Effective Federal System for Canada: Amended Report*, Calgary: Canada West Foundation, 1978.
5. Farihault, Marcel, and Fowler, Robert M., *Ten to One: The Confederation Wager*, Toronto: McClelland and Stewart, 1965.

The following six comprehensive proposals for comprehensive constitutional reform have emanated from Ottawa:

1. Pearson, The Right Honourable Lester B., *Federalism for the Future*, Queen's Printer, Ottawa, 1968.
2. Trudeau, The Right Honourable Pierre Elliott, *The Constitution and the People of Canada*, Queen's Printer, Ottawa, 1969.

In the 1968-1971 period, the government of Canada also issued a series of monographs on more specific aspects of the constitution and constitutional change—the spending power of Parliament, international relations, the constitutional entrenchment of human rights, and federal-provincial powers in respect to taxation and social security.

3. The Special Joint Committee of the Senate and the House of Commons on the Constitution of Canada, *Final Report*, 1972.
4. Trudeau, The Right Honourable Pierre Elliott, *A Time for Action: Towards the Renewal of the Canadian Federation*, Ottawa: Supply and Services, Queen's Printer, 1978.
5. *The Constitutional Amendment Bill, 1978: Text and Explanatory Notes.*
6. *A Future Together: Observations and Recommendations*, Report of the Task Force on Canadian Unity, Ottawa, Supply and Services 1979.

O'Hearn, Peter J.T., *Peace, Order and Good Government: A New Constitution for Canada*, Toronto: Macmillan of Canada, 1964.

Ontario Advisory Committee on Confederation, *First Report*, 1978 and *Second Report*, Toronto 1979. (The first deals with the institutions of the central government, the second with the distribution of legislative powers).

These other works on the Canadian constitution may also be helpful:

Bissonnette, Bernard, *Essai sur la constitution du Canada*, Montréal: Les éditions du jour, 1963.

Brossard, *La Cour Suprême et la constitution*, Montréal: Les presses de l'université de Montréal, 1968.

Browne, G.P., *The Judicial Committee and the British North America Act*, Toronto: University of Toronto Press, 1967.

Cairns, Alan C., "The Judicial Committee and its Critics," *Canadian Journal of Political Science IV*, September 1971, pp. 301-345.

Cairns, Alan C., "The Living Canadian Constitution," in J. Peter Meekison, Editor, *Canadian Federalism: Myth or Reality*. Third Edition, Toronto: Methuen of Canada, 1977, pp. 86-99.

Cairns, Alan C., *From Interstate to Intrastate Federalism in Canada*, Institute Discussion Paper, Kingston: Institute of Intergovernmental Relations, Queen's University, 1979.

Cairns, Alan C., "Recent Federalist Constitutional Proposals: A Review Essay." Vancouver, 1979, mimeo. (To appear in *Canadian Public Policy*.)

Cheffins, R.I., and Tucker, R.N., *The Constitutional Process in Canada*, Second Edition, Toronto: McGraw-Hill Ryerson, 1976.

Favreau, G., *The Amendment of the Constitution of Canada*, Ottawa: Queen's Printer, 1965.

Fletcher, Martha, "Judicial Review and the Division of Powers in Canada," in Meekison *op. cit.*, pp. 100-123.

Forsey, E.A., *Freedom and Order*, Toronto: McClelland and Stewart, 1974.

Hopkins, E.R., *Confederation at the Crossroads*, Toronto: McClelland and Stewart, 1968.

Kennedy, W.P.M., *The Constitution of Canada, 1534-1937*, Second Edition, London: Oxford University Press, 1938.

La Forest, G.V., *Disallowance and Reservation of Provincial Legislation*, Ottawa: Queen's Printer, 1965.

La Forest, G.V., *The Allocation of Taxing Power under the Canadian Constitution*, Toronto: Canadian Tax Foundation, 1967.

Lajoie, A., *Le pouvoir déclaratoire du Parlement*, Montréal: Les presses de l'université de Montréal, 1969.

Laskin, Bora, *The British Tradition in Canadian Law*, London: Stevens, 1969.

L'Écuyer, Gilbert, *La cour suprême du Canada et le partage des compétences 1949-1978*, Quebec: Gouvernement du Quebec, Ministère des affaires intergouvernementales, 1978.

Lederman, W.R., Editor, *The Courts and the Canadian Constitution*, Toronto: McClelland and Stewart, 1964.

Mallory, J.R., *Social Credit and the Federal Power in Canada*, Toronto: University of Toronto Press, 1954. Reprinted in paperback, 1976.

Mallory, J.R., "The Five Faces of Federalism," in Meekison, *op. cit.* pp. 19-30.

McWhinney, Edward, *Quebec and the Constitution 1960-1978*, Toronto: University of Toronto Press, 1979.

O'Connor Report, by the Parliamentary Council of the Senate of Canada on the British North America Act, King's Printer: Ottawa, 1939. Reprinted 1961.

Ontario Advisory Committee on Confederation, *The Confederation Challenge: Background Papers and Reports.*, Toronto: Queen's Printer, 1967 (Volume 1), and 1970 (Volume 2).

Russell, Peter, *Leading Constitutional Decisions: Cases on the British North America Act*, Revised Edition, Toronto: McClelland and Stewart, 1973.

Russell, Peter, *The Supreme Court of Canada as a Bilingual and Bicul-*

tural Institution, Document of the Royal Commission on Bilingualism and Biculturalism, Ottawa: Queen's Printer, 1969.

Scott, Frank, *Civil Liberties and Canadian Federalism,* Toronto: University of Toronto Press, 1959.

Scott, Frank, *Essays on the Constitution,* Toronto: University of Toronto Press, 1977.

Stewart, John, *The Canadian House of Commons, Procedure and Reform,* Montreal: McGill-Queen's University Press, 1977. (The first chapter is a monumental analysis of the parliamentary aspects of the Canadian constitutional system.)

Strayer, Barry, *Judicial Review of Legislation in Canada,* Toronto: University of Toronto Press, 1968.

Tarnopolsky, W.S. *The Canadian Bill of Rights,* Second Edition, Toronto: McClelland and Stewart, 1975.

Tremblay Report, The Report of the Quebec Royal Commission of Inquiry on Constitutional Problems, Queen's Printer, Quebec, 1956.

Weiler, Paul, *In the Last Resort: A Critical Study of the Supreme Court of Canada,* Toronto: Carswell, 1974.

Executive Federalism

Aitchison, J.H., "Interprovincial Cooperation in Canada", in Aitchison, J.H., Editor, *The Political Process in Canada,* Toronto: University of Toronto Press, 1963.

Burns, R.M., *Conflict and its Resolution in the Administration of Mineral Resources in Canada,* Kingston: Centre for Resource Studies, Queen's University, 1976.

Burns, R.M., and Close, Lawrence J., *The Municipal Winter Works Incentive Program: A Study of Government Expenditure Decision-Making,* Toronto and Kingston, Canada Tax Foundation/Institute of Intergovernmental Relations, 1971.

Cairns, Alan C., "The Other Crisis of Canadian Federalism" *Canadian Public Administration* 22, Summer 1979, pp. 175-195.

Careless, Anthony D., *Initiative and Response: The Adaptation of Canadian Federalism to Regional Economic Development,* Montreal: McGill-Queen's University Press, 1977.

Corry, J.A., *Difficulties of Divided Jurisdiction,* Ottawa: King's Printer, 1939.

Dupré, J. Stefan, Cameron, David M., McKechnie, Graeme H., and Rotenberg, Theodore B., *Federalism and Policy Development: The Case of Adult Occupational Training in Ontario,* Toronto: University of Toronto Press, 1973.

Dyck, Rand, "The Canada Assistance Plan: The Ultimate in Cooperative Federalism," *Canadian Public Administration* 19, Winter 1976, pp. 587-602.

Institute of Intergovernmental Relations, Queen's University, *Report: Intergovernmental Liaison on Fiscal and Economic Matters*, 1966.

Johnson, A.W., "The Dynamics of Federalism in Canada," *Canadian Journal of Political Science 1*, March 1968, pp. 18-39.

Leach, Richard H., *Perceptions of Federalism by Canadian and Australian Civil Servants*, Centre for Research on Federal Financial Relations, Canberra, Australian National University, 1976.

Lederman, W.R., "Some Forms and Limitations of Cooperative Federalism," *Canadian Bar Review XLV*, September, 1967, pp. 409-436.

Schultz, Richard, "Federalism and the Regulatory Process," Federal-Provincial Relations Office, Ottawa, 1979, mimeo.

Schultz, Richard, "The Regulatory Process in Federal-Provincial Relations," in Doern, G. Bruce, Editor, *The Regulatory Process in Canada*, Toronto: Macmillan of Canada, 1978, pp. 128-146.

Simeon, Richard, *Federal-Provincial Diplomacy*, Toronto: University of Toronto Press, 1972.

Simeon, Richard, Editor, *Confrontation and Collaboration—Intergovernmental Relations in Canada Today*, Toronto: Institute of Public Administration of Canada, 1979.

Smiley, Donald V., "Canadian Federalism and the Resolution of Federal-Provincial Conflict," in Vaughan, Frederick, Kyba, Patrick, and Dwivedi, O.P., Editors, *Contemporary Issues in Canadian Politics*, Scarborough: Prentice-Hall of Canada, 1970, pp. 48-66.

Smiley, Donald V., "Federal-Provincial Conflict in Canada", *Publius: The Journal of Federalism 4*, Summer 1974, pp. 7-24.

Swainson, Neil, *Conflict over the Columbia*, Montreal: McGill-Queen's University Press, 1979.

Taylor, Malcolm G., *Health Insurance and Canadian Public Policy*, Montreal: McGill-Queen's University Press, 1978.

Veilleux, Gérard, *Les relations intergouvernementales au Canada, 1867-1967*, Montreal: Les presses de l'université du Québec, 1971.

Westmacott, Martin, "The National Transportation Act and Western Canada: A Study in Cooperative Federalism," *Canadian Public Administration XVII, Fall 1973*, pp. 447-468.

Wilson, V. Seymour, "Federal-Provincial Relations and Federal Policy Processes," in Doern, G. Bruce, and Aucoin, Peter, Editors, *Public Policy in Canada*, Toronto: Macmillan of Canada, 1979, pp. 190-212.

The Politics of Canadian Federalism

Berry, Glyn R., "The Oil Lobby and the Energy Crisis", *Canadian Public Administration 17*, Winter 1974, pp. 600-635.

Black, E.R., "Federal Strains within a Canadian Party," *Dalhousie Review XLV*, 1965, pp. 307-323.

Cairns, Alan C., "The Electoral System and the Party System in Canada," *Canadian Journal of Political Science I,* March 1978, pp. 55-80.

Courtney, John C., Editor, *Voting in Canada,* Scarborough: Prentice-Hall of Canada, 1967.

Courtney, John C., *The Selection of National Party Leaders in Canada,* Toronto: Macmillan of Canada, 1973.

Engelmann, F.C., and Schwartz, M.A., *Political Parties and the Canadian Social Structure,* Second Edition, Scarborough: Prentice-Hall of Canada, 1975.

Irvine, William, *Does Canada Need a New Electoral System?* Kingston: Institute of Intergovernmental Relations, Queen's University, 1979.

Lemieux, Vincent, "The Political Party System in Quebec," in Thomson, Dale C., Editor, *Quebec Society and Politics,* Toronto: McClelland and Stewart, 1973, pp. 99-118.

Meisel, John, *Working Papers on Canadian Politics,* Second Edition, Montreal: McGill-Queen's University Press, 1974.

Milner, Henry, *Politics in the New Quebec,* Toronto: McClelland and Stewart, 1978.

Meisel, John, "The Decline of Party," in Thorburn, Hugh G., Editor, *Party Politics in Canada,* Fourth Edition, Scarborough: Prentice-Hall of Canada, 1979, pp. 119-136. (See also in Thorburn, *op. cit.,* Section 5, the series of essays on regional politics in Canada.)

Paltiel, K.Z., *Political Party Financing in Canada,* Toronto: McGraw-Hill of Canada, 1970.

Pross, Paul, Editor, *Pressure Group Behaviour in Canadian Politics,* Toronto: McGraw-Hill Ryerson, 1975. (See particularly essays by Bucovetsky, Dawson and Kwavnick.)

Rayside, David, "Federalism and the Party System: Federal and Provincial Liberals in the Province of Quebec," *Canadian Journal of Political Science XI,* September 1978, pp. 499-528.

Robin, Martin, Editor, *Canadian Provincial Politics,* Second Edition, Toronto: Prentice-Hall of Canada, 1978.

Schultz, Richard, "Interest Groups and Intergovernmental Negotiations: Caught in the Vise of Federalism", in Meekison, J. Peter, Editor, *Canadian Federalism: Myth or Reality.* Third Edition, Toronto: Methuen of Canada, 1977, pp. 340-352.

Schwartz, Mildred, *Politics and Territory: The Sociology of Regional Persistence in Canada,* Montreal: McGill-Queen's University Press, 1974.

Simeon, Richard, and Elkins, David, "Regional Political Culture in Canada," *Canadian Journal of Political Science VII,* December 1968, pp. 373-397.

Smiley, Donald V., "The National Party Leadership Convention: A Preliminary Analysis," *Canadian Journal of Political Science* 1, December, 1968, pp. 373-397.

Smith, David E., *Prairie Liberalism: The Liberal Party in Saskatchewan, 1905-1971*, Toronto: University of Toronto Press, 1975.

Stevenson, H. Michael, Ornstein, Michael, and Williams, A. Paul M., "The State of Mind: Public Perceptions of the Future of Canada," in Byers, R.B., and Reford, Robert W., Editors, *Canada Challenged: The Viability of Confederation*, Toronto: Canadian Institute of International Affairs, 1979, pp. 57-107.

Whitaker, Reginald A., *The Government Party: Organizing and Financing the Liberal Party of Canada, 1930-1958*, Toronto: University of Toronto Press, 1977.

Wilson, John, "The Canadian Political Cultures: Towards a Redefinition of the Nature of the Canadian Political System," *Canadian Journal of Political Science VII*, September, 1974, pp. 438-483.

Winn, Conrad, and McMenemy, John, Editors, *Political Parties in Canada*, Toronto: McGraw-Hill Ryerson, 1976.

(Federal election results by province from 1878-1974 inclusive are in Thorburn, *op. cit.* pp. 304-315. Provincial election results from 1905 to 1976 are presented in Fox, Paul, Editor, *Politics: Canada*, Fourth Edition, Toronto: McGraw-Hill Ryerson, 1977, pp. 599-637.)

The Fiscal and Economic Dimension of Canadian Federalism

Angers, François-Albert, *Essai sur la centralisation*, Montréal: Les presses de l'école des hautes études commerciales, 1960.

Bird, Richard M., *The Growth of Government Spending in Canada*, Toronto: Canadian Tax Foundation, 1970.

Brewis, T.N., *Regional Economic Policies in Canada*, Toronto: Macmillan of Canada, 1969.

Bryden, Kenneth, *Old Age Pensions and Policy-Making in Canada*, Montreal: McGill-Queen's University Press, 1974.

Burns, R.M., "The Operation of Fiscal and Economic Policy", in Doern, G. Bruce, and Wilson, V. Seymour, Editors, *Issues in Canadian Public Policy*, Toronto: Macmillan of Canada, 1974, pp. 286-309.

Canada, *Report of the Royal Commission on Dominion-Provincial Relations*, Ottawa: King's Printer, 1940 (Rowell-Sirois Report).

Canada, *Report of the Royal Commission on Taxation*, Ottawa: Queen's Printer, 1966 (Carter Report). (Particularly Volume 2, Chapter 3, on federal-provincial fiscal relations.)

Careless, A.D., *Initiative and Response: The Adaptation of Canadian Federalism to Regional Development*, Montreal: McGill-Queen's University Press, 1977.

Carter, George E., Canadian Conditional Grants since World War II, Toronto: Canadian Tax Foundation, 1971.

Clark, Douglas H., Fiscal Need and Revenue Equalization Grants, Toronto: Canadian Tax Foundation, 1969.

Courchene, Thomas H., "The New Fiscal Arrangements and the Economics of Federalism," in Options, Proceedings of the Conference on the Future of Federalism, University of Toronto, 1978, pp. 311-346.

Courchene, Thomas H., and Beavis, D.A., "Federal-Provincial Tax Equalization: An Evaluation," Canadian Journal of Economics VI, 1973, pp. 483-502.

Courchene, Thomas H., "Avenues of Adjustment: The Transfer System and Regional Disparities," in Canadian Confederation at the Crossroads, Vancouver: The Fraser Institute, 1978, pp. 145-188.

Cox, Robert W., "Employment, Labour and Future Political Structures," in Byers, R.B., and Reford, Robert W., Editors, Canada Challenged: The Viability of Confederation, Toronto: Canadian Institute of International Affairs, 1979, pp. 262-292.

Debanné, J.G., "Oil and Canadian Policy," in Erickson, Edward W., and Waverman, Leonard D., Editors, The Energy Question Volume II: North America, Toronto: University of Toronto Press, 1974, pp. 125-148.

Dupré, J. Stefan, "Contracting Out: A Funny Thing Happened on the Way to the Centennial," Report of the Proceedings of the Eighteenth Annual Tax Conference, Toronto: Canadian Tax Foundation, 1965, pp. 208-218.

Dupré, J. Stefan, "Tax Powers vs. Spending Responsibilities: An Historical Analysis of Federal-Provincial Finance," in Rotstein, Abraham, Editor, The Prospects for Change: Proposals for Canada's Future, Toronto: McGraw-Hill of Canada, 1965, pp. 83-101.

Economic Council of Canada, Living Together: A Study of Regional Disparities, Ottawa: Supply and Services, 1977.

Fraser Institute, Canadian Confederation at the Crossroads: The Search for Federal-Provincial Balance, Vancouver: The Fraser Institute, 1978.

Graham, John F., Fiscal Adjustment and Economic Development: A Case Study of Nova Scotia, Toronto: University of Toronto Press, 1963.

Graham, John F., Johnson, A.W., and Andrews, J.M., Inter-Government Fiscal Relationships, Toronto: Canadian Tax Foundation, 1964.

Green, Alan, G., "Regional Economic Disparities," in Officer, L.H., and Smith, L.B., Editors, Issues in Canadian Economics, Toronto: McGraw-Hill Ryerson, 1974, pp. 354-370.

Green, Alan G., Regional Aspects of Canada's Economic Growth, Toronto: University of Toronto Press, 1970.

Hanson, E.J., *Fiscal Needs of the Canadian Provinces*, Toronto: Canadian Tax Foundation, 1961.

Hood, William C., "Economic Policy in Our Federal State," in Crepeau, P.-A., and Macpherson, C.B., Editors, *The Future of Canadian Federalism*, Toronto and Montréal: University of Toronto Press/Les presses de l'Université de Montréal, 1965, pp. 58-76.

Lynn, James, *Federal-Provincial Fiscal Relations*, Studies of the Royal Commission on Taxation, No. 23, Ottawa: Queen's Printer, 1967.

Mackintosh, W.A., *The Economic Background of Dominion-Provincial Relations*, Carleton Library, Toronto: McClelland and Stewart, 1964.

Mathews, Philip, *Forced Growth: Five Studies of Government Involvement in the Development of Canada*, Toronto: James Lewis and Samuel, 1971.

Maxwell, J.A., *Federal Subsidies to the Provincial Governments in Canada*, Cambridge, Mass.: Harvard University Press, 1937.

McDougall, Ian, "Energy and the Future of Federalism: National Harmony or Continental Hegomony?" in Byers and Reford, *op. cit.*, pp. 316-345.

Moore, A. Milton, Perry J. Harvey and Beach, Donald I., *The Financing of Canadian Federation: The First Hundred Years*, Toronto: The Canadian Tax Foundation, 1966.

Nowlan, David M., "Centrifugally Speaking: Some Economics of Canadian Federalism," in Lloyd, Trevor, and McLeod, Jack, Editors, *Agenda 1970: Proposals for a Creative Politics*, Toronto: University of Toronto Press, 1966, pp. 177-196.

Ontario Economic Council, *Intergovernmental Relations*, Toronto, 1977. (This is a valuable group of papers on various aspects of fiscal and economic policy and on intergovernmental decision-making.)

Richards, John, and Pratt, Larry, *Prairie Capitalism: Power and Influence in the New West*, Toronto: McClelland and Stewart, 1979.

Reuber, Grant, "Monetary, Fiscal and Debt Management Policies," in Byers and Reford, *op. cit.*, pp. 215-231.

Safarian, A.E., *Canadian Federalism and Economic Integration*, Constitutional Study Prepared for the Government of Canada, Ottawa: Information Canada, 1974.

Scott, Anthony, Editor, *Natural Resource Revenues: A Test of Federalism*, Vancouver: University of British Columbia Press, 1975.

Scott, Anthony, "An Economic Approach to the Federal Structure," in *Options, op. cit.*, pp. 257-280.

Scott, Frank R., "Social Planning and Canadian Federalism," in Oliver, Michael, Editor, *Social Purpose for Canada*, Toronto: University of Toronto Press, 1961, pp. 394-407.

Smiley, Donald V. "The Political Context of Resource Development in Canada," in Scott, *Natural Resources*, pp. 61-72.

Smiley, Donald V., Conditional Grants and Canadian Federalism, Toronto: Canadian Tax Foundation, 1963.

Stevenson, Garth, Unfulfilled Union: Canadian Federalism and National Unity, Toronto: Macmillan of Canada, 1979. (Particularly Chapters 4-7, inclusive.)

Trudeau, The Right Honourable Pierre Elliott, Federal-Provincial Grants and the Spending Power of Parliament, Ottawa: Queen's Printer, 1969.

United States, In Search of Balance: Canada's Intergovernmental Experience, Advisory Committee on Intergovernmental Relations, Washington: Government Printing Office, 1971.

Whalen, Hugh, "Public Policy and Regional Development: The Experience of the Atlantic Provinces," in Rotstein, Abraham, Editor, The Prospect of Change: Proposals for Canada's Future, Toronto: McGraw-Hill of Canada, 1965, pp. 102-148.

Cultural Duality and Canadian Federalism

Arès, Richard, Les positions—éthniques, linguistiques et religieuses des canadiens français à la suite du recensement de 1971, Montréal: Les Éditions Bellarmin, 1975.

Bergeron, Gérard, L'Indépendance oui, mais . . ., Montréal: Les Éditions Quinze, 1977.

Bergeron, Gérard, Ce jour-là . . . le referendum, Montréal: Les Éditions Quinze, 1978.

Bernard André, What Does Quebec Want? Toronto: James Lorimer, 1978.

Brossard, Jacques, L'accession à la souveraineté et le cas du Québec, Montréal: Les presses de l'université de Montréal, 1976.

Brunet, Michel, Québec-Canada anglais: Deux intineraires un affrontement, Montréal: Editions H.M.H., 1978.

Cameron, David R., Nationalism, Self-Determination and the Quebec Question, Toronto: Macmillan of Canada, 1974.

Cameron, David R., "Dualism and the concept of National Unity," in Redekop, John H., Editor, Approaches to Canadian Politics, Scarborough: Prentice-Hall of Canada, 1978, pp. 228-247.

Cook, Ramsay, Editor, French-Canadian Nationalism: An Anthology, Toronto: Macmillan of Canada, 1969.

Cook, Ramsay, Canada and the French-Canadian Question, Toronto: Macmillan of Canada, 1966.

Creighton, Donald, "The Use and Abuse of History," and "The Myth of Biculturalism," in Creighton, Donald, Towards the Discovery of Canada, Toronto: Macmillan of Canada, 1972, pp. 65-82, and pp. 256-270.

Dion, Léon, Quebec: The Unfinished Revolution, Montreal: McGill-Queen's University Press, 1976.

Dumont, Fernand, *The Vigil of Quebec*, Toronto: University of Toronto Press, 1974.

Fournier, Pierre, *The Quebec Establishment: The Ruling Class and the State*, Montreal: Black Rose Books, 1976.

Fullerton, Douglas H., *The Dangerous Delusion: Quebec's Independence Obsession*, Toronto: McClelland and Stewart, 1978.

Guindon, Hubert, "Social Unrest, Social Class and Quebec's Bureaucratic Revolution," *Queen's Quarterly 71*, Summer 1964, pp. 150-162.

Guindon, Hubert, "The Modernization of Quebec and the Legitimacy of the Canadian State," in Glenday, Daniel et al., Editors, *Modernization and the Canadian State*, Toronto: Macmillan of Canada, 1978, pp. 212-246.

Lalande, Gilles, *Pourquoi le fédéralisme* Montréal: Hurtubise, HMH, 1972.

Lamontagne, Maurice, *Le fédéralisme canadien*, Québec, Les presses de l'université Laval, 1954.

Jones, Richard, *Community in Crisis: French-Canadian Nationalism in Perspective*, Toronto: McClelland and Stewart, 1967.

Joy, Richard, *Languages in Conflict*, Toronto: McClelland and Stewart, 1972.

Lanphier, C. Michael, and Morris, Raymond N., *Three Scales of Inequality: Perspectives on French-English Relations*, Don Mills: Longman Canada, 1977.

Lévesque, René, *An Option for Quebec*, Toronto: McClelland and Stewart, 1968.

Lévesque, René, "For an Independent Quebec," *Foreign Affairs 34*, July 1976, pp. 733-744. Toronto.

Lévesque, René, *My Quebec*, Toronto. Totem Books, 1979.

Lieberson, Stanley, *Language and Ethnic Relations in Canada*, New York: John Wiley and Sons, 1970.

McRoberts, Kenneth, and Posgate, Dale, *Quebec: Social Change and Political Crisis*, Toronto: McClelland and Stewart, 1976.

McWhinney, Edward, *Quebec and the Constitution 1960-1978*, Toronto: University of Toronto Press, 1979.

Milner, Henry, *Politics in the New Quebec*, Toronto: McClelland and Stewart, 1978.

Morin, Claude, *Quebec versus Ottawa: The Struggle for Self-Government 1960-1972*, Toronto: University of Toronto Press, 1976.

Murray, Věra, *Le Parti québécois: de la fondation à la prise du pouvoir*, Montréal: Hurtubise HMH, 1976.

Murray, Věra, et Murray, Don, *De Bourassa à Lévesque*, Montréal: Éditions Quinze, 1978.

Paquette, Gilbert, et Charbonneau, Jean-Pierre, *L'Option*, Montréal: Les Éditions de l'homme, 1978.

Quebec, *Report of the Royal Commission of Inquiry on Constitutional Problems*, Four Volumes, Quebec, Queen's Printer 1956. (For an abridgment, see *The Tremblay Report*, Edited and with an Introduction by David Kwavnick, Toronto: McClelland and Stewart, 1973.)

Rioux, Marcel, *Quebec in Question*, Toronto: James Lewis and Samuel, 1971.

Royal Commission on Bilingualism and Biculturalism, Reports, Ottawa: Queen's Printer.
Preliminary Report, 1965.
Book I, The Official Languages, 1967.
Book II, Education, 1968.
Book III, The Work World, 1969.
Book IV, The Cultural Contributions of other Ethnic Groups, 1969.

Ryerson, Stanley, B., *Unequal Union: Confederation and the Roots of Conflict in the Canadas, 1815-1873*, Toronto: Progress Books, 1968.

Smiley, Donald V., *The Canadian Political Nationality*, Toronto: Methuen of Canada, 1967, Chapter 3.

Smith, Denis, *Bleeding Hearts . . . Bleeding Country; Canada and the Quebec Crisis*, Edmonton: M.G. Hurtig, 1971.

Stanley, George F., "Act or Pact? Another Look at Confederation," *Report*, Toronto: Canadian Historical Association, 1956, pp. 1-25.

Thomson, Dale C., Editor, *Quebec Society and Politics: Views from the Inside*, Toronto: McClelland and Stewart, 1973.

Trudeau, Pierre Elliott, *Federalism and the French Canadians*, Toronto: Macmillan of Canada, 1968.

Wade, Mason, *The French-Canadian Outlook*, Carleton Library, Toronto: McClelland and Stewart, 1964.

Wade, Mason, *The French Canadians, 1760-1945*, Toronto: Macmillan of Canada, 1955.

Central Canada-Periphery Relations

Anderson, Owen, and Barr, John, Editors, *The Unfinished Revolt: Some Views on Western Independence*, Toronto: McClelland and Stewart, 1971.

Bercuson, David Jay, Editor, *Canada and the Burden of Unity*, Toronto: Macmillan of Canada, 1977.

Black, E.R., "British Columbia: The Politics of Exploitation," in Shearer, R., Editor, *Exploiting our Economic Potential: Public Policy and the British Columbia Economy*, Toronto: Holt, Rinehart and Winston, 1968, pp. 23-41.

Blackman, W., *The Cost of Confederation: An Analysis of the Costs to Alberta, Part I, Economic Activity*, Calgary, 1974 (mimeo.).

Clark, S.D., *The Developing Canadian Community*, Toronto: University of Toronto Press, 1962.

Clark, S.D., *Movements of Political Protest in Canada 1640-1840*, Toronto: University of Toronto Press, 1957.

Conway, John, "Geo-Politics and the Canadian Union," in *The Confederation Challenge*, Vol. 2., Ontario Advisory Committee on Confederation, Toronto: Queen's Printer, 1970, pp. 28-49.

Fowke, Vernon, *The National Policy and the Wheat Economy*, Toronto: University of Toronto Press, 1957.

Graham, John F., *Fiscal Adjustment and Canadian Development: A Case Study of Nova Scotia*, Toronto: University of Toronto Press, 1963.

Hodgetts, J.E., "Regional Interests and Policy in a Federal Structure," *Canadian Journal of Economics and Political Science XXXII*, February 1966, pp. 3-14.

Innis, Harold A., *Essays in Canadian Economic History*, Edited by Mary Q. Innis, Toronto: University of Toronto Press, 1956.

Irving, John A., *The Social Credit Movement in Alberta*, Toronto: University of Toronto Press, 1959.

Lipset, Martin, *Agrarian Socialism: The Cooperative Commonwealth Federation in Saskatchewan*, Revised and Expanded Edition, Berkeley: University of California Press, 1971.

MacEwan, Paul, *Confederation and the Maritimes*, Windsor, Nova Scotia: Lancelot Press, 1976.

Macpherson, C.B., *Democracy in Alberta: Social Credit and the Party System*, Toronto: University of Toronto Press, 1953.

Mallory, J.R., *Social Credit and the Federal Power in Canada*, Toronto: University of Toronto Press, 1954.

Morton, W.L., *The Progressive Party in Canada*, Toronto: University of Toronto Press, 1950.

Morton, W.L., "The Bias of Prairie Politics," in Swainson, Donald, Editor, *Historical Essays on the Prairie Provinces*, Toronto: McClelland and Stewart, 1970, pp. 289-300.

Pratt, Larry, and Richards, John, *Prairie Capitalism: Power and Influence in the New West*, Toronto: McClelland and Stewart, 1979.

Robin, Martin, *The Rush for Spoils: The Company Province 1871-1933* Toronto: McClelland and Stewart, 1972.

Robin, Martin, *Pillars of Profit: The Company Province, 1934-1972*, Toronto: McClelland and Stewart, 1973.

Smith, David E., *Prairie Liberalism: The Liberal Party of Saskatchewan, 1905-1971*, Toronto: University of Toronto Press, 1975.

Canadian Federalism and Canadian-American Relations

Aitken, H.G.J., *American Capital and Canadian Resources*, Cambridge, Mass.: Harvard University Press, 1961.

Aitken, H.G.J., "Defensive Expansionism: The State and Economic Growth in Canada," in Easterbrook W.T., and Watkins, M.H., Editors, *Approaches to Canadian Economic History*, Carleton Library, Toronto: McClelland and Stewart, 1967, pp. 183-221.

Canada, *Foreign Direct Investment in Canada*, Ottawa: Information Canada, 1972 (Gray Report).

Canada, *Foreign Ownership and the Structure of Canadian Industry*, Ottawa: Information Canada, 1970 (Watkins Report).

Dubuc, Alfred, "The Decline of Confederation and the New Nationalism," in Russell, Peter, Editor, *Nationalism in Canada*, Toronto: McGraw-Hill of Canada, 1966, pp. 112-132.

Fowke, Vernon, "The National Policy—Old and New," in Easterbrook and Watkins, op. cit., pp. 237-258.

Gilpin, Robert, "American Direct Investment and Canada's Two Nationalisms," in Preston, Richard A., Editor, *The Influence of the United States on Canadian Development: Eleven Case Studies*, Durham, N.C.: Duke University Press, 1972, pp. 124-143.

Gilpin, Robert, "Integration and Disintegration on the North American Continent," *International Organization 28*, Autumn 1974, pp. 851-874.

Levy, Thomas, and Holsti, Kal J., "Bilateral Institutions and Trans-governmental Relations between Canada and the United States," *International Organization 28*, Autumn 1974, pp. 875-902.

Levy, Thomas, with Leach, H. and Walker, Donald E., "Province-State Trans-Border Relations: A Preliminary Assessment," *Canadian Public Administration 16*, Fall, 1973, pp. 469-482.

Levitt, Kari, *Silent Surrender: The Multinational Corporation in Canada*, Toronto: Macmillan of Canada, 1970.

Latouche, Daniel, "Quebec and the North American Continent: One Possible Scenario," *International Organization 28*, Autumn 1974, pp. 931-960.

Masson, Claude, "Economic Relations between Quebec, Canada and the United States," in Axline, Andrew et al., Editors, *Continental Community: Independence and Integration in North America*, Toronto: McClelland and Stewart, 1974, pp. 240-249.

Nelles, H.V., "Empire Ontario: The Problems of Resource Development," in Swainson, Donald, Editor, *Oliver Mowat's Ontario*, Toronto: Macmillan of Canada, 1972, pp. 189-210.

Ontario, Legislative Assembly, *Final Report on Economic Nationalism of the Select Committee on Economic and Cultural Nationalism*, Toronto: Queen's Printer 1975.

Smiley, Donald V., "The Federal Dimension of Canadian Economic Nationalism," *Dalhousie Law Journal 1*, October, 1974, pp. 541-579.

Smiley, Donald V., "Canada and the Quest for a National Policy," *Canadian Journal of Political Science VIII*, March 1975, pp. 40-62.

Stevenson, Garth, "Foreign Direct Investment and the Provinces," *Canadian Journal of Political Science VII*, December 1974, pp. 630-647.

Stevenson, Garth, "Continental Integration and Canadian Unity," in *Axline et al, op. cit.*, pp. 194-217.

Normative/Philosophical Analysis

As I have argued in Chapter 9, there is very little written on the Canadian federal system which is even in a broad sense philosophical. Although the boundaries of such a category of writings is arbitrarily made, I would suggest the following:

Cameron, David R., *Nationalism, Self-Determination and the Quebec Question*, Toronto: Macmillan of Canada, 1974.

Cook, Ramsay, *Canada and the French-Canadian Question*, Toronto: Macmillan of Canada, 1976.

Creighton, Donald, *Towards the Discovery of Canada*, Toronto: Macmillan of Canada, 1972.

Dion, Léon, *Quebec: The Unfinished Revolution*, Montreal: McGill-Queen's University Press, 1976.

Kwavnick, David, "Québécois Nationalism and Canada's National Interest," *Journal of Canadian Studies* 12, July 1977, pp. 53-68.

Mathie, William, "Political Community and the Canadian Experience: Reflections on Nationalism, Federalism and Community," *Canadian Journal of Political Science XII*, March 1979, pp. 3-20.

McRae, Kenneth D., "The Plural Society and the Western Political Tradition," Presidential Address to Canadian Political Science Association, May 31, 1979 (mimeo).

Quebec, Report. *Royal Commission of Inquiry on Constitutional Problems*, Queen Printer, Quebec, 1956 (The Tremblay Report).

Rioux, *Quebec in Question*, Toronto: James Lewis and Samuel, 1971.

Smiley, Donald V., *The Canadian Political Nationality*, Toronto: Methuen of Canada, 1967.

Stevenson, Garth, *Unfulfilled Union*, Toronto: Macmillan of Canada, 1979.

Trudeau, Pierre Elliott, *Federalism and the French Canadians*, Toronto: Macmillan of Canada, 1968.

Whitaker, Reginald, "The Competition for Power: Hobbes and the Quebec Question," *Canadian Forum*, February 1979, pp. 6-10.

Postscript

I wrote most of this revision of *Canada in Question* during the first half of 1979 and the manuscript was given to the publishers in the summer of that year. It is trite to say that the succeeding months were featured by great uncertainty in the federal system.

During the federal general election of 1979 and the period immediately after the election there was a polarization between the two major parties in their approach to Canadian federalism. The Progressive Conservative position was that of sensitivity to provincial demands, a relatively low priority for constitutional reform, and a disposition not to involve the central government in the forthcoming Quebec referendum campaign. The Liberal policy was assertive of federal power, urgent about constitutional change, and aggressive in its stance towards the Quebec independence movement. However, in the campaign leading up to the 1980 election these differences were not pressed, except for some inconclusive debate about federal-provincial relations in resource development. The return of the Liberals to power thus gives us few clues about the future behaviour of the central government, most crucially that of Prime Minister Trudeau, in the related matters of constitutional reform and the Quebec referendum.

In the past months the contending forces in Quebec have elaborated and clarified their positions by the publication of the White Paper on Sovereignty-Association by the PQ government in November 1979[1] and the document, "A New Canadian Federation," by the Constitutional Committee of the Quebec Liberal Party in January 1980.[2]

The PQ White Paper reaffirms that party's unequivocal commitment to the political sovereignty of Quebec and to what Peter Leslie has called the "parity principle"[3] of a double veto by the governments of Canada and Quebec over all the important actions of the proposed economic association. There is nothing in this document or in the responses of Canadians outside Quebec which leads me to qualify the conclusion I reached a decade ago that in all likelihood sovereignty-association will be rejected by other Canadians. There appears to be a disposition among some persons in Quebec, even those not committed to independence, that a Yes verdict will give the PQ a lever in pressing for changes short of sovereignty-association. This is not, I believe, so. The likelihood is that outside Quebec such a verdict would be interpreted, and understandably, as support for the White Paper alternative which gave the Quebec authorities no mandate at all to press changes within the federal system. I should thus agree with the judgment of William Johnson that, ". . . a 'yes' vote in the referendum and a vote for the PQ in the next election is a vote for the constitutional status quo not for change."[6] It may be, however, that some of the leaders of the PQ believe that the failure of the Quebec government to negotiate sovereignty-association after a Yes verdict would result in such a raising of the national consciousness that a majority of the Quebec community could be persuaded to accept or demand sovereignty in its fullest legal sense. I have no way of judging whether Premier Lévesque and his colleagues regard this development as the "normal" and "natural" fulfillment of *étapisme*.[4] What is new in the PQ position is the decision announced in December 1979 to put before the Quebec electorate in the referendum the "softest" of all questions to the effect that, even if the government were successful in negotiating a change along the lines of sovereignty-association, such reforms would be subject to popular ratification in a subsequent referendum.[5]

There are, it seems to me, very considerable risks both for Quebec interests and for Canada-Quebec relations in the referendum process that the PQ has put underway. A No verdict—even by a small margin—is likely to give rise to a profound insensitivity to Quebec interests by other Canadians for some time to come, and one can predict the title of the lead editorials in English-language newspapers on the morning after, "The separatist gun was not, (after all), loaded." A Yes vote has its own dangers. I have argued in this book and elsewhere, that sovereignty-association is the "least available alternative" in future Canada-Quebec relations. There is nothing in recent developments which would cause me to change this view.

A New Canadian Federation is sophisticated both from an intellectual and political point of view. Although the two dimensions are inextricably related, I find the general stance of this document towards Confederation and towards constitutional reform more attractive than its substantive proposals. NCF makes a constructive contribution by eschewing some of the slogans which have up to now paralyzed and muddied the constitutional debate—"two nations," "special status," "Quebec's right to self-determination," and so on. In a period when all too many of us have made adverse judgments about the federal experience, the Liberal analysis gives a balanced account of its benefits to our material welfare and to political freedom and stability. Claude Ryan and his colleagues also put by what one might call "the collective bargaining approach to constitutional change" which implies that the participants are involved in a zero-sum game where the losses of one are the gains of others. Most significantly perhaps, NCF asserts that Quebec and Canadian allegiances are complementary rather than conflicting:

> We refuse to choose between Quebec and Canada, as if one should necessarily exclude the other. On the contrary, we choose Quebec AND Canada because each one needs the other to fulfill itself. We are convinced that one can, at the same time, be an authentic Quebecer and a true Canadian.[7]

In terms of substance, there is a considerable congruence between the NCF document and the other sets of proposals for comprehensive constitutional reform elaborated since November 1976. Thus when the federal and provincial governments reactivate the reform process—and presumably this cannot take place with any reasonable hope of success while the PQ is still in office—there may well be a high degree of consensus on the agenda of discussion if not on the details of change. This agenda will in all likelihood include either the elimination or modification of what I call in Chapter 2 the "quasi-unitary" elements of the constitution, the constitutional entrenchment of the jurisdiction of the Supreme Court of Canada along with some form of provincial participation in the choice of its members, a new kind of second chamber of the federal Parliament composed of representatives of the provincial governments, and measures for the constitutional entrenchment of civil and linguistic rights. So far as the distribution of powers is concerned, the thrust of the NCF and other proposals is to enhance the position of the provinces both in increasing their jurisdiction and of establishing procedures by which their governments are directly involved in the exercise of federal powers through a new kind of second chamber.

I have very considerable doubts that the extension of provincial powers suggested by the NCF and other current schemes will leave the central government with the jurisdiction and the will to fulfill what I posit in Chapter 6 as the economic requirements of Canadian nationhood. In the dimension of cultural duality, however, the Ryan document appears to me constructive in spelling out—as did the original Confederation settlement of 1864-1867—what are regarded as the imperatives of such duality in explicit and relatively limited terms rather than erecting the French-English relation as the central consideration of Canadian federalism to which all other considerations and interests should give way.

Whatever progress is made in constitutional reform, the existing constitution has been largely delegitimized. In late 1979 the Federal-Provincial Relations Office released the results of a study that it had made of "activities affecting Quebec that federal departments and agencies carried out chiefly between 1967 and 1977."[8] This report reinforces the assertion that had previously been made by Alan Cairns to the general effect that the participants in federal-provincial relations had come to act outside legal and constitutional norms and that ". . . we are in danger of being left not with a flexible division of powers, but a non-existent division." Some of the findings of the FPRO study are these;

    a) initial departmental responses to the question about the constitutional basis for the activity under review indicated that the majority of federal public servants concerned did not know what the relevant authority was;

  b) further enquiries at subsequent meetings suggested in many cases, if not the majority, the question of the distribution of powers had not been thoroughly considered when the activities were undertaken;

  c) more often than not, departments eventually indicated that the constitutional authority for activities was one or more of the following: the Peace, Order, and Good Government clause of section 91, even though in certain cases there was no enabling legislation justifying the reference to POGG; the federal spending power . . . and Parliament's power to declare works for the general advantage of Canada, Section 92.10 (c)

  d) the British North America Act, and particularly the sections setting out the distribution of powers, did not appear to be a part either of the formal training of the public servants concerned, or, more significantly, of their governmental experience.[9]

The report's explanation of the circumstances mentioned above was that the rapid growth of the federal public service between 1960 and 1975 had led to the recruitment of specialists with degrees in natural science, economics, and management who, in the pursuit of "highly focussed program goals and objectives," were "little interested in questions touching on the philosophy and place of government and the notion of public service, and such matters as the constitutional division of powers."[10] While it is unrealistic to expect federal officials to have a detailed and sophisticated knowledge of the constitutional division of powers, it is disturbing to me at least that many if not most of them are shown not to have an informed concern about the constitutional authority under which their own programs operate.

    Successive federal governments have as yet failed to evolve a national energy policy. There are two sets of considerations, (1) self-sufficiency in petroleum through energy conservation, energy substitution and the development of new sources of domestic energy and (2) the distribution of the economic rents from the production of fossil-fuels among the producing corporations, the governments of the producing provinces, the government of Canada, and Canadian consumers. And a coherent policy in respect to energy must somehow be made compatible with a fiscal regime which gives the federal government the financial capacity to effect the various kinds of interprovincial and interpersonal equalization discussed in Chapter 6.

    In a way which is not understood, the analysis of political systems affects the operation of these systems, even when such commentaries are read by only a relatively small number of people. My fellow professors have continued to busy themselves with writings about Canadian fed-

eralism and in my view the most significant of their efforts published
in the past six months are these:

—Stanley G. French, Editor, *Confederation: Philosophers Look at
Canadian Confederation.*[12]   I pointed out in Chapter 9 that most of
the discourse about Canadian public affairs was historical rather than
philosophical in nature. This is a collection of papers from a symposium held in Montreal in early 1979 under the auspices of the Canadian Philosophical Association at which the philosophers, most of
whom have not been involved in the current debate in their professional capacities, examined the crisis in Confederation. Charles Taylor, one philosopher who *had* been active in this debate, delivered
the extraordinarily perceptive key-note address, "Why Do Nations
Have to Become States?", which makes a valuable, if disturbing, contribution to the question of the viability of multilingual political
communities.

—Garth Stevenson, *Unfulfilled Union: Canadian Federalism and National Unity.*[13] Stevenson's book deals with many of the same subjects as *Canada in Question* but from a somewhat different ideological perspective. It is a thoughtful and lucid analysis which deserves
attention by all serious students of the Canadian federal system.

—William P. Irvine, *Does Canada Need A New Electoral System?*[14]
Electoral reform appears to be now on the agenda of constitutional reform, and it has become increasingly recognized that the procedures
by which members of the House of Commons of Canada are elected
have adverse effects on the workings of the federal system. Apart
from my own proposal[15]—which no one has been disposed to take
seriously—all the current recommendations, including that of Irvine,
suggest the "topping-up" of the present system by adding to the MPs
chosen by the current method a group of members elected from the
provinces by one kind or other of Proportional Representation. Irvine's monograph is a thorough and perceptive analysis of this crucial matter.

—John Richards and Larry Pratt, *Prairie Capitalism: Power and Influence in the New West.*[16] This lucid and thoroughly researched account of the role of the Alberta and Saskatchewan governments in resource development is the most intellectually exciting study of
Canadian public affairs I have read in the past decade. For anyone
wanting to understand the westward shift of power and purpose in
Canada this book is compulsory reading.

—Daniel Bell and Lorne Tepperman, *The Roots of Disunity: A Look at
Canadian Political Culture.*[17] The Bell-Tepperman book is the most
ambitious attempt that has been made to study Canada within the political culture perspective. This perspective assumes that mass atti-

tudes and ways of behaviour are decisive in shaping political systems. Thus political elites—members of legislature, cabinet
ministers, senior public servants, judges, and so on—either share the
political attitudes of those they govern or are responsive to such mass
attitudes that they do not share.[18] The contrary assumptions which
underlie *Canada in Question*, along with the recent writings of Alan
Cairns, suggest that the "roots of disunity" in Canada are more attributable to the way in which political institutions work than to mass
attitudes, that political elites are somewhat unresponsive to such attitudes and that these elites possess somewhat different political values than those held by their fellow citizens. Yet Canadian social scientists have not as yet come forward with conclusive evidence to
demonstrate that one of these sets of assumptions is more valid than
the other.

—Edward McWhinney, *Quebec and the Constitution, 1960-1978.*[19]
Along with Jacques Brossard, Edward McWhinney is one of the few
legal scholars who has written about the Canadian constitution
within a comparative perspective. This is the only coherent analysis
that has been made of the Canadian constitutional debate from 1960
onward. McWhinney's book is a valuable corrective to the current
mania for denigrating the Canadian constitutional experience and
believing that it is possible and desirable to rewrite the constitution
from scratch.

During the time this Edition was being written I continued to learn
from my intellectual association with Alan Cairns, which now extends
over 20 years. He has continued to make distinguished contributions
both to the understanding of the Canadian political system and, even
more notably, to the commentaries on that system. Unfortunately, these
contributions are not as available as easily as they might be because
they are published in various journals and collections of papers. I can
only hope to nudge Alan and some enterprising publisher to gather
those essays together in one or more volumes of Cairnsiana.

D.V.S.
Toronto
February 20, 1980

Notes

1. *Québec-Canada: A New Deal*, Gouvernement du Québec Conseil exécutif,
   Editeur officiel, Québec, 1979.
2. *A New Canadian Federation*, The Constitutional Committee of the Quebec
   Liberal Party, Montreal: The Quebec Liberal Party, 1980.
3. Peter Leslie, *Equal to Equal: Economic Association and the Canadian*

Common Market, Institute Discussion Paper, Kingston: Institute of Intergovernmental Relations, Queen's University, 1979, pp. 26-27.

4. For a more extended analysis see my *The Association Dimension of Sovereignty-Association: A response to the Quebec White Paper*, Institute Discussion Paper, Kingston: Institute of Intergovernmental Relations, Queen's University, 1980.

5. This is the referendum question put before the Quebec National Assembly by the government.

> The government of Quebec has made public its proposals to negotiate a new agreement with the rest of Canada based on the equality of nations;
>
> This agreement would enable Quebec to acquire the exclusive power to make its laws, administer its taxes, and establish relations abroad—in other words, sovereignty—and at the same time, to maintain with Canada an economic association, including a common currency;
>
> any change in political status resulting from these negotiations will be submitted to the people through a referendum; on these terms do you agree to give the government of Quebec the mandate to negotiate the proposed agreement between Quebec and Canada?
>
> Yes ☐
No ☐

6. *The Globe and Mail*, Toronto, November 19, 1979.

7. p.140

8. *Interim Report on Relations between the Government of Canada and the Province of Quebec 1967-1977*, Ottawa: Federal-Provincial Relations office, 1979. In harmony with the policy of the Clark government towards extended freedom of information the Interim Report contains the conclusions of the study made under the previous administration. However, the data on which those conclusions are based has not been made public.

9. pp. 9-10

10. p. 7

11. The position of Alberta of course is crucial here. In October 1979 a symposium for the Alberta Savings Heritage Trust Fund was held in Edmonton under the sponsorship of the Department of Economics of the University of Alberta and some of the results of the symposium are to be published in a forthcoming issue of *Canadian Public Policy*.

12. Stanley G. French, Editor, *Confederation: Philosophers Look at Canadian Confederation*, Montreal: Canadian Philosophical Association, 1979.

13. Garth Stevenson, *Unfulfilled Union: Canadian Federalism and National Unity*, Toronto: Macmillan of Canada, 1979.

14. William P. Irvine, *Does Canada Need a New Electoral System?*, Kingston: Institute of Intergovernmental Offices, Queen's University, 1979.

15. "Federalism and the Legislative Process in Canada," in W.A.W. Neilson and J. C. MacPherson, Editors, *The Legislative Process in Canada*, Montreal: Institute for Research on Public Policy, 1978, pp. 84-87. The elements of my scheme are these, (1) The present system of electing members from

single-member constituencies would remain as now; (2) To the present House would be added 100 "provincial" seats distributed among the provinces in proportion to their respective populations, (3) Provincial members would be chosen by ranking in each province the candidates who had come second in the balloting and sending to Ottawa those whose proportion of the winner's vote in the constituencies was highest up to the province's allotment of such seats.

16. John Richards and Larry Pratt, *Prairie Capitalism: Power and Influence in the New West*, Toronto: McClelland and Stewart, 1979.

17. David Bell and Lorne Tepperman, *The Roots of Disunity: A Look at Canadian Political Culture*, Toronto: McClelland and Stewart, 1979.

18. Harold D. Clarke, Jane Jenson, Lawrence De Duc and Jon H. Pommett, *Political Choice in Canada*, Toronto: McGraw-Hill Ryerson, 1979, is a comprehensive account of what is known about Canadian political attitudes and voting behaviour. But this kind of approach tells us little or nothing about the impact of such "political choice" on the outputs of the Canadian political system—on laws, policies, administrative and judicial decisions, etc. See in this connection, Conrad Winn and John McMenemy, *Political Parties in Canada*, Toronto: McGraw-Hill Ryerson, 1976, particularly pp. 1-6, pp. 206-227 and pp. 267-279.

19. Edward McWhinney, *Quebec and the Constitution 1960-1978*. Toronto: University of Toronto Press, 1978.

Index